D1356848

School Mental Health Services for Adolescents

EDITED BY

JUDITH R. HARRISON

BRANDON K. SCHULTZ

AND

STEVEN W. EVANS

OXFORD
UNIVERSITY PRESS

OXFORD
UNIVERSITY PRESS

Oxford University Press is a department of the University of Oxford. It furthers
the University's objective of excellence in research, scholarship, and education
by publishing worldwide. Oxford is a registered trade mark of Oxford University
Press in the UK and certain other countries.

Published in the United States of America by Oxford University Press
198 Madison Avenue, New York, NY 10016, United States of America.

CIP data is on file at the Library of Congress
ISBN 978-0-19-935251-7

9 8 7 6 5 4 3 2 1
Printed by Sheridan Books, Inc., United States of America

CONTENTS

Judith R. Harrison, PhD, is an assistant professor of educational psychology at Rutgers University. Prior to her career in academia, she spent many years working with youth with emotional and behavioral disorders (EBDs) in public schools. Her research interests and publications focus on the effectiveness, acceptability, and feasibility of services provided to adolescents with EBDs and attention-deficit/hyperactivity disorder, primarily in inclusive settings.

Brandon K. Schultz, EdD, is an assistant professor in the Department of Psychology at East Carolina University (ECU). Dr. Schultz provided school psychological services and clinical supervision during several research projects examining the Challenging Horizons Program, first at James Madison University and then at Ohio University. Currently, Dr. Schultz teaches in the pediatric school psychology doctoral program at ECU and directs the School Behavior Consultation Lab. His current research focuses on technologies to support school mental health implementation in secondary schools.

Steven W. Evans, PhD, is a professor of psychology at Ohio University and co-director of the Center for Intervention Research in Schools. He is the editor-in-chief of the journal *School Mental Health* and has published extensively on a variety of school mental health topics. Dr. Evans has received many federal research grants to support his treatment development and evaluation research on school mental health interventions for adolescents with emotional and behavioral problems.

James J. Appleton
Gwinnett County Public Schools
Gwinnett County, GA

Nora Bunford
Department of Psychology
Ohio University
Athens, OH;
Department of Ethology
Eötvös Loránd University,
   Institute of Biology
Budapest, Hungary

Abby Bode
Department of Psychology
University of South Carolina
Columbia, SC

Sandra L. Christenson
Department of Educational
   Psychology
University of Minnesota
Minneapolis, MN

Erika Coles
Center for Children and Families
Florida International University
Miami, FL

Claire V. Crooks
Centre for School Mental Health
The University of Western Ontario
London, ON, Canada

Beth Custer
College of Education
Lehigh University
Bethlehem, PA

Caely Dunlop
Centre for School Mental Health
The University of Western Ontario
London, ON, Canada

Steven W. Evans
Department of Psychology
Ohio University
Athens, OH

Lois Flaherty
Center for School Mental Health
University of Maryland School
   of Medicine
Baltimore, MD

Catherine C. George
Anderson-Shiro Consolidated
   Independent School District
Anderson, TX

Judith R. Harrison
Graduate School of Education
Rutgers, The State University
   of New Jersey
New Brunswick, NJ

Lisa H. Jaycox
Treatment and Services
    Adaptation Center
Washington, DC

Sheryl H. Kataoka
Treatment and Services
    Adaptation Center
Los Angeles, California

Jennifer S. Kazmerski
Department of Pediatrics
Baylor College of Medicine
Houston, TX

Lee Kern
College of Education
Lehigh University
Bethlehem, PA

Sunny Kim
Koegel Autism Center
University of California, Santa Barbara
Santa Barbara, CA

Rachel Kininger
Department of Psychology
East Carolina University
Greenville, NC

Lynn Kern Koegel
Koegel Autism Center
University of California, Santa Barbara
Santa Barbara, CA

Robert L. Koegel
Koegel Autism Center
University of California, Santa Barbara
Santa Barbara, CA

Walker Krepps
Medical School
University of Minnesota
Minneapolis, MN

Nancy Lever
Center for School Mental Health
University of Maryland School
    of Medicine
Baltimore, MD

Lauren Louloudis
Department of Psychology
East Carolina University
Greenville, NC

Maureen A. Manning
Department of Psychology
Towson University
Towson, MD

Greta M. Massetti
Center for Children and Families
Florida International University
Miami, FL

Matthew P. Mychailyszyn
Department of Psychology
Towson University
Towson, MD

Sean M. O'Dell
Pediatric Psychology Clinic
Geisinger Health Center
Danville, PA

Catherine T. Petrick
Department of Psychology
Towson University
Towson, MD

Angie J. Pohl
Minneapolis Public Schools
Minneapolis, MN

Amy L. Reschly
Department of Educational
    Psychology
University of Georgia
Athens, GA

Brandon K. Schultz
Department of Psychology
East Carolina University
Greenville, NC

Denise A. Soares
Department of Teacher Education
The University of Mississippi
University, MS

Craig F. Spiel
Department of Psychology
Ohio University
Athens, OH

Bradley D. Stein
Treatment and Services
  Adaptation Center
Pittsburgh, PA

Talida M. State
Montclair State University
Montclair, NJ

Sharon Stephan
Center for School Mental Health
University of Maryland School of
  Medicine
Baltimore, MD

Kathryn Van Eck
Department of Psychology
University of South Carolina
Columbia, SC

Kimberly J. Vannest
Department of Education &
  Human Development
Texas A&M University
College Station, TX

Pamela Vona
Treatment and Services
  Adaptation Center
Los Angeles, California

Eric Wagner
Robert Stempel College of Public
  Health & Social Work
Florida International University
Miami, FL

Christy M. Walcott
Department of Psychology
East Carolina University
Greenville, NC

Mark D. Weist
Department of Psychology
University of South Carolina
Columbia, SC

Ken C. Winters
Oregon Research Institute
Eugene, OR

Marleen Wong
Treatment and Services
  Adaptation Center
Los Angeles, California

Imad Zaheer
College of Education
Lehigh University
Bethlehem, PA

INTRODUCTION

School Mental Health for Adolescents

Our intention when conceptualizing this book was to recruit a group of experts who could share their knowledge about school mental health and secondary schools with a broad group of readers, including practitioners, educators, and researchers. We believe that one effective method for improving the quality of care in school mental health is to educate people about best practices, and hopefully inspire them to develop tools that advance our ability to help adolescents with emotional and behavioral problems. With the publication of this volume, we will have certainly achieved part of this goal, as we were fortunate to have an outstanding group of authors agree to contribute chapters. The second part of our goal for this book involves the impact of the book on readers, and this will be determined over the coming years. Thus, we wish each and every one of you "happy reading" and encourage you to engage in high-quality practices that make a difference in the lives of adolescents with emotional and behavioral problems.

For almost two decades, experts have discussed a disheartening gap between the number of adolescents in need of mental health services and the number actually receiving services. In 1999, the U.S. Department of Health & Human Services estimated that 20% of children and adolescents demonstrated mental health needs. Similarly, Merikangas et al. (2010) found that 22.2% of adolescents experienced a mental health disorder associated with severe impairment or distress. However, in 2002, Kataoka, Zhang, and Wells reported that only 20% of children and adolescents in need of services actually received services. This continuing trend of need and lack of service is unfortunate, as evidence-based interventions to help youth with mental health disorders are available; however, service providers with the knowledge and skills to provide those services are lacking in both clinics and schools (Evans, Koch, Brady, Meszaros, & Sadler, 2013). Not surprisingly, one of the common reasons people do not pursue care is a belief that it cannot be helpful. Other obstacles to care include cost, transportation, and convenience. Integrating services into schools has been one way to address some of these barriers for children and adolescents, and educating those providers about evidence-based practices can increase the likelihood that these services will make a difference.

In the first chapter of this book, Mark Weist and colleagues describe this trend of integrating mental health services into schools and provide some history of school mental health. The authors identify and explore events and policies that have increased the development and utilization of school mental health to date. They conclude by describing opportunities for further growth and development of school-based services, including embedding programs within multi-tiered systems of support, improving training and workforce development, improving interdisciplinary and cross-system collaboration, enhancing high-quality and evidence-based practice, and developing effective systems of implementation support.

One impediment to the increasing trend to provide mental health services in schools is the contention that trained individuals with sufficient time to implement school-based services are not available in schools. Although many school mental health professionals may lack knowledge of evidence-based practices, the vast majority have training equivalent or superior to clinic-based practitioners. Unfortunately, in many schools these professionals are relied upon for administrative tasks such as scheduling, proctoring exams, and providing information about colleges. Rachel Kininger and colleagues describe these phenomena and explore the training and skill sets of professionals who could be at the forefront of school mental health, along with their actual roles in schools.

As school mental health continues to expand, the focus of research and practice in school mental health is on (a) efficient and timely identification of students with mental health needs in schools, (b) maximizing the effectiveness of school mental health services with the implementation of evidence-based interventions, and (c) developing feasible models of implementation. The authors of the chapters in Part II address these issues as they focus on various types of common emotional and behavioral problems experienced by adolescents. Problems with disruptive behavior, dysregulated emotions, disorganization, and drug abuse, and their associated school-based interventions, are described. Two chapters focus on strategies for addressing emotion regulation. Mychailyszyn and colleagues provide valuable information specific to assisting students struggling with internalizing disorders, and Bunford and Evans describe emotion regulation in the context of child development and attention-deficit/hyperactivity disorder. Sometimes, and far too frequently, these problems can be caused or exacerbated by experiencing traumatic events. Thus, evidence-based practices for addressing the needs of students who experienced trauma are described by Vona and colleagues. Students with the common problems described in Part II challenge teachers and school mental health professionals on a daily basis, and best practices for these problems are described in these chapters.

Although there is considerable literature on school-based interventions for elementary school–age children with autism, there is very little information available in relation to effective practices for adolescents with autism. Koegel and colleagues provide readers with an excellent update on how to continue to meet the needs of these students when they enter secondary school. Similarly, services that can feasibly and effectively meet the emotional, behavioral, and health needs of adolescents with chronic health problems are also rarely available in the literature. Walcott and Kazmerski provide an outstanding description of the needs of adolescents with chronic health problems and how teachers and school mental professionals can meet those needs at school. These two chapters address problem areas that are insufficiently covered as they apply to adolescents. The chapters provide the latest approaches for practitioners and an excellent starting point for researchers looking to advance intervention development and evaluation research.

Finally, Reschly and colleagues focus on a critically important aspect of helping all of these students. Identifying those with problems and keeping them engaged and connected to school is a prerequisite to the provision of effective school mental health services. This is particularly true with adolescents with emotional and behavioral problems, as dropout, disengagement, and poor attendance are common, regardless of presenting problems. The approaches described in this chapter provide an outstanding alternative to practices in some schools that marginalize these students and push them further away, such as home schooling and computer-based instruction that are sometimes provided to adolescents with emotional and behavioral problems when their problems become difficult to address in the general education setting.

Part III explores the concept of implementing mental health services in secondary schools and in unique situations. Regardless of the problem area identified through assessment, students with mental health concerns will be taught in secondary schools. Kern and colleagues describe evidence-based interventions that can be implemented by secondary teachers within each tier of a three-tiered implementation framework, as well as means of overcoming barriers that might occur during implementation. Taking implementation one step further, Soares, George, and Vannest provide in-depth information regarding systems of progress monitoring to identify students' responses to evidence-based intervention. Simply selecting and implementing interventions is insufficient. As described by these authors, in order to achieve the most benefit for students, teachers, and school mental health professionals must collect data during implementation and adjust interventions as needed.

To translate research to practice and teach professionals to implement interventions in schools, procedures must be in place to provide quality training and feedback. The era of the two-day professional development should be in the past. School psychologists and special educators frequently find themselves in the role of consultant and collaborator, working with each other and with classroom teachers. Research informs the field that without quality consultation, training, and collaboration, school professionals are not likely to implement with fidelity and sustain the use of evidence-based practice.

In addition, one characteristic of mental health services provided in schools is the lack of supervision or mentoring provided to most school-based professionals. The approaches to training and consultation described by Coles and Massetti provide a valuable model for adopting an effective approach to continuing education. Armed with this approach, many school mental health professionals may be able to enhance the practices of teachers and other professionals and thereby improve the outcomes for students with emotional and behavioral problems.

The final chapter of this volume provides an exceptional example of the role of culture in the provision of school mental health services to adolescents. Crooks and Dunlop provide a fascinating description of the unique culture of Aboriginal youth and how school mental health services may be effectively integrated into that context. In addition to learning about this unique culture, readers will be reminded about the importance of considering culture when attempting to provide effective teaching and school mental health practices in any community. Effective interventions are critically important tools, but effectively integrating them into the culture of the school and community is a necessary step before one can benefit the students with emotional and behavioral problems whose families and community shape the manner in which they can be provided.

CONCLUSION

In this book, the authors provide you with the knowledge and expertise of numerous leaders in the field. We address issues that practitioners face daily in schools working with the most challenging students. This task is not an easy one, as school mental health practitioners may be the only hope that many adolescents will have to receive evidence-based services in schools to help them be successful. We hope that we have provided a wealth of information and guidance that you will turn into practice and further research.

REFERENCES

Merikangas, K. R., He, J., Burstein, M., Swanson, S. A., Avenevoli, S., Cui, L., … Swendsen, J. (2010). Lifetime prevalence of mental disorders in U.S. adolescents: Results from the National Comorbidity Survey Replication–Adolescent Supplement (NCS-A). *Journal of the American Academy of Child & Adolescent Psychiatry, 49*, 980–989.

PART I

Foundations

The History and Future
of School Mental Health

MARK D. WEIST, LOIS FLAHERTY, NANCY LEVER,
SHARON STEPHAN, KATHRYN VAN ECK,
AND ABBY BODE ■

As documented in a number of books (e.g., Robinson, 2004; Weist, Evans, & Lever, 2003; Evans, Weist, & Serpell, 2007; Clauss-Ehlers, Serpell, & Weist, 2013; Weist, Lever, Bradshaw, & Owens, 2014), proliferating research and journal articles (see the newer journals *School Mental Health*, published by Springer, and *Advances in School Mental Health Promotion*, published by Routledge), and increasing federal support (President's New Freedom Commission, 2003; U.S. Public Health Service, 2000), the school mental health field is gaining momentum in the United States and around the world (Rowling & Weist, 2004; Weist & McDaniel, 2013). The field is based on several fundamental recognitions. First, in general, children, adolescents, and families have difficulty connecting to, and subsequently do not regularly attend, specialty mental health appointments (see Atkins et al., 1998; Catron, Harris, & Weiss, 1998). Second, although school represents a universal natural setting for youth, schools are under-resourced to meet the mental health needs of students (Nelson, 2003). Third, there are many advantages to augmenting existing school staff efforts to improve student mental health by partnering with community mental health programs to move toward an "expanded" school mental health approach (Weist, 1997). And, when done well, these collaborations demonstrate a range of positive outcomes for schools, students, and families (Weist et al., 2014).

In this chapter, we provide a brief history of the school mental health (SMH) movement, including key themes that have shaped the field's development, review federal investments with an emphasis on the work of the Center for School Mental Health and a connected National Community of Practice (CoP), and present key policy themes and ideas for future development.

HISTORY

Early History

The history of school mental health in the United States has been influenced by changes in society, in schools, in the development of professions, and in the expansion of the knowledge base within education and mental health (Flaherty & Osher, 2003). Just as in the late 19th century, schools in the 21st century are charged with fostering education while facing considerable challenges. In the late 19th and early 20th centuries, schools faced the problems of growing urban immigrant populations, competing work demands of increasing industrialization, and a school year that expanded to include an additional 38 days. The early 21st century presents some new and some old challenges to the school environment, including greater cultural diversity, exposure to trauma, and increased numbers of families living in poverty. Incorporating the wide range of cultural diversity typical of student populations into the learning environment can challenge school staff, particularly when individual schools represent dozens of different cultures and languages. Additionally, school staff must support student learning and well-being for students experiencing various kinds of psychosocial adversity, including poverty and intrafamilial and community violence (Flaherty & Osher, 2003; Truscott & Truscott, 2005).

School mental health services in the current era have been influenced by several factors. First is the knowledge of the high prevalence of psychosocial problems among youth, especially in disadvantaged communities. The extent to which these problems are untreated and undertreated influence the development of SMH services (Weisz, 2004). Second, the long-term implications of these problems in terms of morbidity and mortality have become clear (Aseltine, Gore, & Gordon, 2000; Flaherty, Weist, & Warner, 1996; McWhirter & Page, 1999). Third, the awareness that behavioral problems are often rooted in treatable psychiatric disorders, such as depression, post-traumatic conditions, and anxiety, has grown (Basson et al., 1991; Chiles, Miller, & Cox, 1980). Finally, there has been an "increasing awareness of the barriers posed to optimal development and learning by poverty, racism, gender discrimination, disability, and unsupportive schools," along with a "broadening vision of educational opportunity" (Flaherty & Osher, 2003, p. 20). All these factors have combined to support the development and expansion of SMH.

Current trends in school mental health have their origins in two parallel developments concerned with the well-being of children—the public health movement and the child guidance movement. Public health as a medical field is focused on the prevention of epidemics through screening for communicable diseases and the implementation of population-based approaches, such as ensuring the safety of food and water supplies. From its inception, child guidance has displayed an interdisciplinary orientation and focused on intervening to prevent mental illness and juvenile delinquency.

From School Nurses to School-Based Health Centers

In the early part of the 20th century, schools in urban areas were overwhelmed by large numbers of Eastern European immigrants who lacked access to basic healthcare. The placement of nurses in schools was both a response to these challenges and based on a public health model of detecting and treating illness. Nurses also provided instruction about proper nutrition and sanitation, and thus were engaged in health promotion. The origins of school nursing can be traced to the work of Lina Lavanche Rogers, who began working in the New York City schools in 1902. Soon other school nurses were hired to meet the needs of children whose health problems interfered with their schooling. The impact of these highly skilled and independently functioning professionals was profound—the number of children excluded from school went from 10,567 in September 1902 to 1,101 the following year (Hawkins, Hayes, & Corliss, 1994).

These pioneering efforts led to the establishment of health suites in schools staffed by nurses who oversaw vaccinations, were on hand to detect communicable diseases and treat minor illnesses and injuries, and, in some cases, provided teaching about prevention and health. Although emotional well-being was considered part of health, the field of child and adolescent psychiatry was in its infancy, and there was little recognition of the role that psychiatric disorders played in children's academic, social, and emotional functioning. In fact, depression was not even recognized as occurring in children, first appearing in the third edition of the *Diagnostic and Statistical Manual of Mental Disorders* (*DSM*; American Psychiatric Association, 1980).

School-Based Health Centers

The 1960s saw the establishment of the first school-based health centers (SBHCs), which provided primary healthcare to students who otherwise would have had difficulty accessing it. SBHCs grew out of the traditions of school nursing and public health clinics, and they began to proliferate in the 1980s to meet the need for primary healthcare for adolescents, the most underserved age group. With the recognition that many of the visits to SBHCs were related to mental health concerns (Lear et al., 1991), the centers expanded their scope to include mental health counseling. SBHCs increased from a total of 200 in 1990 to 1,380 in 2000 (Flaherty & Osher, 2003), and there were 1,909 in 45 states in 2010 (U.S. Government Accountability Office, 2010). Typically, these centers are staffed by a full- or part-time nurse practitioner or a physician's assistant, sometimes accompanied by an aide/receptionist, and a master's-level mental health clinician, such as a social worker. Originally located primarily in urban high schools, there was later an expansion of centers into suburban areas and elementary schools (Center for Health and Health Care in Schools, 2003; National Assembly on School-Based Health Care, 2002; U. S. Government Accountability Office, 2010).

From the Child Guidance Movement to Expanded School Mental Health

The guiding principle of the child guidance movement was that intervening in "maladjusted" children's environments could prevent mental illness and juvenile delinquency (Horn, 1989). The first child guidance clinic was established in Chicago in 1909 under William Healy, a neurologist. In 1922 the Commonwealth Fund gave impetus to the movement by funding the establishment of demonstration clinics in eight cities. The clinics were based in communities, not hospitals, and focused on psychological evaluation and therapy for children with behavioral and emotional problems in the context of their families and communities. This approach was based on a developmental perspective, arising from the psychoanalytic view that the origins of mental illness lay in childhood and parent-child relationships. From the beginning, these community-based clinics were an interdisciplinary effort, involving psychologists, social workers, and psychiatrists working together as child study teams (Witmer, 1940). The teams served as consultants providing guidance to teachers about how to better understand and teach children with emotional and behavioral problems. This model held sway into the 1950s.

In the 1960s, the community mental health (CMH) movement came to the fore with the passage of the Community Mental Health Act (CMHA) of 1963 (Public Law 88-164). This act specified that services to children and adolescents and consultation and education were essential services of community mental health centers (CMHCs). Although consultation and education were generally underfunded, CMHCs, such as the Walter P. Carter Center in Baltimore, Maryland, developed liaison relationships with the schools in their service areas by sending staff to meet weekly with school personnel and discuss children being seen at the centers' clinics. In the Baltimore case, these relationships later served as the foundation for the establishment of expanded school mental health (ESMH) programs in the schools in Baltimore City. Please note these close relationships between mental health systems and schools are foundational to ESMH (Weist, 1997) and to programs developed in locations throughout the U.S. (Weist, Lever, Bradshaw & Owens, 2014).

Individuals with Disabilities Education Act (IDEA): Public Law 94-142

Passed in 1975, the IDEA law mandated that schools serve all students, including those with learning or emotional disabilities that become barriers to learning. The law became an important facilitator in moving mental health professionals from outside consultants to integral members of the school staff. Since evaluations had to be performed to determine the degree of disability and necessary educational accommodations, schools added mental health professionals, such as school psychologists, to their staffs (Flaherty & Osher, 2003).

From Fixing Schools to Fixing Students

This shift in educational mandate was accompanied by a shift away from the school consultation model, rooted in the child guidance movement, which focused on helping teachers understand children's psychological needs and doing their work better. As pointed out by Flaherty and Osher (2003), the shift represented movement from fixing the schools to fixing the students. Instead of outside consultants from the various mental health disciplines coming to schools to offer their expertise to teachers and administrators, schools began hiring their own counselors, psychologists, and social workers to provide services directly to students.

Although mental health services were provided to some students who met disability criteria, this did not constitute an organized program of school-based mental health services. The development of SMH programming was driven in large part by youth with emotional and behavioral disorders who required support from many service providers, both in and outside of the school (Flaherty & Osher, 2003). Identified through IDEA as emotionally disturbed (ED), the focus on educational support through IDEA did not produce the improvement in outcomes for youth with ED that was seen among other youth receiving special education services. Furthermore, the unwieldy and costly intervention necessary for these youth taxed the services possible within this new system. As a result, the IDEA was amended in 1997 to expand the learning opportunities and support of students with emotional and/or behavioral disabilities, bringing into the schools an additional influx of mental health professionals. The 1997 amendments allowed for financial investment in collaboration with outside agencies to assist with implementing individualized educational plans (IEPs), as well as working toward broader goals such as promoting a positive school-wide climate and developing and administering prevention programming. Expansion of the goals in the amendments to address prevention in addition to intervention reflected the growing understanding that providing mental health services to students at risk for emotional and behavior disorders may be more effective than waiting to intervene until youth display symptoms severe enough to require a special educational placement. Thus, the 1997 IDEA amendment laid the groundwork for ESMH programs.

Expanded School Mental Health (ESMH) Programs

The concept of "expanded" SMH, which came to the fore in the 1990s, involved building upon programs already in schools by adding additional staff to go beyond the schools' existing focus on crisis management and the needs of students receiving special education services (Weist, 1997). The idea was to provide mental health services to youth in regular as well as special education. ESMH services included diagnostic assessment; individual, group, and family psychotherapy; crisis intervention; medication management; and case management. In addition, some programs implemented preventive services, including classroom consultation and mental health education. Early ESMH successes in Baltimore, Maryland, provided an exemplar model for family-school-community partnerships to support student mental health, and laid the foundation for the receipt of significant federal investment to help advance school mental health programs and policies nationally.

FEDERAL INVESTMENTS

National Center for School Mental Health

Since 1995, the Health Resources and Services Administration, Maternal and Child Health Bureau (MCHB), has pioneered efforts in the area of school health and mental health, funding national centers on school-based health-care (National Assembly on School-Based Health Care, now rebranded as the School-Based Health Alliance), and two centers focused specifically on school mental health.

The School-Based Health Alliance (SBHA) is the national voice for school-based health centers (SBHCs). Its mission is to improve the health of children and adolescents by advancing and advocating for school-based healthcare. The SBHA is a national organization with 17 state affiliates that follow the mission, vision, and core values of the national SBHA. The national SBHA and the state affiliates assist each other in advancing a federal policy agenda that helps to promote and advance school-based and school-linked health services. The School-Based Health Alliance advocates for national policies, programs, and funding to expand and strengthen SBHCs, while also supporting SBHCs at the state and local levels with training and technical assistance.

Between 1995 and 2010, both the University of Maryland, Baltimore, and the University of California, Los Angeles (UCLA) were funded to provide training, technical assistance, and program and policy analysis in school mental health. During this 15 years of funding, school mental health was defined and frameworks for effective school mental health service provision were developed, with increasing emphasis on quality assessment and improvement. Funding decreased in 2010 to support only one center at the University of Maryland, the Center for School Mental Health (CSMH).

Built on the solid foundation of the Baltimore ESMH network, and on an established track record of research, the CSMH mission is to strengthen policies and programs in SMH to improve learning and promote success for America's youth. The CSMH has two overarching goals and several associated objectives, all directed toward facilitating the advancement of a shared family-school-community agenda for advancing three tiers of high-quality SMH programming and related policy to improve academic, behavioral, and socio-emotional outcomes for all students. The first goal of the CSMH is to enhance understanding of SMH policies and programs that are innovative, effective, and culturally and linguistically competent, across the development spectrum (from preschool through postsecondary), across three-tiers of mental health programming (promotion, problem prevention, and intervention), and across levels of scale (international, national, state, and local). The second goal is to enhance implementation of innovative and effective SMH policies and programs through the dissemination and diffusion of analyses and instructive findings via a comprehensive, multifaceted, engaging, and creative communications framework that reaches the full array of invested stakeholders in SMH.

The CSMH team is a committed and diverse stakeholder group with a wealth of experience and a commitment to reducing barriers to learning and promoting academic and social-emotional-behavioral success for *all* students (preschool to postsecondary). CSMH staff serves as clinicians and supervisors for the SMH programs, which provide mental health promotion and intervention to youth and families in schools in four jurisdictions in Maryland. The programs provide a direct connection to "front line" SMH and facilitate a strong research-practice-policy interface.

The CSMH is nationally recognized as a top-ranked training site for SMH professionals, recently receiving three honors: A Graduate Psychology Education Grant through HRSA to support the advancement of psychology training around school mental health, the 2010 American Psychological Association Award for Distinguished Contributions for the Education and Training of Child and Adolescent Psychologists, as well as the highest rated course in the University of Maryland's top-tier graduate social work program (developed by authors N. Lever and M. Weist, along with Michael Lindsay).

National Community of Practice (CoP) on Collaborative School Behavioral Health

A major milestone in the history of the CSMH and in the advancement of SMH nationally occurred in 2004 with the inception of a National Community of Practice (CoP) on Collaborative School Behavioral Health. Étienne Wenger, a pioneer of the CoP concept, defines CoPs as "groups of people who share a concern or a passion for something they do and learn how to do it better as they interact regularly" (Wenger, 2006). A CoP offers an innovative mechanism for doing work across a group of individuals who share similar concerns, problems, or interest in particular areas in an effort to deepen their own knowledge base and effectiveness (Cashman, Linehan, & Rosser, 2007). CoPs enable individuals to synergistically work together with a larger group to advance their knowledge, skills, and effectiveness (Wenger, McDermott, & Snyder, 2002). CoPs emphasize the value of each individual as an expert within his or her own context, while recognizing the importance of the larger group learning process over the individual contributions (Price-Mitchell, 2009).

The National Community of Practice on Collaborative School Behavioral Health is co-facilitated by the Individuals with Disabilities Education Act Partnership (IDEA Partnership) at the National Association of State Directors of Special Education (NASDSE) and CSMH. With the IDEA Partnership, the

CSMH has helped to build, and is committed to providing, ongoing support to advance the CoP. This community includes consumers, educators, practitioners, advocates, researchers, and decision-makers. The mission of the community is to bridge the differences across education and mental health to support youth. The CoP on School Behavioral Health began in 2004 with the convening of a diverse group of stakeholders at a pre-conference meeting to the Annual Conference on Advancing School Mental Health in Dallas, Texas. The group came together to discuss pivotal issues to further a shared mental health agenda involving families, schools, and communities, organized to advance statewide action in SMH. It was agreed that a CoP focused on SMH would be beneficial, and eight "practice groups" formed to pursue special topics at deeper levels. The National CoP currently has 12 Practice Groups, with 17 states, 23 national organizations, and 7 technical assistance centers working together on school mental health.

The National CoP facilitates SMH partnerships and provides practical examples of collaborative successes at the local, state, and national levels. It advances SMH knowledge, policy, and programming through widespread dissemination and diffusion and active, multi-scale communication. The CoP unites and offers collaborations with federal partners, states, and organizations; technical assistance and resource centers with student and family consumers; front-line school-based staff; and policymakers to address intersecting education and mental health priorities to reduce barriers to learning and improve success for all students. Convened annually at the CSMH Annual Conference on Advancing SMH, the CoP provides opportunities to stay connected throughout the year via web-based technology, teleconferences, and shared action (e.g., resource sharing, topical discussions, materials development, and translating knowledge to practice). The National CoP is poised to receive, respond to, and disseminate information through extensive networks.

The CoP has had tremendous impact on the field across the 12 practice groups, states, and organizations. An example of this impact can be highlighted through the Quality and Evidence-Based Practice Group. This group was originally formed during the Dallas landmark meeting of the CoP. From its inception, this practice group has been led by mental health and education professionals, including two authors of this article (M. Weist and S. Stephan), and it has been one of the most productive and impactful practice groups within the CoP. Its mission is to share information across individuals and groups interested in improving the quality of SMH programs and services, and to discuss, promote, and disseminate evidence-based practices in SMH. The practice group strives to bridge the research-practice and practice-research gaps in the field. In addition, the group seeks to understand and identify best student- and program-level evaluation strategies. The diverse stakeholders involved within the National CoP and Quality and Evidence-Based Practice Group collaborate to build a natural laboratory for investigating strategies and resources that could be used to advance evidence-based practices and programming in SMH. Through surveys, focused discussions, newsletters, and the sharing of ideas, resources, and skills through the National CoP, the authors of this article have helped to define the feasibility of and implementation challenges related to the integration of evidence-based practices and programs within school settings. The CoP work has not only influenced the scientific integrity of the project, but also helped in the initial networking that brought some of the leaders of this project together. The CoP models effective communication and collaboration across agencies, systems, programs, universities, and stakeholder groups. Multichanneled communication—via teleconferences, e-mail, webinars, strategic planning meetings, dialogue guides, and wikis—and the appreciation of the expertise across stakeholder groups and systems are contributing to the success of the described studies.

Annual Conference on Advancing School Mental Health

Since 1996, the CSMH has organized an Annual Conference on Advancing SMH, which has drawn up to 1,000 participants each year from most states and several countries. The conference has become the nation's premier conference for advancing high-quality, interdisciplinary school mental health in collaboration with families, schools, and communities. Conference content addresses an array of SMH dimensions, and each conference has featured over 100 sessions, including renowned plenary speakers, intensive trainings, workshops, papers, Community of Practice training, and posters. The conference offers a comprehensive and rich array of training, networking, and partnership building. State, local, and federal officials have endorsed, sponsored, participated in, and used the conference as a platform to advance children's mental health and SMH efforts.

The Annual Conference on Advancing SMH is rapidly evolving via the Community of Practice framework, by allowing participants to stay connected throughout the year in this important shared work. Since 2004, the conference proceedings have been shaped by practice groups of the National CoP, with specialty tracks for each group: Building a Collaborative Culture in SMH; Connecting SMH and PBIS; Connecting SMH with Juvenile Justice and Dropout Prevention; Education: An Essential Component of Systems of Care; Family Partnerships in Mental Health; Improving SMH for Youth with Disabilities; Learning the Language: Promoting Effective Ways for Interdisciplinary Collaboration; Quality and EBP; SMH for Culturally Diverse Youth; Youth Involvement and Leadership; Psychiatry and Schools; and SMH for Military Families. The groups solicit, review, and select proposals for their track, and facilitators serve on the planning committee. EBPs, cultural and developmental sensitivity, and cross-stakeholder relevance are encouraged.

The annual conference is moved throughout the country with strong state leadership and support from a state planning committee each year. Together, the CSMH and the IDEA Partnership have advanced the annual conference and National CoP, with meetings in Cleveland (2005); Baltimore (2006); Orlando (2007); Phoenix (2008); Minneapolis (2009); Albuquerque (2010); Charleston (2011); Salt Lake

City (2012); Crystal City, Virginia (2013); and Pittsburgh (2014), New Orleans (2015), and San Diego (2016).

In their role as facilitators, practice group facilitators lead conference calls for their groups, participate in National CoP calls, develop resources, host webinars, promote dialogue and knowledge exchange, share best practices and resources, and organize a track at the annual conference. Through regular dialogue with facilitators, there is an emphasis on youth and family presence and partnership at the annual meeting and within the overall CoP. The IDEA Partnership and the CSMH have together employed several strategies to ensure youth and family participation. Youth and family attendance and the annual conference and other events are supported through scholarships, grants, and significantly reduced rates. Each conference includes keynotes from youth and/or family. Each state that hosts the conference facilitates a regional youth day to advance understanding and advocacy related to SMH, which serves as a catalyst for helping to build a lasting youth SMH advocacy group in the state. Youth and family are strongly encouraged to participate in the annual conference as presenters. Youth and family participants appear on all state teams. Finally, it is a priority to connect youth and family voice to all practice groups and the larger CoP.

Since the inception of the National CoP, a Community Building Forum has been held each year on the day preceding the annual conference. Attendance has included representation from the state groups, national organizations, TA and resource centers, federal agencies, practice group facilitators, policymakers, and youth and family members. The forum offers an opportunity to review progress and allows participants to discuss strategies to move the community forward. A highlight of the forums has been the opportunity to share knowledge, resources, and best practices and to discuss SMH impacts of major education and mental health research and policy. As part of the Community Building Forums, state teams comprising key system leaders from each state (AZ, HI, MD, MN, MO, MT, NH, NC, NM, OH, PA, SC, VT, IL, SD, UT, and WV) have the opportunity to meet and develop SMH action plans and link shared agenda work to state accountability plans (e.g., state special education performance plans).

To assist the facilitators of each of the practice groups, the CSMH and the IDEA Partnership hold retreats and hosts webinars and phone calls. In addition, facilitators and participants use the IDEA Partnership website and wiki (www.shared-work.org) for ongoing communication, resource development and sharing, and collaboration to build a *Shared Agenda* to advance SMH.

POLICY THEMES

As the CSMH has evolved, in alignment with guidance from federal funders, its focus has shifted from primarily technical assistance and training to the inclusion of program and policy analyses. Since about 2007, major policy foci of the CSMH have included the interplay of health and education reform and their relation to school mental health, application of a public health framework to school mental health, and creating sustainable funding for school mental health.

Mental Health and Education Policy

The CSMH has worked toward a truly integrated approach to the analysis and promotion of effective and impactful mental health and education policies, accounting for different parameters for these policies and programs across the educational spectrum from preschool to postsecondary education. In doing so, the CSMH has specifically considered three critical areas that often run counter to the establishment of integrated policy: marginalization, federalism, and school decision-making.

Marginalization. A critical challenge for the field is effectively addressing the question of why there should be mental health programs and services in schools. School leaders might purposefully resist an agenda to expand attention to mental health issues, based on the belief that schools are not in "the mental health business," or on concerns that schools will need to assume greater responsibility for students' emotional and behavioral problems. Further, stigma and poor understanding of mental health issues clearly interfere with the development of SMH programs and policies. SMH staff and programs may be viewed as "add-ons" that are not central to the academic mission of schools (School Mental Health Alliance, 2004). In addition, school reform efforts generally have not incorporated a focus on addressing noncognitive barriers to development, learning, and teaching (Burke, 2002; Koller & Svoboda, 2002). These noncognitive barriers include environmental and contextual factors (e.g., poor nutrition, family conflict, negative peer influences, exposure to violence, neglect) as well as individual biological and psychological factors (e.g., externalizing and internalizing mental health problems, trauma reactions). Although school reformers acknowledge that academic success promotes overall well-being, they do not often recognize that, in turn, social-emotional well-being is essential to academic success (Klern & Connell, 2004).

Federalism. Perhaps the most significant policy challenge to the SMH field relates to federalism (states' rights, local control), which contributes to tremendous variability in how child-serving systems (including education and mental health) function both across and within states (Weist, Paternite, Wheatley-Rowe, & Gall, 2009). When states and local communities have significant latitude in decisions about policy and practice, outcomes vary. For example, one community in a state may be demonstrating relatively advanced progress in SMH, while the adjacent community shows no progress, with no dialogue or collaboration between these communities. Federalism and the significant variability across child-serving systems contribute to inertia in local and state government in advancing system reform. An important strategy to address the constraints of federalism concerns the organization of state-level initiatives that reform and improve child-serving systems, with SMH at the nexus of such system transformation.

School decision-making. Compounding the challenges of federalism are three major characteristics of school systems in the United States. First, U.S. public schools are characterized by substantial organizational fluidity associated with high rates of mobility and turnover among administrators, teachers, and other school personnel (Guarino, Santibañez, Daley, & Brewer, 2004). Second, school district and building policies and practices are highly reactive to shifting policy and programming realities associated with educational mandates at the local, state, and federal levels. Both necessitate repeated revisiting of agreements made between SMH programs and host schools, as well as ongoing advocacy to sustain services. Third, within most school districts, decentralized decision-making is the norm. In this site-based management approach, substantial decision-making authority is delegated from school boards and superintendents to individual school principals and personnel. Therefore, working agreements regarding roles, functions, and communication between mental health staff and schools typically need to be negotiated and maintained on a building-by-building basis. Policy analyses and dissemination activities of the CSMH will include examination of state and local decision-making processes and their interrelationships.

Healthcare Reform

Related to SMH funding challenges, there are significant considerations within healthcare reform that stand to positively impact SMH. A recent report by the U.S. Department of Health and Human Services (2010) indicated that a disproportionate number of children with mental health problems in the United States do not receive mental health services due to a lack of insurance. It is estimated that 4.7 million children are eligible for Medicaid or the Children's Health Insurance Program (CHIP), but are not currently enrolled in either (Kenney et al., 2010). Implementation of the Patient Protection and Affordable Care Act (ACA), Public Law 111-148 (2010), has had a significant impact on the way that healthcare services are delivered, since many youth who were previously uninsured or underinsured have gained access to services.

With the expansion of health insurance coverage, many of the most vulnerable populations, such as young children, youth aging out of foster care, and children living in poverty now have increased access to preventive services and mental health treatment (English, 2010). In addition, the authorization of funding for home visitation programs to promote improvements in areas such as child development, parenting, and school readiness provides opportunities for families who are in the greatest need. Having already contributed significantly to the national discussion on healthcare reform and implications for SMH, the CSMH continues to analyze healthcare reform policy, disseminate relevant findings to key stakeholder groups, and inform the evolving policy reform at state and national levels related to SMH.

School Mental Health and the Public Health Approach

Since around 2010, several journal articles and federal reports have recommended that the field of children's mental health adopt a public health approach to conceptualizing children's mental health (see Blau, Huang, & Mallery, 2010; Miles, Espiritu, Horen, Sebian, & Waetzig, 2010; Stiffman et al., 2010; U.S. Department of Education, 2010). More specifically, the public health framework applies an ecological approach to conceptualizing children's mental health by recognizing that multiple systems influence children's difficulties and calls for an integration of mental health services across systems, including health, education, mental health, social services, child welfare, and juvenile justice (Blau et al., 2010; Stiffman et al., 2010).

This interdisciplinary and intersystems approach has characterized SMH (and the work of CSMH; see Weist, 2003; Weist, 2005) for years; thus, the SMH field can help to lead broader efforts to infuse a public mental health promotion strategy into services for children (Weist, 2001). This approach is strength-based and suggests a continuum of mental health services ranging from promotion activities that support and maintain positive mental health to prevention and treatment efforts (Blau et al., 2010). The field has not yet fully adopted this framework; only a few instances exist that demonstrate the successful application of the public health model to children's mental health (Miles et al., 2010).

Funding

Even with the significant progress and expansion of SMH programs over the past two decades, the funding for SMH services continues to be a struggle. A 2005 survey of SMH programs across the United States indicated that 70% of school districts reported an increase in need for services, but experienced the same level or decreases in their funding (Foster et al., 2005). It has become increasingly incumbent upon SMH programs to secure funding from multiple sources to sustain their service delivery (Evans et al., 2003; Weist et al., 2009).

While there are some potential funding sources that are underutilized (e.g., from Early and Periodic Screening, Diagnosis, and Treatment; Safe and Drug Free Schools; Title I), other sources of funding (e.g., Medicaid fee-for-service) are highly bureaucratic, unwieldy to obtain, and may not yield sufficient revenue (Center for Health and Health Care in Schools, 2003; Evans et al., 2003). Thus, the process of identifying and securing appropriate funding is difficult for programs. Further, funding provided by education systems is limited, leading to overcommitted and burdened school-employed mental health professionals (Lever, Stephan, Axelrod, & Weist, 2004). When community mental health mechanisms are used, they typically place a significant administrative burden on community providers who work in schools, who are also encumbered with multiple demands. In addition, these fee-for-service approaches have created concerns about overdiagnosis, limited time for prevention activities, and an inability to serve students without Medicaid (Lever et al., 2004; Mills et al., 2006). Exploring collaborative and unique funding arrangements that braid dollars from multiple sources to support shared goals, and to examine methods for assessing cost and cost-effectiveness of SMH, is recommended to help advance school mental health at local, state, and national levels.

FUTURE DIRECTIONS FOR THE FIELD
AND CONCLUSION

This chapter highlights the extensive growth and development in the field of school mental health over the past century and a half. While the school mental health field has had tremendous success in increasing access to a broader array of services, there is room for improvement, with many opportunities for improving the quality and efficiency of mental health services that children receive in school. In the most recent edition of the *Handbook of School Mental Health*, Weist, Lever, Bradshaw, & Owens, et al. (2014) identified eight crosscutting themes in need of attention to escalate progress in the field. These themes summarize the primary challenges that face the field.

Building SMH in the Context of Multi-tiered Systems of Support

Significant attention has been given to the many advantages of integrating school mental health and Positive Behavioral Interventions and Supports (PBIS; see Barrett, Eber, & Weist, 2013). The compelling synergies unleashed recently in these two fields appear to be catalyzing them toward operating as one. Integrating SMH with a multi-tiered system is important for many reasons. First, youth function best in an environment that is consistent, stable, and positive. An important goal of SMH services is to collaborate with school staff to identify effective strategies for supporting optimal student behavior and well-being. When school and SMH staff work within the same multi-tiered system, they share similar goals and communicate with a common language, facilitating collaboration.

Second, multi-tiered systems provide a structured approach for identifying youth with specific mental health needs, which improves the clarity and efficiency of the referral process for SMH services. Third, using a multi-tiered system, such as PBIS, has a powerful prevention capacity with behavioral and emotional problems for children, allowing SMH services to reach youth with mental health concerns and those without current concerns but at risk for future problems. Thus, implementing SMH services within a multi-tiered system is an important next step for the field.

Training and Workforce Development

Extensive developments have occurred in providing training for providers to support the use of evidence-based treatments and in cultivating the skills needed to work in interdisciplinary and collaborative service contexts. A major objective of current training with educators involves increasing knowledge and awareness of childhood development, mental health, and behavioral issues. An example of these development efforts is represented by the Mental Health Education Consortium, which focuses on increased training for preservice and current providers. Training topics include collaborating on interdisciplinary efforts within the school setting, providing empirically supported treatment, and integrating services within the school context (Anderson-Butcher & Weist, 2011).

Interdisciplinary Collaboration

Working within schools requires establishing a shared agenda with other school personnel (Andis et al., 2002), so there is a need to develop training and practice approaches to establish effective teams that emphasize the talents of diverse members coming together to promote youth well-being. Discipline-specific issues can challenge interdisciplinary work, such as language, conceptual frameworks, therapeutic orientation, training models, and other issues. Familiarity with the range of viewpoints across disciplines on these issues can support professionals from different disciplines to engage in effective communication and find ways to strengthen SMH services through the diversity of viewpoints.

Systematic Quality Assessment and Improvement

Given the nature of working in the school context, school-employed mental health staff may benefit from receiving trainings in available resources as well as in school culture, since providing mental health services within schools requires more flexibility in roles than do more traditional service provision. Further, the development of the School Mental Health Quality Assessment Questionnaire (SMHQAQ; Weist et al., 2005; Weist, Ambrose, & Lewis, 2006), a SMH report card that assesses overall progress of SMH work, represents a move to increase efforts surrounding the need to increase quality practices in SMH.

Cultural Competence

A critical future goal of the SMH field is finding effective ways to increase training and practice efforts that foster cultural sensitivity in mental health practices. In terms of mental health treatment within the school environment, cultural considerations, such as identity and labels are important skills to emphasize within the cultural context of the school. Further, cultural beliefs and practices can enhance or conflict with treatment, and the perception that a clinician understands and accepts one's cultural context improves clinical rapport, which is an important component for change in therapy. Thus, finding ways to incorporate cultural competence in training endeavors and cultural sensitivity into SMH services are essential areas of development for the school mental health field.

Family and Youth Engagement and Empowerment

Schools are in a position to readily access youth and families, and so the motivation to change and interest in engaging in SMH services may display greater diversity than is found in clinic-based services. Because the extent to which families are engaged in mental health treatment impacts the quality and clinical outcome of services, identifying effective strategies for supporting family engagement in the SMH context is critical. Furthermore, SMH services have the unique capacity to include youth and families in the development of programs. This point of collaboration is a powerful tool for improving not only the quality of services, but also family engagement by empowering youth and their families to share their voice (Barrett, Eber, & Weist, 2013; Coalition for Psychology in the Schools and Education, 2006).

Evidence-Based Practices

Further research on the effectiveness of evidence-based practices (EBPs) is needed. More research is necessary regarding outcomes when EBPs are implemented in diverse settings rather than traditional laboratory settings. Although EBPs may demonstrate efficacy within the highly controlled context characteristic of many quality research designs, the degree to which these effects translate to the context of the diverse settings that schools can present is often unclear. Additional research is needed to identify the effectiveness of EBPs across developmental stages, across provider and discipline training levels, across various cultural characteristics, and across presenting problems and service provisions.

Implementation Support and Coaching

There is growing emphasis on the need to increase implementation supports for promoting the use of EBPs in schools (Fixsen, Naoom, Blasé, Friedman, & Wallace, 2005). SMH professionals need support beyond training to implement EBPs effectively with children and staff in schools. Thus far, the literature equivocally demonstrates that student outcomes improve with the provision of coaching and implementation supports. More development and investigation in this area is needed to improve SMH services to youth.

INTERNATIONAL EFFORTS

Although much of this chapter focused on the historical context and current practices of SMH on a national level, SMH efforts are gaining momentum on an international level as well. For instance, the growth of the field internationally is evidenced by the development of leadership networks designed with the goal of bringing together like-minded SMH researchers, policymakers, and practitioners from around the world with the common goal of promoting youth mental health within the school context. The International Alliance for Child and Adolescent Mental Health and Schools (INTERCAMHS) was an active network from 2003 to 2010, emphasizing international collaboration in order to bridge efforts from key leaders and policies to guide the development of the field. From the platform of relationships built by INTERCAMHS, and ongoing participation in world conferences on mental health promotion (see below), new international networks focused on SMH are developing, such as the School Mental Health International Leadership Exchange (SMHILE), which is bringing together leaders from regions and countries across the world to share knowledge; co-create dissemination and leadership strategies; and signal best research, policy, and practice directions for the field (Short, Weist, & McDaniel, 2014).

In addition to interagency and international collaboration efforts to enhance the quality of practices in SMH and youth mental health promotion, countries around the world are making strides in developing broad, evidence-based school mental health promotion programs. Of note is the MindMatters program (Wyn, Cahill, Holdsworth, Rowling, & Carson, 2000), a national mental health promotion program implemented in Australian schools. MindMatters is a multi-tiered whole-school approach to mental health promotion that emphasizes a community of health promotion, focusing on addressing the knowledge and awareness of mental health among students and teachers within the school, and on targeted interventions to provide in-house supports to those students who require more focused efforts to address mental health concerns. Similarly, the Resilient Families Program (Shortt, Toumbourou, Chapman, & Power, 2006) is a school-based prevention program implemented within Australian schools that emphasizes linking efforts across the home and school community with the aim of creating environments that reinforce consistent and positive strategies. The Resilient Families Program utilizes the school context and teacher-parent relationships to help increase positive communication and problem-solving approaches to promote mental well-being (Shortt et al., 2006).

In addition to specific school-based interventions gaining support internationally, conferences aimed at bringing like-minded professionals together to share research and knowledge regarding the promotion of mental health are growing in popularity. For instance, the World Conference on the Promotion of Mental Health and Prevention of Mental and Behavioral Disorders was held for the eighth time in London in September 2014. This conference had a number of plenary presentations and a stream of more than 20 presentations on SMH as a prioritized theme in the global mental health promotion movement (see Weist & McDaniel, 2013). Benefitting from the leadership of SMHILE, global networking and collaboration in the advancement of practice, research, and policy in SMH has continued in subsequent world conferences, including a meeting held in Columbia, South Carolina (September 2015). In all of this work, the United States is a clear leader, consistent with progressive and increasing federal policy support for the field (see Anglin, 2003; Cashman, Rosser, & Linehan, 2013).

REFERENCES

American Psychiatric Association. (1980). *Diagnostic and statistical manual of mental disorders* (3rd ed.). Washington, DC: Author.

Anderson-Butcher, D., & Weist, M. D. (2011). The Mental Health-Education Integration Consortium (MHEDIC): A community of practice working to advance school mental health. *The Community Psychologist, 44*(4), 23–25.

Andis, P., Cashman, J., Praschil, R., Oglesby, D., Adelman, H., Taylor, L., & Weist, M. D. (2002). A strategic and shared agenda to advance mental health in schools through family and system partnerships. *International Journal of Mental Health Promotion, 4*, 28–35.

Anglin, T. (2003). Mental health in schools: Programs of the federal government. In M. Weist, S. Evans, & N. Lever (Eds.), *Handbook of school mental health: Advancing practice and research* (pp. 89–106). New York: Springer.

Aseltine, R. H., Gore, S., & Gordon, J. (2000). Life stress, anger and anxiety, and delinquency: An empirical test of general strain theory. *Journal of Health Social Behavior, 41*, 256–275.

Atkins, M. S., McKay, M. M., Arvanitis, P., London, L., Madison, S., Costigan, C., . . . Bennett, D. (1998). An ecological model for school-based mental health services for urban low-income aggressive children. *Journal of Behavioral Health Services & Research, 25*, 64–75.

Barrett, S., Eber, L., & Weist, M.D. (2013). *Advancing education effectiveness: An interconnected systems framework for Positive Behavioral Interventions and Supports (PBIS) and school mental health.* Center for Positive Behavioral Interventions and Supports (funded by the Office of Special Education Programs, U.S. Department of Education). Eugene, OR: University of Oregon Press.

Basson, M. D., Guinn, J. E., McElligott, J., Vitale, R., Brown, W., & Fielding, L. P. (1991). Behavioral disturbances in children after trauma. *Journal of Trauma-Injury Infection and Critical Care, 31*, 1363–1368.

Blau, G. M., Huang, L. N., & Mallery, C. J. (2010). Advancing efforts to improve children's mental health in America: A commentary. *Administration and Policy in Mental Health, 37*, 140–144.

Burke, R. (2002). Social and emotional education in the classroom. *Kappa Delta Pi Record, 38*, 108–111.

Cashman, J., Linehan, P., & Rosser, M. (2007). *Communities of Practice: A new approach to solving complex educational problems.* Alexandria, VA: National Association of State Directors of Special Education.

Cashman, J., Rosser, M., & Linehan, P. (2013). Policy, practice, and people: Building shared support for school behavioral health. In S. Barrett, L. Eber, & M. Weist (Eds.), *Advancing education effectiveness: An interconnected systems framework for Positive Behavioral Interventions and Supports (PBIS) and school mental health* (pp. 96–112). Center for Positive Behavioral Interventions and Supports (funded by the Office of Special Education Programs, U.S. Department of Education). Eugene, OR: University of Oregon Press.

Catron, T., Harris, V. S., & Weiss, B. (1998). Posttreatment results after 2 years of services in the Vanderbilt School-Based Counseling Project. In M. H. Epstein & K. Kutash (Eds.), *Outcomes for children and youth with emotional and behavioral disorders and their families: Programs and evaluation best practices* (pp. 633–656). Austin, TX: PRO-ED, Inc.

Center for Health and Health Care in Schools. (2003). *School-based health centers: Surviving a difficult economy*. Washington, DC: George Washington University.

Chiles, J. A., Miller, M. L., & Cox, G. B. (1980). Depression in an adolescent delinquent population. *Archives of General Psychiatry, 37*, 1179–1184.

Clauss-Ehlers, C., Serpell, Z., & Weist, M. D. (2013). *Handbook of culturally responsive school mental health: Advancing research, training, practice, and policy*. New York, NY: Springer.

Coalition for Psychology in Schools and Education. (2006, August). *Report on the Teacher Needs Survey*. Washington, DC: American Psychological Association, Center for Psychology in Schools and Education.

English, A. (2010). *The Patient Protection and Affordable Care Act of 2010: How does it help adolescents and young adults*. Chapel Hill, NC: Center for Adolescent Health & the Law; and San Francisco, CA: National Adolescent Health Information and Innovation Center.

Evans, S. W., Glass-Siegel, M., Frank, A., vanTreuren, R., Lever, N. A., & Weist, M. D. (2003). Overcoming the challenges of funding school mental health programs. In M. D. Weist, S. W. Evans, & N. A. Lever (Eds.), *Handbook of school mental health: Advancing practice and research* (pp. 73–86). New York, NY: Kluwer Academic/Plenum.

Evans, S. W., Weist, M. D., & Serpell, Z. (2007). *Advances in school-based mental health interventions: Best practices and program models* (Vol. II). New York, NY: Civic Research Institute.

Fixsen, D. L., Naoom, S. F., Blasé, K. A., Friedman, R. M., & Wallace, F., (2005). *Implementation research: A synthesis of the literature*. Tampa, FL: University of South Florida, Louis de la Parte Florida Mental Health Institute, National Implementation Research Network (FMHI Publication #231).

Flaherty, L. T., & Osher, D. (2003). History of school-based mental health services. In M. D. Weist, S. Evans, & N. Lever (Eds.), *Handbook of school mental health: Advancing practice and research* (pp. 11–22). New York, NY: Springer.

Flaherty, L. T., Weist, M. D., & Warner, B. S. (1996). School-based mental health services in the United States: History, current models and needs. *Community Mental Health Journal, 32*, 341–352.

Foster, S., Rollefson, M., Doksum, T., Noonan, D., Robinson, G., & Teich, J. (2005). *School mental health services in the United States 2002–2003* (DHHS Pub. No. [SMA] 05-4068). Rockville, MD: Center for Mental Health Services, Substance Abuse and Mental Health Services Administration.

Guarino, C., Santibañez, L., Daley, G., & Brewer, D. (2004, May). *A review of the research literature on teacher recruitment and retention*. Santa Monica, CA: RAND Corporation.

Hawkins, J. W., Hayes, E. R., & Corliss, C. P. (1994). School nursing in America—1902–1994: A return to public health nursing. *Public Health Nursing, 11*, 416–425.

Horn, M. (1989). *Before it's too late: The child guidance movement in the United States 1922–1945*. Philadelphia: Temple University Press; International Alliance for Child and Adolescent Mental Health and Schools.

Kenney, G., Lynch, V., Cook, A., & Phong, S. (2010). Who and where are the children yet to enroll in Medicaid and the Children's Health Insurance Program? *Health Affairs, 29*, 1920–1929.

Klern, A. M., & Connell, J. P. (2004). Relationships matter: Linking teacher support to student engagement and achievement. *School Mental Health, 74*, 262–273.

Koller, J., & Svoboda, S. (2002). The application of a strengths-based mental health approach in schools. *Journal of the Association for Childhood Education International, 78,* 291–295.

Lear, J. G., Gleicher, H. B., St. Germaine, A., & Porter, P. J. (1991). Reorganizing health care for adolescents: The experience of the School-Based Adolescent Health Care Program. *Journal of Adolescent Health, 12,* 450–458.

Lever, N., Stephan, S., Axelrod, J., & Weist, M. (2004). Fee-for-service revenue for school mental health through a partnership with an outpatient mental health center. *Journal of School Health, 74,* 91–94.

McWhirter, B. T., & Page, G. L. (1999). Effects of anger management and goal setting group interventions on state-trait anger and self-efficacy beliefs among high risk adolescents. *Current Psychology, 18,* 223–237.

Miles, J., Espiritu, R. C., Horen, N., Sebian, J., & Waetzig, E. (2010). *A public health approach to children's mental health: A conceptual framework.* Washington, DC: Georgetown University Center for Child and Human Development, National T.A. Center for Children's Mental Health.

Mills, C., Stephan, S., Moore, E., Weist, M. W., Daly, B. P., & Edwards, M. (2006). The president's New Freedom Commission: Capitalizing on opportunities to advance SMH services. *Clinical Child and Family Psychology Review, 9,* 149–161.

National Assembly on School-Based Health Care. (2002). *School-based health centers: A national definition. Position statement of the National Assembly on School-Based Health Care.* Washington, DC: National Assembly on School-Based Health Care.

Nelson, M. (2003). Through a glass darkly: Reflections on our field and its future. *Behavioral Disorders, 28,* 212–216.

President's New Freedom Commission. (2003). *Achieving the promise: Transforming mental health care in America.* Washington, DC: President of the United States. Retrieved from http://govinfo.library.unt.edu/mentalhealthcommission/reports/reports.htm

Price-Mitchell, M. (2009). Boundary dynamics: Implications for building parent-school partnerships. *School Community Journal, 19,* 9–26.

Robinson, R. (Ed.). (2004). *Advances in school-based mental health interventions: Best practices and program models* (1st ed.). Kingston, NJ: Civic Research Institute.

Rowling, L., & Weist, M. D. (2004). Promoting the growth, improvement and sustainability of school mental health programs worldwide. *International Journal of Mental Health Promotion, 6,* 3–11.

School Mental Health Alliance. (2004). *Working together to promote learning, social-emotional competence and mental health for all children.* New York, NY: Columbia University.

Short, K., Weist, M. D., & McDaniel, H (2014). *The School Mental Health International Leadership Exchange: First foundations.* Unpublished manuscript.

Shortt, A., Toumbourou, J., Chapman, R., & Power, E. (2006). The Resilient Families Program: Promoting health and wellbeing in adolescents and their parents during the transition to secondary school. *Youth Studies Australia, 25,* 33–40.

Stiffman, A., Stelk, W., Horwitz, S., Evans, M., Outlaw, F., & Atkins, M. (2010). A public health approach to children's MH services: Possible solutions to current service inadequacies. *Administration and Policy in Mental Health, 37,* 120–124.

Truscott, D. M., & Truscott, S. D. (2005). Differing circumstances, shared challenges: Finding common ground between urban and rural schools. *Phi Delta Kappan, 87,* 123–130.

U.S. Department of Education. (2010, March). *A blueprint for reform: The reauthorization of the Elementary and Secondary Education Act.* Alexandria, VA: Author. Retrieved from https://www2.ed.gov/policy/elsec/leg/blueprint/blueprint.pdf

U.S. Department of Health and Human Services, Maternal and Child Health Bureau. (2010). *The mental and emotional well-being of children: A portrait of states and the nation 2007.* Washington DC: Author.

U. S. Government Accountability Office. (2010). *School-based health centers: Available information on federal funding* (Publication No. GAO-11-18R). Washington, DC: Author.

U.S. Public Health Service. (2000). *Report of the Surgeon General's Conference on Children's Mental Health: A National Action Agenda* (Publication No. 017-024-01659-4).Washington, DC: Department of Health and Human Services.

Weist, M. D. (1997). Expanded school mental health services: A national movement in progress. In T. H. Ollendick & R. J. Prinz (Eds.), *Advances in clinical child psychology* (pp. 319–352). New York: Plenum.

Weist, M. D. (2001). Toward a public mental health promotion and intervention system for youth. *Journal of School Health, 71,* 101–104.

Weist, M. D. (2005). Fulfilling the promise of school-based mental health: Moving toward a public mental health promotion approach. *Journal of Abnormal Child Psychology, 33,* 735–741.

Weist, M. D., Ambrose, M., & Lewis, C. (2006). Expanded school mental health: A collaborative community/school example. *Children & Schools, 28,* 45–50.

Weist, M. D., Evans, S. W., & Lever, N. (2003). *Handbook of school mental health: Advancing practice and research.* New York, NY: Kluwer Academic/Plenum.

Weist, M. D., Lever, N., Bradshaw, C., & Owens, J. (2014). *Handbook of school mental health: Research, training, practice, and policy* (2nd ed.). New York, NY: Springer.

Weist, M. D., & McDaniel, H. L. (2013). The international emphasis of Advances in School Mental Health Promotion. *Advances in School Mental Health Promotion, 6,* 81–82.

Weist, M. D., Paternite, C. E., Wheatley-Rowe, D., & Gall, G. (2009). From thought to action in school mental health promotion. *International Journal of Mental Health Promotion, 11,* 32–41.

Weist, M. D., Sander, M. A., Walrath, C., Link, B., Nabors, L., Adelsheim, S., . . . Carrillo, K. (2005). Developing principles for best practice in expanded school mental health. *Journal of Youth and Adolescence, 34,* 7–13.

Weisz, J. R. (2004). *Psychotherapy for children and adolescents: Evidence-based treatments and case examples.* New York, NY: Cambridge University Press.

Wenger, E. (2006). Communities of practice: A brief introduction. Retrieved from *http:// wenger-trayner.com/theory/.*

Wenger, E., McDermott, R., & Snyder, W. (2002). *Cultivating communities of practice: A guide to managing knowledge.* Boston, MA: Harvard Business School Press.

Witmer, H. L. (1940). *Psychiatric clinics for children.* New York, NY: Commonwealth Fund.

Wyn, J., Cahill, H., Holdsworth, R., Rowling, L., & Carson, S. (2000). MindMatters: A whole school approach promoting mental health and wellbeing. *Australian and New Zealand Journal of Psychiatry, 34,* 594–601.

Who Are the School Mental Health Professionals?

RACHEL KININGER, BRANDON K. SCHULTZ,
AND JUDITH R. HARRISON ■

The term *school mental health professional* can apply to a wide array of practitioners who play a role in mental health service provision in our nation's public schools. In this chapter, we review the professions that are most often at the forefront of service delivery, including teachers, school counselors, school psychologists, school social workers, and school nurses. We should note at the outset that many more professionals are involved, including the community-based professionals who collaborate or consult on cases. In the interest of conciseness, however, we will focus our discussion on the professionals usually working within public schools. In each section below, we cover the training these professionals typically receive, based on what the relevant professional accrediting bodies recommend, and then discuss the roles these professionals typically assume in the schools, based on published survey results. We end this chapter by examining how these professions have evolved in recent years in regard to ongoing school mental health efforts.

TEACHERS

The responsibilities of teachers are perhaps the most familiar out of all school-based professionals, but their vital role in school mental health service is not as widely understood or appreciated. The role of a teacher is impressed upon all students after years of observing teachers in action. In fact, it has been noted that teacher candidates enter their training programs with preconceptions of what a teacher *should* do based on their own experiences—a phenomenon referred to as the "apprenticeship of observation" (Lortie, as cited in Whitcomb,

2013, p. 450). It is clear, however, that many of these preconceptions are invalid, and training programs are tasked with revising these expectations in the face of a changing profession.

Contemporary training standards are outlined by professional organizations such as the American Association of Colleges for Teacher Education (AACTE, 2009). According to the AACTE, well-prepared teachers need strong verbal skills and general intelligence, must possess sufficient knowledge in the content area taught, must master pedagogical knowledge (specific teaching techniques), must understand learners and learning development, and must be able to make judgments regarding adaptations to accommodate students' needs. Similarly, Darling-Hammond and Bransford (2005) recommended that modern teacher training programs target three important domains of knowledge for beginning teachers: (1) knowledge of learning, human development, and language development; (2) knowledge of specific subject matter; and (3) knowledge of how to teach (including how to teach diverse learners, classroom management strategies, and how to conduct assessments). Such standards have evolved over time in response to increasingly diverse student demographics and rising demands for teacher accountability (Whitcomb, 2013).

At the same time, school-based professionals are increasingly called upon to address student mental health needs because schools are often the only place where children and adolescents can access these services (see Chapter 1, this volume). Teachers—who have the most direct contact with students of any school-based professional—are well-positioned to identify and refer students with unmet mental health needs for services (Reinke, Stormont, Herman, Puri, & Goal, 2011). In this way, teachers can have a dramatic impact on service provision, either in consultation with other school mental health professionals (e.g., school psychologists) or in direct service provision (e.g., designing targeted interventions to address academic impairments). This potential is often unrealized, however, because teachers lack the training and knowledge to identify and address student needs effectively (Kratochwill & Shernoff, 2004).

As mentioned above, several professional agencies establish training standards for teacher education programs, resulting in variability across programs. To demonstrate the degree to which programs differ, we surveyed the coursework in four elementary, three secondary, and three special education undergraduate programs within one state.[1] As anticipated, the majority of required courses were related to developing academic content and pedagogical knowledge. Elementary education programs required courses related to pedagogy across all subject areas, but, in addition, there are requirements for single courses in diversity and education, child development, and students with special needs. Three out of the four elementary education programs required an additional course dedicated to

1. In this and other instances later in this same chapter, we review the course catalogs of training programs in North Carolina. We could have easily chosen any other state, but we chose North Carolina because it is the state most familiar to the first two authors.

classroom management, but none offered a course specific to individual behavioral interventions or techniques. Topics related to school mental health concerns were mentioned in the descriptions of other classes, mostly in relation to instructional interventions for struggling students, but it was unclear how much class time was dedicated to these discussions.

Secondary education programs differ from elementary education programs in that the former require more courses in specific academic content areas (e.g., mathematics, social studies). Secondary education programs also differ in that the course on childhood development is specific to adolescent development. However, only one of the three secondary education programs we surveyed required a course devoted entirely to classroom management. It seemed that the requirement for more coursework in specific subject areas came at the price of training in student mental health needs.

In contrast to elementary and secondary programs, special education programs required specialized coursework relating to school mental health. For instance, special education programs required at least one course addressing exceptional learners, and all programs required at least one course in instructional interventions. All programs surveyed required a course in assessment, and two of the three programs clearly taught behavioral intervention techniques, such as applied behavior analysis, positive behavior support, and functional behavior analysis.

Overall, it appears that general education programs provide preservice teachers with limited school mental health training, despite the rising needs in the field (Rones & Hoagwood, 2000). Special education training programs appear to offer a more solid foundation, based on our small survey, but, unfortunately, special educators work with students only after problems have been identified and academic impairments reach a critical mass. In our view, general education teachers would benefit from receiving more preparation regarding student mental health needs, given the current realities of the field. It is not surprising that teachers' preservice training is primarily geared toward developing teachers' content and pedagogical knowledge, but this consigns teachers to ongoing training needs once they enter the field. Based on the training standards and coursework described above, teachers may not be adequately prepared to implement effective behavior interventions or appropriately refer students for mental health services early in their careers—or perhaps ever—without adequate support from other professionals.

Researchers have examined how teachers perceive their knowledge and skills in fulfilling roles related to mental health promotion. For example, Reinke and colleagues (2011) surveyed 292 early childhood and elementary school teachers in Missouri about their perceptions of mental health concerns in schools and gaps between training in behavioral interventions and implementing interventions in schools. Seventy-five percent of teachers reported working with at least one student with mental health and behavioral concerns in the past year. Disruptive behavior (97%), inattention (96%), family stressors (91%), anxiety problems (76%), and depression (54%) were among the most common concerns reported. Although the majority of teachers (89%) agreed with the statement that schools should be involved in addressing students' mental health issues, only 28% of teachers agreed with the statement that they had adequate knowledge to meet students' mental health needs, and only 34% agreed with the statement that they had the necessary skills to meet students' mental health needs. Furthermore, teachers reported learning about behavioral interventions most often through in-service training (68%) and staff development activities (53%). Only 36% of teachers reported learning about behavioral interventions through undergraduate coursework, and 29% of teachers reported learning about behavioral interventions through graduate coursework. Teachers cited strategies for working with students with externalizing behaviors, recognizing and understanding mental health issues, and training in classroom management and behavioral interventions as the top three areas in which they desired additional training. The authors concluded that teachers perceive the need for mental health services in schools but feel unprepared to provide such services, especially in relation to classroom management and behavior support planning. These findings are not surprising, given the lack of intervention and classroom management coursework in the undergraduate programs we surveyed. Taken together, the results suggest that teachers need ongoing training to be effective school mental health agents.

In summary, teachers have the potential to fulfill a major role in promoting students' mental health. As the members of the school staff who have the most contact with students during the school year, teachers could positively affect students' mental health through the implementation of high-quality interventions and timely referrals. However, because of competing needs, training programs inadequately prepare preservice teachers for addressing student mental health, so ongoing training and support is needed for teachers to realize their true potential as school mental health professionals.

SCHOOL COUNSELORS

School counselors are responsible for promoting the academic achievement, vocational development, and psychosocial development of K–12 students. According to the American School Counselor Association (ASCA, 2012), accredited school counselor training programs target competencies in several domains relevant to mental health services. For example, school counselors receive training in developmental and counseling theories, individual and group counseling techniques, and prevention/intervention services. School counselors are also trained to respond to student and staff mental health needs during crises. Designing and implementing a school-wide school counseling core curriculum that involves structured lessons for students is another important responsibility for school counselors (ASCA, 2014).

In a position statement regarding school counselors' role in student mental health, the ASCA stated that although school counselors are not responsible for providing long-term therapy in schools for students with mental health disorders, school counselors must nevertheless be able to recognize student mental health needs and provide interventions for such students in the short term (ASCA, 2009). In this way, school counselors are integrally involved in addressing student mental health needs. Moreover, school counselors are trained to help identify students who might be eligible for special education as part of a school's multidisciplinary team and provide assistance in developing individualized education plans (IEPs). Overall, school counselors are expected to possess an array of competencies and fulfill a variety of roles related to mental health services in schools, but there are potential limitations to their impact in the school setting relating to training and practice needs.

School counselors must obtain at least a master's degree in school counseling in order to become a certified school counselor. Graduate education agencies, such as the Council for Accreditation of Counseling and Related Educational Programs (CACREP), have established training standards for graduate-level school counselor education programs to ensure that graduate programs provide high-quality training. CACREP outlines eight common-core curricular standards that must be included in any type of counseling program in order for the program to be accredited (CACREP, 2016). Several of the standards required are directly related to promoting student mental health. Table 2.1 contains a list of the most applicable standards and describes how these standards directly relate to fostering competence in providing mental health services. CACREP also created standards specifically for graduate-level school counselor education programs in foundational theories, counselor roles (contextual dimensions), and skills for practice. [2] The school counselor roles and practice skills that involve the school counselors' ability to provide mental health services in schools include: recognizing signs of mental health and behavior disorders; understanding common medications that affect behavior and learning; implementing crisis interventions; examining connections between environmental factors, behavior problems, and academic achievement; and developing counseling techniques. Overall, school counselors whose training program adheres to these standards will be well prepared to address student mental health needs.

Similar to teacher training programs described above, we surveyed selected programs in one state ($N = 11$) to gauge how these training standards translate into typical course loads for students. Two-thirds or more of the core courses in each program surveyed provided training relevant to enhancing students' mental health as per the standards cited above. All programs surveyed included at least two courses related to counseling theories and skills, and a majority of the programs required three or more counseling courses. Five out of 11 programs required a course dedicated to crisis counseling, 5 out of 11 required a course dedicated to substance abuse counseling, and 3 out of 11 required a course dedicated to family counseling. Additionally, all programs surveyed required at least one course in multicultural counseling, group work, and human development— most programs required only one class in each of these domains. Six out of 11

2. Counseling standards include skills in prevention and intervention.

Table 2.1. CACREP STANDARDS RELATED TO MENTAL HEALTH SERVICES

CACREP Standard	Relation to Mental Health
Professional Orientation and Ethical Practice	Students must learn: how school counselors contribute to interdisciplinary emergency management response teams; counseling supervision models, practices, and processes; advocacy processes for clients; ethical standards
Social and Cultural Diversity	Students must: understand multicultural and pluralistic trends; theories of multicultural counseling; know strategies for working with and advocating for diverse populations; develop cultural self-awareness; understand counselors' roles in eliminating biases, oppression, and discrimination
Human Growth and Development	Students must understand: theories of development, learning, personality, resilience, and wellness; effects of crises on individuals; understand human behavior, psychopathology, disability, developmental crises, and environmental impacts
Counseling and Helping Relationships	Students must understand: the counseling process; counselor characteristics and behavior that impact the helping process; essential counseling skills; counseling theories to inform selection of appropriate interventions; consultation; crisis intervention and suicide prevention
Group Counseling and Group Work	Students must learn: theories of group purpose; principles of group dynamics; group leadership styles; theories and techniques for group counseling

programs required a core course in psychopathology, and in some cases psychopathology courses were offered as electives. In terms of professional collaboration and consultation, 6 out of 11 programs required courses that were clearly focused on consultation. Finally, all programs required at least one course pertaining to foundations and ethics in school counseling. Overall, CACREP accredited programs appeared to provide a strong knowledge and skill base in mental health topics, as over 60% of typical course loads were in areas directly related to mental health (at least nominally). As would be expected, counseling knowledge and techniques were the courses required most often in each program.

Although school counselors appear to be trained to provide high-quality mental health services in schools, research has shown that most cannot devote much time to these services once they enter the field. In one survey, school counselors reported they spend 37% of their time counseling students, 24% of their time working with teachers to implement guidance curriculum for classrooms, and about 14% of their time providing crisis response support (Vandegrift, 1999). Taken together, these results suggests that school counselors spend about 75% of their time performing duties related to promoting students' mental health, while the remainder of their time is spent in system support (e.g., preparing budgets, attending meetings) and other non-guidance-related activities. A more recent survey of 361 school counselors from two southern states revealed that there were significant differences between school counselors' actual and desired roles within schools (Scarborough & Culbreth, 2008). Specifically, significant discrepancies between school counselors' desire to engage in student counseling, coordination (i.e., identifying and referring students for services), and consultation and their actual engagement in these activities were found. Working in secondary schools accounted for a significant proportion of the discrepancy between preferred and actual engagement in intervention activities, and fewer years of experience accounted for an additional portion of the discrepancy. Furthermore, school counselors were engaging in significantly more clerical and administrative duties than they desired. Overall, school counselors may not be able to implement their full range of mental health skills in schools consistently, depending on the expectations placed on them in their individual schools.

Additionally, administrators may not be aware of the role that school counselors can play in meeting student mental health needs. For instance, in a survey of 20 principals and 33 school counselors in middle and high schools in the Midwest, school counselors rated their ability to provide group counseling to students and identify students who require mental health services significantly higher compared to administrator ratings of these same abilities (Brown, Dahlbeck, & Sparkman-Barnes, 2006). Seventy-five percent of counselors and administrators combined believed it was school counselors' responsibility to address students' academic, career, personal, and mental health issues, but 25% of these participants believed the school counselors' primary role should only require academic, mediation, and career counseling. These discrepancies in perceptions of school counselor duties could be a major barrier in school counselors' provision of mental health services in schools. Administrators may not be aware of the knowledge and skills school counselors possess, and as a result they may not fully capitalize on school counselors' training. In short, school counselors may represent an underutilized resource within school mental health.

SCHOOL PSYCHOLOGISTS

School psychologists are responsible for helping students succeed academically, socially, behaviorally, and emotionally (National Association of School Psychologists [NASP], 2010a). With a knowledge base in both psychology and education, school psychologists implement direct and indirect educational and mental health services in schools. There are several ways in which school psychologists are involved in providing school mental health services, including conducting psychological assessments; consulting and collaborating with parents, educators, and other professionals to enhance the students' environment; implementing specific interventions and preventive services; and evaluating programs and interventions (NASP, 2010a). These skills enable school psychologists to be integrally involved in promoting students' mental health in schools. In a position statement regarding appropriate behavioral, social, and emotional supports in schools, NASP stated that school psychologists are responsible for advocating for students' mental health needs by providing leadership in universal screening, targeted interventions, and intensive interventions (NASP, 2009).

An examination of school psychology training programs reveals adequate requirements regarding the provision of mental health services. School psychologists are required to possess at least a specialist-level degree (which requires a minimum of three years of study, 60 credit hours, and a full-time internship) in school psychology in order to become a certified school psychologist (NASP, 2010b). NASP accredits specialist-level school psychology training programs and has established expectations for programs to ensure high-quality training. Examining these expectations allows for an understanding of the knowledge and skills acquired in accredited graduate programs.

The NASP Model for Comprehensive and Integrated School Psychological Services (2010a) outlines 10 domains of general competencies (basic knowledge and skills) that are addressed in graduate-level training programs accredited by NASP. The NASP Standards for Graduate Preparation of School Psychologists (NASP, 2010b) parallel the NASP Model and provide specific examples of the skills targeted in accredited training programs. A list of the seven domains relevant to promoting mental health in schools is presented in Table 2.2, along with examples as to how each domain relates to the provision of mental health services. To the degree that these training domains are realized in training programs, school psychologists are prepared to ensure high-quality mental health services in schools.

Again, to assess how these standards translate into course content, we surveyed relevant programs within one state. In this instance, we examined course requirements for four specialist-level programs accredited by the NASP. All four programs required one course in emotional and behavioral assessment, one course in consultation, and at least one course covering legal, ethical, and professional practice. All four programs required at least one course in interventions related to mental health. Three programs required a course in applied behavior analysis, and one program required a course in counseling theories and techniques. Two programs required a course related to the psychology of families and parenting. In regard to foundational knowledge in education and psychology, two out of the four schools required an advanced educational psychology course, all four programs required a course related to biological psychology, three programs required a course in child psychopathology, and three programs required a course in developmental psychology. Finally, two programs required courses in cultural counseling. Although variability persists, the NASP training domains appear to have influenced what the training programs target in their curriculum.

Historically, school psychologists have been viewed as psychometricians whose primary role is to determine if students are eligible for special education services (Fagan & Wise, 2007). With the advent of the latest training domains and

Table 2.2. A Selection of the National Association
of School Psychologists Practice Domains

Domain	Relation to Mental Health
Data-Based Decision Making and Accountability	School psychologists are skilled in administering psychological assessments, use assessment data to select evidence-based mental health services, and design assessments to evaluate the implementation and effectiveness of interventions.
Consultation and Collaboration	School psychologists are knowledgeable about models and strategies of consultation; use consultation to plan, implement and evaluate mental health services; and facilitate communication among school staff, families, and community professionals.
Interventions and Mental Health Services to Develop Social and Life Skills	School psychologists are knowledgeable about biological, cultural, developmental, and social impacts on behavior and mental health; implement and evaluate services to promote socialization and mental health; and provide a continuum of mental health services (e.g., individual/group counseling, behavior coaching, social-emotional learning programs, parent education/support).
Preventive and Responsive Services	School psychologists are knowledgeable about resilience and risk factors in relation to mental health and design and implement preventions and interventions based on this knowledge. They know evidence-based practices for crisis response and provide direct and indirect interventions for students with mental health issues.
Family-School Collaboration Services	School psychologists are knowledgeable about family systems, strategies to promote home-school-community collaboration to enhance students' mental health, and evidence-based practices to support family influences on students' mental health.
Diversity in Development and Learning	School psychologists have the knowledge base and skills necessary to provide services that enhance functioning for individuals with diverse characteristics.
Legal, Ethical, and Professional Practice	School psychologists are knowledgeable about the history of school psychology; ethical, legal, and professional standards; and multiple service models and methods. They advocate for effective mental health services for students.

NOTE: Three additional domains are targeted in graduate training programs: (1) implementing school-wide practices to promote learning; (2) research and program evaluation; and (3) providing interventions and instructional support to develop students' academic skills. However, these domains are not directly related to the provision of mental health services in schools.

other developments, the role of the school psychologist has expanded to include counseling and intervention implementation. School psychologists are currently trained to provide an array of mental health services in schools, but research has shown that these skills are not fully realized. In a recent survey sponsored by NASP, Castillo, Curtis, and Gelley (2010) found that school psychologists spent an average of 47% of their time conducting initial special education evaluations and revaluations. Much of this assessment time is spent administering intelligence tests, even though the practical utility of the results have been questioned for well over a decade (e.g., Gresham & Witt, 1997). Nevertheless, school psychologists reported devoting some of their time to the provision of mental health services. For instance, school psychologists spent an average of about 25% of their time developing and implementing interventions for individual students, 11% of their time promoting school-wide social-emotional supports, and 6% of their time in individual student counseling (serving an average of about 10 students each school year). However, 32% of school psychologists reported that they did not engage in individual counseling at all. Furthermore, most school psychologists (80–90%) did not conduct student groups addressing mental health issues, and 67% reported they did not conduct student groups addressing problem behaviors. In regard to consultation and collaboration, school psychologists reported spending an average of 16% of their time in consultation, mostly involving individual students' needs. Although school psychologists are spending more time in intervention-focused services than was reported in the past, they are still spending the majority of their time conducting assessments to determine eligibility for special education.

Researchers have also examined the factors that permit and limit school psychologists' ability to provide mental health services in schools. For instance, Suldo, Friedrich, & Michalowski (2010) interviewed 39 school psychologists through 11 focus groups in two southeastern school districts to analyze their perceptions of mental health services in schools. One major barrier to school psychologists' provision of mental health services was schools' primary focus on academics and educational accountability. Educators were perceived as being more concerned about academics and less concerned about students' mental health. Fifty-five percent of focus groups discussed inconsistent mental health treatment due to scheduling constraints in schools as another barrier. Seventy-three percent of focus groups also perceived insufficient support from their department and administration in providing mental health services. More specifically, 64% of focus groups felt that their department assigned them roles and responsibilities not directly related to the provision of mental health services. School psychologists also reported that their assessment caseloads prevented them from providing mental health services. Low parent support for mental health services was another perceived barrier that was discussed in 45% of focus groups. Finally, 73% of focus groups discussed insufficient training as a perceived barrier, with 64% of groups citing a lack of knowledge, 36% citing inexperience, and 55% reporting a lack of confidence. The last finding is particularly surprising given the aforementioned training goals, but it highlights the importance of continuing professional development in the 10 domains of practice after school psychologists enter the field.

SCHOOL SOCIAL WORKERS

The mission of school social workers is to establish connections between schools, families, and communities in order address students' academic, social, emotional, and behavioral needs (National Association of Social Workers [NASW], 2012). School social workers approach problems with an ecological perspective, taking into account the influence of home, school, and community environments on students' behavior (Frey et al., 2013). School social workers typically provide a variety of services in schools, ranging from individual clinical casework to designing and implementing school-wide programs (School Social Work Association of America [SSWAA], 2014).

According to the School Social Worker Practice Model, direct service roles include implementing evidence-based educational, behavioral, and mental health services to both students and families (Frey et al., 2013). For example, many social workers conduct mental health assessments, with a focus on psychosocial factors, and implement individual, group, and family counseling (Bronstein, Anderson, Terwilliger, & Sager, 2012). School social workers may also be involved in crisis response (Jozefowicz-Simbeni, 2008) and implementing skill-building or support groups for students and parents (Lebya, 2009). Another important direct service role according to the School Social Worker Practice Model is consulting with school staff to assist in intervention implementation (Frey et al., 2013). School social workers provide indirect services by coordinating school-based and community-based resources such as health, mental health, juvenile justice, and child welfare systems. This responsibility involves determining if referrals to outside agencies are necessary and assisting students and families with the process of accessing community services (Leyba, 2009). As a result of this coordination, students and families are provided access to a continuum of services. Finally, school social workers strive to establish and promote positive psychosocial school environments (Frey et al., 2013). Each school social worker's specific responsibilities are likely to vary based on the needs of the school, and most school social workers seem to shape their own roles to some degree (Leyba, 2009).

According to the National Association of Social Workers (NASW) Standards for School Social Work Services (2012), it is recommended that school social workers have at least a master's degree in social work from a program accredited by the Council on Social Work Education (CSWE); however, there is not a specific master's degree in school social work. Instead, school social workers attend a training program in social work and then take extra courses or seek out additional training in order to specialize in social work related to schools. In other words, some programs offer a concentration or specialty in school social work. Such schools require candidates to take extra classes in topics relevant to providing social services in schools. Other programs may not offer such concentrations, and, according to the NASW Standards, individuals who attend such programs must seek out additional training in school-related issues. Consequently, there are different paths to becoming a school social worker, and hence a variety of training experiences (Sabatino, Alvarez, & Anderson-Ketchmark, 2011).

The expected competencies for social workers outlined by the CSWE and the standards created specifically for school social workers by the NASW provide some clarity. For example, the CWSE outlines several domains of competency, including diversity and differences in practice; knowledge of the social environment; human behavior across development; the interplay between environment and behavior; research-informed practice; social policies and structures; and interventions for individuals, families, groups, organizations, and communities (CSWE, 2012). The core curriculum competencies are complemented by the NASW Standards for School Social Work Services (2012). These standards define the expected competencies and roles of school social workers. Furthermore, the standards are intended "to provide a basis for the preparation of school social workers and the development of continuing education materials and programs related to school social work services" (NASW, 2012, p. 6). Table 2.3 outlines the standards that directly apply to the provision of mental health services in schools and provides an explanation as to how these competencies and roles relate to mental health services. Overall, the CWSE and NASW standards require that school social workers receive sufficient training in areas related to the provision of mental health services in schools.

Table 2.3. NATIONAL ASSOCIATION OF SOCIAL WORKERS (NASW) STANDARDS

NASW Standard	Relation to Mental Health
Qualifications	School social workers shall have specialized knowledge of: education systems, historical and current trends in public education
Assessment	School social workers shall: have skills in individual, family, and systems assessment, data gathering, and interpretation; use ecological perspectives and functional approaches in assessment
Intervention	School social workers shall: use evidence-informed practices in delivering services; apply interventions within a multi-tier framework; address relevant ecologies through intervention
Cultural Competence	School social workers shall: use evidence-based techniques that reflect an understanding of how culture impacts the helping process; be knowledgeable of culturally appropriate resources
Interdisciplinary Leadership and Collaboration	School social workers shall: consult with parents, school personnel, community members, and other professionals; provide leadership and collaboration to implement school-based and school-linked programs

An issue with school social worker training is the lack of enforced national guidelines for curriculum in training programs (Mumm & Bye, 2011). Although the standards and competencies outlined above suggest that school social worker training programs produce high-quality mental health professionals, there is no guarantee that every school social worker will receive adequate training, because certification requirements vary rather dramatically from state to state. Several researchers have investigated this issue by looking at the ways in which coursework requirements vary across school social work courses and programs. For example, Berzin and O'Connor (2010) examined syllabi for school social work courses in 31 schools with an accredited social work master's program. The authors calculated the percentage of themes covered in syllabi across the different programs. In regard to student mental health, 62% of schools incorporated relevant content, with specific curricula covering substance abuse (43%), attention-deficit/hyperactivity disorder (31%), self-harm/suicide (31%), pervasive developmental disorders (21%), depression (17%), oppositional defiant disorder/conduct disorder (17%), anxiety (12%), and eating disorders (7%). Fifty-five percent of courses included information on evidence-based practices, but courses inconsistently offered information on specific evidence-based interventions. Ninety-five percent of courses covered topics in special education, such as assessment (71%), individualized education programs (55%), functional behavior assessment (43%), referral (22%) and early intervention (21%). In regard to clinical interventions, 62% of courses addressed clinical groups, 47% addressed crisis intervention, 29% covered mediation, 28% addressed home visits, 26% covered solution-focused therapy, and less than 20% addressed grief work, play therapy, and cognitive behavioral therapy. Finally, 52% of courses covered community linkages, 41% addressed school-wide intervention programs, 17% addressed changing school culture and school-wide intervention, and only 5% covered school-based health clinics. The authors concluded that coursework seemed to be geared more toward clinical preparation and less toward orienting school social workers to the educational context. In other words, the courses appeared to provide limited training in current educational trends related to students' social-emotional needs or in recent evidence-based practices.

Mumm and Bye (2011) examined the websites of the 195 accredited Master of Social Work programs in the United States. Out of 118 graduate schools in social work, 30% offer a school social work concentration. When graduate programs and bachelor's degree programs offering a concentration in school social work were examined, 86% of these programs required a field experience placement in a school setting, and 23% required a course on exceptional children. The concentration in some programs consisted of a field placement in a school and one elective course on school-based practice, whereas others required more extensive coursework relating to children, families, and schools. The authors stated that an understanding of school system structure and an ability to select, implement, and evaluate evidence-based practices are of critical importance in school social work, but based on their review, some school social workers are not being adequately trained in these domains. Although the CSWE and the NASW have appropriate standards in place to ensure high-quality mental health services, the diversity in training requirements across programs may mean that many school social workers fail to receive adequate training.

Another area of interest is how school social work training translates into actual practice. In a survey of 1,639 school social workers from across the United States, 60% reported spending most of their time in individual counseling, 31% reported spending most of their time doing group counseling, and 21% reported spending most of their time doing family work (Kelly et al., 2010). Thus, individual clinical work seems to be school social workers' primary responsibility. The majority of school social workers reported that most of their referrals were for students with behavioral (58%) and emotional problems (55%), and 30% indicated that more than half of their cases involved students with IEPs. Furthermore, 87% of school social workers reported a discrepancy between the amount of time they would like to be involved in primary prevention activities and the amount of time they actually spend in these activities. Specifically, social workers reported spending about 25% of their time in primary prevention and about 60% of their time in tertiary prevention (e.g., special education), whereas ideally they would split this time evenly between the two. Finally, school social workers reported spending 30% of their time on administrative tasks, which—similar to other school mental health professionals (e.g., school counselors)—suggests that they may not regularly apply their skill set in schools.

SCHOOL NURSES

School nurses work in schools to address student health issues that can hinder academic achievement. One of the most common responsibilities of school nurses is the administration of medications, including psychiatric medications (Maughan & Mangena, 2014). In addition, school nurses commonly participate on interdisciplinary teams to promote positive school climates, help to implement intervention plans (e.g., the health portion of IEPs), and provide a liaison between schools and community mental health providers (National Association of School Nurses [NASN], 2013). In all, it has been estimated that school nurses spend roughly a third of their time addressing student mental health concerns in some capacity (Foster et al., 2005).

The training background of school nurses shares some similarities with that of school social workers, in that there are no programs specific to the profession. Rather, school nurses are nurses who are hired to work in schools. The NASN has put forth standards for the profession, recommending at least a bachelor's degree in nursing and state licensure as a registered nurse (RN), but requirements for specialized training are ultimately defined at the state level. Some states require specialized training for school nurses, including specific coursework or continuing education credits, experience in the field, or a passing grade on the National

School Nurse Certification Exam. For example, some states require school nurses to have continuing education credits in the area of child abuse and neglect detection (e.g., California). Other states have no requirements other than an RN (National Association of State Boards of Education [NASBE], n.d.).

To assess the degree to which nurses are trained to address child and adolescent mental health needs, we surveyed the course requirements for traditional bachelor's degrees in nursing in one state ($N = 15$)[3]. Of these programs, most (80%) required at least one class in development, and most (75%) appeared to require at least one advanced class in psychiatric nursing (or mental health nursing). Of course, preservice school nurses can opt to take additional classes in psychology or development, but additional coursework in these areas did not appear to be a requirement for the bachelor's degree. Related topics may also be discussed as part of other classes (e.g., "Current Issues in Nursing"), but this is not clear from course catalogs alone.

In a recent survey of 6,841 school nurses across the country (Maughan & Mangena, 2014), it was found that the vast majority were RNs (93.5%), with a plurality holding a bachelor's degree in nursing (44.4%). Most school nurses were hired directly by a public school district (84%), with others working in settings such as private schools and military bases. Roughly half (49.6%) were split across two or more buildings, and caseloads for most school nurses exceeded 750 students for a majority (51%) of respondents. The 750-student caseload is an important threshold, as this is the recommended ratio of students in the general population to a single school nurse (NASN, 2010). The recent survey also asked practicing school nurses about their training, and respondents reported wanting additional information in the areas of intervention planning (e.g., IEPs, 504 plans) and behavioral health (e.g., attention-deficit/hyperactivity disorder). Taken together, these results suggest that although school nurses who attain a bachelor's degree are very likely to receive training in mental health nursing and child development, practicing school nurses feel inadequately prepared to address some common needs of school mental health services provision and are likely to be confronted with large caseloads. Perhaps most troubling, many of the survey respondents (16.2%) reported that their positions were under threat of being cut from school budgets (Maughan & Mangena, 2014).

CONCLUSION

It is clear from our literature review that some of the most readily available school mental health professionals have training comparable to community-based mental health professionals (cf. marriage and family therapists, drug abuse counselors, case managers); however, the skill sets of school mental health practitioners

3. We chose to survey the course catalogs of bachelor's programs based on NASN recommendations for the field. One additional degree-conferring university in the state did not make their catalog readily available online.

appear underutilized in practice. For example, school counselors and school social workers report spending roughly 30% of their time in administrative tasks unrelated to their training. Other school mental health professionals appear limited by traditional and outmoded roles, limiting their effectiveness. For example, school psychologists spend the majority of their time in psychoeducational assessment to determine student eligibility for special education, even though their training prepares them to be effective behavior consultants and interventionists. Still other school mental health professionals are confronted with caseloads larger than recommended by professional organizations (e.g., school nurses).

What does this mean for the future of school mental health initiatives? Our impression is that to increase school mental health service capacity, one of three things will need to occur: (1) the current roles of school-based professionals will need to change to better meet student mental health needs, (2) community-based mental health professionals will need to consult with school professionals to a greater degree than they do now, or (3) some combination of the first two options. Our hope for the field is the third option. We believe that substantial progress can be made on behalf of at-risk students by shifting the current job descriptions of school-based professionals away from time-consuming services that could be managed by inexpert staff (e.g., administrative tasks), and replacing those burdens with more training-consistent activities. In our opinion, this would represent a more effective allocation of resources. At the same time, we believe that increased support from community-based professionals—clinical psychologists, social workers, pediatricians, and psychiatrists—could vastly improve school mental health efforts. For community-based professionals to be successful, however, they will need to know how to navigate school systems effectively and arrange ways to be reimbursed for these services—two challenges that require careful consideration.

REFERENCES

American Association of Colleges for Teacher Education. (2009). *Teacher preparation makes a difference*. Washington, DC: Author. Retrieved from http://aacte.org/pdf/Publications/Resources/Teacher%20Preparation%20Makes%20a%20Difference.pdf

American School Counselor Association. (2009). The school counselor and student mental health. Alexandria, VA: Author. Retrieved from https://www.schoolcounselor.org/school-counselors-members/about-asca-(1)/position-statements

American School Counselor Association. (2012). ASCA school counselor competencies. Alexandria, VA: Author. Retrieved from http://www.schoolcounselor.org/asca/media/asca/home/SCCompetencies.pdf

American School Counselor Association. (2014). *The role of the school counselor*. Alexandria, VA: Author. Retrieved from: https://www.schoolcounselor.org/school-counselors-members/careers-roles

Berzin, S. C., & O'Connor, S. (2010). Educating today's social workers: Are school social work courses responding to the changing context? *Children & Schools, 32*, 237–249.

Bronstein, L. R., Anderson, E., Terwilliger, S. H., & Sager, K. (2012). Evaluating a model of school-based health and social services: An interdisciplinary community-university collaboration. *Children & Schools*, *34*, 155–165.

Brown, C., Dahlbeck, D. T., & Sparkman-Barnes, L. (2006). Collaborative relationships: School counselors and non-school mental health professionals working together to improve the mental health needs of students. *Professional School Counseling*, *9*, 332–335.

Castillo, J. M., Curtis, M. J., & Gelley, C. (2010). School psychology 2010—Part 2: School psychologists' professional practices and implications for the field. *Communiqué*, *40*(8), 4–6.

Council for Accreditation of Counseling and Related Educational Programs. (2016). 2016 CACREP Standards. Alexandria, VA: Author. Retrieved from http://www.cacrep.org/for-programs/2016-cacrep-standards/

Council on Social Work Education. (2012). Educational Policy and Accreditation Standards. Alexandria, VA: Author. Retrieved from: http://www.cswe.org/File.aspx?id=13780

Darling-Hammond, L. & Bransford, J. (2005). *Preparing teachers for a changing world: What teachers should learn and be able to do*. San Francisco, CA: Jossey-Bass.

Fagan, T., & Wise, P. S. (2007). *School psychology: Past, present, and future* (3rd ed.). Bethesda, MD: NASP.

Foster, S., Rollefson, M., Doksum, T., Noonan, D., Robinson, G., & Teich, J. (2005). *School Mental Health Services in the United States, 2002–2003*. DHHS Pub. No. (SMA) 05-4068. Rockville, MD: Center for Mental Health Services, Substance Abuse and Mental Health Services Administration. Retrieved from http://store.samhsa.gov/shin/content//SMA05-4068/SMA05-4068.pdf

Frey, A. J., Alvarez, M. E., Dupper, D. R., Sabatino, C. A., Lindsey, B. C., Raines, J. C., . . . Norris, M. A. (2013). School Social Work Practice Model. London< KY: School Social Work Association of America. Retrieved from http://sswaa.org/displaycommon.cfm?an=1&subarticlebr=459

Gresham, F. M., & Witt, J. C. (1997). Utility of intelligence tests for treatment planning, classification, and placement decisions: Recent empirical findings and future directions. *School Psychology Quarterly*, *12*, 249–267.

Jozefowicz-Simbeni, D. M. H. (2008). An ecological and developmental perspective in dropout risk factors in early adolescence: Role of school social workers in dropout prevention. *Children & Schools*, *30*, 49–62.

Kelly, M. S., Berzin, S. C., Frey, A., Alvarez, M., Shaffer, G., & O-Brien, K. (2010). The state of school social work: Findings from the national school social work survey. *School Mental Health*, *2*, 132–141.

Kratochwill, T. R., & Shernoff, E. S. (2004). Evidence-based practice: Promoting evidence-based interventions in school psychology. *School Psychology Review*, *33*, 34–48.

Leyba, E. G. (2009). Tools to reduce overload in the school social worker role. *Children & Schools*, *31*, 219–228.

Maughan, E., & Mangena, A. S. (2014). The 2013 NASN School Nurse Survey: Advancing school nursing practice. *NASN School Nurse*, *29*, 76–83. doi: 10.1177/1942602X14523135

Mumm, A. M., & Bye, L. (2011). Certification of school social workers and curriculum content of programs offering training in school social work. *Children & Schools, 33*, 17–23.

National Association of School Nurses. (2010). *Caseload assignments* (Position statement). Silver Spring, MD: Author. Retrieved from http://www.nasn.org/Portals/0/positions/2010pscaseload.pdf

National Association of School Nurses. (2013). *Mental health of students* (Position statement). Silver Spring, MD: Author. Retrieved from http://www.nasn.org/Portals/0/positions/2013psmentalhealth.pdf

National Association of School Psychologists. (2009). *Appropriate Behavioral, Social, and Emotional Supports to Meet the Needs of All Students* (Position Statement). Bethesda, MD: Author.

National Association of School Psychologists. (2010a). *Model for Comprehensive and Integrated School Psychological Services*. Bethesda, MD: Author.

National Association of School Psychologists. (2010b). *Standards for Graduate Preparation of School Psychologists*. Bethesda, MD: Author.

National Association of Social Workers. (2012). *NASW Standards for School Social Work Services*. Washington DC: Author. Retrieved from http://www.naswdc.org/practice/standards/NASWSchoolSocialWorkStandards.pdf

National Association of State Boards of Education. (n.d.). *State School Health Policy Database: Requirement for school nurses*. Retrieved from http://www.nasbe.org/healthy_schools/hs/bytopics.php?topicid=2130

Reinke, W. M., Stormont, M., Herman, K. C., Puri, R., & Goel, N. (2011). Supporting children's mental health in schools: Teacher perceptions of needs, roles, and barriers. *School Psychology Quarterly, 26*, 1–13.

Rones, M., & Hoagwood, K. (2000). School-based mental health services: A research review. *Clinical Child and Family Psychology Review, 3*, 223–241.

Sabatino, C. A., Alvarez, M. E., & Anderson-Ketchmark, C. (2011). "Highly qualified" school social workers. *Children & School, 33*, 189–192.

Scarborough, J. L., & Culbreth, J. R. (2008). Examining discrepancies between actual and preferred practice of school counselors. *Journal of Counseling & Development, 86*, 446–459.

School Social Work Association of America (2014). *School social workers' role in addressing students' mental health needs and increasing academic achievement*. London: KY: Author. Retrieved from http://sswaa.org/displaycommon.cfm?an=1&subarticlenbr=600

Suldo, S. M., Friedrich, A., & Michalowski, J. (2010). Personal and systems-level factors that limit and facilitate school psychologists' involvement in school-based mental health services. *Psychology in the Schools, 47*, 354–373.

Vandegrift, J. A. (1999). Are Arizona public schools making the best use of school counselors? Results of a three-year study of counselors' time use. (Report No. CG028489; ERIC Document Reproduction Service No. ED430178). Tempe: Arizona State University.

Whitcomb, J. (2013). Learning and pedagogy in initial teacher preparation. In W. M. Reynolds & G. E. Miller (Eds.). *Handbook of Psychology: Vol. 7. Educational Psychology* (pp. 441–463). Hoboken, NJ: John Wiley & Sons.

PART II

School Mental Health Interventions

3

Engaging Adolescents
in Secondary Schools

AMY L. RESCHLY, ANGIE J. POHL,
SANDRA L. CHRISTENSON,
AND JAMES J. APPLETON ■

Student engagement at school and with learning is the rare construct that appeals to scholars and educators across disciplines, such as public health and developmental, educational, and school psychology, as well as nations (e.g., Australia, Finland, Portugal, United States). Thus, the characterization of student engagement as a "meta-construct" (Fredricks, Blumenfled, & Paris, 2004) is fitting. Views of engagement have been evolving since the topic was first introduced almost 30 years ago. Student engagement has been described as "the attention . . . investment, and effort students expend in the work of school" (Marks, 2000, p. 155), and it is characterized as the "bottom line" in programs to promote school completion (Grannis, 1994) and school reform efforts (National Research Council & Institute of Medicine [NRC & IOM], 2004). In summarizing various definitions and research on student engagement, Christenson, Reschly, and Wylie (2012) concluded that

> [s]tudent engagement refers to the student's active participation in academic and co-curricular or school-related activities and commitment to educational goals and learning. Engaged students find learning meaningful and are invested in their learning and future. . . . [It] drives learning; requires energy and effort; is affected by multiple contextual influences; and can be achieved for all learners. (pp. 816–817)

Students have fundamental, basic human needs for autonomy, belonging, and competence (Ryan & Deci, 2000), or, in other words, the need to feel that "I can, I want to, and I belong" (NRC, 2004). Student engagement may be viewed as the manifestation of the extent to which these fundamental psychological needs are met. Student engagement is associated with myriad outcomes of interest across social-emotional, behavioral, and academic domains (Christenson et al., 2012). This is true whether engagement is investigated as part of the learning process, which tends to associate with how much students learn, or more generally as engagement with school, which associates with persistence in school (Janosz, 2012). Thus, the appeal to both scholars and practitioners is clear. For educators, however, student engagement and disengagement is compelling because it accurately describes the students and conditions present in schools (Christenson et al., 2008; Finn & Zimmer, 2012; Fredricks et al., 2004), has clear relevance across ages and levels of schooling (Finn & Zimmer, 2012; Reschly & Christenson, 2012), and has strong ties to student achievement (Finn & Zimmer, 2012). In sum, engagement is relevant for all students in all types of schools (NRC, 2004). Thus, when an engagement lens is adopted vis-à-vis mental health service delivery, it is applicable to a range of students, from those showing early warning signs of disengagement to those with diagnosable psychological disorders. Irrespective of student characteristics (or student placement on the continuum of mental health service delivery), the central point is to engage students more effectively and motivate them to acquire the academic and effort/persistence skills (sometimes referred to as *noncognitive skills*) needed to be college and career ready (Farrington et al., 2012).

Student engagement has wide appeal, with implications for theory and interventions to enhance students' functioning across academic, behavioral, and social-emotional domains. Student engagement in this chapter is examined as a global, multidimensional construct,[1] with a focus on important areas of consensus among scholars and implications for conceptualizing interventions. A description of these important aspects is followed by a summary of engagement research and intervention recommendations specific to adolescents and the integration of measurement and intervention in a comprehensive model of service delivery.

STUDENT ENGAGEMENT

There are several points regarding the conceptualization of student engagement that have implications for intervention and mental health. A model of engagement (Figure 3.1) illustrates important aspects of the construct as well as relationships among contextual variables, engagement, and both proximal and distal student outcomes.

Dimensions of Student Engagement

It is widely agreed that engagement is a multidimensional construct that includes aspects of students' behavior, emotion, and cognition. Fredericks and colleagues

---

1. Discussion of nuances in different conceptualizations of engagement may be found in Reschly and Christenson (2012).

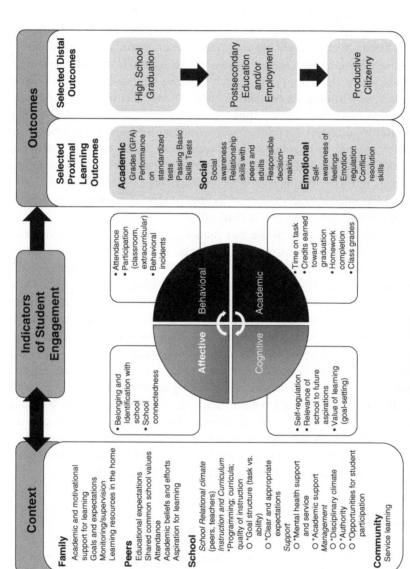

Figure 3.1 Model of context, engagement, and student outcomes.

NOTE: Adapted from Appleton et al., 2006; Christenson et al., 2008; and Reschly & Christenson, 2012.

(2004) explain that "[t]he fusion of behavior, emotion, and cognition under the idea of engagement is valuable because it may provide a richer characterization of children than is possible in research on single components. . . . In reality, these factors are dynamically interrelated within the individual" (p. 61). Although there are some differences among scholars in the operationalization of each of these types of engagement, one may generally view *behavioral engagement* as encompassing school-related conduct, involvement in learning, and participation in school-related activities (Fredricks et al., 2004). In our work, we further differentiated *academic engagement* (e.g., involvement in learning) from the larger behavioral engagement class to more accurately describe the engagement of students we worked with in dropout prevention efforts in an effort to refine and match interventions to student needs (Appleton, Christenson, Kim, & Reschly, 2006; Christenson et al., 2008). *Cognitive engagement* may be described as investment and effort devoted to learning and self-regulation during learning (Fredricks et al., 2004). *Affective engagement*, also referred to as *emotional* and *psychological engagement*, refers to emotional experiences at school or while learning. Affective engagement is often operationalized as feelings of identification with, or belonging at, school (Reschly, Appleton, & Pohl, 2014).

These types of engagement are not mutually exclusive, but rather interrelated aspects of a larger construct, a contention clearly supported in research (e.g., Appleton et al., 2006; Finn & Zimmer, 2012; Ladd & Dinella, 2009). Furthermore, in our early work, we speculated that there is a sequence to these subtypes of engagement wherein the more internal forms—cognitive and affective engagement—precede the more objective, observable forms—behavioral and academic engagement (Reschly & Christenson, 2006a). Although evidence suggests mutual influence among the internal and external engagement types (e.g., Ladd & Dinella, 2009), there is also support for a general, indirect sequence wherein internal engagement affects behavioral (including academic) engagement, which in turn is more directly related to outcomes, such as achievement (Christenson & Anderson, 2002; Voelkl, 2012). In any event, the literature clearly underscores the importance of students' thoughts and emotions in understanding student behavior and academic performance (e.g., Cleary & Zimmerman, 2012; Fredricks et al., 2004; Pekrun & Linnenbrink-Garcia, 2012; Schunk & Mullen, 2012).

Contexts and Amenability to Intervention

Two of the most important properties of the student engagement construct are the influence of contexts, such as homes, schools, and communities (see Figure 1), on students' engagement, and the amenability of engagement to intervention. There is agreement among engagement scholars that engagement serves as a mediator between contexts and student outcomes across social, academic, and behavioral domains (Christenson et al., 2008; Connell & Wellborn, 1991; Fredricks et al., 2004; Furrer, Skinner, Marchand, & Kindermann, 2006). In other words, students' engagement is affected by contexts, which in turn are related to outcomes, such as achievement or high school graduation.

The influence of contexts on students' engagement illustrates a point that is at the heart of the widespread interest in the engagement construct. That is, student engagement is amenable to intervention and environmental (contextual) manipulations. A common distinction in the dropout literature may be useful for illustration. Hundreds of variables have been examined relative to dropout and school completion. Some of these are demographic in nature, such as race-ethnicity, socioeconomic status (SES), and the region of the country in which students reside, while others may be more easily affected through intervention, such as parental monitoring, homework completion, or student attendance (Reschly & Christenson, 2006b, 2012). Understanding which demographic variables are associated with greater risk conditions is useful, but, from an intervention perspective, knowing a student's race or socioeconomic status does little to inform what intervention strategy is needed to increase self-regulation, belonging/identification, or homework completion. In other words, there is a difference between demographic and functional risk wherein indicators of functional risk (engagement/disengagement) are most useful for determining imminent need for support and intervention (Christenson, 2008). In this vein, those variables that are amenable to intervention have been differentiated according to contexts, such as families and schools. Furthermore, given links between these contextual variables and both proximal and distal outcomes (e.g., between time on task or attendance and achievement), these variables are logical targets for intervention efforts (Reschly & Christenson, 2006b).

Student Engagement and Development

An early, influential model of student engagement and disengagement as it relates to high school dropout and completion was advanced by Finn (1989). In this conceptualization, engagement comprises two main components: behavior and identification/valuing of school. As students participate, they experience success and feel like they belong and identify with school, which in turn promotes their ongoing participation, thereby creating a cycle of participation-success-valuing that endures in the face of minor setbacks through the completion of schooling. For other students, including those most at risk for negative school outcomes, the participation-success-valuing cycle breaks down over time, becoming one of poorer performance and withdrawal. Students may not have the attitudes or behaviors required for successful participation at the start of schooling, thereby reducing the likelihood of success and undermining valuing over time (Finn, 1989). Alternatively, students may encounter academic problems, have difficulty interacting with teachers, or develop relationships with disengaged peers who disrupt the participation-success-valuing cycle (Finn & Zimmer, 2012).

The idea that there are cycles of engagement and disengagement over time, beginning at school entry or even earlier, garners support from a range of research studies. There have been studies of dropout, for example, that find consistencies from early elementary school when variables such as attendance, behavior, academic performance, and attachment to school are examined (e.g., Alexander, Entwisle, & Horsey, 1997; Barrington & Hendricks, 1989; Ensminger

& Slusarcick, 1992). Other support may be drawn from studies of model preschool programs, such as Perry Preschool (Schweinhart & Weikart, 1999) and the Chicago Parent-Child Center (Reynolds, 2001), which have been shown to be associated with later school outcomes, presumably through the effect these programs have on preparing students for school, thereby facilitating the participation-success-valuing cycle (Reschly & Christenson, 2012). Studies indicate that engagement is related to achievement and outcomes across ages and levels of schooling (e.g., Alexander et al., 1997; Balfanz, Herzog, & Iver, 2007; Finn, 2006; Lovelace, Reschly, Appleton, & Lutz, 2014).

Although this volume is devoted to adolescence, the development of engagement and disengagement across years of schooling is an important facet of engagement theory and intervention planning. A central tenet of Finn's model (1989) is that engagement changes as students progress in school, with greater opportunities for involvement and more responsibility. In other words, successful participation is different in eighth grade than it is in first grade. Thus, there are age-related changes in the environment that must also be considered as part of students' cycles of engagement or disengagement. In this vein, there are two additional considerations. The first is that the typical developmental pattern is for students to exhibit both seasonal and grade-related declines in student engagement. Data from a large, diverse school district indicate that all students' reported levels of engagement decline from fall to spring within each school year, and that engagement declines in each subsequent year of schooling (e.g., ninth graders report lower engagement than eighth graders; Appleton, 2012; Lovelace, Reschly, & Appleton, 2017). The elementary to middle school transition in particular has received attention as being a particularly difficult one for many students, with declines in attendance, behavior, motivation, and achievement following the transition (Eccles et al., 1993). This period includes numerous changes, including physical and social-emotional development, as well as school and social changes associated with the transition. In some cases, there is a mismatch between school settings and students' needs for autonomy, relatedness, belonging, and competence. Likewise, a mismatch may also exist between intervention strategies and students' needs and development. As noted by the NRC and IOM (2004), "adolescents are too old and too independent to follow teachers' demands out of obedience and many are too young, inexperienced, or uninformed to fully appreciate the value of succeeding in school" (p. 2). Age-related declines in engagement may be compounded by an environment that is less supportive of engagement (e.g., larger, more impersonal classes; more transmissive teaching). For some students, these declines become persistent and stable, developing into a pattern of disengagement with negative long-term effects.

The other intervention consideration that arises is the stability of patterns of student engagement. Many students exhibit relatively stable patterns of engagement over time, with only small decreases with age (Archambault, Janosz, Morizot, & Pagani, 2009). For example, a longitudinal study by Wylie and Hodgen (2012) found that 17% of their sample sustained high, stable levels of engagement across several years, while 13% demonstrated low, stable levels of engagement. Given that the interest in student engagement is rooted largely in its amenability to intervention, this stability may seem antithetical to intervention efforts. Instead, it should be viewed as what occurs in the absence of significant contextual changes, thereby resulting in environments that sustain high or low levels of student engagement. Despite many students demonstrating stability, not all do. Studies reveal distinct trajectories associated with different patterns of engagement (Archambault et al., 2009; Wylie & Hodgen, 2012). Of particular concern are those students with stable, low levels of engagement and those showing rapid declines in the first years of high school.

Student Engagement and Mental Health

Youth mental health is described as "the achievement of expected developmental cognitive, social, and emotional milestones" and functioning well in the home, school, and community (U.S. Department of Health and Human Services, 1999, p. 123). Practically speaking, mentally healthy students relate well to others, regulate their emotions, and perceive themselves as capable of learning and performing. Given that mental health is strongly influenced by the contexts in which youth develop, such as the family, school, peer group, and neighborhood, it is logical for schools to play a role in supporting mental health.

In schools, promoting mental health entails promoting healthy social-emotional development, preventing mental health problems, and enhancing resiliency (Adelman & Taylor, 2010). This may be best accomplished through reducing risk factors for poor social, emotional, and behavioral outcomes, and by developing or enhancing the protective factors that buffer against risks, including both environmental protective factors (e.g., safe, caring, and supportive schools) and personal protective factors (e.g., sense of autonomy, belonging, and competence; social, coping, and problem-solving skills) (Adelman & Taylor, 2010; O'Connell, Boat, & Warner, 2009). Such efforts presume that the primary causes for most social, emotional, and behavioral problems in youth are not biological factors, but rather environmental and person factors that are often amenable to change, providing natural targets for prevention and intervention efforts.

Student engagement in school and learning is widely acknowledged as a protective factor for youth—protecting them from risks that emerge during elementary, middle, and high school (Finn & Zimmer, 2012; Skinner & Pitzer, 2012). Students who feel connected at school, identify with school, value school, participate in the classroom and in extracurricular activities, attend regularly, and perform well academically are more likely than disengaged peers to experience social, emotional, and behavioral health. Moreover, engaged students are less likely than their disengaged peers to experience mental health problems or engage in health risk behaviors (Bond et al., 2007; Li & Lerner, 2011; O'Connell et al., 2009; Wang & Peck, 2013; World Health Organization [WHO], 2005). Table 3.1 provides examples of indicators of the four subtypes of engagement—academic, behavioral, cognitive, and affective—and their relation to aspects of mental health, such as depressive symptoms, emotional distress, and engagement in risky behaviors. It follows then that by promoting student engagement for all students, schools are also making strides toward promoting healthy social-emotional development and enhancing resiliency.

Table 3.1. EXAMPLES OF INDICATORS OF ENGAGEMENT AS PROTECTIVE FACTORS
AND INDICATORS OF DISENGAGEMENT AS RISK FACTORS FOR OUTCOMES RELATED
TO MENTAL HEALTH

Engagement Subtype	Protective Factors	Risk Factors
Academic	• Academic achievement is a protective factor against mental health problems (WHO, 2005) • Improvements in school academic performance were significantly associated with improvements in problem behavior (Najaka, Gottfredson, & Wilson, 2001). • Student-reported engagement in classroom tasks such as completing homework and taking part in classroom discussions was associated with reported engagement in fewer problem behaviors (Morrison et al., 2002)	• Poor academic functioning was identified as early sign of emerging or existing mental health problems during childhood and adolescence (DeSocio & Hootman, 2004) • Youth who experience school failure are more likely to abuse substances (Arthur et al., 2002; National Research Council & Institute of Medicine, 2009) • Academic failures can lead to negative emotions (Roeser, Eccles, & Strobel, 1998) • Low school achievement predicts delinquency (Maguin & Loeber, 1996)
Behavioral	• Participation in extracurricular activities is associated with lower involvement in major health risk behaviors (Resnick, 2000), absence of behavioral or emotional disorders (Rae-Grant, Thomas, Offord, & Boyle, 1989), and substance use (Arthur et al., 2002) • The more schooling people have the better their health is likely to be (Freudenberg & Ruglis, 2007) • Students with positive behavioral engagement trajectories were less depressed, and were less likely to be involved in delinquency and drug abuse (Li & Lerner, 2011) • Youth who were positively engaged in two or more settings had higher self-esteem and lower depression (Seidman & Pedersen, 2003)	• Inconsistent school attendance was identified as an early sign of emerging or existing mental health problems during childhood and adolescence (DeSocio & Hootman, 2004) • Truancy is a risk indicator for substance abuse among adolescents (Hallfors et al., 2002; Henry, 2007) • Perpetrating bullying should be seen as an indicator of risk of various mental health disorders in adolescence (Kaltiala-Heino, Rimpelä, Rantanen, & Rimpelä, 2000; Nansel et al., 2001) • Adolescents who drop out of school are at increased risk for depression, drug involvement, and suicidal behavior (Eggert, Thompson, Randell, & Pike, 2002)

Table 3.1. CONTINUED

Engagement Subtype	Protective Factors	Risk Factors
Cognitive	• Valuing education and seeing the need for educational attainment is considered a protective factor against mental health problems (Roeser et al.,1998; WHO, 2005) • Engagement in "meaningful instrumental activity" was significantly related to adolescents' life satisfaction, well-being, and overall self-esteem (Maton, 1990) • Adolescents who felt academically competent and valued school also reported less frequent symptoms of sadness and anger concurrently (Roeser et al., 1998) • High level of problem-solving ability is considered a protective factor against mental health problems (WHO, 2005) • Self-efficacy has been identified as a predictor of adolescent success in life (Perry, DeWine, Duffy, & Vance, 2007) • Cognitive engagement was found to have a significant weak negative relationship with depression in adolescents (Wang & Peck, 2013)	• Low commitment to school is related to adolescent drug use (Hawkins et al., 1992) • Adolescents who felt academically incompetent and devalued school were more likely to report symptoms of sadness and anger concurrently (Roeser et al., 1998) • To the extent that schooling is not seen as valuable, a sense of hopelessness or alienation from self and the sanctioned ways of being successful might ensue, causing emotions of dismay and distress (Roeser et al., 1998)
Affective	• Identifying with school is considered a protective factor against mental health problems (WHO, 2005) • Bonding to school was positively related to effects on problem behaviors (Najaka et al., 2001)) • Youth who feel connected to their school are less likely to engage in delinquent or violent behavior, to drink alcohol, to use drugs, to	• Difficulties in social integration and problems adjusting to school are among the early signs of emerging psychotic disorders in adolescents (McClellan, Breiger, McCurry, & Hlastala, 2003) • Students with low school connectedness are more likely to experience anxiety, depressive symptoms, mental health problems, and low self-esteem, and to engage in substance use and violence

(continued)

Table 3.1. CONTINUED

Engagement Subtype	Protective Factors	Risk Factors
	initiate sexual activity at earlier ages, and to experience depressive symptoms, emotional distress, and suicidality (Blum et al., 2004; Brookmeyer, Fanti, & Henrich, 2006; Catalano et al., 2004; Li & Lerner, 2011; Loukas, Roalson, & Herrera, 2010; McNeely & Falci, 2004; Resnick et al., 1997; Wang & Dishion, 2012) • When students are able to form positive relationships with adults at school, they are less likely to report engaging in troubling and risky behaviors (Griffiths, Liles, Furlong, & Sidhwa, 2012)	(Hagborg, 1994; Jacobson & Rowe, 1999; Kuperminc et al., 2001; Resnick et al., 1997; Shochet et al., 2006) • Young people who are not engaged with learning or who have poor relationships with peers and teachers are more likely to use drugs and engage in socially disruptive behaviors, report anxiety/depressive symptoms, have poorer adult relationships, and fail to complete secondary school (Bond et al., 2007)

INTERVENTIONS TO ENHANCE STUDENT ENGAGEMENT

Many features of student engagement, such as (a) engagement across development and levels of schooling; (b) strong links between engagement and outcomes, including mental health, and the amenability of student engagement to intervention; and (c) the emergence of student engagement as a meta-construct (Fredricks et al., 2004), clearly establish student engagement as a practical framework for designing school-based interventions across universal, targeted, and intensive levels. The description of interventions in the sections that follow illustrate this unified framework, bringing together promising and evidence-based interventions, such as those that target engaged time, self-regulation, attendance, and behavior, to maximize the impact of interventions on students. It should be noted, however, that research and interventions that address various subtypes of engagement are extensive in some areas but not in others. Furthermore, the unification of these types into one framework is relatively recent. Thus, more research is needed to understand the outcomes of comprehensive engagement interventions. Educators and other interventionists may draw from promising and evidence-based practices and should evaluate the effects of recommended strategies and interventions with specific populations and sites (Christenson et al., 2012).

Multi-tiered System of Supports

Schools are increasingly taking a multi-tiered service-delivery approach to promote academic and behavioral success in school. In this approach, multiple tiers of increasingly intense interventions are directed at correspondingly smaller population segments so that a continuum of support is available to students based on their needs (Mellard & Johnson, 2008). In their seminal article, Walker and colleagues (1996) provided a framework for preventing and reducing school problems based on the U.S. Public Health Service's tiered model of prevention. The model uses a three-tiered approach, with primary, secondary, and tertiary levels of intervention that help match the intensity of prevention and intervention strategies to the severity of the problem. Although originally adapted to address behavior problems, this model is now implemented to ensure appropriate supports are in place to support students' academic, social, and emotional needs as well. Adelman and Taylor (2010) suggest that the primary level includes universal interventions that promote healthy development and prevent problems for all students; the secondary level provides early, targeted interventions for students who are demonstrating the onset of emotional, behavior, and learning problems; and the third level consists of intensive interventions for those students with chronic or severe problems.

Student engagement interventions are organized here in alignment with the multi-tiered system of supports (MTSS) and with Adelman and Taylor's model for promoting mental health in schools, offering universal interventions to enhance engagement in school and learning for all students (contributing to students' healthy development and preventing problems in the school context), and targeted/intensive interventions to re-engage those students showing initial signs of disengagement or those demonstrating more severe or chronic disengagement (enhancing protective factors and reducing risks that may contribute to mental health problems). The interventions are also organized by student engagement subtype (academic, affective, behavioral, cognitive). It should be noted that interventions are interrelated. For example, an intervention to address self-regulation (cognitive) may also affect time on task or homework completion (academic).

Interventions

Academic. Academic engagement refers to participation in instruction, academic work, and tasks. Academic engagement is easily observed in the classroom (e.g., time on task, completing school work, and attending to instruction) and indicated by academic data readily available to school personnel, such as homework completion, grades, and credits earned toward graduation (Appleton et al, 2006; Reschly & Christenson, 2012).

Researchers have posited that cognitive and affective engagement mediate the relationship between self-processes and academic and behavioral engagement

(Reschly & Christenson, 2006a). Given the directional nature of engagement models, this mediation suggests that cognitive and affective engagement precede academic and behavioral engagement. Therefore, interventions to foster academic engagement may be the same interventions needed to foster students' cognitive and affective engagement. For example, the amount of time students are actively engaged in learning has been linked consistently to students' academic achievement (Gettinger & Walter, 2012), indicating the need for universal interventions to focus on promoting students' sustained engagement in learning. Student engagement with a task is largely determined by a student's motivation to work on the task (Gettinger & Walter, 2012), and interest is a source of motivation to engage and sustain engagement with that task (Ainley, 2012). By providing academic tasks known to be of interest to students, teachers are promoting students' cognitive engagement in the task (putting forth effort and sustaining their effort), and thus time engaged in the task, which is an indicator of academic engagement.

Universal interventions to promote academic engagement for all students generally target environmental influences, particularly instructional quality and delivery and classroom structures (See Box 3.1). Class-wide strategies to encourage students' active participation in learning include matching instruction to student level, providing explicit instructions for tasks, checking for understanding, providing feedback, facilitating smooth transitions, and establishing classroom routines (Gettinger & Walter, 2012). Examples of individualized interventions to increase academic engagement include providing supplemental academic support for students based on their academic areas of need through tutoring, peer tutoring, or after-school programming (Rodriguez et al., 2004; Sáenz, Fuchs, & Fuchs, 2005), monitoring homework completion (Cooper, 1989); and increasing home support for learning (Klem & Connell, 2004). Specific strategies and interventions appear in Box 3.1.

Affective. Students' emotions at school or when involved in learning are representative of their affective engagement. Indicators of affective engagement typically include identification, school connectedness, and belonging (Appleton et al., 2006; Christenson et al., 2008). Affectively engaged students are those who experience a sense of belonging and emotional support and who value the benefits learning affords them (Finn & Zimmer, 2012; Voelkl, 2012). These students tend to have more positive emotional reactions to learning itself, and toward the people with whom they interact while learning, including teachers, other students, support staff, and administrators (Fredricks & McColskey, 2012). Positive emotional experiences appear to incentivize continued and deeper involvement in learning and the activities endorsed and provided by the school.

Although other subtypes of engagement (academic, behavioral, cognitive) appear directly linked to achievement outcomes (Appleton et al., 2006; Finn & Zimmer, 2012; Lovelace et al., 2014), affective engagement tends to indirectly influence achievement (Finn & Zimmer, 2012; Osterman, 2000; Voelkl, 2012). Specifically, affective engagement appears to influence motivation, persistence with rigorous academic work, and expectations for success (Goodenow, 1993a, 1993b; Goodenow

Box 3.1

STRATEGIES AND INTERVENTIONS TO ENHANCE ACADEMIC ENGAGEMENT

UNIVERSAL STRATEGIES

Enhance classroom managerial strategies such as establishing classroom routines, decreasing class and group sized, reducing transition time, and managing off-task behavior (Gettinger & Walter, 2012)

Utilize student-mediated strategies such as promoting goal setting, use of metacognitive and study strategies, and supporting students' self-management skills (Gettinger & Walter, 2012)

Apply principles of effective instruction such as facilitating active student responding, providing frequent feedback, ensuring appropriate instructional match, scaffolding learning, and providing clear instruction (Gettinger & Walter, 2012)

Facilitate home support for learning
- Provide home support for learning strategies to content area
- Enhance bidirectional communication with families
- Encourage parents to volunteer in the classroom (Lee & Smith, 1993)

Utilize a variety of interesting texts and resources (Ainley, 2012)

Support student autonomy by providing choices within courses and assignments (Skinner et al., 2005)

Ensure appropriateness of homework assignments (Cooper, 1989)

Ensure that there are both high expectations and support for learning (Lee & Smith, 1999; Williamson & Blackburn, 2010)

Utilize cooperative learning (Greenwood et al., 2002) and peer-assisted learning strategies (Boudah, Schumacher, & Deshler, 1997; Lee & Smith, 1993) to increase opportunities for student academic response and time on task

TARGETED/INTENSIVE STRATEGIES

Ensure the student has the academic skills needed to complete the assigned task, and if the student does not, explicitly teach the academic skills

Enhance student's personal belief in self through repeated contacts, goal setting, problem solving, and relationship building (Lehr et al., 2004)

Aid the student in defining goals for the future; discuss the connection between education and those goals for the future (Miller & Brickman, 2004)

Explicitly teach cognitive and metacognitive strategies such as managing time, chunking assignments, studying for tests, using mnemonic devices, taking notes, making outlines, and comprehending textbooks (Hattie, 2013)

(continued)

Box 3.1

CONTINUED

Implement self-monitoring interventions (e.g., graph progress toward goals; Rock, 2005)

Discuss the link between student's effort and the outcome/behavior/success achieved to increase the student's perceived self-control, self-efficacy, and self-determination (Schunk & Mullen, 2012)

Provide specific, positive feedback emphasizing student effort and the strategies used to master a skill or complete a task (Schunk & Mullen, 2012)

Help the student set challenging but reachable goals so that he or she can experience success and draw on that success for motivation (Schunk & Mullen, 2012)

FORMAL INTERVENTIONS

Formal Reading and Math Interventions
- Information about evidence-based academic interventions to teach reading and math skills can be found in the What Works Clearinghouse at http://ies. ed.gov/ncee/wwc/

Concept-Oriented Reading Instruction (CORI; Guthrie et al., 2004)
- Instructional framework that promotes reading engagement through strategy instruction, modeling of strategies, opportunities for practice, and motivational support
- Results from several studies showed that students receiving CORI demonstrated superior motivation, strategy use, and reading comprehension compared to students receiving traditional reading instruction

Homework, Organization, and Planning Skills Interventions (HOPS)
- A collection of evidence-based organization skill interventions
- Can be implemented at the universal or targeted level
- A randomized trial of middle school students with ADHD found significant effects of the program over wait-list control students in terms of parent-rated organized action, planning, and homework completion (Langberg, Epstein, & Becker, 2012).

NOTE: Adapted from Christenson et al., 2008 and Reschly et al., 2014.

& Grady, 1993), which in undesirable conditions can lead to misbehavior, sexual activity, and involvement in criminal activities (Kuperminc, Leadbeater, & Blatt, 2001; Resnick et al., 1997; Shochet, Dadds, Ham, & Montague, 2006). Interventions to enhance affective engagement at the universal and targeted/intensive levels focus on promoting student belonging and bonding with school; enhancing beliefs regarding the value of school, and ensuring that the push for improving academic achievement is paired with social support (Reschly et al. 2014). Specific strategies and interventions to enhance affective engagement appear in Box 3.2.

Box 3.2

UNIVERSAL STRATEGIES

To address concerns regarding school size and impersonal environments
- implement small learning communities
- implement advisement programs with advisors (teachers) frequently monitoring student engagement and risk data
- enhance number of and access to school-based extracurricular clubs and activities

Look for ways to build relationships and connections with students
- Identify students who may not have a connection with a staff member in the building and match staff and alienated or neglected students for "mentor-like" contact

Enhance peer connections through peer assisted learning strategies

Implement mentoring programs (e.g., with college students, staff)

Increase access and participation in extracurricular activities

TARGETED/INTENSIVE STRATEGIES

For students who are at greatest risk for alienation and disengagement, educators should focus on
- enhancing personal relationships with at least one caring adult
- personalizing education to students' individual interests and goals
- providing assistance for students' personal problems when needed (e.g., counseling, small groups)

FORMAL INTERVENTIONS

Check & Connect (see full description in text)
- Structured school-based mentoring program to address engagement comprehensively (academic, behavioral, cognitive, affective)
- Typically delivered at intensive level; 1:1 mentor-student ratio
- Multiple studies of effectiveness; listed in the What Works Clearinghouse (ies.ed.gov/ncee/wwc/interventionreport.aspx?sid=78)

ALAS
- Structured school-based mentoring program (Larson & Rumberger, 1995)

Counselors/mentors
- track student behavior, attendance, grades; provide feedback
- coordinate interventions, connect with families and teachers
- work with families to facilitate participation and communication, behavior management
- help students develop problem-solving, task and social skills
- effects on staying in school, progressing in school, and graduation/dropout (ies.ed.gov/ncee/wwc/pdf/intervention_reports/WWC_Project_ALAS_100506.pdf)

NOTE: Adapted from Christenson et al., 2008 and Reschly et al., 2014.

Behavioral. Indicators of behavioral engagement have been extensively researched and consistently demonstrate strong associations with current and later achievement and with school exit outcomes (Finn & Zimmer 2012; Rumberger & Lim, 2008). For example, student attendance is highly predictive of current achievement (Gottfried, 2010) and later dropout (Alexander et al., 1997). Also, comprehensive reviews and meta-analyses of extracurricular participation (Feldman & Matjasko, 2005) and programs that enhance students' out-of-school time (Lauer et al., 2006) generally indicate desired effects. Specifically, participation in extracurricular activities has generally been associated with achievement, better social-emotional adjustment, and reduced delinquency (Feldman & Matjasko, 2005), whereas summer- and after-school programs are only likely to improve achievement if implemented with high rigor and focus (Shernoff, 2010). Further, severe behavioral difficulties are associated with poorer outcomes for students in terms of suspensions, expulsions (Wagner, Kutash, Duchnowski, Epstein, & Sumi, 2005) and high school dropout (U.S. Department of Education, n.d.)

Strategies and interventions to address behavioral engagement at the universal level typically include fostering student and staff attendance; maximizing student participation in class and school governance (see also academic engagement); enhancing students' productive use of time in terms of extracurricular participation and time outside of school (i.e., before/after school, in the summer); and promoting an effective school and disciplinary climate through school-wide and class-wide management strategies, such as Positive Behavior Interventions and Supports (PBIS). Interventions at the targeted and intensive levels focus on individualized support that is tailored to a student's particular needs, such as behavioral contracting and reinforcement-based individual interventions, as well as more intensive efforts to partner with families, connect students to and coordinate with available services, and fostering connections between adults and students through mentoring, counseling, and so on (Reschly et al., 2014; see Box 3.3).

Cognitive. Students' investment in their learning, effort directed toward learning, and use of self-regulated learning strategies to understand material, accomplish tasks, and master skills is referred to broadly as cognitive engagement (Appleton et al., 2006; Fredricks et al., 2004). Indicators of cognitive engagement include perceiving oneself as competent, persisting in the face of challenging tasks, maintaining motivation, interest in learning, valuing learning, perceiving learning as relevant to future goals, planning, setting goals, self-monitoring progress, and reflecting on task performance.

Various aspects of cognitive engagement, such as self-regulated learning, self-efficacy, and goal orientation, are interrelated and associated with positive academic outcomes for students (Greene, Miller, Crowson, Duke, & Akey, 2004; Pintrich & DeGroot, 1990; Wolters & Taylor, 2012). The use of self-regulated learning strategies such as planning, setting goals, self-monitoring progress, self-evaluation appears to predict academic achievement for students at the elementary, secondary, and postsecondary levels (Cleary, 2006; Pintrich & DeGroot,

Box 3.3

STRATEGIES AND INTERVENTIONS TO ENHANCE BEHAVIORAL ENGAGEMENT

UNIVERSAL STRATEGIES

Examine school discipline policies
- Eliminate out-of-school suspensions due to concerns regarding punitive nature, ineffectiveness, and exclusion from instruction
- Ensure understanding by students; perceptions of fairness
- Switch or enhance focus on positive rather than punitive consequences of behavior

Encourage staff and peer interaction and planning for the future through small learning communities and student-selected vocational interests
(also addresses cognitive and affective engagement)

Implement social skills, conflict resolution, social emotional learning, or anti-bullying curricula for all students

Increase number and type of extracurricular activities available to students

Facilitate participation in extracurricular activities
- Address barriers such as levels of competition, fees, and transportation

Connect with families (Epstein & Sheldon, 2002)
- Enhance forms of communication
- Establish a regular school contact
- Provide educational workshops (e.g., behavior management)

Involve students in hands-on, active learning directly related to future paths and interests
(also addresses cognitive and academic engagement)

Examine and strive to create an orderly, consistent school environment
Offer in-service and support to improve classroom management
(also addresses academic and affective engagement)

Accept and encourage student participation in class and school governance (e.g., assignments, grading, activities); use feedback to make appropriate changes

Ensure that school climate or culture is safe and respectful of student differences

TARGETED/INTENSIVE STRATEGIES

Develop and implement intensive and individualized interventions to address attendance, participation, and behavioral issues at school
- Behavior contracts
- Self-management interventions
- Reinforcement-based interventions that target appropriate or alternative behaviors
- Partner with families to monitor, supervise, and reinforce student behavior

(continued)

Box 3.3

Utilize programs that work to develop specific skills that will help students more effectively self-manage and navigate school and community environments, such as problem-solving, anger management, and communication

Provide intensive wrap-around services

Consider implementing structured mentoring programs (e.g., Check & Connect) to monitor and enhance student engagement

Collaborate with and assist families in development of skills for behavior management and supervision

Provide alternative programs for those students who have not completed school or who will not attend the traditional program

Implement school-to-work programs to foster success and relevant educational opportunities

FORMAL INTERVENTIONS

Good Behavior Game (universal)
- Introduced over 40 years ago; researched across ages and diverse student demographics
- Effectively increases on-task behavior and decreases disruptive behavior; Long-term effects found years later on graduation, drug use, etc. (Bradshaw, Zmuda, Kellam, & Ialongo, 2009; Poduska et al., 2008)
- Students divided into teams; teams earn points for appropriate behaviors as defined by the teacher (e.g., following rules, time on task); teams compete for rewards

PBIS (universal)
- In use across the United States
- Widely researched; effects found for improving academic achievement and school climate, and for reducing problem behaviors, bullying, and peer victimization (Sugai & Simonsen, 2012)
- Tier 1 goals are to teach appropriate behavior and create a consistent environment (e.g., common language); specific focus is on encouraging and rewarding appropriate behavior

Behavior Education Program (targeted)
- Time and cost-efficient; effective for reducing disruptive behavior and improving academic performance (Hawken & Horner, 2003; Todd, Campbell, Meyer, & Horner, 2008)
- For students with nonviolent persistent disruptive behavior who did not respond to Tier 1 support
- Daily check-in/check-out system (before and after school) to ensure students receive positive adult attention; also used to foster home-school collaboration
- Consistent with school goals; feedback given immediately after each class and at the end of each day/week; performance toward goals graphed

Box 3.3

CONTINUED

Check & Connect (intensive)
- Increases likelihood of staying in school; also effects on truancy, suspension, course passing, attendance, and credits earned (Christenson, Stout, & Pohl, 2012)
- Structured school-based mentoring program to promote school completion; addresses engagement comprehensively (academic, behavioral, cognitive, affective)
- Typically delivered at intensive level; 1:1 mentor-student ratio
- Engagement routinely monitored, more intensive interventions delivered at first signs of concern; Interventions are individualized based on student need and may include tutoring, behavior contracts, promoting connections to community, facilitating extracurricular involvement, etc.

NOTE: Adapted from Christenson et al., 2008 and Reschly et al., 2014.

1990). Self-efficacy beliefs, or students' beliefs in their ability to succeed on a task and/or reach their goals, are associated with student engagement in learning, use of self-regulated learning strategies, putting forth effort, persisting in the face of challenges, and academic achievement (Miller, Greene, Montalvo, Ravindran, & Nichols, 1996; Schunk & Mullen, 2012). A mastery goal orientation, in which students strive to learn and master a concept or skill, is associated with engagement in self-regulated learning behaviors, effort and persistence, self-efficacy, and academic achievement (Ames, 1992; Pintrich & DeGroot, 1990; Wolters, 2004). Additionally, students who perceive their schoolwork as instrumental to achieving their future goals are more likely to value the work and engage cognitively in order to move closer to reaching their short-term goals and ultimately their future goals (Miller & Brickman, 2004; Walker & Greene, 2009).

Universal and targeted strategies for promoting cognitive engagement for students are informed by these research findings. At the universal level, educators can teach and promote self-regulated learning strategies; enhance students' self-efficacy beliefs; promote a mastery goal orientation in the classroom; ensure academic tasks and activities are meaningful, relevant, and interesting to students; and facilitate future-oriented thinking and connecting of current schoolwork to future goals (see Box 3.4). For students who do not respond to the universal strategies, a more individualized approach may be taken to target the specific aspects of cognitive engagement with which the student is struggling. For example, a student with low self-efficacy, particularly one who has experienced repeated school failure, may benefit from someone helping him or her set short-term achievable goals for academic progress, so that as the student reaches his or her goals and starts to experience academic success and increase in self-efficacy (Schunk & Mullen, 2012). See Box 3.4 for more universal and targeted strategies to promote cognitive engagement.

Box 3.4

Strategies and Interventions to Enhance Cognitive Engagement

UNIVERSAL STRATEGIES

Teach, model, and promote the use of self-regulated learning strategies such as planning, goal setting, self-monitoring of progress, strategy selection, and self-evaluation (Zimmerman, 2002)

Facilitate the goal setting process (Greene et al., 2004; Miller & Brickman, 2004)

Promote a mastery goal orientation; keep the focus on understanding, skill development, and personal improvement (Anderman & Patrick, 2012)

Encourage educators and administrators to foster a mastery oriented goal structure in the classroom and school; remind them of TARGET—ensure *tasks* are meaningful and relevant, the *authority* is shared between the teacher and students, all students are *recognized* for progress and effort, *grouping* is heterogeneous and flexible, *evaluation* is criterion-referenced, and *time* is flexible in the class allowing for self-pacing when needed (Epstein, 1989)

Provide students with authentic, challenging assignments that relate to life outside of school and to their interests (Ainley, 2012)

Model learning strategies when teaching specific concepts; provide student models when possible (Schunk & Mullen, 2012)

Encourage parents to deliver messages related to motivational support for learning (high expectations, talk to students about school and schoolwork, valuing of education) (Blum, 2005; Christenson, 2004)

TARGETED/INTENSIVE STRATEGIES

Utilize after-school programs (tutoring, homework help)

Implement evidence-based academic interventions to build students' academic skills, especially reading and math (Finn, 1993)

Implement individual self-monitoring interventions (Rock, 2005)

Foster positive teacher-student relationship for marginalized students (Hughes & Kwok, 2006)

Intensify partnering and communication efforts with families (e.g., home-school notes, assignment notebooks, enrichment activities) (Klem & Connell, 2004)

FORMAL INTERVENTIONS

Peer Assisted Learning Strategies (PALS) (Barton-Arwood, Wehby, & Falk, 2005; Fuchs, Fuchs, & Burish, 2000)
• Class-wide peer tutoring combining proven instructional principles and practices

Box 3.4

<small>CONTINUED</small>

- Teachers pair students in the class, so that partners work simultaneously and productively on different activities that address the problems they are experiencing
- Evidence supports effectiveness for students with and without disabilities and ELL students
- Effective in improving reading and math skills, on-task behavior, social acceptance

Self-Regulated Strategy Development
- Instructional approach in which the instructor explains, models, and prompts students' use of self-regulated strategies in completing an academic task
- Results from numerous studies with elementary and secondary students with and without disabilities demonstrated that the Self-Regulated Strategy Development is effective in helping students to improve their quality of, knowledge of, approach to, and self-efficacy in writing (Harris, Graham, Mason, & Friedlander, 2008)

Self-Regulation Empowerment Program
- Developed to help secondary students become more strategic, motivated, and regulated during more complex and comprehensive academic activities
- Focuses on training students in task analysis, goal setting and strategic planning, self-recording, self-evaluation, strategic attributions, and adaptive inferences
- Initial research findings suggest that the intervention leads to increased behavior self-management, self-efficacy, and academic achievement (Cleary, Platten, & Nelson, 2008)

<small>NOTE:</small> Adapted from Christenson et al., 2008 and Reschly et al., 2014.

Check & Connect

Check & Connect is an example of a targeted intervention designed to promote engagement in school and learning across engagement subtypes. The structured mentoring intervention pairs caring adults with students in grades K–12 who are demonstrating signs of disengagement (e.g., course failures, attendance below 90%, poor credit accrual; Balfanz, Bridgeland, Bruce, & Fox, 2013). The mentor conducts regular *checks* on the student's educational progress and levels of engagement, using academic and behavioral data regularly collected by the school. The mentor then utilizes that *check* data and knowledge of the student to *connect* with the student, personalizing interventions to the student's needs in order to re-establish and maintain the students' connection to school and learning, promote student resilience through increasing protective factors and reducing risk factors, and enhance the student's academic and social competencies. Recognizing the importance of multiple contextual influences—home, school, and community—on student engagement, Check & Connect mentors work to create positive relationships in and among all three environments in order to encourage congruent and consistent messages about educational expectations and goals and ensure supports are in place for students to attain them (Christenson, Stout, & Pohl, 2012).

Check & Connect has met the evidence-based standards of the U.S. Department of Education's What Works Clearinghouse (WWC, 2006) for students with disabilities who were at risk of disengagement and dropout. In the two random assignment studies upon which that conclusion was based, the students receiving Check & Connect were "significantly less likely than similar control group students to have dropped out of school at the end of the first follow-up year (corresponding to the end of the freshman year)—9% compared with 30%." Moreover, students were "significantly less likely to have dropped out of school at the end of the fourth follow-up year (corresponding to the senior year for students making normal progress—39% compared with 58%)" (Sinclair et al., 1998; Sinclair et al., 2005, as quoted in WWC, 2006, p. 3). These two studies also demonstrated treatment-control differences in critical student engagement indicators such as attendance, behavior, credits earned, and ultimately a five-year graduation rate for students with disabilities, indicating the necessity of sustained intervention for students who are disengaged from learning. Research continues for Check & Connect, with three efficacy trials currently underway to examine for whom and under what conditions the program is most effective.

General Recommendations

Drawing on the research for Check & Connect specifically, and student engagement more generally, the following recommendations should be taken into consideration when designing systems to engage all students in school and learning and re-engage those who have disengaged.

Screening and monitoring of key variables. Key to the implementation of tiered models of support (i.e., MTSS, RTI) following the word support is screening of the student population (Reschly & Bergstrom, 2009). Comprehensive screening may include academics, behavior, and mental health concerns (e.g., depression, suicidality). Other population variables that should be regularly monitored include attendance, homework completion rates, extracurricular participation, student self-reported affective and cognitive engagement, and student isolation and withdrawal (Christenson et al., 2008; Reschly et al., 2014). Selection of monitoring variables should be guided by underscoring alterable variables, as they represent students' functional behavior within the classroom and school context and most readily link to intervention. Drawing upon our intervention and theoretical work in engagement, we have underscored the importance of student self-report of their engagement and school experiences, even among elementary-age students (Appleton et al., 2006; Carter, Reschly, Lovelace, Appleton, & Thompson, 2012; Reschly & Christenson, 2012) These data must be considered comprehensively to gain a more complete picture of student risk, and they may help inform the link to interventions (e.g., student isolation, no extracurricular participation). Finally, response must be timely to ensure student safety in the case of mental health concerns and to address disengagement and academic and behavior problems before problems worsen and become more difficult to address.

Linking assessment to intervention. The collection of data—whether it comprises those variables regularly maintained by schools, such as attendance and behavioral incidents, the collection of screening instruments, or more in-depth group-administered and individually administered measures—is an enormous and time-intensive enterprise. Unfortunately, these data are often compartmentalized, underutilized, or fail to inform intervention planning or monitoring. Tiered service-delivery models are based on the use of data for screening, monitoring, and decision-making; thus, timeliness and utility of data are keys to the implementation of interventions. Some variables are better suited to this endeavor than others. Student engagement variables, because of links to important outcomes and inherent amenability to intervention, are well suited to identification and monitoring (e.g., homework completion, time on task, attendance, behavioral incidents, belonging; see Christenson et al., 2008; Reschly et al., 2014).

Engagement theory and research have other implications for interventions. In particular, to improve generalizability and impact, it is helpful when interventions are coordinated across peer, family, school, and community contexts (Reschly et al., 2014). In addition, school personnel, families, and mental health professionals should plan for and closely monitor students following normative transitions, such as those between elementary and middle school, and those that are not normative, such as changing schools and experiencing illnesses. An understanding of typical developmental patterns is critical to these efforts. For example, students generally decline in their affective and cognitive engagement from fall to spring and in subsequent academic years (Lovelace, Reschly, & Appleton, 2017). Thus, typical declines within an average range may not warrant additional support, while changes in other variables, such as an increase in behavioral incidents or missed homework, may trigger a more immediate response. Many of the intervention recommendations in Box 3.1, Box 3.2, Box 3.3, and Box 3.4 target the provision of additional support to students based on specific needs.

Consider both the content and process of the intervention. Box 3.1, Box 3.2, Box 3.3, and Box 3.4 provide examples of universal and targeted/intensive strategies for the four engagement subtypes. These intervention examples promote protective factors, reduce risks and obstacles for students, and teach skills to help students meet the demands of the classroom. While the content, or "what," of the interventions is illustrated, the process, or "how," by which the selected intervention is implemented is not apparent. In Check & Connect research, we have learned that for disengaged students it is not only the intervention per se that is important, but also that an intervention is implemented within a relationship consistently and persistently, supporting the student to attain personal goals. Hence, understanding students' perspectives, engaging in active reflection and problem solving with the student, and attending to developmental issues are critical considerations for intervention success.

Monitoring both fidelity of interventions and student responses. Tiered models of service delivery are data- and intervention-focused. Given that student progress is used to determine whether interventions are discontinued or modified, it is imperative that the integrity with which the intervention is implemented is monitored, along with the student's response to the support or services provided. Intervention integrity is typically assessed through direct observation, a review of intervention products (e.g., work completed, workbooks), and interventionist self-report (e.g., checklist of steps; Sanetti & Kratochwill, 2011). As mentioned in the previous section, many engagement variables are well suited to intervention progress monitoring.

CONCLUSION

Mental health is not simply the absence of mental illness. Mental health refers to adolescents' ability to function well socially, emotionally, and cognitively across contexts. It is impacted by both the environment and person factors, many of which are amenable to change. Promoting mental health for adolescents requires a positive, proactive approach targeting those alterable factors in the contexts in which adolescents grow and develop, including the home, school, and community. In working within the school environment to promote mental health, student engagement is a factor with wide appeal as a possible target for intervention because of its potential for enhancing students' functioning across academic, behavioral, and social-emotional domains. Student engagement in school and learning is amenable to intervention and environmental (contextual) manipulations and is tied to a host of positive outcomes for youth, including those directly related to adolescent mental health. By attending to the contextual influences of communities, families, and peers on student engagement, in addition to working to meet student needs for competence, autonomy, and relatedness, schools promote student engagement in school and learning while also taking necessary steps toward preventing mental health problems and enhancing students' social, emotional, and cognitive functioning and well-being.

REFERENCES

Adelman, H. S., & Taylor, L. (Eds.). (2010). *Mental health in schools: Engaging learners, preventing problems, and improving schools.* Thousand Oaks, CA: Corwin Press.
Ainley, M. (2012). Students' interest and engagement in classroom activities. In S. Christenson, A. Reschly, & C. Wylie (Eds.), *Handbook of research on student engagement* (pp. 283–302). New York, NY: Springer.

Alexander, K. L., Entwisle, D. R., & Horsey, C. S. (1997). From first grade forward: Early foundations of high school dropouts. *Sociology of Education, 70,* 87–107.

Ames, C. (1992). Classrooms: Goals, structures, and student motivation. *Journal of Educational Psychology, 84,* 261–271.

Anderman, E. M., & Patrick, H. (2012). Achievement goal theory, conceptualization of ability/intelligence, and classroom climate. In S. Christenson, A. Reschly, & C. Wylie (Eds.), *Handbook of research on student engagement* (pp. 173–191). New York, NY: Springer.

Appleton, J. J. (2012). Systems consultation: Developing the assessment-to-intervention link with the Student Engagement Instrument. In S. Christenson, A. Reschly, & C. Wylie (Eds.), *Handbook of research on student engagement* (pp. 725–742). New York, NY: Springer.

Appleton, J. J., Christenson, S. L., Kim, D., & Reschly, A. L. (2006). Measuring cognitive and psychological engagement: Validation of the Student Engagement Instrument. *Journal of School Psychology, 44,* 427–445.

Archambault, I., Janosz, M., Fallu, J. S., & Pagani, L. S. (2009). Student engagement and its relationship with early high school dropout. *Journal of Adolescence, 32*(3), 651–670.

Arthur, M. W., Hawkins, J. D., Pollard, J. A., Catalano, R. F., & Baglioni, A. J. (2002). Measuring risk and protective factors for use, delinquency, and other adolescent problem behaviors: The Ccommunities That Care Youth Survey. *Evaluation Review, 26,* 575–601.

Balfanz, R., Bridgeland, J., Bruce, M., & Fox, J. H. (2013). *Building a grad nation: Progress and challenge in ending the high school dropout epidemic—2013 annual update.* Washington, DC: Civic Enterprises, the Everyone Graduates Center at Johns Hopkins University School of Education, America's Promise Alliance, and the Alliance for Excellent Education.

Balfanz, R., Herzog, L., & Mac Iver, D. J. (2007). Preventing student disengagement and keeping students on the graduation path in urban middle-grades schools: Early identification and effective interventions. *Educational Psychologist, 42,* 223–235.

Barrington, B. L., & Hendricks, B. (1989). Differentiating characteristics of high school graduates, dropouts, and nongraduates. *Journal of Educational Research, 89,* 309–319.

Barton-Arwood, S. M., Wehby, J. H., & Falk, K. B. (2005). Reading instruction for elementary age students with emotional and behavioral disorders: Academic and behavioral outcomes. *Exceptional Children, 72,* 7–27.

Blum, R. (2005). *School connectedness: Improving the lives of students.* Baltimore, MD: Johns Hopkins University School of Public Health.

Blum, R. W., Libbey, H. P., Bishop, J. H., & Bishop, M. (2004). School connectedness: Strengthening health and education outcomes for teenagers. *Journal of School Health, 74,* 231–235.

Bond, L., Butler, H., Thomas, L., Carlin, J., Glover, S., Bowes, G., & Patton, G. (2007). Social and school connectedness in early secondary school as predictors of late teenage substance use, mental health, and academic outcomes. *Journal of Adolescent Health, 40,* 357.e9–18.

Boudah, D. J., Schumacher, J. B., & Deshler, D. D. (1997). Collaborative instruction: Is it an effective option for inclusion in secondary classrooms? *Learning Disability Quarterly, 20*(4), 293–316.

Bradshaw, C. P., Zmuda, J. H., Kellam, S. G., & Ialongo, N. S. (2009). Longitudinal impact of two universal preventive interventions in first grade on educational outcomes in high school. *Journal of Educational Psychology, 101*, 926–937.

Brookmeyer, K. A., Fanti, K. A., & Henrich, C. C. (2006). Schools, parents, and youth violence: A multilevel, ecological analysis. *Journal of Clinical Child and Adolescent Psychology, 35*, 504–514.

Carter, C., Reschly, A. L., Lovelace, M. D., Appleton, J. J., & Thompson, D. (2012). Measuring student engagement among elementary students: Pilot of the Elementary Student Engagement Instrument. *School Psychology Quarterly, 27*, 61–73.

Catalano, R. F., Oesterle, S., Fleming, C. B., & Hawkins, J. D. (2004). The importance of bonding to school for healthy development: Findings from the Social Development Research Group. *Journal of School Health, 74*(7), 252–261.

Christenson, S. L. (2004). The family-school partnership: An opportunity to promote the learning competence of all students. *School Psychology Review, 33*(1), 83–104.

Christenson, S. L. (2008, January 22). Engaging students with school: The essential dimension of dropout prevention programs [Webinar]. National Dropout Prevention Center for Students with Disabilities.

Christenson, S. L., & Anderson, A. R. (2002). Commentary: The centrality of the learning context for students' academic enabler skills. *School Psychology Review, 31*, 378–393.

Christenson, S. L., Reschly, A. L., Appleton, J. J., Berman, S., Spanjers, D., & Varro, P. (2008). Best practices in fostering student engagement. In A. Thomas & J. Grimes (Eds.). *Best practices in school psychology* (5th ed., pp. 1099–1199). Bethesda, MD: National Association of School Psychologists.

Christenson, S. L., Reschly, A. L., & Wylie, C. (Eds). (2012). *Handbook of research on student engagement*. New York, NY: Springer.

Christenson, S. L., Stout, K., & Pohl, A. (2012). Check & Connect: A comprehensive student engagement intervention. Minneapolis, MN: University of Minnesota.

Cleary, T. J. (2006). The development and validation of the self-regulation strategy inventory self-report. *Journal of School Psychology, 44*, 307–322.

Cleary, T. J., Platten, P., & Nelson, A. C. (2008). Effectiveness of self-regulation empowerment program with urban high school students. *Journal of Advanced Academics, 20*, 70–107.

Cleary, T. J. & Zimmerman, B. J. (2012). A cyclical self-regulatory account of student engagement: Theoretical foundations and applications. In S. L. Christenson, A. L. Reschly, & C. Wylie (Eds.), *Handbook of research on student engagement* (pp. 237–257). New York, NY: Springer.

Connell, J. P., & Wellborn, J. G. (1991). Competence, autonomy, and relatedness: A motivational analysis of self-system processes. In M. R. Gunnar & L. A. Stroufe (Eds.), *Self processes in development: Minnesota Symposium on Child Psychology* (Vol. 23, pp. 43–77). Hillsdale, NJ: Erlbaum.

Cooper, H. (1989). Synthesis of research on homework. *Educational Leadership, 47*, 85–91.

DeSocio, J., & Hootman, J. (2004). Children's mental health and school success. *Journal of School Nursing, 20*, 189–196.

Eccles, J. S., Midgley, C., Wigfield, A., Buchanan, C. M., Reuman, D., Flanagan, C., & Mac Iver, D. (1993). Development during adolescence: The impact of stage-environment fit on young adolescents' experiences in schools and in families. *American Psychologist, 48*, 90–101.

Eggert, L. L., Thompson, E. A., Randell, B. P., & Pike, K. C. (2002). Preliminary effects of brief school-based prevention approaches for reducing youth suicide—Risk behaviors, depression, and drug involvement. *Journal of Child and Adolescent Psychiatric Nursing, 15*, 48–64.

Ensminger, M. E., & Slusarcick, A. L. (1992). Paths to high school graduation or dropout: A longitudinal study of a first-grade cohort. *Sociology of Education, 65*, 95–113.

Epstein, J. (1989). Family structures and student motivation: A developmental perspective. *Research on Motivation in Education, 3*, 259–295.

Epstein, J. L., & Sheldon, S. B. (2002). Present and accounted for: Improving student attendance through family and community involvement. *Journal of Educational Research, 95*, 308–318.

Farrington, C. A., Roderick, M., Allensworth, E., Nagaoka, J., Keyes, T. S., Johnson, D. W., & Beechum, N. O. (2012). *Teaching adolescents to become learners: The role of noncognitive factors in shaping school performance: A critical literature review.* Chicago: University of Chicago Consortium on Chicago School Research.

Feldman, A. F., & Matjasko, J. L. (2005). The role of school-based extracurricular activities in adolescent development: A comprehensive review and future directions. *Review of Educational Research, 75*, 159–210.

Finn, J. D. (1989). Withdrawing from school. *Review of Educational Research, 59*, 117–142.

Finn, J. D. (1993). *School engagement and students at risk.* National Center for Educational Statistics, U.S. Department of Education.

Finn, J. D. (2006). *The adult lives of at-risk students: The roles of attainment and engagement in high school.* NCES 2006-328). Washington, DC: National Center for Education Statistics, U.S. Department of Education.

Finn, J. D., & Zimmer, K. (2012). Student engagement: What is it? Why does it matter? In S. L. Christenson, A. L. Reschly, & C. Wylie (Eds.), *Handbook of research on student engagement* (pp. 97–131). New York, NY: Springer.

Fredricks, J. A., Blumenfeld, P. C., & Paris, A. H. (2004). School engagement: Potential of the concept, state of the evidence. *Review of Educational Research, 74*, 59–109.

Fredricks, J. A., & McColskey, W. (2012). The measurement of student engagement: A comparative analysis of various methods and student self-report instruments. In S. Christenson, A. Reschly, & C. Wylie (Eds.), *Handbook of research on student engagement* (pp. 763–782). New York, NY: Springer.

Freudenberg, N., & Ruglis, J. (2007). Peer reviewed: Reframing school dropout as a public health issue. *Preventing Chronic Disease, 4*(4), 1–11.

Fuchs, D., Fuchs, L. S., & Burish, P. (2000). Peer-assisted learning strategies: An evidence based practice to promote reading achievement. *Learning Disabilities Research & Practice, 15*, 85–91.

Furrer, C. J., Skinner, E., Marchand, G., & Kindermann, T. A. (2006, March). *Engagement vs. disaffection as central constructs in the dynamics of motivational development.* Paper presented at the Annual Meeting of the Society for Research on Adolescence, San Francisco, CA.

Gettinger, M., & Walter, M. (2012). Classroom strategies to enhance academic engaged time. In S. Christenson, A. Reschly, & C. Wylie (Eds.), Handbook of research on student engagement (pp. 653–673). New York, NY: Springer.

Goodenow, C. (1993a). Classroom belonging among early adolescent students: Relationship to motivation and achievement. *Journal of Early Adolescence, 13,* 21–43.

Goodenow, C. (1993b). The psychological sense of school membership among adolescents: Scale development and educational correlates. *Psychology in the Schools, 30,* 79–90.

Goodenow, C., & Grady, K. E. (1993). The relationship of school belonging and friends' values to academic motivation among urban adolescent students. *Journal of Experimental Education, 62,* 60–71.

Gottfried, M. A. (2010). Evaluating the relationship between student attendance and achievement in urban elementary and middle schools: An instrumental variables approach. *American Educational Research Journal, 47,* 434–465.

Grannis, J. C. (1994). The dropout prevention initiative in New York City: Educational reforms for at-risk students. In R. J. Rossi (Ed.), *Schools and students at risk: Context and framework for positive change* (pp. 182–206). New York, NY: Teachers College.

Greene, B. A., Miller, R. B., Crowson, H. M., Duke, B. L., & Akey, K. L. (2004). Predicting high school students' cognitive engagement and achievement: Contributions of classroom perceptions and motivation. *Contemporary Educational Psychology, 29,* 464–482.

Greenwood, C. R., Horton, B. T., & Utley, C. A. (2002). Academic engagement: Current perspectives in research and practice. *School Psychology Review, 31,* 328–349.

Griffiths, A., Liles, E., Furlong, M. J., & Sidhwa, J. (2012). The relations of adolescent student engagement with troubling high-risk behaviors. In S. L. Christenson, A. L. Reschly, & C. Wylie (Eds.), *Handbook of research on student engagement* (pp. 563–584). New York, NY: Springer.

Guthrie, J. T., Wigfield, A., Barbosa, P., Perencevich, K. C., Taboada, A., Davis, M. H., ... Tonks, S. (2004). Increasing reading comprehension and engagement through concept-oriented reading instruction. *Journal of Educational Psychology, 96*(3), 403.

Hagborg, W. J. (1994). An exploration of school membership among middle- and high-school students. *Journal of Psychoeducational Assessment, 12,* 312–323.

Hallfors, D., Vevea, J. L., Iritani, B., Cho, H., Khatapoush, S., & Saxe, L. (2002). Truancy, grade point average, and sexual activity: A meta-analysis of risk indicators for youth substance use. *Journal of School Health, 72,* 205–211.

Harris, K. R., Graham, S., Mason, L. H., & Friedlander, B. (2008). *Powerful writing strategies for all students.* Baltimore, MD: Paul H. Brookes.

Hattie, J. (2013). *Visible learning: A synthesis of over 800 meta-analyses relating to achievement.* New York, NY: Routledge.

Hughes, J. N., & Kwok, O. (2006). Classroom engagement mediates the effect of teacher-student support on elementary students' peer acceptance: A prospective analysis. *Journal of School Psychology, 43,* 465–480.

Hawken, L. H., & Horner, R. H. (2003). Evaluation of a targeted intervention within a schoolwide system of behavior support. *Journal of Behavioral Education, 12,* 225–240.

Hawkins, J. D., Catalano, R. F., & Miller, J. Y. (1992). Risk and protective factors for alcohol and other drug problems in adolescence and early adulthood: Implications for substance abuse prevention. *Psychological Bulletin, 112,* 64–105.

Henry, K. L. (2007). Who's skipping school: Characteristics of truants in 8th and 10th grade. *Journal of School Health, 77*, 29–35.

Jacobson, K. C., & Rowe, D. C. (1999). Genetic and environmental influences on the relationships between family connectedness, school connectedness, and adolescent depressed mood: Sex differences. *Developmental Psychology, 35*, 926.

Janosz, M. (2012). Commentary: Outcomes of engagement and engagement as an outcome: Some consensus, divergences, and unanswered questions. In S. L. Christenson, A. L. Reschly, & C. Wylie (Eds). *Handbook of research on student engagement* (pp. 695–703). New York, NY: Springer.

Kaltiala-Heino, R., Rimpelä, M., Rantanen, P., & Rimpelä, A. (2000). Bullying at school—An indicator of adolescents at risk for mental disorders. *Journal of Adolescence, 23*, 661–674.

Klem, A. M., & Connell, J. P. (2004). Relationships matter: Linking teacher support to student engagement and achievement. *Journal of School Health, 74*, 262–273.

Kuperminc, G. P., Leadbeater, B. J., & Blatt, S. J. (2001). School social climate and individual differences in vulnerability to psychopathology among middle school students. *Journal of School Psychology, 39*, 141–159.

Ladd, G. W., & Dinella, L. M. (2009). Continuity and change in early school engagement: Predictive of children's achievement trajectories from first to eighth grade? *Journal of Educational Psychology, 101*, 190–206.

Langberg, L. M., Epstein, J. N., & Becker, S. P. (2012). Evaluation of the Homework, Organization, and Planning Skills (HOPS) intervention for middle school students with Attention Deficit Hyperactivity Disorder as implemented by school mental health providers. *School Psychology Review, 41*, 342–364.

Larson, K. A., & Rumberger, R. W. (1995). ALAS: Achievement for Latinos through Academic Success. In H. Thorton (Ed.), *Staying in school: A technical report of three dropout prevention projects for junior high school students with learning and emotional disabilities* (pp. A-1-A-71). Washington, DC: U.S. Department of Education.

Lauer, P. A., Akiba, M., Wilkerson, S. B., Apthorp, H. S., Snow, D., & Martin-Glenn, M. L. (2006). Out-of-school-time programs: A meta-analysis of effects for at-risk students. *Review of Educational Research, 76*, 275–313.

Lee, V. E., & Smith, J. B. (1993). Effects of school restructuring on the achievement and engagement of middle-grade students. *Sociology of Education, 66*(3), 164–187.

Lee, V. E., & Smith, J. B. (1999). Social support and achievement for young adolescents in Chicago: The role of school academic press. *American Educational Research Journal, 36*, 907–945.

Lehr, C. A., Sinclair, M. F., & Christenson, S. L. (2004). Addressing student engagement and truancy prevention during the elementary school years: A replication study of the Check & Connect model. *Journal of Education for Students Placed at Risk, 9*, 279–301.

Li, Y., & Lerner, R. M. (2011). Trajectories of school engagement during adolescence: implications for grades, depression, delinquency, and substance use. *Developmental Psychology, 47*, 233–247.

Loukas, A., Roalson, L. A., & Herrera, D. E. (2010). School connectedness buffers the effects of negative family relations and poor effortful control on early adolescent conduct problems. *Journal of Research on Adolescence, 20*, 13–22.

Lovelace, M., Reschly, A. L., Appleton, J. J., & Lutz, M. (2014). Concurrent and predictive validity of the Student Engagement Instrument. *Journal of Psychoeducational Assessment, 32*, 509–520.

Lovelace, M., Reschly, A. L., & Appleton, J. J. (2017). *Stability and change in cognitive and affective student engagement.* Manuscript in preparation.

Marks, H. M. (2000). Student engagement in instructional activity: Patterns in the elementary, middle, and high school years. *American Educational Research Journal, 37*, 153–184.

Maton, K. I. (1990). Meaningful involvement in instrumental activity and well-being: Studies of older adolescents and at-risk teen-agers. *American Journal of Community Psychology, 18*, 297–320.

Maguin, E., & Loeber, R. (1996). Academic performance and delinquency. *Crime and Justice, 20*, 145–264.

McClellan, J., Breiger, D., McCurry, C., & Hlastala, S. A. (2003). Premorbid functioning in early-onset psychotic disorders. *Journal of the American Academy of Child & Adolescent Psychiatry, 42*, 666–672.

McNeely, C., & Falci, C. (2004). School connectedness and the transition into and out of health-risk behavior among adolescents: A comparison of social belonging and teacher support. *Journal of School Health, 74*, 284–292.

Mellard, D., & Johnson, E. (2008). *RTI: A practitioner's guide to implementing response to intervention.* Thousand Oaks, CA: Corwin Press.

Miller, R. B., & Brickman, S. J. (2004). A model of future-oriented motivation and self regulation. *Educational Psychology Review, 16*, 9–33.

Miller, R. B., Greene, B. A., Montalvo, G. P., Ravindran, B., & Nichols, J. D. (1996). Engagement in academic work: The role of learning goals, future consequences, pleasing others, and perceived ability. *Contemporary Educational Psychology, 21*, 388–422.

Morrison, G. M., Robertson, L., Laurie, B., & Kelly, J. (2002). Protective factors related to antisocial behavior trajectories. *Journal of Clinical Psychology, 58*, 277–290.

Najaka, S. S., Gottfredson, D. C., & Wilson, D. B. (2001). A meta-analytic inquiry into the relationship between selected risk factors and problem behavior. *Prevention Science, 2*(4), 257–271.

Nansel, T. R., Overpeck, M., Pilla, R. S., Ruan, W. J., Simons-Morton, B., & Scheidt, P. (2001). Bullying behaviors among US youth: Prevalence and association with psychosocial adjustment. *JAMA, 285*, 2094–2100.

National Research Council & Institute of Medicine (2004). *Engaging schools: Fostering high school students' motivation to learn.* Washington, DC: National Academies Press.

O'Connell, M. E., Boat, T., & Warner, K. E. (Eds). (2009). *Preventing Mental, Emotional, and Behavioral Disorders Among Young People: Progress and Possibilities.* Washington, DC: The National Academies Press.

Osterman, K.F. (2000). Students' need for belonging in the school community. *Review of Educational Research, 70*, 323–367.

Pekrun, R. & Linnenbrink-Garcia, L. (2012). Academic emotions and student engagement. In S. L. Christenson, A. L. Reschly, & C. Wylie (Eds.), *Handbook of Research on Student Engagement* (pp. 259–282). New York, NY: Springer.

Perry, J. C., DeWine, D. B., Duffy, R. D., & Vance, K. S. (2007). The academic self-efficacy of urban youth: A mixed-methods study of a school-to-work program. *Journal of Career Development, 34*, 103–126.

Pintrich, P. R., & De Groot, E. V. (1990). Motivational and self-regulated learning components of classroom academic performance. *Journal of Educational Psychology, 82*, 33–40.

Poduska, J. M., Kellam, S. G., Wang, W., Brown, C. H., Ialongo, N. S., & Toyinbo, P. (2008). Impact of the Good Behavior Game, a universal classroom-based behavior intervention, on young adult service use for problems with emotions, behavior, or drugs or alcohol. *Drug and Alcohol Dependence, 95*(Suppl. 1), 29–44.

Rae-Grant, N., Thomas, B. H., Offord, D. R., & Boyle, M. H. (1989). Risk, protective factors, and the prevalence of behavioral and emotional disorders in children and adolescents. *Journal of the American Academy of Child & Adolescent Psychiatry, 28*, 262–268.

Reschly, A. L., Appleton, J. J., & Pohl, A. (2014). Best practices in fostering student engagement. In A. Thomas and P. Harrison (Eds.), *Best practices in school psychology* (6th ed.). Bethesda, MD: National Association of School Psychologists.

Reschly, A. L., & Christenson, S. L. (2006a). Prediction of dropout among students with mild disabilities: A case for the inclusion of student engagement variables. *Remedial and Special Education, 27*, 276–292.

Reschly, A. L., & Christenson, S. L. (2006b). Promoting school completion. In G. Bear & K. Minke (Eds.), *Children's needs III: Understanding and addressing the developmental needs of children*. Bethesda, MD: National Association of School Psychologists.

Reschly, A. L., & Christenson, S. L. (2012). Jingle, jangle, and conceptual haziness: Evolution and future directions of the engagement construct. In S. L. Christenson, A. L. Reschly, & C. Wylie (Eds). *Handbook of research on student engagement.* (pp. 3–19). New York: Springer.

Reschly, D. J., & Bergstrom, M K. (2009). Response to intervention. In T. B. Gutkin & C. R. Reynolds (Eds.), *The handbook of school psychology* (4th ed.) (p. 434–460). Hoboken, NJ: Wiley.

Resnick, M. D. (2000). Protective factors, resiliency, and healthy youth development. *Adolescent Medicine: State of the Art Reviews, 11*, 157–164.

Resnick, M. D., Bearman, P. S., Blum, R. W., Bauman, K. E., Harris, K. M., Jones, J., . . . Udry, J. R. (1997). Protecting adolescents from harm: Findings from the National Longitudinal Study on Adolescent Health. *JAMA, 278*, 823–832.

Reynolds, A. J. (2001). *Study: Early Childhood Intervention Cuts Crime, Dropout Rates.* Retrieved from http://www.waisman.wisc.edu/cls/PRESS01.PDF.

Rock, M. L. (2005). Use of strategic self-monitoring to enhance academic engagement, productivity, and accuracy of students with and without exceptionalities. *Journal of Positive Behavior Interventions, 7*, 3–17.

Rodriguez, J. L., Jones, E. B., Pang, V. O., & Park, C. D. (2004). Promoting academic achievement and identity development among diverse high school students. *High School Journal, 87*, 44–53.

Roeser, R. W., Eccles, J. S., & Strobel, K. R. (1998). Linking the study of schooling and mental health: Selected issues and empirical illustrations at. *Educational Psychologist, 33*, 153–176.

Rumberger, R. W., & Lim, S. A. (2008). *Why students drop out of school: A review of 25 years of research* (Project Report No. 15). Santa Barbara: University of California, California Dropout Research Project.

Ryan, R. M., & Deci, E. L. (2000). Self-determination theory and the facilitation of intrinsic motivation, social development, and well-being. *American Psychologist, 55*(1), 68–78.

Sáenz, L. M., Fuchs, L. S., & Fuchs, D. (2005). Peer-assisted learning strategies for English language learners with learning disabilities. *Exceptional Children, 71*, 231–247.

Sanetti, L. M. H., & Kratochwill, T. R. (2011). The evaluation of the "Treatment Integrity Planning Protocol" and two schedules of treatment integrity self-report: Impact on implementation and report accuracy. *Journal of Educational and Psychological Consultation, 21*, 284–308

Schunk, D. H., & Mullen, C. A. (2012). Self-efficacy as an engaged learner. In S. L. Christenson, A. L. Reschly, & C. Wylie (Eds.), *Handbook of research on student engagement* (pp. 219–235). New York, NY: Springer.

Schweinhart, L. J., & Weikart, D. P. (1999, September). The advantages of High/Scope: Helping children lead successful lives. *Educational Leadership, 57*, 77–78.

Seidman, E., & Pedersen, S. (2003). Holistic contextual perspectives on risk, protection, and competence among low-income urban adolescents. In S. S. Luthar (Ed.), *Resilience and Vulnerability: Adaptation in the Context of Childhood Adversities* (pp. 318–342). Cambridge, England: Cambridge University Press.

Shernoff, D. J. (2010). Engagement in after-school programs as a predictor of social competence and academic performance. *American Journal of Community Psychology, 45*(3-4), 325–337.

Shochet, I. M., Dadds, M. R., Ham, D., & Montague, R. (2006). School connectedness is an underemphasized parameter in adolescent mental health: Results of a community prediction study. *Journal of Clinical Child and Adolescent Psychology, 35*, 170–179.

Sinclair, M. F., Christenson, S. L., Evelo, D. L., & Hurley, C. M. (1998). Dropout prevention for youth with disabilities: Efficacy of a sustained school engagement procedure. *Exceptional Children, 65*, 7–21.

Sinclair, M. F., Christenson, S. L., & Thurlow, M. L. (2005). Promoting school completion of urban secondary youth with emotional or behavioral disabilities. *Exceptional Children, 71*, 465–482.

Skinner, E. A. & Pitzer, J. R. (2012). Developmental dynamics of student engagement, coping, and everyday resilience. In S. L. Christenson, A. L. Reschly, & C. Wylie (Eds). *Handbook of research on student engagement* (pp. 21–44). New York, NY: Springer.

Skinner, C. H., Pappas, D. N., & Davis, K. A. (2005). Enhancing academic engagement: Providing opportunities for responding and influencing students to choose to respond. *Psychology in the Schools, 42*, 389–403.

Sugai, G., & Simonsen, B. (2012). Positive behavioral interventions and supports: History, defining features, and misconceptions. Storrs: Center for Positive Behavioral Interventions and Supports, University of Connecticut. Retrieved from http://www.pbis.org/common/cms/files/pbisresources/PBIS_revisited_June19r_2012.pdf

Todd, A. W., Campbell, A. L., Meyer, G. G., & Horner, R. H. (2008). The effects of a targeted intervention to reduce problem behaviors elementary school implementation of Check In–Check Out. *Journal of Positive Behavior Interventions, 10*, 46–55.

U.S. Department of Education, Office of Special Education and Rehabilitative Services, Office of Special Education Programs (2016), 38th Annual Report to Congress on the Implementation of the Individuals with Disabilities Education Act, 2016. Washington, D.C. https://ed.gov/about/reports/annual/osep/2016/parts-b-c/38th-arc-for-idea.pdf

U.S. Department of Health and Human Services. (1999). *Mental Health: A Report of the Surgeon General*. Rockville, MD: U.S. Department of Health and Human Services,

Substance Abuse and Mental Health Services Administration, Center for Mental Health Services, National Institutes of Health, National Institute of Mental Health.

Voelkl, K. E. (2012). School identification. In S. L. Christenson, A. L. Reschly, & C. Wylie (Eds.), *Handbook of research on student engagement* (pp. 193–218). New York, NY: Springer.

Wagner, M., Kutash, K., Duchnowski, A. J., Epstein, M. H., & Sumi, W. C. (2005). The children and youth we serve: A national picture of the characteristics of students with emotional disturbances receiving special education. *Journal of Emotional and Behavioral Disorders, 13*, 79–96.

Walker, C. O., & Greene, B. A. (2009). The relations between student motivational beliefs and cognitive engagement in high school. *Journal of Educational Research, 102*, 463–472.

Walker, H. M., Horner, R. H., Sugai, G., Bullis, M., Sprague, J. R., Bricker, D., & Kaufman, M. J. (1996). Integrated approaches to preventing antisocial behavior patterns among school-age children and youth. *Journal of Emotional and Behavioral Disorders, 4*, 194–209.

Wang, M. T., & Dishion, T. J. (2012). The trajectories of adolescents' perceptions of school climate, deviant peer affiliation, and behavioral problems during the middle school years. *Journal of Research on Adolescence, 22*, 40–53.

Wang, M. T., & Peck, S. C. (2013). Adolescent educational success and mental health vary across school engagement profiles. *Developmental Psychology, 49*, 1266–1276.

What Works Clearinghouse. (2006). *WWC intervention report: Dropout prevention: Check & Connect*. Washington, DC: U.S. Department of Education, Institute of Education Sciences. Retrieved from http://ies.ed.gov/ncee/wwc/interventionreport.aspx?sid=78

Williamson, R., & Blackburn, B. (2010). *Rigorous schools and classrooms: Leading the way*. Larchmont, NY: Eye on Education.

Wolters, C. A. (2004). Advancing achievement goal theory: Using goal structures and goal orientations to predict students' motivation, cognition, and achievement. *Journal of Educational Psychology, 96*, 236–250.

Wolters, C. A., & Taylor, D. J. (2012). A self-regulated learning perspective on student engagement. In S. L. Christenson, A. L. Reschly, & C. Wylie (Eds.), *Handbook of research on student engagement* (pp. 635–652). New York, NY: Springer.

World Health Organization. (2005). Mental health policy and service guidance package: Child and adolescent mental health policies and plans. Retrieved from http://www.who.int/mental_health/policy/essentialpackage1/en/

Wylie, C., & Hodgen, E. (2012). Trajectories and patterns of student engagement: Evidence from a longitudinal study. In S. L. Christenson, A. L. Reschly, & C. Wylie (Eds.), *Handbook of research on student engagement* (pp. 585–600). New York, NY: Springer.

Zimmerman, B. J. (2002). Becoming a self-regulated learner: An overview. *Theory into Practice, 41*, 64–70

4

Supporting Students Following School Crises

From the Acute Aftermath Through Recovery

PAMELA VONA, LISA H. JAYCOX, SHERYL H. KATAOKA, BRADLEY D. STEIN, AND MARLEEN WONG ■

Unfortunately, catastrophic events in and near schools have become familiar incidents in the lives of children, families, and communities across the nation (Dean et al., 2008; Hoven et al., 2005; Pfefferbaum et al., 1999). As a result, school systems must be prepared to respond to school shootings, disasters, and other school crises, and to effectively support students during and after such traumatic events (Jaycox, Kataoka, Stein, Wong, & Langley, 2005). This chapter will provide a definition of *school crisis*, describe the impact of school crises on students and the broader school system, and offer a historical perspective on crisis response in schools. Current school-based trauma interventions will be discussed, followed by a discussion about how schools can be prepared to implement psychological supports alongside their school's comprehensive emergency management strategies for prevention, crisis response, and long-term recovery.

ISSUES RELATED TO IDENTIFICATION, HISTORY, AND MENTAL HEALTH SERVICES

A school crisis is a sudden, unexpected, or unanticipated event that not only disrupts a school's daily functioning, but also often involves short-term shock, confusion, and fear among the school community (Wong, 2004). Many crises occur on or in proximity to the school campus, such as an accident on school grounds, a violent crime near a school that jeopardizes the safety of students and staff, a suicide of a student or staff, or the sudden death of a student. Other events, however, such as an earthquake, hurricane or tornado, or man-made disaster such as a terrorist attack, may not be directly linked to the school setting. However, both types of incidents have a profound effect on school children and the broader school community. Although each student, teacher, parent, or family member experiences a crisis differently, school crises have a broad and immediate impact on many children and adults sufficient to interfere with teaching, learning, attendance, and behavior.

Schools can play a critical role in supporting students following a school crisis (Chemtob, Nakashima, & Hamada, 2002; Pfefferbaum, Call, & Sconzo, 1999; Pfefferbaum et al., 1999; Stuber et al., 2002; Weist et al., 2002), especially given the significant effects that these traumatic events can have on adolescents' social, emotional and cognitive development. Studies have found that traumatic events, including terrorism, natural disasters, mass shootings, and student suicide, can result in significant emotional distress, such as post-traumatic stress, anxiety, and depression (Brent et al., 1995; Galea et al., 2002; North, Smith, & Spitznagel, 1994; Schuster et al., 2001; Stein et al., 2004; Weisler, Barbee, & Townsend, 2006). Furthermore, research has identified a link between trauma and poor school functioning (Hurt, Malmud, Brodsky, & Giannetta, 2001). For example, exposure to violence has been shown to be associated with lower grade-point average (GPA); more days of school absence (Hurt, et al., 2001); decreased rates of high school graduation (Grogger, 1997); and significant deficits in attention, IQ, and reading ability (Delaney-Black et al., 2002). These links between traumatic events and learning illustrate the importance of providing supports that address both students' academic and emotional needs.

Similar to the effects on students, school staff can be directly and indirectly impacted by a school crisis (Daniels, Bradley, & Hays, 2007; North et al., 1999; North et al., 2002; Schwarz & Kowalski, 1991; Sloan, Rozensky, Kaplan, & Saunders, 1994). In schools, teachers and school counselors often find themselves in the role of providing social-emotional support for students who have experienced a crisis; however, those same individuals can be at risk for developing compassion fatigue or secondary traumatic stress themselves. *Secondary traumatic stress* occurs when individuals learn about the firsthand traumatic experiences of another and subsequently experience symptoms that mirror PTSD. Secondary traumatic stress has been observed in helping professionals, including counselors and teachers, following traumatic events (Alisic, 2012; Craig & Sprang, 2010). Thus, restoring teachers, counselors, and school staff to prior levels of functioning is a key component of crisis intervention and recovery, as is treating those who continue to be negatively affected by the event itself or who may be experiencing secondary traumatic stress. However, while supporting school staff is essential to this process, describing the specific interventions for adults extends beyond the scope of this chapter. Thus, this chapter will primarily focus on services provided before, during, and after a crisis to assist adolescents affected by a traumatic event.

History of School Preparedness and Crisis Intervention Strategies

Educators and the American public have not always recognized the gravity of school crises and the negative impacts of such events on students and families. For example, a 1927 school massacre by a school board member in Bath, Michigan, causing the death of 38 children and 7 adults, was viewed as an atypical occurrence, for which no coordinated school response was implemented and no counseling was provided for students.

One of the first systematic attempts to understand the impact of a school crisis on students occurred in 1984 following a shooting that occurred at the 49th Street Elementary School in South Los Angeles (Wong, 2006). In response, the Los Angeles Unified School District (LAUSD) partnered with two child psychiatrists (Robert Pynoos and Spencer Eth) to assess the impact of the event on students and staff. As a result of this partnership, the LAUSD created a two-tiered crisis intervention strategy, consisting of school-based and district-level crisis teams. The school-based crisis team included the school principal, who led the team of school social workers, school psychologists, nurses, counselors, school police, and support staff (such as custodians and school secretaries). The team provided a first level of response for "life events," such as the accidental death or serious injury of students or staff, and worked to ameliorate the distress of students and teachers by encouraging students to remain in school in an enhanced environment of social and emotional supports. The district-level team responded to the school principal's request when events overwhelmed the resources and training of the school-based team. Comprising experienced school mental health professionals and regional administrators, the district team help to organize a response after a high-profile event that draws the attention of media, such as gang-related shootings or incidents of mass injury and death. This "LAUSD" model came to serve as a prototype for crisis response for school districts nationally.

The American public and the U.S. Department of Education began recognizing the need for crisis management in schools following a wave of school shootings in the 1990s. In this climate, the Office of Safe and Drug-Free Schools (OSDFS) was created as part of the Improving America's Schools Act (IASA) of 1994. Following the school shooting at Columbine High School in Littleton, Colorado in 1999, national awareness and calls for more widespread dissemination of crisis management strategies and tools accelerated (Vossekuil, 2004). The OSDFS also responded after the bombing of the Murrah Federal Building in 1995. District-wide, students and staff were provided mental health services by the Oklahoma City Public School District (Pfefferbaum, Call, & Sconzo, 1999; Pfefferbaum et al., 1999) Similarly, following the terrorist attacks on September 11, 2001, OSDFS funded and assisted with recovery services with the New York Board of Education. Across a wide variety of school-based settings, more than 50% of the children received counseling within months of the attack (Stuber et al., 2002). Following both incidents, interventions such as psychological first aid and crisis counseling were provided to promote the psychological recovery of students and staff.

In addition, the OSDFS funded Project SERV (School Emergency Response to Violence) in 2001, supporting response and recovery services in schools. In 2003, with the increased acceptance and use of crisis management in schools across the nation, funds were appropriated by the U.S. Department of Education through the Readiness and Emergency Management for Schools (REMS) program. REMS grants support schools and school districts in developing emergency response and preparedness plans and helps to identify and train the necessary personnel to implement these activities.

Six years later, public awareness that young adults are also in need of school-based response and recovery services was raised. Following the school shooting at Virginia Polytechnic Institute and State University (Virginia Tech) in 2007, the Emergency Management for Higher Education (EMHE) grant program was developed to support programs tailored to young adult students exposed to severe trauma.

Despite the promising strides made in school emergency response and pre-paredness over the past two decades, most schools across the country continue to lack the strategic planning and resources to implement a comprehensive strategy to implement a spectrum of services from prevention through long-term recov-ery. In 2011, President Obama's Presidential Policy Directive (PPD-8; see U.S. Department of Education, 2013) provided an overall approach to disaster pre-paredness, representing an accumulation of the lessons learned over decades of crisis response to terrorism, natural and man-made disasters, and school-related incidents such as mass school shootings.

On December 14, 2012, the deadliest school shooting in the United States since the Bath, Michigan, disaster of 1927 occurred at Sandy Hook Elementary School in Newtown, Connecticut. The president responded by issuing the "Now Is the Time" initiative (White House, 2014). While a major focus of the initiative is on reducing gun violence, it also includes elements that aim to facilitate the imple-mentation of PPD-8 in school settings. For example, "Now Is the Time" aims to make schools safer by providing schools with additional personnel, includ-ing trained resource officers and counselors. It also promotes access to expanded mental health coverage for students (White House, 2014).

Despite these recent advances in policy and practice in emergency prepared-ness (U.S. Department of Education, 2013), the progress has not yet been matched by successful implementation in schools nationally. There is still much work to do in specifying how these recommendations can be applied to all school settings nationally, taking into account the great variation in schools and districts and surrounding community resources. The following section outlines ways in which school crisis and mental health supports can align with key components of PPD-8 to improve school safety and crisis response.

PPD-8 emphasizes actions that occur in three timeframes: *before*, *during*, and *after* a crisis. Before a crisis, strategies should aim to deter a threatened or actual incident from occurring and put in place processes to reduce the physical and/ or psychological impact on the school community. During a crisis, interven-tions should aim to restore a safe and secure school environment and facilitate the transition to recovery. After a crisis, interventions should focus on identify-ing students and staff who continue to experience symptoms in order to facilitate long-term recovery.

EVIDENCE-BASED PRACTICES

In this section, we describe interventions, along with their evidence bases, that can be implemented within schools, including secondary schools, to meet the aims of each of the PPD-8 time frames described above. It should be recognized, however, that optimal efforts to address emotional and behavioral issues in schools often require that interventions address the level of need for each individual (Bradshaw, Koth, Bevans, Ialongo, & Leaf, 2008), frequently determined by staff referral and/ or screening efforts. Figure 4.1 combines the PPD-8 time frames with a com-mon school framework (Positive Behavior Interventions and Supports, or PBIS) that includes universal programs (Tier 1), interventions for those at risk (Tier 2), and services delivered to those in need of intensive services (Tier 3). For each intervention described, we provide information about its effectiveness, as many of the interventions presented have been demonstrated to be effective, while others have limited evidence of effectiveness but are currently considered to be "best" or "promising" practices.

Before a Crisis

There are a number of strategies that a school can implement before a crisis to prevent or mitigate its impact. To date, a majority of these activities are univer-sal approaches that aim to impact the entire school community, with fewer early intervention and targeted approaches developed to identify students who are

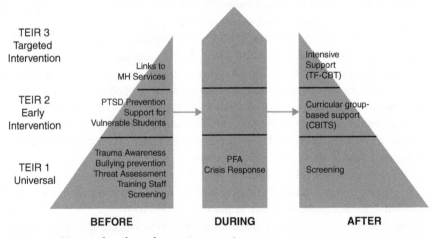

Figure 4.1 Universal, early, and target interventions.

currently experiencing or at risk for experiencing mental health difficulties. The development of early intervention and targeted approaches that can be implemented in advance of a school crisis is a promising approach for both preventing students with emotional and mental health difficulties from engaging in violent acts and/or strengthening emotionally vulnerable students in advance of a crisis occurring. Strategies to use prior to a crisis fit within all three tiers of the PBIS framework (Bradshaw et al. 2008).

Universal approaches. In this section we will discuss five strategies directed toward the entire school community that can be implemented before a school crisis occurs. These strategies aim to prevent or reduce the impact of a traumatic event on the school community.

Threat assessment. Threat assessment involves a set of strategies and procedures to help identify potential threats and the likelihood that they will occur. The threat assessment process often involves convening a committee comprising school community stakeholders to assess all hazards to the school community, including natural disasters and neighborhood and community risks and vulnerabilities, such as high rates of crime, drug use and/or sales, and poverty.

In 1999 the U.S. Department of Education's Office of Safe and Drug Free Schools and the U.S. Secret Service began working together to better understand and ultimately help prevent school shootings. The findings from this joint effort, published in *The Final Report and Findings of the Safe School Initiative: Implications for the Prevention of School Attacks in the United States* (Vossekuil, 2004), constitute a best practice approach and reveal that targeted violence in school is rarely impulsive. The students who have perpetrated these attacks usually planned them in advance—with planning behavior that was often observable. Additionally, prior to most attacks, other students knew that the attack was going to occur and may have participated in the planning of the attack or the identification of the victims.

Threat assessment is a safety measure that requires the establishment of multisystem relationships. The educator, law enforcement, and mental health professional constituencies bring unique and often complementary attitudes, skills, and knowledge. These differences are valued in the process of threat assessment because no single person should make a decision about whether a student poses or does not pose a credible threat to the safety of the school (Wong, 2007). Building and maintaining relationships across disciplines and agencies is an essential component of effective threat assessment (Vossekuil, 2004; Wong, 2007).

Bullying prevention. Preventing bullying on campus is another key strategy for preventing violence and other traumatic events from occurring. Studies suggest that bullying is estimated to effect approximately 20–25% of adolescents, with higher rates of prevalence for younger adolescents (Carlyle & Steinman, 2007; Seals & Young, 2002) Students who engage in bullying behavior and aggressive behavior are at increased risk for delinquency and school dropout, whereas victims of bullying are more likely to have depression, anxiety, and suicidality (Berthold & Hoover, 2000). Therefore, bullying prevention programs aim to reduce antisocial and/or aggressive behavior in would-be perpetrators and mitigate the negative consequences of these behaviors on victims.

Although there has been much research about bullying over the last several decades, bullying prevention and intervention programs have had mixed results, with the best evidence existing for whole school approaches (Merrell, Gueldner, Ross, & Isava, 2008). These whole school approaches aim to create a school-wide culture of acceptance and communication, empowering students to find positive ways to resolve conflicts. It also trains administrators, teachers, and other staff to support students in making constructive decisions and respond proactively when aggression of any kind exists on the school campus. Despite promising studies, the evidence for bullying programs remains weak, with many programs lacking evidence or showing mixed results. For example, more targeted interventions that rely on classroom curriculum and isolated social skills efforts have not been effective in reducing bullying on campuses (Merrell, Gueldner, Ross, & Isava, 2008). Thus, this is an area that demands continued research and refinement of programs.

Training key school personnel. Training school staff (e.g., mental health clinicians, school resource officers) who may be involved in the immediate response to a crisis or long-term recovery process is an important activity that schools can undertake in advance of a crisis. As stated above, the Now Is the Time initiative promotes the training of onsite resource officers and school counselors who can be ready to secure the school campus and provide counseling services immediately following a school crisis (White House, 2014).

For the longer-term mental health recovery of students, training of mental health staff in evidence-based interventions is best done in periods of stability, or the before phase, as well. This recommendation stems from work in the New Orleans region following Hurricanes Katrina and Rita, showing that schools with an existing infrastructure, including trained staff, were more successful in implementing interventions following the disaster (Jaycox et al., 2007).

Enhancing trauma awareness. There is increasing attention focused on creating trauma-aware school systems. For a school community to be prepared for a crisis, schools and districts should provide ongoing trauma awareness and skills training as part of the fabric of the school organizational culture, practices, and policies. A school community with this level of enhanced trauma awareness may help to build resilience for students and the school system more broadly by preparing and educating schools to be responsive to the needs of their constituents with seamless, accessible, and effective child and family services, involving all school community members. While enhancing trauma awareness among the school community may be a promising approach to potentially preventing a school crisis from occurring or preparing schools to be responsive following a crisis, there are no studies to date documenting this relationship. This is a strategy that warrants increased attention from researchers.

Assessing and promoting mental health. A number of strategies can be employed to promote the mental health of the school community. For example, regular screenings that assess the wellness of students and school staff could help to identify individuals who may be struggling and in need of support. The results of these screening efforts would help to link students and staff with early intervention or targeted treatments depending on their level of need. Currently, there is no evidence demonstrating that screening improves the wellness of the school community and/or prevents school crises from occurring. Therefore, it may be valuable for researchers to explore whether identifying and subsequently linking vulnerable students and staff to evidence-based interventions strengthens the school community and prevents potential violent events or other tragedies from occurring on campus.

Early intervention. Below we describe interventions that can be implemented in advance of a school crisis to support vulnerable adolescents. The primary aim of these early intervention strategies is to provide support to adolescents who are at risk for developing PTSD or other mental health difficulties following a traumatic event or who may be more likely to engage in behaviors that may traumatize the school community. Students that have been identified as needing mental health support, whether identified by universal screening or through a referral process, should have access to evidence-based mental health interventions on or near the school campus. Often, these early intervention approaches are conducted in group settings.

Interventions to support vulnerable students. A number of interventions for a variety of mental health conditions, including depressive disorders, anxiety disorders, and conduct disorders, have been developed and implemented in school settings, and have been shown to be effective for children and adolescents of varying cultural and ethnic backgrounds. Interpersonal psychotherapy for depressed adolescents (IPT-A) has been implemented in school-based health clinics and has been shown to significantly reduce depressive symptoms and improve social and general functioning of adolescents (Mufson et al., 2004). A school-based, group cognitive behavioral therapy (CBT) intervention has been shown to be effective in the treatment of anxiety for adolescents (Ginsburg & Drake, 2002). Additionally, the Coping Power intervention, a school-based group treatment that focuses on anger management and problem solving, has been shown to reduce aggressive behaviors in preadolescent boys (Lochman & Wells, 2004). Linking vulnerable students to evidence-based early intervention strategies on campus may reduce the likelihood of a traumatic event and/or help to bolster students' resilience if a crisis were to occur.

Interventions to prevent post-traumatic stress. Taking steps that aim to prevent the onset of PTSD if a crisis were to occur is another intervention that should be implemented before a school crisis. This may be particularly relevant for communities at high risk for a traumatic event, such as inner-city schools where crime or gang-related violence is more common, or regions of the country where natural disasters like hurricanes and tornadoes more frequently occur. This type of intervention aims to train students in effective coping skills prior to trauma exposure. An example of this type of intervention was developed and tested in Israel and was found to reduce symptoms of post-traumatic stress in the intervention group following a rocket attack as compared to a control group that did not receive the intervention (Wolmer, Hamiel, & Laor, 2011).

Targeted support. It is probable that there are adolescents experiencing symptoms of depression, anxiety, or other mental health problems prior to the occurrence of any traumatic event on or near their school. For these students, more intensive mental health services may be required. In many cases, these services are not provided on campus in a group setting. Rather, students may be referred to a local community mental health agency to receive these more intensive one-on-one services.

Multisystemic Therapy (MST) is typically delivered in a clinic setting and involves targeted intervention within the family, peer, and school systems. This approach has been shown to reduce antisocial behavior in adolescents (Schoenwald & Henggeler, 2005). Treating adolescents with substance abuse issues is also vital to the safety of the school community. Multidimensional Family Therapy (MDFT) and the Adolescent Community Reinforcement Approach (A-CRA) place an emphasis on problem solving and improving interpersonal skills. Both have been shown to reduce substance abuse among adolescents (Barrett, Slesnick, Brody, Turner, & Peterson, 2001; Liddle, 2004; Liddle et al., 2001). A strong infrastructure of mental health services that provides both easy access and a high quality of mental health services for those in need may be a strategy for preventing school crisis, but it is not routinely incorporated into school crisis planning.

During a Crisis

School crises usually produce one or more of the following conditions: temporary, intermittent, or prolonged disruptions of regular school functions and routines; high rates of absenteeism; student and faculty distress that interfere with the ability of students and staff to focus on learning; physical and or psychological injury to students and/or staff; disruption to regular school routines from parental concern; and concentrated attention from the community and news media.

Universal approaches. The approaches used during a school crisis are primarily universal in that they are delivered to the entire school community. The aim of these school-wide approaches is to mitigate the severity of the crisis and to help students, staff, and the larger school community return to "a new normal" of functioning as soon as possible. Below we describe several school-wide approaches that can be used during a school crisis.

Operation of school crisis teams. Many school districts employ the use of a school or district crisis team in an attempt to restore order and calm in the learning environment after the disruption caused by a crisis on school grounds. The response of school or district crisis teams can be divided into several phases following a traumatic event on or near a school campus. In the first phase, the principal of a school or the superintendent of the district convenes the members of the crisis team, which includes one or more teacher representatives, school counselors, school psychologists, school social workers, school nurses, custodians, and school secretaries. In some districts, child mental health and other social services workers are established members of the team and have been part of the preparedness/response training. The facts of the incident or event are reviewed and the crisis team members are given a short script of a few paragraphs to share confirmed public information with students. They are also given information about possible police activity on campus; the bell schedule, if revised; the location of crisis counseling services on campus; and the approved means (usually hall passes) by which students will be released from the classroom to participate in counseling sessions.

In the second phase, the crisis team triages the needs of students, faculty, and staff by identifying those that might have been eyewitnesses to the incident. The triage process is based on levels of exposure to violence and the risk of psychological trauma. For example, services to those students who witnessed the event (after the police investigation has been completed) and to those who knew the victim(s) are a priority.

During a crisis response, the principal, teachers, and crisis team members will determine how long acute crisis counseling services may continue at the school site. The objective of counseling services is to assist students with achieving an understanding of how crises may cause social, emotional, and behavioral changes, and of how students can utilize coping skills to achieve self-regulation of thoughts and emotions. Crisis team members may remain at the school for a few days, a week, or longer periods of time, depending upon factors such as continuing acute counseling needs balanced with the need for members to return to their regular assignments at other schools and offices within the district.

Psychological First Aid. The concept of Psychological First Aid (PFA) was first introduced into the literature by the American Psychological Association in 1954 (Schreiber, Gurwitch, & Wong, 2006). The APA acknowledged that interventions were necessary to alleviate stress of a "severity and quality not generally encountered . . . due to the 'forces of nature or from enemy attack.'" (Everly, Phillips, Kane, & Feldman, 2006).

PFA is a widely used school-based approach that acknowledges the disruptive aspects of the crisis events to the school community. It is intended to protect survivors from further physical harm and to triage survivors in an attempt to identify and support those who are most distressed. Teachers, administrators, and other school staff are then directed to actively work to help students to restore social and emotional equilibrium and order to the learning environment. Re-establishing "social connectedness" is a critical component of the process. Strategies include reuniting friends, teachers, and returning students to school; providing information and linkage with local resources on school campuses; and returning students to school and familiar routines with the aim of full student attendance and participation in the learning process, as well as helping students to resume extracurricular school and community activities.

Another component of PFA is helping survivors to understand common crisis-related emotions and reactions. School nurses, school psychologists, and school social workers serve important roles in this process. They work to stabilize the emotions and behaviors of students, school staff, and parents; provide education about the expected psychological responses to stressful and traumatic events; and teach and support constructive coping behaviors.

To accommodate school staff variation, PFA is available in two different versions. For mental health professionals with experience in trauma, *Psychological First Aid for Schools* (PFA-S) provides guidelines for intervening with students exposed to mass causality events. For educators and other school staff, *Psychological First Aid for Schools: Listen, Protect, Connect* is available. This approach prioritizes improving communication with recently traumatized students and staff (Schreiber, Gurwitch, & Wong, 2006).

Research on the effectiveness of PFA interventions has lagged behind their dissemination due in large part to the challenges of testing interventions in a group of acutely affected adolescents. Additionally, because of the sudden and unexpected nature of these events, it is likely that only naturalistic studies may be possible to implement. A randomized controlled trial of a PFA intervention may not only be infeasible, but it may also raise many ethical questions about what is received by students in the comparison group.

After a Crisis

Following the culmination of immediate response efforts during a school crisis, most students return to typical functioning. It is common, however, for a subset of students to remain symptomatic, in which case additional services are often needed. It is not unusual for schools to experience high rates of absenteeism after an act of violence on the school campus because of a fear of recurrence among students and parents. Some students may exhibit more easily identifiable trauma-related external symptoms, such as aggressive or self-destructive behavior, while others may experience internalized symptoms that are more difficult for educators and mental health professionals to recognize, such as a distorted sense of blame or disturbances in memory. Identifying and providing services to students and staff still experiencing symptoms of trauma following a traumatic event are the focus of interventions after a school crisis has occurred.

Universal approaches. Although not a common practice in most schools, developing and implementing a universal screening process may help to identify students who remain symptomatic following a school crisis. In schools, ideal measures should be easy to administer and score, but they should also be suitable for large-scale screenings that include a full range of traumatic events and trauma-related symptoms (Pagano, Cassidy, Little, Murphy, & Jellinek, 2000). Based on a number of factors, including size of the school, resources, and personnel, schools have developed varying strategies for identifying students in need (Hallfors et al., 2006; Scott et al., 2009) Districts and schools must consider the capacity of their mental health workforce prior to determining the extent of the screening. Schools or districts may mandate that all students in a particular grade receive screening (Kataoka, 2012). However, when resources are limited, schools may choose to conduct this screening with a few classrooms so as not to identify more students than can be served.

However, in these instances it may be more ethical to conduct the screening on all students and refer symptomatic students to local community agencies.

Early intervention. Students who remain symptomatic in the weeks following a crisis may benefit from early interventions. Most commonly, these interventions employ components of cognitive behavioral therapy (CBT), including psycho-education, relaxation skills, cognitive restructuring, trauma narrative, safety planning, affect modulation, conjoint parent sessions, and in vivo mastery of trauma reminders (Cohen, Mannarino, & Deblinger, 2006). As described above, early interventions are commonly delivered in a group setting on the school grounds. These interventions are less intensive than the individual therapy a student may receive in a more traditional service setting. The format of early-intervention trauma services in schools tend to be briefer and may not allow for the same level of processing of the traumatic event. Parents also tend to be less involved in school-based interventions than they are in services provided in a more traditional service setting like a community clinic.

While there has been an emphasis on the development of school-based trauma interventions, these efforts have not been matched with rigorous evaluation, with only a small number of studies employing experimental or quasi-experimental designs to test the impact of such interventions (Jaycox, Stein, & Amaya-Jackson, 2008). A review of school-based interventions for children and adolescents with PTSD symptoms found positive results for 19 studies, 16 of which employed a CBT approach (Rolfsnes & Idsoe, 2011).

Cognitive Behavioral Intervention for Trauma in Schools (CBITS). One intervention that exemplifies many of the components described above is the Cognitive Behavioral Intervention for Trauma in Schools (CBITS). Created in partnership with school staff and administrators, CBITS was specifically designed for school-based delivery. This school-community research collaborative team designed the implementation of CBITS to fit during one class period (Stein et al., 2002).

CBITS is delivered on school campuses to students who have been exposed to trauma and exhibit symptoms of PTSD in the clinical range (see Stein et al., 2003 for details). During one-hour weekly group sessions over the course of about 10 weeks, students learn the core components of cognitive behavioral skills. Separate psycho-educational sessions for parents and teachers are also offered. CBITS has been studied in a quasi-experimental trial (Kataoka et al., 2003) with students from fourth through eighth grade, and a randomized controlled trial (Stein et al., 2003) with sixth-grade students. In both trials CBITS was delivered by school-based clinicians. CBITS has been shown to result in improvements in post-traumatic stress disorder (PTSD) and depression among pre-adolescent and early-adolescent students exposed to violence. It is also associated with improved school performance (Kataoka et al., 2011). While CBITS has not undergone a randomized controlled trial with high school students, it has been adapted for older adolescents and is currently being implemented with ninth grade students (www.cbitsprogram.org).

Support for Students Exposed to Trauma (SSET). Support for Students Exposed to Trauma (SSET) is an adaptation of the CBITS intervention, developed in recognition of the scarcity of mental health clinicians in many schools. The intervention is a series of 10 lessons delivered by teachers or school counselors to reduce students' trauma-related distress. SSET includes a wide variety of CBT-based skill-building techniques geared toward changing maladaptive thoughts and promoting positive behaviors. It is also intended to increase levels of peer and parent support for affected students. In a preliminary study, SSET was found to reduce trauma-related mental health symptoms in preadolescent students in sixth and seventh grade (Jaycox et al., 2009).

Targeted. Students who remain symptomatic following early intervention approaches may benefit from more intensive individualized treatment. A number of interventions borne out of cognitive behavioral theory have been shown to be effective in supporting individuals suffering from post-traumatic stress. The most rigorously tested and widely disseminated intervention is Trauma-Focused Cognitive Behavioral Therapy (TF-CBT).

TF-CBT comprises 12–16 sessions of individual and parent-child therapy. However, it can also be adapted for use in a longer-term treatment approach. The key component of TF-CBT are outlined by the acronym "PRACTICE: Psychoeducation and Parenting skills; Relaxation skills; Affective regulation skills; Cognitive coping skills; Trauma narrative and cognitive processing of the traumatic event(s); *In vivo* mastery of trauma reminders; Conjoint child-parent sessions; and Enhancing safety and future developmental trajectory" (Cohen & Mannarino, 2008).

TF-CBT was originally designed and shown to be effective in supporting children and adolescents who had suffered sexual abuse (Cohen, Deblinger, Mannarino, & Steer, 2004; Cohen, Mannarino, & Knudsen, 2005). However, the intervention has since been adapted and has been used to support children and adolescents (ages 3–17) suffering with PTSD, depression, and other emotional disorders resulting from a variety of traumatic experiences, such as domestic violence and traumatic grief (Cohen & Mannarino, 2008). It has also been used successfully to support children and adolescents following large-scale disasters that would be considered school crises, as defined earlier in this chapter. In fact, TF-CBT was used to successfully support children and adolescents following the 9/11 attacks (Hoagwood et al., 2007) and Hurricane Katrina (Cohen et al., 2009; Jaycox et al., 2012).

SERVICE DELIVERY MODEL

Above we outlined the President's Disaster Directive (PDD-8) and described the universal, early intervention, and targeted strategies that schools can implement to provide a continuum of care, from disaster preparedness to long-term recovery. However, beyond understanding the interventions that fall within each time frame, schools must develop a strategy for integrating these services into their school community. Given the broad diversity of schools and districts across the country, a single service delivery model of crisis response and recovery is unlikely to work across all schools. Rather, key contextual factors will impact implementation of interventions in schools within each time frame, and below we discuss how these contextual factors can facilitate or impede implementation, using an established framework developed by Mendel and colleagues (Mendel, Meredith, Schoenbaum, Sherbourne, & Wells, 2008). According to Mendel's model, a system's readiness and ability to implement new strategies is a function of its *norms and attitudes, organizational structure and process*, and *resources.* Other important implementation factors include *media and change agents, policies and incentives*, and *networks and linkages.*

According to this model, *norms and attitudes* refers to the knowledge and beliefs about particular mental health conditions, treatment options, and the perception that particular interventions or treatments will successfully alleviate a particular health problem. These norms significantly impact whether an issue is going to receive attention and whether there is broad support for specific interventions. *Organizational structure and process* refers to the modes of communication within a school, how knowledge is shared, and how services are provided. These processes can significantly facilitate or impede successful implementation. *Resources* are another critical contextual factor. In this model resources can refer to human capital (e.g., staff time), infrastructure, and funding. *Policies and incentives* at the federal, state, and local level significantly impact a school's ability to implement new interventions. In addition, such policies are helpful because organizations such as schools are unlikely to change without external influence (Burns & Wholey, 1993; Scott, 1995). *Media and change agents* represent another key component of the implementation process. The efforts of motivated and persuasive individuals are often necessary for new ideas and interventions to be adopted and implemented. Finally, *networks and linkages* with stakeholders and partnering organizations are key to garnering support and procuring key resources not available within the school setting. In the section below, we describe how these contextual factors play a role in implementing the interventions that make up the continuum of care from disaster preparedness to long-term recovery (see Table 4.1 for details).

Before a Crisis

Attitudes or "implicit norms" of an organization are key variables that impact the implementation process (Mendel, Meredith, Schoenbaum, Sherbourne, & Wells, 2008). One aspect inherent in the norms and attitudes present before a crisis is the potential stigma regarding mental health issues and need for services that can be a significant attitudinal barrier in delivering social-emotional supports in the schools. This is particularly true in some racial and ethnic minority communities where stigma about mental health and medical treatment is quite strong (Corrigan, 2004). Before a crisis, school communities may not perceive the importance of prevention efforts or longer-term mental health supports. Helping the school community make the link between social-emotional supports and academic mission of schools can help to build support for these services (Domitrovich et al., 2008).

Table 4.1. CONTEXTUAL FACTORS OF IMPLEMENTATION BY TIME FRAME

	Before	During	After
Norms and Attitudes	Shared vision for creating a safe and supportive school	School leadership providing clear messages to parents, students, and staff about the crisis and aligning that message with emergency response team and law enforcement	Understanding the need for short-term and long-term recovery approaches
Organizational Structure and Process	Organized screening and referral process Regular professional development for staff on MH needs of students	Crisis teams providing crisis counseling and assisting school in supporting roles	Organizing screening and referral process
Resources	Staff time for screening Staff time for in-services Trained MH clinicians Supervision	Resource officers Crisis counselors Project SERV	Staff to screen school following trauma MH clinicians trained in trauma-focused EBPs Supervision
Policies and Incentives	Federal initiatives District policies	Federal initiatives District policies	Federal initiatives District policies
Media and Change Agents	Administrator MH clinician champion	Crisis team providing education and support to media so that responsible reporting occurs during crisis	Television Newspapers
Networks and Linkages	Law enforcement Community mental health agencies	Law enforcement	Community mental health agencies

Developing a shared vision across the school community, which includes students, family members, administrators, teachers, counselors, coaches, and other school staff, often requires a number of staff in-services and parent information sessions. These educational sessions should include information about the impact of traumatic events on students, families, and school communities, and on how adopting a continuum of care can both mitigate the deleterious impact of a school crisis on the school community and help those who are negatively affected recover and return to normal school functioning. A number of online resources have been developed and can be used to facilitate this discussion among the school community (e.g., www.nctsn.org, www.cbitsprogram.org, www.traumaawareschools.org).

A variety of **organizational processes** can help to promote the implementation of preventative strategies in the phase before a crisis. These processes include the following:

1. Prioritization by the school administration to schedule regular in-services related to trauma awareness and bullying prevention for all school staff.
2. Regular annual or biannual training of crisis team members, which are essential for understanding the individual and interagency roles of the members.
3. A universal screening process to assess the wellness of the school community. Informing parents about this screening and obtaining parental consent is an organizational process that often requires additional resources, coordination with teaching staff, and collaboration with parent groups on campus.
4. Onsite early intervention resources and/or a referral processes to targeted interventions to local community mental health agencies. Having an organizational site referral process mapped out and shared with all school staff can facilitate referrals into designated entry points in care.

However, to successfully carryout the activities listed above, key **resources** including financial support for specific tasks, staff with relevant expertise and infrastructure must be assembled. Access to these resources can be a unique challenge within schools, a setting that isn't designed to deliver psychological supports and interventions (Ringeisen, Henderson, & Hoagwood, 2003).

We encourage schools to build upon the resources they currently have and think about how they can leverage these resources to support prevention, crisis response, and long-term recovery efforts. As technology, such as web-based learning, advances in the field of behavioral health, schools may be able to access these tools and training, some of which have shown to be just as effective as in-person trainings (DeRosier, McMillen, Davis, Kameny, & Hoffend, 2011; Dimeff et al., 2009; Weingardt, Cucciare, Bellotti, & Lai, 2009) and are more cost-effective. **Resources** that can help to promote the implementation of preventative strategies before a crisis include:

1. Time for all staff to attend in-services related to bullying and trauma awareness.
2. Training support for school personnel who will be involved in crisis response activities.
3. If schools choose to conduct a universal screening to assess the overall wellness of their students and staff, schools must provide school counselors with dedicated time to conduct the screening and evaluate the results. This activity often requires the support of additional school staff and/or interns (Kataoka, 2012).

4. Clinical staff trained in evidence-based practices (EBPs) are necessary to provide early intervention and targeted support to students experiencing or at risk for experiencing mental health difficulties.
5. Supervision for clinicians providing evidence-based care to students. Studies reveal that supervision is a key component to supporting implementation (Fixsen, Blase, Naoom, & Wallace, 2009).
6. Infrastructure support such as dedicated space is necessary for these activities to be conducted successfully.

There are a variety of models that schools use to provide these services. One of the most common models is having community agencies provide services on campus. This can be a sustainable model if agency providers have dedicated staff for school-based activities and can be reimbursed for their services. Districts and schools may also employ clinicians full or part time to provide services. Another less common but growing model of care is school-based health centers, which frequently have health and mental health providers trained to be an on-site referral source for the host school, and for feeder schools in the local area. Coordination with these valuable school resources and preparation with them regarding crisis intervention and ongoing recovery services on a school campus in important before a crisis occurs.

Policies and incentives at the federal, state, and local level and targeted funds for training and implementation of prevention activities during the "before" stage are critical to the implementation of these activities. There is clear evidence that funds targeted for specific interventions and activities are more likely to enhance subsequent adoption and implementation (Aarons, Sommerfeld, & Walrath-Greene, 2009). Below we outline specific policies and incentives that can help to promote the implementation of preventative strategies before a crisis.

1. Current federal initiatives such as Safe Schools/Healthy Students (SS/HS) have supported schools, districts, and communities to engage in partnerships to facilitate more comprehensive youth violence prevention efforts.
2. A number of additional federal programs have been proposed that aim to support schools and districts in their efforts to prevent and prepare for a crisis.
   a. The Successful, Safe, and Healthy Students Program aims to support the mental and physical well-being of students. A portion of the funds is targeted specifically for developing more comprehensive emergency management plans and promoting school climates ensure that students are "ready to learn" (Office of Elementary and Secondary Education, 2014).
   b. Another federal program, Project Prevent, provides grants to help schools in communities with high rates of violence to overcome the cycle. These grants would provide resources and technical

      assistance to schools and clinicians to support students' social
      and emotional well-being (Office of Elementary and Secondary
      Education, 2014).

   c. The President's "Now Is the Time" initiative to reduce gun violence
      has a number aims, two of which apply directly to schools and
      adolescents. The first is to enhance the use of trained resource officers
      and counselors and develop emergency management plans. The
      second is to expand access to mental health coverage for children
      and adolescents with the intention of supporting vulnerable students
      before a violent event occurs (White House, 2014).

3. State policies may also facilitate prevention activities. For example, all
   states have laws or policies that mandate bullying prevention on each
   school campus. The specific policies for each state can be found at www.
   stopbullying.org.

4. District level policies can also impact the implementation of prevention
   activities. For example, in Wisconsin, the Madison Unified School
   District, has screened all sixth grade students for exposure to trauma and
   symptoms of PTSD and depression (Kataoka, 2012). These activities help
   to link vulnerable students to early intervention services.

Before a school crisis, a number of individuals can serve as *change agents*, whose
mission is to enhance the safety of the school system and call for the implementation of a comprehensive emergency management approach.

1. Administrator support has been cited as a key facilitator of
   implementation (Gottfredson, Jones, & Gore, 2002; Pagoto
   et al., 2007).

2. In other instances, school-based mental health clinicians have stepped
   into this role and advocated for prevention and early intervention
   services on the school campus.

3. External funders such as private organizations may also influence the
   implementation of key prevention and recovery efforts. An example
   of this can be seen in Madison, Wisconsin, where a private funder
   has partnered with the school district to support efforts to screen
   and provide early intervention to students with mental health needs
   (Kataoka, 2012).

Networks and Linkages throughout the community are also key to supporting
implementation. Partnerships with law enforcement and local community mental
health agencies are key during the "before" stage of crisis response, since such
partnerships, particularly with organizations using EBPs, increase the likelihood
of a school exploring or adopting EBPs (Aarons, Sommerfeld, & Walrath-Greene,
2009). Schools may also want to partner with local advocacy groups. For example,
if a student is being bullied for his or her sexual orientation, schools may benefit
from partnering with an LGBTQ organization.

During a Crisis

The *organizational structure and processes* of an organization are critical to how it responds to a crisis. During a crisis, seamless communication between the school staff, law enforcement, and mental health providers is critical for effective implementation, but this can only be achieved if joint training and skills development have preceded an actual crisis event.

Additional *resources* can be acquired immediately following a disaster. For example, Project SERV (School Emergency Response to Violence) is funded by the U.S. Department of Education to help provide local students and education staff with academic and mental health services following a crisis. School districts may apply online at the department's website.

During a crisis, *policies* help to provide a roadmap for helping to direct the actions of staff and students. A district bulletin can provide guidelines for how district staff can be pulled from their regular assignments and called together at the site of a school crisis. A full understanding at all levels of all district faculty and staff can only be achieved if procedures and delegation of authority to act in response to a crisis are encoded in a district policy bulletin, which will survive the administration of any superintendency (unless it is rewritten). Otherwise, the operation of the crisis team is left to the changing views of leadership. As an example, the typical tenure of a school district superintendent is two years in office.

The *media* can have a significant impact on how schools are supported. For example, media attention may impact additional services and supports to the affected school or district. In instances were a crisis receives extensive media coverage, school personnel and clinicians should work with the media to make sure messaging serves to support the community, and that it helps the community to understand the changes that may be needed.

Similar to the *networks and linkages* that should be in place before a crisis, it is important that schools maintain partnerships with law enforcement, community mental health agencies, advocacy groups, and families. It is also possible that new partnerships will form following a crisis. Additional organizations may want to provide support to the school community in recovery. In this case, it is important that these organizations understand the mission and strategy of the school, and that their work compliments these efforts.

After a Crisis

Despite efforts made before a crisis to provide education about the impact of trauma on students and the broader school community, as well as the need for support services, it often takes a significant crisis for this information to truly resonate within the school community and to impact the organization's *norms and attitudes*. Results from a survey conducted following the Newtown shooting revealed that 59% of respondents supported increased government spending on mental health care, and 61% favored greater spending on such care as a strategy for reducing gun violence. Fifty eight percent viewed discrimination against people with mental illness as a serious problem, while 56% believed that, with treatment, individuals can adapt and return to productive lives (Barry, McGinty, Vernick, & Webster, 2013).

After a crisis there are a number of ***organizational processes*** that can help to promote the implementation of recovery efforts. These key strategies include

- a universal screening in the weeks and months following the crisis,
- the implementation of early intervention strategies like CBITS to support students still experiencing symptoms, and
- targeted treatments like TF-CBT for students in need of more intensive services.

A number of ***key resources*** are necessary to successfully implement long-term recovery strategies. These include

- dedicated staff to implement the screening to detect students and staff still experiencing symptoms (possibly addition staff such as interns or school counselors),
- teachers trained to implement SSET,
- clinicians trained to implement CBITS and TF-CBT, and
- supervision for teachers and clinicians providing services.

Following a major crisis with national impact, such as 9/11 or the tragedy at Newton, Connecticut, it is not uncommon for ***policies*** to change and for additional funding streams (public and private) to emerge. The Substance Abuse and Mental Health Services Administration (SAMHSA)-funded National Child Traumatic Stress Network, a federal initiative since 2001, has provided training and dissemination to community agencies and schools across the United States for all stages of crisis response, before, during, and especially after a crisis. The network was created to support mental health recovery following the terrorist attacks on 9/11 and has been active is responding to disasters ever since, including Katrina and Newtown.

CONCLUSION

Significant progress has been made in conceptualizing a comprehensive emergency management approach for schools. Many of these advances have resulted from major school crises after which public and government awareness is enhanced. The lessons learned from each tragedy have helped to inform the field's understanding of the necessary components of crisis response and long-term recovery. However, despite these recent advances in policy (U.S. Department of Education, 2013) progress has not yet been matched by consistent implementation in schools nationally.

In this chapter, we have described a number of interventions and strategies that fall along the continuum of care from prevention to long-term recovery. A great deal of research has demonstrated the effectiveness of interventions for students following a traumatic event (Cohen & Mannarino, 2008; Cohen, Mannarino, & Deblinger, 2006; Kataoka et al., 2003; Liddle, 2004; Liddle et al., 2001; Lochman & Wells, 2004; Mufson et al., 2004; Stein et al., 2003). However, less evidence exists related to interventions and strategies that aim to prevent or provide immediate response to a crisis. This may be attributed to limited feasibility and ethical concerns for conducting randomized controlled trials during disaster situations. In the case of bullying, findings on the effectiveness of prevention have been mixed (Merrell, Gueldner, Ross, & Isava, 2008). To the extent that it is possible and feasible, additional research is needed to identify effective prevention and response strategies before or during a crisis that may help to reduce the number of school crises and/or mitigate the deleterious impact of these events on students if one does occur.

Implementing a comprehensive emergency management strategy that includes a variety of interventions from prevention to long-term recovery is a considerable task that may take schools years to accomplish. We have provided a framework that helps to organize the key contextual factors that may facilitate implementation. It is critical that schools build upon the work that they are already doing in the area of supporting the emotional well-being of their students and the broader school community. Additionally, as new technologies emerge, such as web-based platforms for training in evidence-based practices (DeRosier, McMillen, Davis, Kameny, & Hoffend, 2011; Vona et al., 2014), schools may have access to more cost-effective resources that facilitate implementation and supervision of trauma-informed interventions. Finally, schools will benefit from identifying strategic partnerships within the community. These linkages will likely help them garner additional support and resources not directly available on campus.

REFERENCES

Aarons, G. A., Sommerfeld, D. H., & Walrath-Greene, C. M. (2009). Evidence-based practice implementation: The impact of public versus private sector organization type on organizational support, provider attitudes, and adoption of evidence-based practice. *Implementation Science, 4*(1), 83.

Alisic, E. (2012). Teachers' perspectives on providing support to children after trauma: A qualitative study. *School Psychology Quarterly, 27*(1), 51–59.

Barrett, H., Slesnick, N., Brody, J. L., Turner, C. W., & Peterson, T. R. (2001). Treatment outcomes for adolescent substance abuse at 4- and 7-month assessments. *Journal of Consulting and Clinical Psychology, 69*(5), 802–813.

Barry, C. L., McGinty, E. E., Vernick, J. S., & Webster, D. W. (2013). After Newtown: public opinion on gun policy and mental illness. *New England Journal of Medicine, 368*(12), 1077–1081.

Berthold, K. A., & Hoover, J. H. (2000). Correlates of bullying and victimization among intermediate students in the Midwestern USA. *School Psychology International, 21*(1), 65–78.

Bradshaw, C. P., Koth, C. W., Bevans, K. B., Ialongo, N., & Leaf, P. J. (2008). The impact of School-Wide Positive Behavioral Interventions and Supports (PBIS) on the organizational health of elementary schools. *School Psychology Quarterly*, *23*(4), 462.

Brent, D. A., Perper, J. A., Moritz, G., Liotus, L., Richardson, D., Canobbio, R., . . . Roth, C. (1995). Posttraumatic stress disorder in peers of adolescent suicide victims: Predisposing factors and phenomenology. *Journal of the American Academy of Child & Adolescent Psychiatry*, *34*(2), 209–215.

Burns, L. R., & Wholey, D. R. (1993). Adoption and abandonment of matrix management programs: Effects of organizational characteristics and interorganizational networks. *Academy of Management Journal*, *36*(1), 106–138.

Carlyle, K. E., & Steinman, K. J. (2007). Demographic differences in the prevalence, co-occurrence, and correlates of adolescent bullying at school. *Journal of School Health*, *77*(9), 623–629.

Chemtob, C. M., Nakashima, J. P., & Hamada, R. S. (2002). Psychosocial intervention for postdisaster trauma symptoms in elementary school children: A controlled community field study. *Archives of Pediatrics & Adolescent Medicine*, *156*(3), 211–216.

Cohen, J. A., Deblinger, E., Mannarino, A. P., & Steer, R. A. (2004). A multisite, randomized controlled trial for children with sexual abuse–related PTSD symptoms. *Journal of the American Academy of Child & Adolescent Psychiatry*, *43*(4), 393–402.

Cohen, J. A., Jaycox, L. H., Walker, D. W., Mannarino, A. P., Langley, A. K., & DuClos, J. L. (2009). Treating traumatized children after Hurricane Katrina: Project Fleur-de Lis. *Clinical Child and Family Psychology Review*, *12*(1), 55–64.

Cohen, J. A., & Mannarino, A. P. (2008). Trauma-focused cognitive behavioural therapy for children and parents. *Child and Adolescent Mental Health*, *13*(4), 158–162.

Cohen, J. A., Mannarino, A. P., & Deblinger, E. (2006). *Treating trauma and traumatic grief in children and adolescents*. New York, NY: Guilford Press.

Cohen, J. A., Mannarino, A. P., & Knudsen, K. (2005). Treating sexually abused children: 1 year follow-up of a randomized controlled trial. *Child Abuse & Neglect*, *29*(2), 135–145.

Corrigan, P. (2004). How stigma interferes with mental health care. *American Psychologist*, *59*(7), 614–625.

Craig, C. D., & Sprang, G. (2010). Compassion satisfaction, compassion fatigue, and burnout in a national sample of trauma treatment therapists. *Anxiety, Stress, & Coping*, *23*(3), 319–339.

Daniels, J. A., Bradley, M. C., & Hays, M. (2007). The impact of school violence on school personnel: Implications for psychologists. *Professional Psychology: Research and Practice*, *38*(6), 652.

Dean, K. L., Langley, A. K., Kataoka, S. H., Jaycox, L. H., Wong, M., & Stein, B. D. (2008). School-based disaster mental health services: Clinical, policy, and community challenges. *Professional Psychology: Research and Practice*, *39*(1), 52.

Delaney-Black, V., Covington, C., Ondersma, S. J., Nordstrom-Klee, B., Templin, T., Ager, J., . . . Sokol, R. J. (2002). Violence exposure, trauma, and IQ and/or reading deficits among urban children. *Archives of Pediatrics & Adolescent Medicine*, *156*(3), 280–285.

DeRosier, M. E., McMillen, J., Davis, N. O., Kameny, R., & Hoffend, C. (2011). Tools to support career advancement of diverse social, behavioral, and mental health researchers: Comparison of in-person and online training delivery modes. *Journal of Online Learning and Teaching*, *7*(1), 43–56.

Dimeff, L. A., Koerner, K., Woodcock, E. A., Beadnell, B., Brown, M. Z., Skutch, J. M., . . . Harned, M. S. (2009). Which training method works best? A randomized controlled trial comparing three methods of training clinicians in dialectical behavior therapy skills. *Behaviour Research and Therapy, 47*(11), 921–930.

Domitrovich, C. E., Bradshaw, C. P., Poduska, J. M., Hoagwood, K., Buckley, J. A., Olin, S., . . . Ialongo, N. S. (2008). Maximizing the implementation quality of evidence-based preventive interventions in schools: A conceptual framework. *Advances in School Mental Health Promotion, 1*(3), 6–28.

Everly, G. S., Jr., Phillips, S. B., Kane, D., & Feldman, D. (2006). Introduction to and overview of group psychological first aid. *Brief Treatment and Crisis Intervention, 6*(2), 130–136.

Fixsen, D. L., Blase, K. A., Naoom, S. F., & Wallace, F. (2009). Core implementation components. *Research on Social Work Practice, 19*(5), 531–540.

Galea, S., Ahern, J., Resnick, H., Kilpatrick, D., Bucuvalas, M., Gold, J., & Vlahov, D. (2002). Psychological sequelae of the September 11 terrorist attacks in New York City. *New England Journal of Medicine, 346*(13), 982–987.

Ginsburg, G. S., & Drake, K. L. (2002). School-based treatment for anxious African-American adolescents: A controlled pilot study. *Journal of the American Academy of Child & Adolescent Psychiatry, 41*(7), 768–775.

Gottfredson, G. D., Jones, E. M., & Gore, T. W. (2002). Implementation and evaluation of a cognitive-behavioral intervention to prevent problem behavior in a disorganized school. *Prevention Science, 3*(1), 43–56.

Grogger, J. (1997). Local violence and educational attainment. *Journal of Human Resources, 32*(4), 659–682.

Hallfors, D., Brodish, P. H., Khatapoush, S., Sanchez, V., Cho, H., & Steckler, A. (2006). Feasibility of screening adolescents for suicide risk in a real-world high school settings. *American Journal of Public Health, 96*(2), 282.

Hoagwood, K. E., Vogel, J. M., Levitt, J., D'Amico, P. J., Paisner, W. I., Kaplan, S. J., & Hamilton, J. D. (2007). Implementing an evidence-based trauma treatment in a state system after September 11: the CATS project. *Journal of the American Academy of Child & Adolescent Psychiatry, 46*(6), 773–779.

Hoven, C. W., Duarte, C. S., Lucas, C. P., Wu, P., Mandell, D. J., Goodwin, R. D., . . . Susser, E. J. (2005). Psychopathology among New York City public school children 6 months after September 11. *Archives of General Psychiatry, 62*(5), 545–551.

Hurt, H., Malmud, E., Brodsky, N. L., & Giannetta, J. (2001). Exposure to violence: Psychological and academic correlates in child witnesses. *Archives of Pediatrics & Adolescent Medicine, 155*(12), 1351–1356.

Jaycox, L. H., Cohen, J. A., Mannarino, A. P., Walker, D. W., Langley, A. K., Gegenheimer, K. L., . . . Schonlau, M. (2012). Children's mental health care following Hurricane Katrina: A field trial of trauma-focused psychotherapies. *Journal of Traumatic Stress, 23*(2), 223–231.

Jaycox, L. H., Kataoka, S. H., Stein, B. D., Wong, M., & Langley, A. (2005). Responding to the needs of the community: A stepped-care approach to implementing trauma-focused interventions in schools. *Emotional and Behavioral Disorders in Youth, 5*, 85–103.

Jaycox, L. H., Langley, A. K., Stein, B. D., Wong, M., Sharma, P., Scott, M., & Schonlau, M. (2009). Support for students exposed to trauma: A pilot study. *School Mental Health, 1*(2), 49–60.

Jaycox, L. H., Stein, B. D., & Amaya-Jackson, L. (2008). School-based treatment for children and adolescents. In E. B. Foa, T. M. Keane, M. J. Friedman, & J. A. Cohen

(Eds.), *Effective treatments for PTSD: Practice guidelines from the International Society of Traumatic Stress Studies* (pp. 327–345). New York, NY: Guilford.

Jaycox, L. H., Tanielian, T. L., Sharma, P., Morse, L., Clum, G., & Stein, B. D. (2007). Schools' mental health responses after Hurricanes Katrina and Rita. *Psychiatric Services, 58*(10), 1339–1343.

Kataoka, S. (2012). *Disseminating trauma services in schools: Voices from the school community.* Paper presented at the 28th Annual International Society for Traumatic Stress Studies Meeting, Los Angeles, CA.

Kataoka, S., Jaycox, L. H., Wong, M., Nadeem, E., Langley, A., Tang, L., & Stein, B. D. (2011). Effects on school outcomes in low-income minority youth: Preliminary findings from a community-partnered study of a school trauma intervention. *Ethnicity & Disease, 21*(S1-71-7).

Kataoka, S., Stein, B. D., Jaycox, L. H., Wong, M., Escuerdo, P., Tu, W., . . . Fink, A. (2003) A school-based mental health program for traumatized Latino immigrant children. *Journal of the American Academy of Child & Adolescent Psychiatry, 42*(3), 311–318.

Liddle, H. A. (2004). Family-based therapies for adolescent alcohol and drug use: Research contributions and future research needs. *Addiction, 99*(Suppl. 2), 76–92.

Liddle, H. A., Dakof, G. A., Parker, K., Diamond, G. S., Barrett, K., & Tejeda, M. (2001). Multidimensional family therapy for adolescent drug abuse: Results of a randomized clinical trial. *American Journal of Drug and Alcohol Abuse, 27*(4), 651–688.

Lochman, J. E., & Wells, K. C. (2004). The coping power program for preadolescent aggressive boys and their parents: Outcome effects at the 1-year follow-up. *Journal of Consulting and Clinical Psychology, 72*(4), 571.

Mendel, P., Meredith, L. S., Schoenbaum, M., Sherbourne, C. D., & Wells, K. B. (2008). Interventions in organizational and community context: A framework for building evidence on dissemination and implementation in health services research. *Administration and Policy in Mental Health and Mental Health Services Research, 35*(1–2), 21–37.

Merrell, K. W., Gueldner, B. A., Ross, S. W., & Isava, D. M. (2008). How effective are school bullying intervention programs? A meta-analysis of intervention research. *School Psychology Quarterly, 23*(1), 26.

Mufson, L., Dorta, K. P., Wickramaratne, P., Nomura, Y., Olfson, M., & Weissman, M. M. (2004). A randomized effectiveness trial of interpersonal psychotherapy for depressed adolescents. *Archives of General Psychiatry, 61*(6), 577–584.

National Child Traumatic Stress Network. Psychological First Aid for Schools. (n.d.). http://www.nctsn.org/content/psychological-first-aid-schoolspfa

North, C. S., Nixon, S. J., Shariat, S., Mallonee, S., McMillen, J. C., Spitznagel, E. L., & Smith, E. M. (1999). Psychiatric disorders among survivors of the Oklahoma City bombing. *JAMA, 282*(8), 755–762.

North, C. S., Smith, E. M., & Spitznagel, E. L. (1994). Posttraumatic stress disorder in survivors of a mass shooting. *American Journal of Psychiatry, 151*(1), 82–88.

North, C. S., Tivis, L., McMillen, J. C., Pfefferbaum, B., Spitznagel, E. L., Cox, J., . . . Smith, E. M. (2002). Psychiatric disorders in rescue workers after the Oklahoma City bombing. *American Journal of Psychiatry, 159*(5), 857–859.

Office of Elementary and Secondary Education. (2014). *Federal Partner Update.* Washington, DC: Department of Education. Retrieved from https://www.nasmhpd.org/sites/default/files/FedPartnersOESE.pdf

Pagano, M. E., Cassidy, L. J., Little, M., Murphy, J. M., & Jellinek, M. S. (2000). Identifying psychosocial dysfunction in school-age children: The Pediatric Symptom Checklist as a self-report measure. *Psychology in the Schools, 37*(2), 91–106.

Pagoto, S. L., Spring, B., Coups, E. J., Mulvaney, S., Coutu, M. F., & Ozakinci, G. (2007). Barriers and facilitators of evidence-based practice perceived by behavioral science health professionals. *Journal of Clinical Psychology, 63*(7), 695–705.

Pfefferbaum, B., Call, J. A., & Sconzo, G. M. (1999). Mental health services for children in the first two years after the 1995 Oklahoma City terrorist bombing. *Psychiatric Services, 50*(7), 956–958.

Pfefferbaum, B., Nixon, S. J., Krug, R. S., Tivis, R. D., Moore, V. L., Brown, J. M., . . . Gurwitch, R. H. (1999). Clinical needs assessment of middle and high school students following the 1995 Oklahoma City bombing. *American Journal of Psychiatry, 156*(7), 1069–1074.

Ringeisen, H., Henderson, K., & Hoagwood, K. (2003). Context matters: Schools and the "research to practice gap" in children's mental health. *School Psychology Review, 32*(2), 153–168.

Rolfsnes, E. S., & Idsoe, T. (2011). School-based intervention programs for PTSD symptoms: A review and meta-analysis. *Journal of Traumatic Stress, 24*(2), 155–165.

Schoenwald, S. K., & Henggeler, S. W. (2005). Multisystemic therapy for adolescents with serious externalizing problems. In J. Lebow (Ed.), *Handbook of clinical family therapy* (pp. 103–127). Hoboken, NJ: John Wiley.

Schreiber, M., Gurwitch, R., & Wong, M. (2006). *Listen, protect, connect—Model & teach: Psychological First Aid (PFA) for students and teachers.* Washington, DC: U.S. Department of Homeland Security. Retrieved from https://www.ready.gov/sites/default/files/documents/files/PFA_SchoolCrisis.pdf

Schuster, M. A., Stein, B. D., Jaycox, L. H., Collins, R. L., Marshall, G. N., Elliott, M. N., . . . Berry, S. H. (2001). A national survey of stress reactions after the September 11, 2001, terrorist attacks. *New England Journal of Medicine, 345*(20), 1507–1512.

Schwarz, E. D., & Kowalski, J. M. (1991). Malignant memories: PTSD in children and adults after a school shooting. *Journal of the American Academy of Child & Adolescent Psychiatry, 30*(6), 936–944.

Scott, M. A., Wilcox, H. C., Schonfeld, I. S., Davies, M., Hicks, R. C., Turner, J. B., & Shaffer, D (2009). School-based screening to identify at-risk students not already known to school professionals: The Columbia suicide screen. *American Journal of Public Health, 99*(2), 334–339.

Scott, W. R. (1995). *Institutions and organizations.* Thousand Oaks, CA: SAGE.

Seals, D., & Young, J. (2002). Bullying and victimization: Prevalence and relationship to gender, grade level, ethnicity, self-esteem, and depression. *Adolescence, 38*(152), 735–747.

Sloan, I. H., Rozensky, R. H., Kaplan, L., & Saunders, S. M. (1994). A shooting incident in an elementary school: Effects of worker stress on public safety, mental health, and medical personnel. *Journal of Traumatic Stress, 7*(4), 565–574.

Stein, B. D., Jaycox, L. H., Elliott, M. N., Collins, R., Berry, S., Marshall, G. N., . . . Schuster, M. A. (2004). The emotional and behavioral impact of terrorism on children: Results from a national survey. *Applied Developmental Science, 8*(4), 184–194.

Stein, B. D., Jaycox, L. H., Kataoka, S. H., Wong, M., Tu, W., Eliot, M. N., & Fink, A. (2003). A mental health intervention for schoolchildren exposed to violence. *JAMA, 290*(5), 603–611.

Stein B. D., Kataoka S. H., Jaycox, L. H., Wong, M., Fink, A., Escudero, P., & Zaragoza, C. (2002). Theoretical basis and program design of a school-based mental health intervention for traumatized immigrant children: a collaborative research partnership. *Journal of Behavioral Health Services & Research, 29*(3), 318–326.

Stuber, J., Fairbrother, G., Galea, S., Pfefferbaum, B., Wilson-Genderson, M., & Vlahov, D. (2002). Determinants of counseling for children in Manhattan after the September 11 attacks. *Psychiatric Services, 53*(7), 815–822.

U.S. Department of Education, Office of Elementary and Secondary Education, & Office of Safe and Healthy Students. (2013). *Guide for developing high-quality school emergency operations plans.* Washington, DC: Author.

Vona, P., Wilmoth, P., Jaycox, L. H., McMillen, J. S., Kataoka, S. H., Wong, M., . . . Stein, B. D. (2014). A web-based platform to support an evidence-based mental health intervention: Lessons from the CBITS web site. *Psychiatric Services, 65*(11), 1381–1384.

Vossekuil, B. (2004). *The final report and findings of the Safe School Initiative: Implications for the prevention of school attacks in the United States*: Washington, DC: U.S. Secret Service and Department of Education. Retrieved from https://www2.ed.gov/admins/lead/safety/preventingattacksreport.pdf

Weingardt, K. R., Cucciare, M. A., Bellotti, C., & Lai, W. P. (2009). A randomized trial comparing two models of web-based training in cognitive behavioral therapy for substance abuse counselors. *Journal of Substance Abuse Treatment, 37*(3), 219–227.

Weisler, R. H., Barbee, J. G., & Townsend, M. H. (2006). Mental health and recovery in the Gulf Coast after Hurricanes Katrina and Rita. *JAMA, 296*(5), 585–588.

Weist, M. D., Sander, M. A., Lever, N., Rosner, L. E., Pruitt. D. B., Lowie, J. A., . . . Christodulu, K.V. (2002). School mental health's response to terrorism and disaster. *Journal of School Violence, 1*(4), 5–31.

White House. (2014). Now Is the Time. http://www.whitehouse.gov/sites/default/files/docs/wh_now_is_the_time_full.pdf

Wolmer, L., Hamiel, D., & Laor, N. (2011). Preventing children's posttraumatic stress after disaster with teacher-based intervention: A controlled study. *Journal of the American Academy of Child & Adolescent Psychiatry, 50*(4), 340–348.

Wong, M. (2004). *Jane's safe school planning guide.* London: Jane's Information Group.

Wong, M. (2006). Commentary: Building partnerships between schools and academic partners to achieve a health-related research agenda. *Ethnicity and Disease, 16*(1), S1.

Wong, M. (2007). Managing threats: Safety lessons learned from school shootings. *UrbanEd: The University of Southern California School of Education Magazine.*

5

Enhancing Attention and Organization in Adolescents

CRAIG F. SPIEL, JUDITH R. HARRISON
AND TALIDA M. STATE ■

Attention and organization are essential skills for academic success in secondary schools. Difficulties attending in classroom settings can lead to serious academic impairment and may result in poor grades, grade retention, and school dropout. Obviously, such outcomes can be very costly, spiraling into a host of negative outcomes for adults, such as a high risk of under- or unemployment, financial difficulties, and relationship challenges. Attempts to alter the negative effects of inattention and disorganization on academic progress have resulted in the development of interventions and services to target those areas.

In this chapter we will describe these interventions, review the evidence for each, and describe service delivery in schools. We will first discuss (a) attention and organization as they relate to academic achievement; (b) the impact that lack of these skills might have on individuals, schools, and the community; (c) methods schools can use to screen for difficulties with attention and organization; and (d) services adolescents with deficits typically can receive through special education.

DEFINING THE PROBLEM

What Is Attention?

Attention is the ability to expend mental energy on a specific stimulus or group of stimuli perceived by the senses. It includes attending to a stimulus, sustaining attention, inhibiting responses to distraction, and shifting attention as needed (Riccio, Reynolds, Lowe, & Moore, 2002). Individuals can experience difficulties with any of these four phases of attention. Attention is a prerequisite to memory and learning. In an academic setting, attention can include the act of mentally following or taking notice of instruction and instructional activities. When adolescents are inattentive, they may appear to not listen, to make careless mistakes, or to be forgetful. Inattention can be common and, to a limited degree, expected among adolescents (Power et al., 1998). For some students, however, inattention can be at a level that is so pervasive and significant that it causes problems for the student and his or her academic learning and achievement. This can be particularly true as students' transition from elementary school to middle or high school, because cognitive demands increase and students are expected to function independent of adult supervision (Barkley, Anastopoulos, Guevremont, & Fletcher, 1991).

What Is Organization?

Similar to attention, organization is vital for academic success. Organization is the ability to arrange or structure items for efficient use and to approach a task in an orderly manner. In middle or high school settings, organization is demonstrated through material management (e.g., backpack, notebook, or locker) and time management (e.g., knowing when assignments are due, keeping a daily planner). When adolescents struggle with organization, they may often be unaware of projects and assignments due dates, frequently misplace homework assignments and materials, and have many unrelated items stuffed haphazardly into a backpack or locker. As with attention, the expectation for students to organize their time and materials independently increases from childhood to adolescence. Compared with elementary school children, who may be closely supervised by a teacher in a single classroom for most of the school day, middle and high school youth are exposed daily to multiple teachers and classes, and both the amount and difficulty of homework assignments increase. The increased expectations may result in significant academic impairment for adolescents with poor organization skills.

Attention-Deficit/Hyperactivity Disorder (ADHD)

Attention-deficit/hyperactivity disorder (ADHD) can be considered an extreme form of inattention and disorganization[1]. ADHD is characterized by symptoms of inattention, hyperactivity, and impulsivity, and is one of the most common disorders in youth, affecting 8.8% of the population (Visser et al., 2014). Because ADHD is a chronic disorder, the diagnosis persists for the majority of individuals into adolescence (Barkley, Murphy, & Fischer, 2008). Compared to students without ADHD, students with ADHD often experience academic impairment (including lower grades on core academic classes), are more likely to be placed

1. Although these problems are not unique to ADHD and may be demonstrated by adolescents who experience other challenges (e.g., depression, anxiety), we will focus on ADHD in the remainder of this chapter.

in lower-level classrooms (e.g., remedial vs. honors), and are more likely to be rated by teachers as not working up to potential (Kent et al., 2010). Adolescents with ADHD also turn in a significantly lower percentage of assignments, are more likely to be absent or tardy from class, and are more likely to drop out of school before graduation from high school than adolescents without ADHD (Barkley, Fischer, Smallish, & Fletcher, 2006; Kent et al., 2010). Inattention is associated with academic impairments and frequently manifests as problems with completing and submitting assignments, completing long-term assignments, taking notes in class, and exhibiting off-task behavior in the classroom (DuPaul & Stoner, 2003; Hoza, Pelham, Waschbusch, Kipp, & Owens, 2001; Mash & Barkley, 2003; Raggi & Chronis, 2006). These academic impairments frequently experienced by adolescents with ADHD can have devastating impacts on success in school.

IDENTIFICATION AND TREATMENT

Identifying Risk

Difficulties associated with ADHD, including inattention and disorganization, are often diagnosed prior to adolescence. Thus, the job of educators is to target impairment that is interfering with school performance. On occasion, a student who demonstrates symptoms of impairment associated with ADHD might arrive at a middle or high school without a prior diagnosis. Although a few secondary schools screen for mental health challenges using screening instruments described later in this chapter, it is more likely that teachers will be the first to notice and mention students in their class who frequently do not turn in assignments, act impulsively and inattentively in the classroom, and struggle with organization (Sax & Kautz, 2003). When secondary teachers notice students struggling with these challenges, they should first make sure that the adolescent does not have a prior diagnosis, a 504 plan, or an individualized education plan (IEP). If the student does have a plan, then the teacher should implement the strategies. If the student does not have a diagnosis or a plan, then teachers can implement targeted classroom-based intervention (such as those described later in this chapter) to assist the student. Depending on school procedures, these strategies may be selected individually by the teacher or through a Response to Intervention (RtI) team (e.g., Student Assistance Team). Should difficulties persist following the implementation of evidence-based strategies, the student should be referred for an evaluation to determine eligibility for section 504 or special education services. It is important to note that schools should make this referral in a timely manner, as a recent "Dear Colleague" letter (U.S. Department of Education, 2016) indicated that schools have a tendency to delay referral, which is both harmful and in direct opposition to mandates made by the Individuals with Disabilities Education Improvement Act (IDEIA, 2004). As previously mentioned, this evaluation might be a response to results from a school-wide broadband screener that can be followed by a narrow-band instrument to help pinpoint the specific difficulties the child is experiencing, with the aim of matching appropriate interventions. Although secondary schools rarely utilize mental health screeners, it is probable that this will change in the near future.

One common screener that school professionals use is the BASC-3 Behavioral and Emotional Screening System (BESS; Kamphaus & Reynolds, 2015). The BESS is a screening tool that collects information from parents, teachers, and youth ages 3 through 18 and can be completed in 5 to10 minutes. The BESS identifies behavioral and emotional strengths and weaknesses and can screen for internalizing problems, externalizing problems, school problems, and adaptive skills. Another option is the Strengths and Difficulties Questionnaire (SDQ; Goodman, 1997). The SDQ is a behavioral screening questionnaire for parents or teachers of children ages 4 through 16 and can be completed in 5 minutes. The 25-item measure identifies emotional symptoms, conduct problems, hyperactivity-inattention, peer problems, and prosocial behavior. Another option is the Systematic Screening for Behavior Disorders (SSBD; Walker & Severson, 2014). The SSBD-2 is a gated screening process that involves teachers nominating students, followed by teachers completing a Critical Events Inventory and a short adaptive and maladaptive behavior checklist for students identified as the most at risk. Finally, students who score high on these checklists are given 15-minute observations to gather information on their performance in social and classroom interactions. There are other screeners available as well (see Harrison, Vannest, & Reynolds, 2013 for a review), and, altogether, these broadband screeners provide options for an efficient way for school psychologists and other school professionals to screen for potential issues with inattention and disorganization.

If elevated levels of inattention or disorganization are identified with broadband screeners, it is recommended that they are followed by narrow-band instruments such as the Vanderbilt ADHD Diagnostic Parent Rating Scale (VADPRS; Wolraich et al., 2003) and the Vanderbilt ADHD Diagnostic Teacher Rating Scale (VADTRS; Wolraich, Feurer, Hannah, Baumgaertel, & Pinnock, 1998). The VADPRS and the VADTRS include all 18 *DSM-IV* criteria for ADHD, in addition to 8 criteria for oppositional defiant disorder (ODD), 12 criteria for conduct disorder (CD), and 7 criteria that screen for anxiety and depression. Another narrow band questionnaire is the Disruptive Behavior Disorder Rating Scale (DBD; Pelham, Gnagy, Greenslade, & Milich, 1992). The DBD is a 45-item scale that also assesses the presence and severity of symptoms of inattention, hyperactivity/impulsivity, oppositionality, and conduct problems according to *DSM-IV* criteria. Parents and Teachers rate the severity of each item on a 4-point scale ranging from 0 (not at all present) to 3 (very much present). They are available at no cost through the authors of the measures.

Informants

In addition to considering the types of instruments that can be utilized within an ADHD evaluation, there are many sources of information that are important to consider. ADHD symptoms must be present in two or more settings (American Psychiatric Association, 2013); thus, it is likely to be necessary to gather ratings from at least two individuals. Beyond this formality, it is important to gather ratings from individuals who observe student behavior in different contexts. Teacher report, parent report, and student self-report can provide rich information to help understand whether the primary concerns related to inattention and disorganization are due to ADHD, another disability or disorder, or a combination. However, it may be difficult to determine when to use parent, teacher, or student self-report, whether the reliability of these sources changes based on the student's development, and how to integrate varying reports from multiple informants. We will discuss each of these issues in turn.

Teacher report. Teachers have a unique and important perspective on a student's challenges with attention and/or organization. Generally, teacher report is more helpful to identify or assess progress for *externalizing problems*, such as ADHD or other common comorbid problems, compared with *internalizing problems*, simply because of the overt/covert behaviors associated with these problems (McMahon & Frick, 2005; Pelham, Fabiano, & Massetti, 2005; Silverman & Ollendick, 2005). For example, teachers may more easily observe and report when a student is consistently forgetting to bring needed materials to class or out of the chair (externalizing problems) than observe when a student feels hopeless or worried (internalizing problems). Thus, we recommend relying on teacher report to help assess for symptoms of ADHD and to monitor treatment outcomes for externalizing disorders.

Parent report. Evidence-based assessment recommendations for children and adolescents all include the use of parent report for *both* internalizing and externalizing disorders (Mash & Hunsley, 2005). Thus, collecting parent reports can greatly inform assessments. However, caution should be given to specific characteristics that could influence parent ratings. For example, mothers with depression have been found to over-report symptoms of ADHD (Pelham et al., 2005) and symptoms of depression in children (Klein, Dougherty, & Olino, 2005). In cases where parent psychopathology is suspected, teacher ratings can be used to supplement and confirm parent ratings.

Self-report. As a general rule, child or adolescent self-report is less reliable for externalizing problems compared with internalizing problems. Children and adolescents often underestimate aggressive behaviors, symptoms, and overall impairment as they pertain to externalizing disorders (McMahon & Frick, 2005; Pelham et al., 2005). However, child or adolescent self-report can be useful when assessing covert forms of conduct problems, such as drug use, risky sexual behavior, and dangerous driving behaviors. For internalizing problems, such as anxiety and depression, child and adolescents self-report are prioritized above teacher and parent report. However, one caution regarding self-report of internalizing problems is that some groups of children and adolescents (e.g., younger children, African American youth, Hispanic American youth) may be more likely to respond in a socially desirable fashion (i.e., a tendency to rate oneself in very optimistic ways; Silverman & Ollendick, 2005) instead of in a straightforward, honest fashion. Some rating scales, such as the Revised Children's Manifest Anxiety Scale (RCMAS-2; Reynolds & Richmond, 2008), include "Lie" scales that can be helpful for detecting social desirability. If a child or adolescent gets a high score on a "Lie" scale, it may be important to question the accuracy of the child's self-report and consider other reports.

Combining reports from multiple informants. As is evidenced by the following sections describing the benefits and challenges of using different informants, the most efficient means of determining if symptoms exist is to combine the reports of multiple informants. However, SMH professionals have to grapple with integration of reports from different individuals. This may be especially difficult, since low agreement is frequently the case (Achenbach, McConaughy, & Howell, 1987). However, disagreement between raters does not necessarily mean that the reports are invalid. Differences between raters could be due to real differences in the child's behavior across situations. Thus, variations in report across informants could offer a valuable insight into the child's or adolescent's behavior.

To integrate reports from multiple informants, several suggestions have been made (Klein et al., 2005). The most sensitive strategy for integrating reports is the "or" rule, which assumes that a feature of diagnosis is present if any informant reports it. A stringent strategy is the "and" rule, which requires at least two informants to confirm a feature of diagnosis. A third approach that more closely resembles clinical practice is the "best estimate" strategy, which relies on clinical judgment to integrate varying reports from informants. Although it is possible that the best-estimate strategy opens the possibility of clinician bias, there is evidence that the reliability of the best-estimate strategy can be high (Klein, Ouimette, Kelly, Ferro, & Riso, 1994).

Developmental Changes

Assessing ADHD in adolescents may be more challenging than assessing children. Parents and adults often supervise children closely. In school, children often have only one teacher, who is able to observe the child's behaviors and provide rich information that can aid assessments. In contrast, adolescents often have multiple teachers, who observe only a limited portion of each school day. In addition, there are many locations at schools, such as the hallway, lunchroom, or parking lot, where peer interactions occur under limited adult supervision. Outside of school, adolescents often participate in activities where parents are unable to observe strengths and problems. Thus, the importance of multiple informants cannot be overstated when working with adolescents.

SCHOOL-BASED SERVICES FOR ADHD

Once adolescents with ADHD have been identified, the next issue becomes what services to provide to enhance the students' competencies, teach skills, and minimize the negative effects these symptoms might have on academic performance. In the following sections, we will discuss services frequently found on Section 504 and individualized education programs (IEPs) of youth with ADHD. The IEP is the roadmap for services implemented through special education. Services and supports included in IEPs are mandated to be research-based to the greatest extent possible and specific to the individual needs of the child. Although these criteria are specific to students served by special education, it should be considered best practice for the selection of all school-based services. Next, we will describe evidence-based interventions that are available to teach students to overcome difficulties with attention and organization.

Frequently Provided Services

Approximately one-quarter (28%; Bussing, Zima, Mason, Hou, & Wilson, 2005) to one half (57%; Reid, Maag, Vasa, & Wright, 1994) of students with ADHD receive targeted or specialized education services in schools. Students in high school with ADHD are greater than six times more likely than same-aged peers to receive services at school through special education, Section 504 of the Rehabilitation Act of 1973 (Section 504 plans), or other specialized services (Murray et al., 2014). Although ADHD is not recognized as a specific IDEIA disability category, a large portion of all students who receive special education services have a diagnosis of ADHD, including a majority of students in the Other Health Impaired (OHI; 65.8%) and Emotional Disturbance (ED; 57.9%) categories, and 20.2% and 20.6% in the Learning Disability and Intellectual Disability categories, respectively (Schnoes, Reid, Wagner, & Marder, 2006).

There are a limited number of studies investigating the types of services provided to adolescents with ADHD in special education. One study conducted by Schnoes and colleagues (2006) investigated the types of services provided to 467 (33%) of students with ADHD and 952 (67%) of other students in special education who did not have ADHD. The authors reported that the most common services provided to youth with ADHD were extended time on tests and assignments, tests read aloud, modified tests, shorter or different assignments, slower-paced instruction, and more frequent feedback. Similarly, Spiel, Evans, and Langberg (2014) reviewed services on IEPs and Section 504 plans for 97 youth with ADHD and found the six most common services included on IEPs and Section 504 plans were extended time on tests and assignments, small group instruction, prompting/cueing, the use of a calculator or notes during test, having tests and quizzes read aloud, and additional breaks. Murray and colleagues (2014) investigated the services provided to high school students with ADHD and found the five most frequent services were extended time on tests and assignments, student progress monitored by special education staff, learning strategies/study skills assistance, more frequent feedback, and use of a calculator when otherwise not permitted.

In theory, some of these accommodations might be well suited to target inattention and disorganization, but no empirical evidence exists to support their use with youth with ADHD. Harrison, Bunford, Evans, and Owens (2013) completed a large literature review of services with the potential to be educational accommodations and found no evidence that the strategies frequently used provided students with a differential boost or met the definition of an accommodation. Research is lacking that compares the effects of these services for youth with ADHD or other emotional or behavioral disorders to the effects for students without emotional or behavioral disorders. Such comparisons are necessary to determine if accommodations provide a differential boost for youth with ADHD when compared to those without. A differential boost effectively "levels the playing field" between those with and without ADHD. Since that review, the results of one study completed by Spiel and colleagues (2016) provided preliminary evidence that reading tests aloud to students with ADHD might fit the criteria of an evidence-based accommodation. Spiel and colleagues found that reading tests aloud in small groups significantly improved the test scores of youth with ADHD but not youth without ADHD, suggesting a differential boost. However, this is the only preliminary evidence supporting the use of any accommodation with this population; others (Harrison, Kwong, & Evans, in review; Lewandowski, Lovett, Parolin, Gordon, & Codding 2007; Pariseau, Fabiano, Massetti, Hart, & Pelham, 2010) call into question the effectiveness of extended time (i.e., the most frequent service provided to youth with ADHD; Murray et al., 2014; Schnoes et al., 2006; Spiel et al., 2014) on homework assignments and tests and quizzes. Lewandowski and colleagues (2007) found that, when given extended time, youth with and without ADHD completed more problems correctly; however, the youth without ADHD answered more items correctly than the group with ADHD during both standard (12 minutes) and extended time (18 minutes). Pariseau and colleagues (2010) found that youth with ADHD actually completed more problems correctly per minute with the standard amount of time (30 minutes) compared to extended time (45 minutes). In a single case experimental design study, Harrison et al. (in review) found no relationship between the provision of extended time and task engagement, accuracy, or completion. The results of these studies indicate that much more research is needed to evaluate the services that are frequently provided to youth with ADHD in schools to ensure that problems of inattention and disorganization are truly addressed.

In addition, it should be noted that accommodations are not designed to address skill deficits, such as organization and self-regulation of attention. Instead, accommodations are designed to level the playing field between those with and without disabilities by removing content-irrelevant variance (i.e., variance created by skills not being directly taught or assessed), such as the skills needed to complete a task on time. Thus, if a student is given extra time as an accommodation, then the accommodation actually reduces the expectation for the student to attend to the task and manage time. This is an important distinction, as adolescents need many skills that might not be taught (i.e., note-taking instruction, time management, self-management of attention) to function independently in the present and in the future. Thus, the best first line of intervention would be the implementation of strategies to teach students needed skills.

Evidence-Based Services

The most frequently *recommended* treatment for children and adolescents with ADHD is not implementation of accommodations, but rather medication, behavioral interventions, and/or psychosocial interventions (Evans, Owens, & Bunford, 2014; Pelham & Fabiano, 2008; Wolraich et al., 2005). We will not discuss medication in this chapter, not because it is ineffective or because we recommend again its use, but primarily because it is beyond the scope of school-based interventions. In addition, when children reach adolescence, they are frequently reluctant to continue medication, and a majority completely discontinue use by age 15 (Charach, Ickowicz, & Schachar, 2004). Therefore, we will focus on behavioral/psychosocial interventions with empirical or promising support.

Several reviews of the literature on effectiveness of interventions for children and adolescents with ADHD have been completed over time (e.g., Owens, Storer, & Girio-Herrera, 2011; Pelham & Fabiano, 2008; Pelham, Wheeler, & Chronis, 1998; Sadler & Evans, 2011). The most recent and thorough systematic review of the literature was completed by Evans et al. (2014). This review adds information regarding the level of empirical evidence and factors with potential to influence the outcomes to the findings of Pelham and Fabiano (2008). Pelham and Fabiano categorized interventions into three groups: behavioral parent training, behavioral classroom management, and behavioral peer interventions. The authors concluded that behavioral parent training and behavioral classroom management are well-established treatments for ADHD. In addition, behavioral peer interventions in recreation settings, such as summer treatment programs had sufficient evidence to be considered well-established interventions. Evans and colleagues (2014) categorized studies of psychosocial interventions into four categories: behavioral parent training, behavioral classroom management, combined behavioral treatment studies, and training interventions published after 2008. The authors concluded that behavioral parent training, behavioral classroom management, training interventions, and combined behavior management are considered well-established treatments. It should be noted that much more research has been conducted with children than with adolescents. Thus, in the following sections, we describe each treatment identified as well-established by the review authors that has empirical support from research with adolescents or is considered promising with adolescents and three select promising interventions, not covered in previous reviews, with empirical support that can be implemented to address adolescents skill deficits (i.e., self-management, note-taking intervention, and homework management training).

Behavioral parent training. Although not frequently implemented or considered by IEP teams, behavioral parent training strategies have a great deal of potential for implementation in schools and have been developed and evaluated by many well-known teams of researchers and experts in the field (Chronis, Chacko, Fabiano, Wymbs, & Pelham, 2004; DeNisco, Tiago, & Kravitz, 2005). Behavioral parent training is a process in which parents are taught effective parenting strategies utilizing behavioral techniques, such as modeling appropriate behavior, and positive and negative reinforcement and extinction techniques (see Pfiffner & Kaiser, 2010). Parents are taught to establish and reinforce clear and precise expectations and how to determine and modify antecedents and consequences to inappropriate behavior. They are taught negotiation and contacting procedures to use with teens, how to increase effectiveness of commands, how to reinforce desired behaviors with positive attention and tangible rewards, and how to modify unwanted behaviors with the use of response cost and time out. Finally, parents monitor progress made toward established goals. The use of behavioral parent training has been found to increase organizational skills, homework completion, and materials management, and to decrease symptoms of hyperactivity and impulsivity as rated by parents (see Evans et al., 2014). Since many parents of adolescents with ADHD express frustration with adolescent behavior, this intervention would be an excellent option to be added to adolescent behavior plans.

Behavior management (point systems). Contingency management in the form of a point system or token economy is one form of behavior management that addresses the needs of many students who exhibit behavior problems such as those associated with ADHD. Token economy strategies have been discussed in the literature for many decades (e.g., Kazdin, 1971; Soares, Harrison, Vannest, & McClelland, 2016) and encompass strategies based on behavioral principles in which points (primary reinforcers) are earned and traded in at a specified date and time for a backup reinforcer that the student values (Kazdin, 1971; Simonsen, Fairbanks, Briesch, Myers, & Sugai, 2008). Procedures for implementing token economies can be simple or complex. Typically, teachers design the point system by describing the target behavior in observable and measurable terms and determining tokens and backup reinforcers to be used. After the token economy has been developed, the teacher explains the procedures to the student. The student earns tokens for the target behavior and trades them for a desired reinforcer at a designated time point (Vannest, Reynolds, & Kamphaus, 2015). Some teachers include response cost in the token economy, in which student can lose tokens for demonstrating inappropriate behavior. The use of point systems has been found to increase adaptive behaviors, positive social behaviors, and academic performance (Dickerson, Tenhual, & Green-Paden, 2005; Matson & Boisjoli, 2009).

Training interventions. These interventions focus on training children with ADHD to overcome their difficulties in organizing school materials. Materials organization is an intervention used to teach students to physically organize materials in their book bags, binders, and lockers. Students also learn to accurately record homework and tests in a planner and plan for long-term tests and projects. The first step in teaching students to organize their materials is to start from scratch. Together with the student, the instructor takes everything out of his or her book bag and binder, and they organize each of them following a designated checklist. The checklist includes labeled folders with pockets for each subject. The pockets are also labeled for completed and incomplete work. Each day, the teacher checks the binder against the checklist, and the student corrects any problems.

This is a scaffolded process, with teacher assistance being slowly faded from the process. The student receives positive reinforcement for organization. This procedure continues daily until the checklist indicates that the binder and/or book bag are 100% organized according to the criteria for four days. After these four days, the teacher begins to fade the positive reinforcement and the student completes the checklist with the instructor reading the checklist, and the only verification coming from the instructor. Finally, the student completes his or her own sheet at 100% for another four days. The student is then allowed to independently complete the checklist daily.

Organization training has been found to increase independent materials organization and academic performance (Evans et al., 2009). In addition, in a small randomized controlled trial, Harrison et al. (in progress) found that sixth- and seventh-grade students could be taught to independently organize their materials and maintain that organization better than when their materials were organized for them by an adult—a common accommodation provided to students with ADHD. The importance of organization training with students struggling to organize their materials cannot be overstated. This is a lifelong skill needed for independent functioning.

Combined behavior management. Combined behavior management interventions are those that address multiple areas of impairment simultaneously. The Challenging Horizons Program (CHP) is one multicomponent school-based treatment program that has sufficient empirical support to be considered a probably efficacious treatment (Evans, et al., 2014). Specifically, CHP is a program conducted after school that addresses organizational impairment, academic impairment, and social impairment (Evans, Schultz, DeMars, & Davis, 2011; Molina et al., 2008). Procedural steps are embedded within each component. In this section, we will describe the four typical components experienced daily by adolescents with ADHD in a CHP identified by Evans, Axelrod, and Langberg (2004).

Youth meet with their primary counselors (i.e., master's-level professionals) to build relationships, identify goals, monitor progress, and negotiate and implement interventions. Youth participate in an Interpersonal Skills Group to work on gaining knowledge, demonstrating skills, and improving relationship skills (i.e., parent, teacher, and peer relationships). Youth learn and practice social skills needed to work cooperatively in competitive situations during a recreational period. Finally, youth participate in educational groups in which they are taught note-taking and study skills, to record assignments in daily assignment planners and gather materials for homework completion, written language skills, and to maintain organization of their binders, book bags, and lockers. Results of a randomized controlled trial indicated that the symptoms and impairment of adolescents who participated in CHP improved in comparison to students in the control group.

Self-management. Self-management is an intervention used to teach youth to control their own behavior. It can be used to target a multitude of behaviors, such as academic engagement and task completion and submission. Through the self-management process, youth monitor and evaluate their behavior (Mace, Belfiore, & Hutchinson, 2001) and self-instruct and reinforce themselves (Shapiro & Cole, 1994). The number and exact components necessary for self-management to be effective have been questioned and are the focus of emerging research. Therefore, the procedures discussed here are those of Fantuzzo and colleagues (1987), with the acknowledgement that research has identified that all included steps may not be necessary (Briesch & Chafouleas, 2009; Fantuzzo & Polite, 1990), and that further research with youth with ADHD is needed to determine which steps are important.

Self-management involves identifying and operationally defining a target behavior. A form is then developed that includes the target behavior and a method for students to indicate if they performed the target behavior within a specified time period. For example, a student can self-monitor if he or she attended to the task every five minutes. At the end of a predetermined amount of time, this student would receive a reinforcer if he or she attended to the task for a certain number of five-minute intervals. The teacher can simultaneously monitor student behavior and compare his or her ratings to student ratings. If the ratings match, then the student would receive an additional reinforcer for accurate ratings. Students do not lose points when ratings do not match.

In a review of 30 single case experimental design (SCED) studies that studied self-management as a behavioral strategy, Briesch and Chafouleas (2009) found a very strong overall effect size. Self-management was found to increase attention to task and decrease disruptive behavior. In a similar SCED meta-analysis with 47 source studies, Briesch and Briesch (2016) also found a large effect. The authors found no difference in effect between elementary and second students, but they found that the effects for students with ADHD and those with learning disabilities, while still large, were lower than those for students with emotional and behavioral disorders and those with intellectual disabilities. Self-management of attention and completion is an excellent alternative to providing extra time for task completion.

Note-taking intervention. Note-taking instruction is an intervention used to teach students to take effective notes during classroom discussions, which ultimately improves on-task behaviors in the classroom. One approach to note-taking instruction is a scaffolded, modeling approach (Evans, Pelham, & Grudberg, 1995). Using this approach, teachers instruct students to take notes by modeling note-taking during instruction. The students copy the notes as written. Through a scaffolded process, teachers begin by writing all the main ideas and details for students to see and prompting students. Slowly, the teacher removes assistance by providing fewer details and less prompting. Evans et al. (1995) evaluated the effectiveness of the note-taking instruction with 30 adolescents with ADHD in a Summer Day Treatment Program (STP) and found that student comprehension increased and disruptive behavior decreased. The feasibility of implementation of note-taking instruction in schools has not been evaluated; however, it is likely that teaching students to take notes would be feasible and would fit within the context of teaching routines and expectations.

Homework management training. Homework management training is an intervention to teach parents to help their children complete their homework (Raggi, Chronis-Tuscano, Fishbein, & Groomes, 2009). Through the training, parents are taught to use appropriate negotiation strategies, create monthly contingencies, and establish a homework management plan contract with his or her adolescent. Parents are taught the basic behavioral techniques (i.e., reinforcement, punishment) and how to write specifics within the plan and contract, such as rules/expectations, rewards to be used, and who will be responsible for the homework management plan. Importantly, parents are taught to negotiate the specifics of the plan with the adolescent and to troubleshoot issues that arrive during homework time. In a multiple baseline design study with 11 middle school students with ADHD, Raggi and colleagues (2009) found that parent training resulted in improved homework problems, grade point average, and academic productivity. This is an excellent strategy to be included on student behavior management plans and can be incorporated with parent behavior management training.

SERVICE DELIVERY MODEL

As can be seen by the research previously discussed, enhancing the attention and organization of adolescents can be achieved in middle and high schools without reducing expectations. Models to complete this process come from the fields of education and psychology, and interventions are best delivered through a collaborative model. It might be unlikely that a classroom teacher can implement all of the interventions discussed above. The teacher will need assistance from experts within the school. Through collaboration, teachers, school mental health professionals, and others working with students come together to provide services needed for individual students. Collaboration begins before intervention selection, continues through intervention selection, and is essential during intervention implementation.

Interventions with preliminary evidence of support to address inattention and disorganization (e.g., behavior management, note-taking instruction, organization training, self-management, homework management training) can be implemented during the school day or within an after-school program. Implementation within or after the school day requires a plan that specifies (a) who will implement the strategy, (b) when will it be implemented, (c) where will training occur, (d) how implementation fidelity will be measured, and (d) how progress will be monitored. We suggest that the procedures be a written plan even when the student does not have an RtI team, section 504, or IEP. For example, for an adolescent who is receiving organization training, the plan could be implemented before school, in school, or after school. It would be necessary to identify who is going to implement the organization training and when and how often it will occur. Organization training can be implemented by a paraprofessional or staff in a program before or after school in about 15 minutes. Organization training could easily be a component of a Check In/Check Out program. Note-taking instruction and self-management can also be implemented during the day or after school, with a little more training and time devoted to the intervention. Thus, it is essential for all team players to work together and know the plan for implementation. Evidence-based interventions such as these have the potential to significantly decrease problems caused inattention and disorganization and help set students on a course to success.

CONCLUSION

This chapter began with a discussion of challenges with attention and organization, both skills necessary for academic success, experienced by some secondary-age students, including those with ADHD. Also discussed were methods of identifying those challenges. A majority of the chapter focused on assessment and selection of evidence-based interventions to address the challenges for students with ADHD. The importance of these strategies cannot be overstated. By identifying problems areas and providing interventions to adolescent students, school professionals can help students learn skills to independently meet age-appropriate academic expectations.

REFERENCES

Achenbach, T. M., McConaughy, S. H., & Howell, C. T. (1987). Child/adolescent behavioral and emotional problems: Implications of cross-informant correlations for situational specificity. *Psychology Bulletin, 101*, 213–232.

American Psychiatric Association. (2013). *Diagnostic and statistical manual of mental disorders* (5th ed.). Arlington, VA: American Psychiatric Publishing.

Barkley, R. A., Anastopoulos, A. D., Guevremont, D. C., & Fletcher, K. E. (1991). Adolescents with ADHD: Patterns of behavioral adjustment, academic functioning, and treatment utilization. *Journal of the American Academy of Child & Adolescent Psychiatry, 30*(5), 752–761.

Barkley, R., Fischer, M., Smallish, L., & Fletcher, K. (2006). Young adult outcome of hyperactive children: Adaptive functioning in major life activities. *Journal of the American Academy of Child and Adolescent Psychiatry, 45*(2), 192–202.

Barkley, R. A., Murphy, K. R., & Fischer, M. (2008). *ADHD in adults: What the science says.* New York: Guilford.

Briesch, A. M., & Briesch, J. M. (2016). Meta-analysis of behavioral self-management interventions in single-case research. *School Psychology Review, 45*(1), 3–18.

Briesch, A. M., & Chafouleas, S. M. (2009). Development and validation of the Children's Usage Rating Profile for Interventions (CURP-I). *Journal of Educational and Psychological Consultation, 19*, 321–336.

Bussing, R., Zima, B. T., Mason, D., Hou, W., & Wilson, G. C. (2005). Use and persistence of pharmacotherapy for elementary school students with attention-deficit/hyperactivity disorder. *Journal of Child and Adolescent Psychopharmacology, 15*(1), 78–87.

Charach, A., Ickowicz, A., & Schachar, R. (2004). Stimulant treatment over five years: Adherence, effectiveness, and adverse effects. *Journal of the American Academy of Child & Adolescent Psychiatry, 43*, 559–567. doi:10.1097/00004583-200405000-00009

Chronis, A. M., Chacko, A., Fabiano, G. A., Wymbs, B. T., & Pelham, W. E., Jr. (2004). Enhancements to the behavioral parent training paradigm for families of children with ADHD: Review and future directions. *Clinical Child and Family Psychology Review, 7*(1), 1–27.

DeNisco, S., Tiago, C., & Kravitz, C. (2005). Evaluation and treatment of pediatric ADHD. *The Nurse Practitioner, 30*(8), 14–23.

Dickerson, F. B., Tenhual, W. N., & Green-Paden, L. D. (2005). The token economy for schizophrenia: Review of the literature and recommendations for future research. *Schizophrenia Research, 75,* 405–416. doi:10.1016/j.schres.2004.08.026

DuPaul, G. J., & Stoner, G. (2003). *ADHD in the schools: Assessment and intervention strategies* (2nd ed.). New York, NY: Guildford.

Evans, S. W., Axelrod, J. L., & Langberg, J. M., (2004). Efficacy of a school-based treatment program for middle school youth with ADHD: Pilot data. *Behavior Modification, 28,* 528–547.

Evans, S. W., Owens, J. S., & Bunford, N. (2014) Evidence-based psychosocial treatments for children and adolescents with attention-deficit/hyperactivity disorder. *Journal of Clinical Child and Adolescent Psychology, 43*(4), 527–551. doi:10.1080/15374416.2013.850700

Evans, S. W., Pelham, W. E., & Grudberg, M. V. (1995). The efficacy of notetaking to improve behavior and comprehension with ADHD adolescents. *Exceptionality, 5,* 1–17.

Evans, S. W., Schultz, B. K., DeMars, C. E., & Davis, H. (2011) Effectiveness of the Challenging Horizons After-School Program for young adolescents with ADHD. *Behavior Therapy, 42,* 462–474.

Evans, S. W., Schultz, B. K., White, L. C., Brady, C., Sibley, M. H., & Van Eck, K. (2009). A school-based organization intervention for young adolescents with attention deficit/hyperactivity disorder. *School Mental Health, 1,* 78–88.

Fantuzzo, J. W., & Polite, K. (1990). School-based self-management interventions with elementary school children: A component analysis. *School Psychology Quarterly, 5,* 180–198.

Fantuzzo, J. W., Stovall, A., Schachtel, D., Goins, C., & Hall, R. (1987). The effects of peer social initiations on the social behavior of withdrawn maltreated preschool children. *Journal of Behavior Therapy and Experimental Psychiatry, 18,* 357–363.

Goodman, R. (1997). The Strengths and Difficulties Questionnaire: A research note. *Journal of Child Psychology and Psychiatry, 38*(5), 581–586. doi:10.1111/j.1469-7610.1997.tb01545.x

Harrison, J. R., Bunford, N., Evans, S. W., & Owens, J. S. (2013). Educational accommodations for students with behavioral challenges: A systematic review of the literature. *Review of Educational Research, 83*(4), 551–597.

Harrison, J. R., Evans, S. W., & Belmonte, C. (in progress). Evaluation of services selected for IEPs of youth with ADHD.

Harrison, J. R., Vannest, K. J., & Reynolds, C. R. (2013). Social acceptability of five screening instruments for social, emotional, and behavioral challenges. *Behavioral Disorders, 38*(3), 171–189.

Hoza, B., Pelham, W. E., Waschbusch, D. A., Kipp, H., & Owens, J. S. (2001). Academic task persistence of normally achieving ADHD and control boys: Performance, self-evaluation, and attributions. *Journal of Consulting and Clinical Psychology, 69,* 271–283.

Kamphaus, R. W., & Reynolds, C. R. (2015). *Behavior Assessment System for Children (BASC-3): Behavioral and Emotional Screening System (BESS)* (3rd ed.). Bloomington, MN: Pearson.

Kazdin, A. E. (1971). The effect of response cost in suppressing behavior in a pre-psychotic retardate. *Journal of Behavior Therapy and Experimental Psychiatry, 2*(2), 137–140.

Kent, K. M., Pelham, W. E., Molina, B. S. G., Sibley, M. H., Waschbusch, D. A., Yu, J., . . . Karch, K. M. (2010). The academic experience of male high school students with ADHD. *Journal of Abnormal Child Psychology, 39,* 451–462.

Klein, D. N., Dougherty, L. R., & Olino, T. M. (2005). Toward guidelines for evidence-based assessment of depression in children and adolescents. *Journal of Clinical Child and Adolescent Psychology, 34,* 412–432. doi:10.1207/s15374424jccp3403_3

Klein, D. N., Ouimette, P. C., Kelly, H. S., Ferro, T., & Riso, L. P. (1994). Test-retest reliability of team consensus best-estimate diagnoses of axis I and II disorders in a family study. *American Journal of Psychiatry, 151*(7), 1043–1047.

Lewandowski, L., Lovett, B., Parolin, R., Gordon, M., & Codding, R. (2007). Extended time accommodations and the mathematics performance of students with and without ADHD. *Journal of Psychoeducational Assessment, 25*(1), 17–28.

Mace, F. C., Belfiore, P. J., & Hutchinson, J. M. (2001). Operant theory and research on self-regulation. In B. Zimmerman & D. Schunk (Eds.), *Learning and academic achievement: Theoretical perspectives* (pp. 39–65). Mahwah, NJ: Lawrence Erlbaum.

Mash, J., & Barkley, R. A. (2003). *Child psychopathology* (2nd ed.). New York: Guilford.

Mash, E. J., & Hunsley, J. (2005). Evidence-based assessment of child and adolescent disorders: Issues and challenges. *Journal of Clinical Child and Adolescent Psychology, 34*(3), 362–379.

Matson, J. L., & Boisjoli, J. A. (2009). The token economy for children with intellectual disability and/or autism: A review. *Research in Developmental Disabilities, 30*(2), 240–248.

McMahon, R. J., & Frick, P. J. (2005). Evidence-based assessment of conduct problems in children and adolescents. *Journal of Clinical Child and Adolescent Psychology, 34*(3), 477–505.

Molina, B. S. G., Flory, K., Bukstein, O. G., Greiner, A. R., Baker, J. L, Krug, V., & Evans, S. W. (2008). Feasibility and preliminary efficacy of an after-school program for middle schoolers with ADHD: A randomized trial in a large public middle school. *Journal of Attention Disorders, 12,* 207–217.

Murray, D. W., Molina, B.S.G., Glew, K, Houck, P., Greiner, A., Fong, D., . . . Jensen, P. S. (2014). Prevalence and characteristics of school services for high school students with attention-deficit/hyperactivity disorder. *School Mental Health, 6,* 267–278. doi:10.1007/s12310-014-9128-6

Owens, J. S., Storer, J. L., & Girio-Herrera, E. (2011). Psychosocial interventions for elementary school-aged children with attention deficit hyperactivity disorder. In S. W. Evans & B. Hoza (Eds.), *Treating attention-deficit-hyperactivity disorder: Assessment and intervention in developmental context* (pp. 10-1–10-36). New York, NY: Civic Research Institute.

Pariseau, M., Fabiano, G., Massetti, G., Hart, K., & Pelham, W. (2010). Extended time on academic assignments: Does increased time lead to improved performance for children with attention-deficit/hyperactivity disorder? *School Psychology Quarterly, 25*(4), 236–248.

Pelham, W. E., & Fabiano, G. A. (2008). Evidence-based psychosocial treatments for attention-deficit/hyperactivity disorder. *Journal of Clinical Child & Adolescent Psychology, 37*(1), 184–214.

Pelham, W. E., Fabiano, G. A., & Massetti, G. M. (2005). Evidence-based assessment of attention deficit hyperactivity disorder in children and adolescents. *Journal of Clinical Child and Adolescent Psychology, 34*(3), 449–476.

Pelham, W. E., Gnagy, E. M., Greenslade, K. E., & Milich, R. (1992). Teacher ratings of *DSM-III-R* symptoms for the disruptive behavior disorders. *Journal of the American Academy of Child & Adolescent Psychiatry, 31*(2), 210–218.

Pelham, W. E., Wheeler, T., & Chronis, A. (1998). Empirically supported psychosocial treatments for attention deficit hyperactivity disorder. *Journal of Clinical Child Psychology, 27*(2), 190–205.

Pfiffner, L. J., & Kaiser, N. M. (2010). Behavioral parent training. In M. K. Dulcan (Ed.), *Dulcan's textbook of child and adolescent psychiatry* (1st ed., pp. 845–868). Washington DC: American Psychiatric Publishing.

Power, T. J., Doherty, B. J., Panichelli-Mindel, S. M., Karustis, J. L., Eiraldi, R. B., Anastopoulos, A. D., & DuPaul, G. J. (1998). The predictive validity of parent and teacher reports of ADHD symptoms. *Journal of Psychopathology and Behavioral Assessment, 20*, 57–81.

Raggi, V., & Chronis, A. (2006). Interventions to address the academic impairment of children and adolescents with ADHD. *Clinical Child and Family Psychology Review, 9*(2), 85–111.

Raggi, V. L., Chronis-Tuscano, A., Fishbein, H., & Grooms, A. (2009). Development of a brief, behavioral homework intervention for middle school students with attention-deficit/hyperactivity disorder. *School Mental Health, 1*(2), 61–77.

Reid, R., Maag, J., Vasa, S., & Wright, G. (1994). Who are children with ADHD: A school-based survey. *Journal of Special Education, 28*, 117–137.

Reynolds, C. R., & Richmond, B. O. (2008). *Revised Children's Manifest Anxiety Scale (RCMAS-2)* (2nd ed.). Los Angeles, CA: Western Psychological Services.

Riccio, C. A., Reynolds, C. R., Lowe, P., & Moore, J. J. (2002). The continuous performance test: A window on the neural substrates for attention? *Archives of Clinical Neuropsychology, 17*(3), 235–272.

Sadler, J., & Evans, S. W. (2011). Psychosocial interventions for adolescents with ADHD. In S. W. Evans & B. Hoza (Eds.), *Treating attention-deficit-hyperactivity disorder: Assessment and intervention in developmental context* (pp. 11-1–11-21). New York, NY: Civic Research Institute.

Sax, L., & Kautz, K. J. (2003). Who first suggests the diagnosis of attention-deficit/hyperactivity disorder? *Annals of Family Medicine, 1*(3), 171–174.

Schnoes, C., Reid, R., Wagner, M., & Marder, C. (2006). ADHD among students receiving special education services: A national survey. *Exceptional Children, 72*(4), 483–496.

Shapiro, E., & Cole, C. L. (1994). *Behavior change in the classroom: Self-management interventions*. New York, NY: Guilford.

Silverman, W. K., & Ollendick, T. H. (2005). Evidence-based assessment of anxiety and its disorders in children and adolescents. *Journal of Clinical Child and Adolescent Psychology, 34*(3), 380–411.

Simonsen, B., Fairbanks, S., Briesch, A., Myers, D., & Sugai, G. (2008). Evidence-based practices in classroom management: Considerations for research to practice. *Education and Treatment of Children, 31*(3), 351–380.

Soares, D. A., Harrison, J. R., Vannest, K. V., & McClelland, S. S. (2016). Effect size for token economy use in contemporary classroom settings: A meta-analysis and moderator analysis of single case research. *School Psychology Review, 45*(4), 379–399.

Spiel, C. F., Evans, S. W., & Langberg, J. M. (2014). Evaluating the content of individualized education programs and 504 plans of young adolescents with attention deficit/hyperactivity disorder. *School Psychology Quarterly, 29*(4), 452–468. doi:10.1037/spq0000101

Spiel, C. F., Mixon, C. S., Holdaway, A. S., Evans, S. W., Harrison, J. R., Zoromski, A. K., & Yost, J. S., (2016). Is reading tests aloud an accommodation for youth with or at risk for ADHD? *Remedial and Special Education, 37*(2), 101–102.

U.S. Department of Education. (2016). *Dear colleague letter and resource guide on students with ADHD.* Washington, DC: Author.

Vannest, K. J., Reynolds, C., & Kamphaus, R. (2015). *BASC-2 Intervention Guide.* Minneapolis, MN: Pearson.

Visser, S. N., Danielson, M. L., Bitsko, R. H., Holbrook, J. R., Kogan, M. D., Ghandour, R. M., . . . Blumberg, S. J. (2014). Trends in the parent-report of health care provider-diagnosed and medicated attention-deficit/hyperactivity disorder: United States, 2003–2011. *Journal of the American Academy of Child & Adolescent Psychiatry, 53*(1), 34–46.

Walker, H. M., & Severson, H. H. (2014). *Systematic Screening for Behavior Disorders (SSBD)* (2nd ed.). Longmont, CO: Sopris West.

Wolraich, M. L., Feurer, I. D., Hannah, J. N., Baumgaertel, A., & Pinnock, T. Y. (1998). Obtaining systematic teacher reports of disruptive behavior disorders utilizing *DSM-IV*. *Journal of Abnormal Child Psychology, 26*(2), 141–152.

Wolraich, M. L., Lambert, W., Doffing, M. A., Bickman, L., Simmons, T., & Worley, K. (2003). Psychometric properties of the Vanderbilt ADHD Diagnostic Parent Rating Scale in a referred population. *Journal of Pediatric Psychology, 28*(8), 559–568.

Wolraich, M. L., Wibbelsman, C. J., Brown, T. E., Evans, S. W., Gotlieb, E. M., Knight, J. R., . . . Wilens, T. (2005). Attention-deficit/hyperactivity disorder among adolescents: A review of the diagnosis, treatment, and clinical implications. *Pediatrics, 115*(6), 1734–1746.

6

Managing Disruptive Behavior

SEAN M. O'DELL AND LAUREN LOULOUDIS ■

In the context of schools, disruptive behaviors negatively impact the ability of teachers to deliver instruction and students to learn in the classroom. These behaviors are not bound to any particular diagnostic category, and indeed a mental health diagnosis is not a prerequisite for the exhibition of disruptive behavior in any setting. Disruptive behaviors are associated with a variety of learning, behavioral, and social-emotional difficulties. The goal of this chapter is to focus on the mental health conditions with which disruptive behaviors are an associated behavioral manifestation. Specifically, this chapter will discuss attention-deficit/hyperactivity disorder (ADHD), oppositional defiant disorder (ODD), and conduct disorder (CD) in the context of adolescents in schools. First, a framework for conceptualizing identification and treatment concerns relevant to these populations is discussed. Next, evidence-based practices are reviewed for each disorder. Last, recommendations for service delivery are offered. The evidence, models, and suggestions presented herein are intended to be readily applicable for a variety of mental health professionals across diverse school organizational structures and cultures.

IDENTIFICATION AND TREATMENT CONCERNS

Recent estimates suggest that 7.3% of youth between the ages of 5 and 17 exhibit clinically elevated levels of ADHD symptoms and functional impairment when rated by classroom teachers (DuPaul, Reid, Anastopoulos, & Power, 2014), and as many as 79% of individuals diagnosed with ADHD in childhood continue to meet clinical criteria in late adolescence and adulthood (Cheung et al., 2015). Of note, the most recent version of the *Diagnostic and Statistical Manual of Mental Disorders* (*DSM-5*; American Psychiatric Association [APA], 2013) states that ADHD symptoms must have an onset before age 12. Although boys are five times more likely than girls to be diagnosed with ADHD, overall prevalence rates show that the ratio of boys to girls who meet diagnostic criteria for ADHD to be closer to 2:1 (Barkley, 2015).

Oppositional defiant disorder and conduct disorder are often researched and discussed together because of their high overlap in symptomology and developmental trajectory. To be diagnosed, ODD must have symptom onset before age 18. It is defined by developmentally inappropriate patterns of angry/irritable mood, argumentative/defiant behavior, or vindictiveness toward one or more individuals who are not siblings (APA, 2013). The lifetime prevalence for ODD is 11.2% for males and 9.2% for females (Nock, Kazdin, Hiripi, & Kessler, 2007). In the *DSM-5*, the criteria for CD include persistent patterns of major societal norm violations, such as aggression toward people and/or animals, destruction of property, deceitfulness or theft, and serious rule breaking at home or school (APA, 2013). There is a specifier in the *DSM-5* criteria for limited prosocial behavior characterized by diminished guilt following negative actions, lack of empathy and fear, impaired ability to recognize stress in others, considerable focus on reward relative to consequences, and insensitivity to punishment. CD is present in 0.8% of girls and 2.1% of boys overall; however, these rates increase with age to over 3% of girls and over 5% of boys in adolescence (Nock et al., 2007).

Developmental and Contextual Factors

From a developmental psychopathology perspective (see Cicchetti, 2006), there is scientific and practical value in understanding the transactional relationships between the biological, psychological, and contextual aspects of development that lead to both adaptive and maladaptive outcomes. Understanding more about these factors affords school mental health professionals the opportunity to identify risk and protective factors as well as the differential impact of these factors throughout the course of development. This enables practitioners to target those factors that are amenable to intervention at opportune times during the life course to ultimately improve developmental outcomes. In the *DSM-5*, ADHD is classified as a neurodevelopmental disorder, and both ODD and CD are classified as disruptive behavior disorders (APA, 2013). However, there are many areas of overlap between ADHD, ODD, and CD in terms of onset, symptomology, comorbidities, associated functional impairments, and long-term outcomes. Therefore, it is instructive to discuss some of the similarities and differences between these conditions before discussing the evidence base for treatment of these disorders and outlining assessment and intervention considerations with these populations in schools.

Attention-deficit/hyperactivity disorder. The average heritability of ADHD in identical twins across 20 studies was shown to be 0.76, indicating that when one twin met criteria for ADHD, there was a 76% chance the other twin also met diagnostic criteria for ADHD (Faraone et al., 2005). Such high yet imperfect heritability among individuals with identical genetics indicates that there are complex genetic and environmental factors that contribute to the expression of the constellation of behaviors currently categorized as ADHD. Nigg, Nikolas, and Burt (2010) found that although psychosocial factors (e.g., child inattentive and hyperactive symptoms, marital conflict and instability, family adversity) are twice as strong predictors of ADHD diagnosis compared with prenatal or perinatal factors, research is not entirely clear about how these environmental factors serve as pathways to ADHD.

Adolescents who exhibit clinically significant ADHD symptoms experience a variety of impairments compared with their nondisabled peers. Academically, adolescents with ADHD underperform on standardized achievement tests and are at increased risk for school dropout (Barkley, 2015; Loe & Feldman, 2007), as well as incomplete school work, increases in suspensions and expulsions, and grade retention, even when controlling for other salient personal and contextual factors associated with achievement (Fergusson, Bolden, & Horwood; 2007; Martin, 2014). These academic difficulties occur along with impaired attention, study and organizational skills, and procrastination, as well as elevated rates of disruptive classroom behavior, including calling out, violation of classroom rules, difficulty staying seated, and completing work school work quickly but with low accuracy (DuPaul & Stoner, 2014). Consistent patterns of relationship problems with parents, teachers, and peers have also been associated with ADHD (Stormont, 2001).

Oppositional defiant disorder and conduct disorder. ODD and CD share substantial symptomology and developmental trajectory. Compared with ADHD, far less research has been conducted in these populations to determine the genetic and environmental bases of etiology. What is presently known is that dysfunction in specific regions of the brain (e.g., the amygdala and hippocampus) has been shown to interact with harsh and intrusive parenting styles to predict later conduct problems (Willoughby, Mills-Koonce, Propper, & Waschbusch, 2013).

Interestingly, Willoughby and colleagues (2013) appear to have elucidated a sensitive period of development, such that the presence of harsh parenting is only predictive of child conduct problems at age three when exhibited within the first year of life. These findings are consistent with Patterson's coercive family process model, which purports that conduct problems develop and are maintained due to patterns of behavior in which both parents and children are reinforced for exhibiting aversive behaviors toward one another (Patterson, 1982). Taken together, these findings suggest that when parents frequently resort to harsh parenting practices early in a child's development, the result is an increase in later conduct problems in the home and increased long-term risk for antisocial behavior in school and community settings.

The developmental trajectory and diagnostic criteria of ODD and CD have considerable overlap. Some studies have found that rates of ODD decline into adolescence at the same time that rates of CD begin to increase, suggesting that ODD is a developmental precursor to CD, and that CD typically emerges from ODD as youth enter adolescence (Lahey et al., 2000; Rowe, Maughan, Pickles, Costello, & Angold, 2002). However, apparent declining rates of ODD and increasing rates of CD into adolescence have been at least partially distorted by previous iterations of the *DSM* precluding comorbid ODD diagnoses when CD is diagnosed. In fact, 62% of those meeting criteria for CD also exhibit clinically significant levels of ODD symptoms (Maughan, Rowe, Messer, Goodman, & Meltzer, 2004). The *DSM-5* has removed this diagnostic constraint. Early childhood onset of conduct problems, coercive familial interactions, academic underachievement, prenatal exposure to toxins, parental psychopathology and poor quality child care, peer rejection, association with a deviant peer group, and exposure to violence have been identified as psychosocial risk factors associated with worse outcomes within these populations (Dodge & Pettit, 2003; Frick, 1998; Loeber & Farrington, 2000; Raine, 2002). It is important to thoroughly assess for the multiple psychosocial risk factors that may serve as barriers to treatment, or that may require treatment adjunctive to school-based services, as lower educational attainment, school refusal and truancy, and school dropout are common outcomes within this population (Esch et al., 2014).

Comorbidities. It is also important for school mental health professionals and other educators to understand that disruptive behaviors, although distinct from one another in a categorical diagnostic sense, rarely occur in isolation from other mental disorders. In a recent cross-sectional survey study, Larson, Russ, Kahn, and Halfon (2011) found that 33% of youth with ADHD had at least one comorbid diagnosis, 16% had two, and 18% had three or more. Larson and colleagues found high rates of comorbid anxiety and depression within this sample (18% and 14%, respectively), and comorbid ODD or CD were also found in 27% of cases. This appears to be a relatively conservative estimate, as other studies have found comorbidity rates between 45% and 84% (Barkley, 2015; DiTrani, Di Roma, Scatena, & Donfrancesco, 2013).

With regard to ODD, Nock, Kazdin, Hirpi, and Kessler (2007) found a 92% lifetime prevalence of at least one comorbid diagnosis, ranging from mood and anxiety disorders (45.8% and 62.3%, respectively) to ADHD (35.0%), CD (42.3%), and substance use disorders (47.2%). Although a total of 70% of individuals in the Nock and colleagues (2007) sample were found to no longer meet diagnostic criteria for ODD by age 18, onset before age 7 was associated with a 50% slower recovery rate. With the exception of CD, the presence of any of the comorbid diagnoses mentioned above were also found to be predictive of between 40% and 70% more chronic course of ODD. Taken together, these findings clearly indicate the need for thorough assessment when evaluating adolescents referred for disruptive behavior problems. Failing to find or attend to comorbid problems may lead to failed interventions, or potentially to unwanted side effects, from otherwise evidence-based treatments.

EVIDENCE-BASED PRACTICES IN SCHOOL SETTINGS

This section reviews preventive school-based interventions, as well as the available psychosocial intervention packages for ADHD, ODD, and CD that can be implemented in school settings. In addition, we discuss research on psychopharmacological interventions in these populations. Although school mental health professionals do not and cannot prescribe medication, a thorough understanding of medication commonly prescribed to youth with disruptive behavior problems, as well as the associated treatment concerns, will help practitioners to collaborate effectively with physicians and community mental health providers. We have drawn from adolescent research whenever possible, and from extended findings from research with the school-age population where such research is not yet available.

Foundational and Preventive Interventions

Classroom management is an effective way to decrease disruptive behaviors and establish a positive learning environment. School environments that foster positive student behavior have structured and explicit rules, strong teacher-student relationships, and reward systems (Reinke & Herman, 2002). Similarities across grade levels in classroom behavior management include having clear expectations and classroom rules that are accompanied by consistent consequences (Reinke, Lewis-Palmer, & Merrell, 2008). When implemented correctly, effective behavioral management should allow the teacher more teaching time and less time disciplining students who are being disruptive. Motivational strategies such as the Classroom Check-Up (CCU) provide class-wide consultation with self-monitoring of implementation of behavioral strategies to teachers to ensure treatment fidelity (Reinke et al., 2008).

Other preventive programs promote and reward prosocial behaviors that are incompatible with any delinquent, oppositional, or conduct problems. One such program, the Expect Respect program, aims to reduce bullying through a positive behavior approach (Nese, Horner, & Dickey, 2014). Components of this program include three 1-hour lesson plans to shape student behavior. Signals for stopping bullying were identified, as well as bystander and seeking support routines. Research on the Expect Respect program suggests that it results in the reduction of physical and verbal aggression among participating students.

Interventions for ADHD

Specific to the adolescent population, Sibley, Kuriyan, Evans, Waxmonsky, and Smith (2014) concluded that there is evidence for psychostimulant medications and behavior therapy, and that behavior therapy may be required to address the functional impairments in this population. Psychosocial treatments also have substantial support for improving academic outcomes. DuPaul, Eckert, and Vilardo (2012) conducted a meta-analysis of school-based interventions for ADHD. The authors found a mean effect size of 3.48 when single-subject designs were employed to evaluate the effects of academic interventions, indicating strong evidence of efficacy. More modest support was found for academic interventions in studies that used within- and between-subjects designs. Others have found more support for psychosocial treatment packages using between-subjects designs, with average effect sizes of 0.63 on academic productivity and 0.32 on academic achievement (Fabiano et al., 2009).

Treatment protocols with the most empirical support for adolescents with ADHD are rooted in a behavioral orientation, but vary in dosage, setting, implementation format, and specific targets of intervention. These interventions are upward extensions of interventions for ADHD initially developed with school-age populations, and contain developmentally appropriate adaptations where needed (see Chapter 5, this volume, for discussion of interventions to enhance attention and organization with this population). With regards to behavioral peer interventions, the first upward extension of the Summer Treatment Program (Pelham et al., 2010) has recently been developed and evaluated in a sample of adolescents with ADHD (Pelham et al., 2010; Sibley, Smith, Evans, Pelham, & Gnagy, 2012). This intensive, eight-week day-treatment program ran for nine hours daily, Monday through Friday, and included academic, organizational, occupational/life skills, leadership, and substance use prevention components. Efforts were made to include parents in a collaborative manner in order to enhance generalization of skills learned during the intervention. The results showed between 60% and 90% parent-rated improvements on a variety of social and behavioral aspects of functioning (Sibley et al., 2012). Although these results are promising, the availability of this intervention is presently limited to a handful of regions across the United States.

Supporting Teens' Academic Needs Daily-Group (STAND-G) is a collaborative parent-teen group intervention for high school students with ADHD (Sibley et al., 2014). STAND-G is an eight-session program that targets teen autonomy, fostering collaboration between parent and child, as well as skills training and coaching in organization and problem-solving skills. Sibley and colleagues (2014) concluded that promising results were found on outcomes related to organization, time management, academic habits, and home behavior. Also of note, changes in report card outcomes (i.e., GPA) were not consistently found across iterations of the groups, and those participants with comorbidities and oppositional behavior did not benefit as much from STAND-G as those without such comorbidities.

Dosage and sequencing of pharmacological and psychosocial treatments for ADHD. Although the efficacy of both pharmacological and behavioral interventions is established, considerable debate continues in the field regarding optimal dosage and sequencing of interventions. At present, there is a dearth of literature to guide practitioners in this matter. Research has shown that when combination treatment is used (i.e., medications and behavior therapy), lower medication dosages are required to achieve comparable outcomes (Conners et al., 2001). Yet, some professional agencies have taken the position that psychostimulant medications should be used as first line treatment for youth with ADHD (e.g., American Academy of Pediatrics, 2011), and that behavior therapies should only be considered after medications have not worked to alleviate the symptoms of ADHD.

There are many reasons why this view is limited in its validity and applicability to adolescents with ADHD in a school setting. First, no studies have been conducted with adolescents with ADHD to compare the effects of dosage and sequencing of psychopharmacological and psychosocial interventions. In the elementary school–age population, only one such study has been conducted (Pelham et al., 2014). Key findings from this study are as follows: (a) as level of intensity of behavior modification increased, the level of functional improvements increased; (b) a low dose (5 mg) of methylphenidate in combination with low-intensity behavior modification evidenced substantial treatment effects, while increasing intensity of behavior modification when combined with a low dose of medication did not substantially add to treatment effects; and (c) a high dose of medication (20 mg) combined with any level of behavior modification led to improvements in functioning compared with a high dose of medication alone. These findings suggest complex interactions between dosages of medication and behavior therapy, but it is clear that many ADHD-related impairments are not addressed by a treatment approach in which medications are the first-line therapy. Still, more research is needed with individuals with ADHD from other points in the life span, and across home and school contexts, before explicit recommendations can be made in terms of dosage and sequencing.

Another shortcoming in using medications as a front-line treatment is that the evidence supporting medication use is derived from large randomized controlled trials that use tightly controlled medication titration procedures that do not represent the level of care available in community settings. Also, such recommendations do not take family stakeholders' preferences for treatment into consideration. In a recent randomized controlled trial, when given the option to complete a medication trial before entering a family-school psychosocial intervention for ADHD, families opted out over 40% of the time (Power et al., 2012). Family choice should be a priority when treatments are of comparable efficacy, as is the case in the ADHD population. Finally, there is not sufficient evidence to suggest psychostimulant medications alone are effective in treating academic difficulties and social functioning. Even when ADHD symptoms are reduced with medication, academic and social performance do not necessarily improve (Sibley, Kuriyan, Evans, Waxmonsky, & Smith, 2014).

Interventions for ODD and CD

Recent reviews of the literature have classified the evidence for both psychopharmacological and psychosocial treatments for youth with ODD and CD (Eyberg, Nelson, & Boggs, 2008; Nevels, Dehon, Alexander, & Gontkovsky, 2010). Psychosocial treatments for conduct problems vary widely across theoretical orientation, and are typically implemented in community settings as opposed to schools. No treatment packages were considered *well-established* in these reviews, and only Multisystemic Therapy (MST; Henggeler & Lee, 2003) met criteria for a *probably efficacious* treatment. With regard to long-term outcomes following MST, a two-year follow up showed results of lower parental report of problem behaviors and a decrease in youth reports on delinquent behaviors (Ogden & Hagen, 2006). Unfortunately, MST is unlikely to be feasible for implementation solely by school-based professionals, as it provides intensive family- and community-based treatments in order to prevent out-of-home placements for youth with severe conduct problems and to restore family functioning.

Wilson and Lipsey (2007) conducted a meta-analysis of treatments targeting aggressive and disruptive behavior in schools. The results showed small to moderate effect sizes on a variety of educationally relevant outcomes, including aggression and other problem behaviors, hyperactivity and inattention, social skills and adjustment, internalizing problems, and school performance and participation. The effects of interventions did not differ significantly based on theoretical orientation (e.g., behavioral, cognitive behavioral, social skills), though programs implemented at a school-wide level to those at risk for or already experiencing problems were associated with better outcomes. Considering the dearth of evidence on school-based psychosocial approaches tailored specifically for youth with ODD and CD, the reader is encouraged to determine the educational needs at the individual level throughout the evaluation process, work to implement needed skill-building and performance support interventions in the school setting, and connect systems of care as appropriate in order to achieve the best outcomes when intervening with these youth.

With regard to pharmacotherapy, the most common medications used in children with conduct problems and/or significant aggressive behaviors are antipsychotics (Rapp & Wodarski, 1997). Antipsychotic medications purportedly target symptoms of aggression and oppositional behavior in adolescents with ODD and CD. However, concerns related to the safety and efficacy of long-term use of these medications, along with scarce research, make this a less than ideal approach to reducing symptoms of CD. Psychostimulants are another prevalent type of medication used in the treatment of overt aggression, irritability, impulsivity, and antisocial behaviors associated with ODD and CD. According to a recent review by Nevels, Dehon, Alexander, and Gontkovsky (2010), stimulants are most often used to treat children with ADHD and comorbid ODD or CD who exhibit aggressive symptoms. When ADHD is not present and the treatment of CD is the main concern, Nevels and colleagues (2010) report that antipsychotics and antidepressants are the medications of choice for many prescribing physicians. Several options (e.g., risperidone, lithium) can be effective for the treatment of aggressive behaviors; however, there are considerable side effects with these medications that must be weighed against the potential benefits.

SCHOOL MENTAL HEALTH SERVICE DELIVERY

The day-to-day activities and responsibilities of a school-based mental health practitioner are often demanding and hectic, leaving little time for reflection on the overarching purpose and goals of assessment and intervention. Yet adopting a guiding framework can provide a solid foundation to work from when conceptualizing cases, planning and conducting assessments, and linking assessment data to both intervention planning and progress monitoring.

One useful framework that can be applied to a service delivery model of school mental health is *contextual behavioral science*, which states that the prediction and influencing of behavior with precision, scope, and depth is a useful main objective for psychological intervention (see Biglan & Hayes, 1996). This framework has utility for school-based mental health practitioners because it champions those interventions that are well matched to the functional needs of the target student. It also espouses maintaining a particular sensitivity throughout the assessment and intervention process to the transactional processes affecting behavior that are evident between all aspects of an individual's unique ecology, from genetics to the highest levels of social ecology. Although the goals of contextual behavior science are similar to those of a behavior analytic perspective as applied to the individual, these goals are inclusive of any theoretical perspective or intervention strategy to the extent that effective prediction and influence of behavior is the goal.

As discussed previously, the treatment literature to date has shown that psychopharmacological and psychosocial interventions developed from a behavioral-theoretical orientation have the most support for the treatment of ADHD, ODD, and CD if the goal is to influence the symptoms and functional impairments associated with these disorders. However, a range of comorbid conditions is common among youth with disruptive behavior problems, and may require conjunctive or even primary treatment in some cases. In addition, the potential influences of the family system and family-school interactions on educational outcomes must be taken into consideration. Considering the potential complexities of assessing and treating disruptive behavior in school settings, such a guiding framework for treatment planning is warranted.

The next sections provide several service delivery considerations for adolescents with disruptive behaviors, based on the literature. The goal of these recommendations is to enhance the ability of school-based mental health professionals to conduct comprehensive evaluations that lead to interventions that are well matched to the context of the target child. The intent is to provide these recommendations in a fashion that will be applicable regardless of whether an organization currently employs a population-based system of supports or uses a referral system.

Implications for Assessment

Considering the range of presentations and comorbidities of ADHD, ODD, and CD in adolescents, there are several considerations that should be made when assessing these youth in the school setting. An approach to assessment that includes stakeholders from both the home and school settings throughout the process affords the opportunity to better understand the developmental context of the target individual, and thereby better predict behaviors that are likely to be exhibited across settings under particular conditions. Multiple methods of assessment, including a combination of clinical interviews of all relevant stakeholders, reliable and valid rating scales of relevant areas of functioning, and direct observations of functioning in the classroom setting, can be used to facilitate the information gathering process.

A comprehensive discussion of all evidence-based assessments is beyond the scope of this chapter. DuPaul and Stoner (2014) provide a comprehensive, practitioner-friendly guide for the assessment and treatment of ADHD in school settings, and many of the strategies recommended in this volume translate well to the ODD and CD populations. A diagnosis of ADHD requires assessment of both symptoms and impairment across home and school settings (APA, 2013). With regard to diagnosis of ODD and CD, assessment of home functioning is not a requisite for diagnosis if behavioral concerns involve only a school stakeholder (e.g., teacher, administrator). However, factors related to functioning in the home environment often serve as initiating and maintaining factors for conduct problems (Patterson, 1982), and if present they often require intensive, multisystemic treatment (Henggler & Lee, 2003). An additional advantage of formally assessing for both symptoms and impairment affords the opportunity to use repeated assessments as outcome measurement for any subsequent interventions. For practitioners working in settings using a population-based approach to school mental health, adding these outcomes for youth receiving secondary or tertiary preventive interventions may enhance progress monitoring if comparable measures are not already a part of progress monitoring.

Teachers are crucial stakeholders in the assessment process, as these school professionals spend the majority of the day with the student. In middle and high schools, where students typically interact with multiple teachers throughout the day, the assessment process becomes more challenging to navigate for mental health professionals. One heuristic is to obtain teacher ratings from the teacher who made the referral, if applicable. Other assessment information, including classroom observations and clinical interviews, can be conducted across the remaining classrooms, and the assessment information can be integrated to determine any patterns across classroom settings. In terms of predictors of teacher referral, stigma and knowledge related to ADHD have not been shown to predict referral patterns; rather, teacher self-efficacy, perceived benefit, value, personal responsibility to refer, ease of referral process, and administrative support related to the referral have been shown to predict referral likelihood (Lee, 2014).

When interpreting norm-referenced rating scale data from multiple raters, it is important to keep in mind that there are generally weak to moderate correlations between caregivers and teachers when assessing ADHD (Narad et al., 2015). Using an averaging method for the number of symptoms across settings when interpreting home and school ratings presently has the best evidence for validity of ADHD diagnosis (Martel, Schimmack, Nikolas, & Nigg, 2015). With regard to involving the target child in the assessment process at this stage, there is evidence that youth with ADHD generally report themselves to be less impaired than other stakeholders (Mikami, Calhoun, & Abikoff, 2010; Sibley et al., 2014). Therefore, obtaining self-report measures of functioning may have more utility for understanding the perspective of the target child than for informing diagnosis. Despite the limitation of self-report data for diagnosis and assessment of functional impairment, obtaining the perspective of adolescents with ADHD can still be useful in treatment planning and obtaining buy-in to intervention procedures (Evans, Owens, & Bunford, 2014; Sibley et al., 2014).

Connecting Assessment to Intervention

A disconnect between evaluation procedures and intervention planning for students with disruptive behaviors undermines the utility of information gathered during the assessment process and reduces the likelihood of effective and efficient treatment for the target student. When using assessment information to develop an intervention plan, it is essential that the goals of interventions are matched to the educational needs of the student, and that these needs are captured in any written plan, such as the student's individualized education program (IEP) or 504 plan. A recent review of these documents (Spiel, Evans, & Langberg, 2014) showed that although 85% of youth with ADHD had nonacademic behavior problems (e.g., social impairments), less than half had measurable annual goals and objectives that related to these problems. This study also showed a pervasive lack of evidence-based interventions, as only 25% of IEPs and 5% of 504 plans listed a behavioral intervention as a treatment component. Clearly, there is room for improvement in this area, and school mental health professionals are in an ideal position to make such improvements.

Once a treatment plan is developed, it is important to select meaningful outcome measures. For the treatment of disruptive behavior, functional impairments are arguably the most clinically important global outcome of treatment, and they may be more amenable to change than psychiatric symptoms for some individuals. In the case of ADHD, Fabiano and colleagues' meta-analysis (2009) showed that between-group intervention studies in the ADHD population result in large effects of behavioral treatments on parent ratings of ADHD-related impairment in functioning and parenting behaviors, yet had less impact on ADHD and other externalizing symptoms. These outcomes highlight the importance of using measurements that extend beyond psychiatric symptoms, and suggest that reductions in symptoms do not necessarily precede improvements in functional outcomes. This is also supported by findings suggesting that there is a subset of up to 16% of youth with ADHD who evidence improvements in functional outcomes without evidence of reliable change in ADHD symptoms (Owens, Johannes, & Karpenko, 2009). Targeting functional outcomes is also more attuned to the reasons families refer children for treatment (Becker, Chorpita, & Daleiden, 2011), and may be a more ecologically valid measure of treatment outcome across settings than psychiatric symptoms alone.

Connecting Systems of Care

The need for comprehensive and coordinated care for disruptive behavior in schools cannot be overstated. A one-size-fits-all approach for intervention with this population, or one that fails to effectively coordinate across systems and across development for these youth, is unlikely to produce favorable outcomes. Family decisions to seek treatment are often multiply determined, but the availability of treatment, along with a description of the potential risks and benefits, is most influential overall (Schatz et al., 2015). Schools provide an advantageous setting for intervention for youth with disruptive behavior problems, and these findings indicate that it is important for service providers to be well versed in the empirically supported treatments for these conditions.

Coordination of intervention efforts and collaboration with other professionals within the organization should be a goal for any school-based mental health professional. Organizations differ in the definition of roles for school psychologists, special education teachers, school counselors, social workers, behavior specialists, paraprofessionals, and other professionals who have relevant training and experience to assist in intervention implementation. Organizations also differ in terms of administrative support for facilitating collaboration in assessment, treatment delivery, and progress monitoring. Mental health professionals in schools who carefully consider caseload, training and experience, and interest and willingness to participate are more likely to achieve better treatment outcomes.

Of course, not all mental health services can be made available in school settings. For youth with serious conduct problems, school-based treatment may not be appropriate as a stand-alone treatment option. Referral to a community agency, preferably one implementing MST, is recommended if significant conduct problems and problematic parent-child interactions are found during the assessment process.

Psychotropic Medications

Given that physicians are the professionals qualified to recommend medication as a treatment option, information provided in this section is restricted to ways that school mental health practitioners can work in a consultation-liaison role to facilitate appropriate medication use for the treatment of disruptive behavior problems.

Generally, it is within the scope of practice of school mental health practitioners to recommend further evaluation by a physician during the assessment process if the family has not already obtained these services. When youth who are already engaged with a community mental health provider for treatment present for assessment in the schools, school-based mental health professionals can (a) assist the community practitioners with diagnostic decision-making and determining the need for medication, as appropriate; (b) coordinate the evaluation of medication effects in the school setting to determine optimal dosage; and (c) act as the liaison to connect the care across any medical, psychosocial, and educational interventions that follow the evaluation. When coordinating these services, however, it is important that school mental health professionals not recommend that a family start or discontinue medication; this is the role of a physician. When communicating with physicians, it is vital to correspond in a brief, no-nonsense manner (DuPaul & Carlson, 2005).

Despite the growing availability of school mental health services, primary care physicians often are a family's primary mental health provider (Cooper, Valleley,

Polaha, Begeny, & Evans, 2006; Magill & Garrett, 1988). In line with physicians' expertise, psychotropic medications are the primary mode of treatment provided in this setting, and assessments leading to diagnoses are often less thorough than those typically conducted by mental health professionals. Presently, there is not enough research to provide evidence-based guidelines to school mental health practitioners for the dosage or sequencing of pharmacological, psychosocial, or combined treatment for youth with disruptive behavior problems.

However, considering the available evidence through a contextual behavioral lens, recommendations can be made to guide collaborative efforts, depending on the identified target of intervention. Disruptive behavior symptoms are most likely to be severely impairing at very high levels (Nock et al., 2007). Because the symptoms of these disorders are the primary treatment targets of medications, they may be an appropriate primary treatment target when severity of symptoms is high, when psychosocial interventions have not produced improvement, or both. Similarly, medications may be an appropriate treatment component to consider if the assessment data show that the target child possesses the requisite skills (e.g., academic, self-regulatory, social) to function well in the school context, suggesting that behavioral performance is the main deficit. When it is assessed that the primary functional need for the target child relates to a skill deficit in any educationally relevant domain, there is no known evidence that medication alone will remediate this deficit. In this case, it is likely more advantageous to select the most feasible psychosocial or educational interventions with empirical support. When youth present with a combination of skills and performance deficits, astute clinical judgment is required. In this case, the balance of treatment decisions should encompass all available assessment data, priority of treatment concerns, and the evidence for and feasibility of implementation for all interventions under consideration.

Stakeholder Engagement

Engaging families in treatment is of critical importance. Even when treatment concerns are only present in school settings, factors related to family functioning have an impact on school-based intervention outcomes. A consistent and positive parenting and family routine has been shown to be a strong protective factor against negative functional outcomes in the population with disruptive behavior problems (Steinberg & Drabick, 2015). Conversely, negative and coercive parenting practices are particularly salient risk factors for negative outcomes (Hinshaw et al., 2000; Patterson, 1982). If intensive, family-based services are indicated but are not available through the school, then referral to community agencies using evidence-based psychosocial treatments are recommended. Regular two-way communication with parents regarding both positive and negative progress toward the goals of intervention efforts (i.e., not just when the student has violated school norms), and engagement of families in the intervention process whenever possible, is also recommended (Sheridan & Kratochwill, 2008).

Finally, it is important to provide guidance for other school professionals, especially teachers, when youth are involved in pharmacologic treatment. Teacher training is often cursory in terms of student behavioral and mental health concerns. Moreover, teachers often report that communication regarding the use of medications or associated side effects is limited (Lien, Carlson, Hunter-Oehmke, & Knapp, 2007). As a result, teachers frequently have misconceptions that lead them to be less likely to be accepting of medications as a treatment option (Sciutto, 2013). However, training and communication can impact both perceptions of medication as a treatment component and teacher participation in the intervention (Canu & Mancil, 2012).

CONCLUSION

This chapter has reviewed identification and treatment concerns, evidence-based treatments, and service delivery considerations for adolescents with ADHD, ODD, and CD. Adolescents with significant disruptive behavior problems make up a prevalent population within secondary schools that often require additional supports from school mental professionals in order to benefit from educational programming and avoid negative long-term life outcomes. The factors related to the development of these problems often involve a complex interplay between genetic and environmental factors throughout development. Mental health professionals in schools are in a unique position to assist in the identification, assessment, treatment, and progress monitoring of this population.

It is imperative that thorough assessments involving multiple methods across all relevant stakeholders from the home, school, and medical settings be conducted. The evidence bases for the treatment of adolescents with disruptive behavior problems include a range of medications, psychosocial interventions, and academic interventions that can be delivered in the school setting. However, relative to literature in the school-age population with these disorders, much less is currently known. Future research in these areas should focus on increasing the evidence base for upward and downward extensions of psychosocial treatment protocols in school settings, determining an evidence base for dosage and sequencing of pharmacological and psychosocial treatments, and improving the continuity of services across the life span. In schools, the performance of students can also be best supported by ensuring that foundational and preventive interventions are in place in classrooms, and by working as a liaison to involve other stakeholders from the school, as well as home and medical systems, to coordinate the intervention.

REFERENCES

American Academy of Pediatrics (2011). ADHD: Clinical practice guidelines for diagnosis, evaluation, and treatment of attention deficit/hyperactivity disorder in children and adolescents. *Pediatrics, 128,* 1–16.

American Psychiatric Association (2013). *Diagnostic and statistical manual of mental disorders* (5th ed.). Washington, DC: Author.

Barkley, R. A. (Ed.), (2015). *Attention-deficit/ hyperactivity disorder: A handbook for diagnosis and treatment* (4th ed.). New York, NY: Guilford.

Becker K. D., Chorpita, B. F., & Daleiden, E. L. (2011). Improvements in symptoms versus functioning: How do our best treatments measure up? *Administration and Policy in Mental Health and Mental Health Services Research, 38,* 440–458.

Biglan, A., & Hayes, S. C. (1996). Should the behavioral sciences become more pragmatic? The case for functional contextualism in research on human behavior. *Applied and Preventive Psychology, 5,* 47–57. doi:10.1016/S0962-1849(96)80026-6

Canu, W. H., & Mancil, E. B. (2012). An examination of teacher trainees' knowledge of attention-deficit/hyperactivity disorder. *School Mental Health, 4*(2), 105–114. doi:10.1007/s12310-012-9071-3

Cheung, C. H. M., Rijdijk, F., McLoughlin, G., Faraone, S. V., Asherson, P., & Kuntsi, J. (2015). Childhood predictors of adolescent and young adult outcome in ADHD. *Journal of Psychiatric Research, 62,* 92–100. doi:10.1016/j.jpsychires.2015.01.011

Cicchetti, D. (2006). Developmental psychopathology. In D. Cicchetti & D. J. Cohen (Eds.), *Developmental psychopathology* (Vol. 1, *Theory and Method,* 2nd ed., pp. 1–23). Hoboken, NJ: John Wiley & Sons.

Conners, C. K., Epstein, J. N., March, J. S., Angold, A., Wells, K. C., Klaric, J., . . . Wigal, T. (2001). Multimodal treatment of ADHD in the MTA: An alternative outcome analysis. *Journal of the American Academy of Child & Adolescent Psychiatry, 40,* 159–167.

Cooper, S., Valleley, R. J., Polaha, J., Begeny, J., & Evans, J. H. (2006). Running out of time: Physician management of behavioral health concerns in rural pediatric primary care. *Pediatrics, 118,* 132–138.

Di Trani, M., Di Roma, F., Scatena, M. C., & Donfrancesco, R. (2013). Severity of symptomatology and subtypes in ADHD children with comorbid oppositional defiant and conduct disorders. *International Journal on Disability and Human Development, 12*(3), 283–287. doi:10.1515/ijdhd-2012-0106

Dodge, K.A., & Pettit, G.S. (2003). A biopsychosocial model of the development of chronic conduct problems in adolescence. *Developmental Psychology, 39,* 349–371.

DuPaul, G. J., & Carlson, J. S. (2005). Child psychopharmacology: How school psychologists can contribute to effective outcomes. *School Psychology Quarterly, 20*(2), 206–221. doi:10.1521/scpq.20.2.206.66511

DuPaul, G. J., & Eckert, T. L., & Vilardo, B. V. (2012). The effects of school-based interventions for attention deficit hyperactivity disorder: A review of the literature. *School Psychology Review, 41*(4), 387–412.

DuPaul, G. J., Reid, R., Anastopoulos, A. D., & Power, T. J. (2014). Assessing ADHD symptomatic behaviors and functional impairment in school settings: Impact of student and teacher characteristics. *School Psychology Quarterly, 29*(4), 409–421. doi:10.1037/spq0000095

DuPaul, G. J. & Stoner, G. (2014). *ADHD in the schools: Assessment and intervention strategies* (3rd ed.). New York, NY: Guilford.

Esch, P., Bocquet, V., Pull, C., Couffignal, S., Lehnert, T., Graas, M., . . . Ansseau, M. (2014). The downward spiral of mental disorders and educational attainment: A systematic review on early school leaving. *BMC Psychiatry, 14,* 237. doi:10.1186/s12888-014-0237-4

Evans, S. W., Owens, J. S., & Bunford, N. (2014). Evidence-based psychosocial treatments for children and adolescents with attention-deficit/hyperactivity disorder. *Journal of Clinical Child and Adolescent Psychology*, 43(4), 527–551. doi:10.1080/15374416.2013.850700

Eyberg, S. M., Nelson, M. M., & Boggs, S. R. (2008). Evidence-based psychosocial treatments for children and adolescents with disruptive behavior. *Journal of Clinical Child and Adolescent Psychology*, 37(1), 215–237. doi:10.1080/15374410701820117

Fabiano, G. A., Pelham, W. E., Coles, E. K., Gnagy, E. M., Chronis-Tuscano, A., & O'Connor, B. C. (2009). A meta-analysis of behavioral treatments for attention-deficit/hyperactivity disorder. *Clinical Psychology Review*, 29(2), 129–140. doi:10.1016/j.cpr.2008.11.001

Faraone, S. V., Perlis, R. H., Doyle, A. E., Smoller, J. W., Goralnick, J. J., Holmgren, M. A., & Sklar, P. (2005). Molecular genetics of attention-deficit/hyperactivity disorder. *Biological Psychiatry*, 57, 1313–1323.

Fergusson, D. M., Boden, J. M., & Horwood, L. J. (2007). Exposure to single parenthood in childhood and later mental health, educational, economic, and criminal behavior outcomes. *Archives of General Psychiatry*, 64, 1089–1095.

Frick, P. J. (1998). *Conduct disorders and severe antisocial behavior*. New York: Plenum.

Henggeler, S. W., & Lee, T. (2003). Multisystemic treatment of serious clinical problems. In A. E. Kazdin & J. R. Weisz (Eds.), *Evidence-based psychotherapies for children and adolescents* (pp. 301–322). New York: Guilford.

Hinshaw, S. P., Owens, E. B., Wells, K. C., Kraemer, H. C., Abikoff, H. B., Arnold, L. E., . . . Wigal, T. (2000). Family processes and treatment outcome in the MTA: Negative/ineffective parenting practices in relation to multimodal treatment. *Journal of Abnormal Child Psychology*, 28(6), 555–568.

Loe, I. M., & Feldman, H. M. (2007). Academic and educational outcomes of children with ADHD. *Journal of Pediatric Psychology*, 32, 643–654. doi:10.1093/jpepsy/jsl054

Lahey, B. B., Schwab-Stone, M., Goodman, S. H., Waldman, I. D., Canino, G., Rathouz, P. J., . . . Jensen, P. S. (2000). Age and gender differences in oppositional behaviour and conduct problems: A cross-sectional household study of middle childhood and adolescence. *Journal of Abnormal Psychology*, 109, 488–503.

Larson, K., Russ, S. A., Kahn, R. S., & Halfon, N. (2011). Patterns of comorbidity, functioning, and service use for US children with ADHD. *Pediatrics*, 127, 462–470. doi:10.1542/peds.2010-0165.

Lee, J. (2014). Predictors of teachers' intention to refer students with ADHD to mental health professionals: Comparison of U.S. and South Korea. *School Psychology Quarterly*, 29(4), 385–394. doi:10.1037/spq0000046

Loeber, R., & Farrington, D. P. (2000). Young children who commit crime: Epidemiology, developmental origins, risk factors, early interventions, and policy implications. *Development and Psychopathology*, 12, 737–762.

Lien, M. T., Carlson, J. S., Hunter-Oehmke, S., & Knapp, K. A. (2007). A pilot investigation of teachers' perceptions of psychotropic drug use in schools. *Journal of Attention Disorders*, 11(2), 172–177. doi:10.1177/1087054707300992

Magill, M. K., & Garrett, R. W. (1988). Behavioral and psychiatric problems. In R. B. Taylor (Ed.), *Family medicine* (3rd ed., pp. 534–562). New York: Springer-Verlag.

Martel, M. M., Schimmack, U., Nikolas, M., & Nigg, J. T. (2015). Psychological assessment integration of symptom ratings from multiple informants in ADHD diagnosis: A psychometric model with clinical utility. *Psychological Assessment*, 27(3), 1060–1071. doi: 10.1037/pas0000088

Martin, A. J. (2014). The role of ADHD in academic adversity: Disentangling ADHD effects from other personal and contextual factors. *School Psychology Quarterly*, 29(4), 395–408. doi:10.1037/spq0000069

Maughan, B., Rowe, R., Messer, J., Goodman, R., & Meltzer, H. (2004). Conduct disorder and oppositional defiant disorder in a national sample: Developmental epidemiology. *Journal of Child Psychology and Psychiatry*, 45(3), 609–621.

Mikami, A. Y., Calhoun, C. D., & Abikoff, H. B. (2010). Positive illusory bias and response to behavioral treatment among children with attention-deficit/hyperactivity disorder. *Journal of Clinical Child & Adolescent Psychology*, 39, 373–385.

Narad, M. E., Garner, A. A., Peugh, J. L., Tamm, L., Antonini, T. N., Kingery, K. M., . . . Epstein, J. N. (2015). Parent-teacher agreement on ADHD symptoms across development. *Psychological Assessment*, 27(1), 239–248.

Nese, R., Horner, R., & Dickey, C. (2014). Decreasing bullying behaviors in middle school: Expect Respect. *School Psychology Review*, 29(3), 272–286.

Nevels, R. M., Dehon, E. E., Alexander, K., & Gontkovsky, S. T. (2010). Psychopharmacology of aggression in children and adolescents with primary neuropsychiatric disorders: A review of current and potentially promising treatment options. *Experimental and Clinical Psychopharmacology*, 18(2), 184–201. http://doi.org/10.1037/a0018059

Nigg, J., Nikolas, M., & Burt, S. A. (2010). Measured gene-by-environment interaction in relation to attention-deficit/hyperactivity disorder. *Journal of the American Academy of Child and Adolescent Psychiatry*, 49(9), 863–873. doi:10.1016/j.jaac.2010.01.025

Nock, M. K., Kazdin, A. E., Hiripi, E., & Kessler, R. C. (2007). Lifetime prevalence, correlates, and persistence of oppositional defiant disorder: Results from the National Comorbidity Survey Replication. *Journal of Child Psychology and Psychiatry and Allied Disciplines*, 48(7), 703–713. doi:10.1111/j.1469-7610.2007.01733.x

Ogden, T., & Hagen, K. A. (2006). Multisystemic treatment of serious behaviour problems in youth: Sustainability of effectiveness two years after intake. *Child and Adolescent Mental Health*, 11(3), 142–149. doi:10.1111/j.1475-3588.2006.00396.x

Owens, J. S., Johannes, L. M., & Karpenko, V. (2009). The relation between change in symptoms and functioning in children with ADHD receiving school-based mental health services. *School Mental Health*, 1(4), 183–195. doi:10.1007/s12310-009-9020-y

Patterson, G. R. (1982). *Coercive family process.* Eugene, OR: Castalia.

Pelham, W. E., Burrows-MacLean, L., Gnagy, E. M., Fabiano, G. A., Coles, E. K., Wymbs, B. T., . . . Waschbusch, D. A. (2014). A dose-ranging study of behavioral and pharmacological treatment in social settings for children with ADHD. *Journal of Abnormal Child Psychology*, 42(6), 1019–1031.

Pelham, W. E., Gnagy, E. M., Greiner, A. R., Waschbusch, D. A., Fabiano, G. A., & Burrows-MacLean, L. (2010). Summer treatment programs for attention deficit/hyperactivity disorder. In A. E. Kazdin & J. R. Weisz (Eds.), *Evidence-based psychotherapies for children and adolescents* (2nd ed., pp. 277–292). New York, NY: Guilford.

Pelham, W. E., Sibley, M. H., Evans, S. W., Smith, B. H., Gnagy, E. M., & Greiner, A. R. (2010). Summer treatment program for adolescents. Available from authors.

Power, T. J., Mautone, J. A., Soffer, S. L., Clarke, A. T., Marshall, S. A., Sharman, J., . . . Jawad, A. F. (2012). A family–school intervention for children with ADHD: Results of a randomized clinical trial. *Journal of Consulting and Clinical Psychology*, *80*(4), 611–623. doi:10.1037/a0028188

Raine, A. (2002). Biosocial studies of antisocial and violent behavior in children and adults: A review. *Journal of Abnormal Child Psychology*, *30*, 311–326.

Rapp, L. A., & Wodarski, J. S. (1997). The comorbidity of conduct disorder and depression in adolescents. *Family Therapy*, *24*(2), 81–100.

Reinke, W. M., & Herman, K. C. (2002). Creating school environments that deter antisocial behaviors in youth. *Psychology in the Schools*, *39*(5), 549–559. doi:10.1002/pits.10048

Reinke, W. M., Lewis-Palmer, T., & Merrell, K. (2008). The Classroom Check-Up: A classwide teacher consultation model for increasing praise and decreasing disruptive behavior. *School Psychology Review*, *37*(3), 315–332.

Rowe, R., Maughan, B., Pickles, A., Costello, E., & Angold, A. (2002). The relationship between *DSM-IV* oppositional defiant disorder and conduct disorder: Findings from the Great Smoky Mountains Study. *Journal of Child Psychology and Psychiatry*, *43*, 365–373.

Schatz, N., Fabiano, G., Cunningham, C., dosReis, S., Waschbusch, D., Jerome, S., . . . Morris, K. (2015). Systematic review of patients' and parents' preferences for ADHD treatment options and processes of care. *The Patient—Patient-Centered Outcomes Research*, *8*(6), 483–497. doi:10.1007/s40271-015-0112-5

Sciutto, M. J. (2013). ADHD knowledge, misconceptions, and treatment acceptability. *Journal of Attention Disorders*, *19*(2), 91–98. doi:10.1177/1087054713493316

Sheridan, S. M., & Kratochwill, T. R. (2008). *Conjoint behavioral consultation: Promoting family-school connections and interventions* (2nd ed.). New York: Springer Science + Business Media.

Sibley, M. H., Altszuler, A. R., Ross, J. M., Sanchez, F., Pelham, W. E., & Gnagy, E. M. (2014). A parent-teen collaborative treatment model for academically impaired high school students with ADHD. *Cognitive and Behavioral Practice*, *21*(1), 32–42. doi:10.1016/j.cbpra.2013.06.003

Sibley, M. H., Kuriyan, A. B., Evans, S. W., Waxmonsky, J. G., & Smith, B. H. (2014). Pharmacological and psychosocial treatments for adolescents with ADHD: An updated systematic review of the literature. *Clinical Psychology Review*, *34*(3), 218–232. doi:10.1016/j.cpr.2014.02.001

Sibley, M. H., Smith, B. H., Evans, S. W., Pelham, W. E., & Gnagy, E. M. (2012). Treatment response to an intensive summer treatment program for adolescents with ADHD. *Journal of Attention Disorders*, *16*(6), 443–448.

Spiel, C. F., Evans, S. W., & Langberg, J. M. (2014). Evaluating the content of individualized education programs and 504 plans of young adolescents with attention deficit/hyperactivity disorder. *School Psychology Quarterly*, *29*(4), 452–468. doi:10.1037/spq0000101

Steinberg, E. A., & Drabick, D. A. G. (2015). A developmental psychopathology perspective on ADHD and comorbid conditions: The role of emotion regulation. *Child Psychiatry & Human Development*, *46*(6), 951–966. doi:10.1007/s10578-015-0534-2

Stormont, M. (2001). Social outcomes of children with AD/HD: Contributing factors and implications for practice. *Psychology in the Schools*, *38*, 521–531.

Willoughby, M. T., Mills-Koonce, R., Propper, C. B., & Waschbusch, D. A. (2013). Observed parenting behaviors interact with a polymorphism of the brain-derived neurotrophic factor gene to predict the emergence of oppositional defiant and callous-unemotional behaviors at age 3 years. *Development and Psychopathology, 25*(4.1), 903–917. doi:10.1017/S0954579413000266

Wilson, S. J., & Lipsey, M. W. (2007). School-based interventions for aggressive and disruptive behavior: Update of a meta-analysis. *American Journal of Preventive Medicine, 33,* S130–S143.

7

Regulating Emotions

MATTHEW P. MYCHAILYSZYN, MAUREEN A. MANNING,
AND CATHERINE T. PETRICK ■

Adolescents face many challenges in today's fast-paced and changing world, including increasing educational demands (Harris, 2008), rising rates of divorce (Heckel, Clarke, Barry, McCarthy, & Selikowitz, 2009; Messner, Bjarnason, Raffalovich, & Robinson, 2006), and media exposure to messages of violence and terrorism (Comer, Furr, Beidas, Weiner, & Kendall, 2008; Comer & Kendall, 2007), among others. These stressors contribute to youth's vulnerability to a wide range of associated mental health difficulties.

IDENTIFICATION AND TREATMENT CONCERNS

Internalizing disorders represent an area of marked concern for youth, particularly during the developmental stage of adolescence. Indeed, in one of the most recent and largest epidemiological efforts, the National Comorbidity Survey Replication Adolescent Supplement (NCS-A), internalizing problems were found to be the most prevalent mental health difficulty among a nationally representative sample of adolescents between the ages of 13 and 18 in the United States (Merikangas et al., 2010). Specifically, anxiety disorders were found to be the most common, with nearly one in every three adolescents (31.9%) meeting criteria for a diagnosis, while mood disorders had the third-highest lifetime prevalence, creating impairment for 14.3% of the overall sample. Regarding the latter, particularly troublesome is empirical evidence that suggests an increasing prevalence rate of depression among youth (Hammen & Rudolph, 2003). Moreover, such contemporary prevalence data are relatively consistent with epidemiological studies over the last 30 years (e.g., Costello, Egger, & Angold, 2005; Viken, 1985), reflecting the persistent threat of internalizing psychopathology to the mental health well-being of youth over time.

Adolescents who struggle with emotion regulation difficulties experience a host of associated negative outcomes and sequelae. Although these youth may be perceived as less troublesome than those exhibiting disruptive/oppositional behavior, they are nevertheless comparably distressed and impaired. In the realm of academics, internalizing disorders have been found to represent a major obstacle to educational progress. For instance, it has been found that "elevated anxiety produces a state of physiological arousal and a narrowing focus of attention on perceived threat. This arousal tends to impair concentration on nonthreat stimuli such as academic tasks" (Wood, 2006, p. 345). Indeed, over the course of the last three decades, investigators have documented the deleterious effects of anxiety on academic performance (e.g., Ialongo, Edelsohn, Werthamer-Larsson, Crockett, & Kellam, 1995; Mychailyszyn, Mendez, & Kendall, 2010; Strauss, Frame, & Forehand, 1987), which often manifests as early as elementary school and persists into adolescence. The negative association between depression and school grades has been the subject of similar investigation over the last 30 years, with researchers obtaining temporally stable findings regarding the impairing influence of teen depression on academic achievement (e.g., Fauber, Forehand, Long, Burke, & Faust, 1987; Jaycox et al., 2009).

Beyond the educational domain, internalizing disorders have been found to adversely affect quality of life in a multitude of other ways. Anxiety disorders increase vulnerability to the development of comorbid conditions and, if left untreated, may persist into adulthood and lead to the development of substance abuse problems (Kendall, Safford, Flannery-Schroeder, & Webb, 2004). Depression is similarly associated with a range of impairments for youth struggling with this condition (Collins & Dozois, 2008). Though the symptoms (e.g., diminished interest, hopelessness) are sufficiently troublesome unto themselves, they often lead to additional problems of functioning, with evidence suggesting that even youth with subclinical levels of depressive symptoms experience a wide range of impairment (Georgiades, Lewinsohn, Monroe, & Seeley, 2006). Furthermore, and of major concern, depression among adolescents tends to be recurrent, with episodes of earlier onset having a longer duration and being a significant predictor for the experience of later episodes and adult depression.

The devastating consequences of failure to effectively regulate emotions is perhaps most evident when adolescents take their own lives. The prevention of youth suicide is a national public health priority, as evidenced by initiatives such as the National Strategy for Suicide Prevention (U.S. Department of Health and Human Services [HHS] Office of the Surgeon General and National Action Alliance for Suicide Prevention, 2012) and the Garrett Lee Smith Memorial Act (Miller, 2011). Given the high percentage of students who think about, plan, attempt, or complete suicide, the barriers that suicidal behavior poses to student learning, and the significant amount of time students spend in school, secondary schools represent natural environments to provide suicide prevention to adolescents. Comprehensive school-based suicide prevention programs include a continuum of services, as discussed briefly below and further elsewhere (Desrochers & Houck, 2013; Mazza & Reynolds, 2007).

Notwithstanding the substantial prevalence of internalizing disorders among adolescents, the prospect of effective and efficient identification of such youth can present a considerable challenge. Of primary concern is that, because of their less visible nature (e.g., versus externalizing disorders), anxiety and depression have a greater likelihood of not being detected by adults. Yet despite this well-recognized obstacle, it remains a common convention (e.g., in school-based intervention research) to depend on classroom teachers for identification, assuming that, due to their regular interaction with students, they might (or perhaps *should*) know if and when a student is feeling distressed. Unfortunately, however, the research on the efficacy of this practice is scant, and that which has been conducted seems to be less encouraging in terms of its utility. For instance, Auger (2004) found limited agreement between teachers' ratings and students' self-reports of depression. Perhaps of most concern was the study's finding of teachers' limited ability to accurately identify those students experiencing the highest level of depression symptoms—a group that the author points out we might assume could be recognized even if general mood evaluation of students as a whole is more difficult. The research of Moor and colleagues (2007) only adds to the concern in this area: this study investigated the effectiveness of a psychoeducational intervention to help teachers recognize the signs of clinical depression in their adolescent students. Based on their evaluation, however, the authors concluded

that training teachers with this package did not improve their ability to recognize their depressed pupils. Recognizing depressive illness in adolescence is one of the main public health challenges for adolescent mental health services and this study adds to the growing literature on the difficulties in achieving this. (p. 81)

Certainly, teacher nominations are not the only vehicle by which anxious and depressed students can be identified within school systems. Indeed, as described above, because such internalizing difficulties are often so difficult to recognize through simple observation, they may often not come to light unless some form of more standardized direct evaluation is conducted. A comprehensive review of such measures is beyond the scope of this chapter, however, and interested readers should refer to reports elsewhere in the literature (e.g., Muller & Erford, 2012; Mychailyszyn et al., 2011). While such assessment tools have demonstrated sound psychometric properties, their practicality in the context of day-to-day school operations may be limited. For instance, in considering pre-existing school-based intervention research that has utilized large-scale—sometimes universal—school screenings to determine which individuals were referred for services in those investigations, Warner and Fox (2012) came to the following conclusion:

The encouraging news is that self-report school screenings have been effective in detecting anxious and depressed children who otherwise would likely not have been identified. On the other hand, because school screenings of this nature are probably not feasible without researcher support, referral remains a major obstacle to the sustainability of our school-based interventions for anxiety and depression. (p. 194)

Clearly, many challenges remain unaddressed in the realm of school-based detection of internalizing symptomatology. Ultimately, the most efficient and effective manner of identifying students with such mental health concerns will likely involve initial screening followed by a combination of the two aforementioned strategies, in some type of multiple-gating assessment process. Specifically, teachers can be asked for nominations of students that are believed to be experiencing anxiety or depression. Those individuals can then be referred for more formalized assessment in order to distinguish the true from false positives. The process may be further enhanced by incorporating knowledge about factors that confer a greater risk for development of disorders. While such a method is admittedly not without its flaws (e.g., potential for missed cases, or "false negatives"), until further research provides solutions that can be built into the infrastructure of school mental health, the practical achievement of identification will remain a limited and imperfect process.

Many challenges exist when it comes to the identification of anxiety and depression for adolescents. This reality becomes especially frightening when the most extreme of outcomes—suicide—is contemplated in the context of internalizing struggles. Given the high stakes of this behavior, we devote space below to an individualized consideration of suicide assessment.

Screening Procedures

Screening students for risk of suicide occurs through the administration of self-report questionnaires that ask students about suicidal thoughts, intentions, and previous attempts. A significant body of research indicates that screening is effective in identifying students at risk for suicide who would not have been identified otherwise (e.g., through teacher, peer, or self-referrals). When asked questions regarding suicidal behavior, adolescents tend to disclose this information honestly, even when they have not shared it with others. Because many of the risk factors for suicide, such as depression, involve internalizing symptoms that are not readily observable by others, self-report measures can be an effective and time-efficient way of eliciting such symptoms. Effective school-based suicide screening programs include the Columbia University TeenScreen Program (McGuire & Flynn, 2003) and the Signs of Suicide (SOS) program (Substance Abuse and Mental Health Services Administration [SAMHSA], 2008), both of which are recognized as evidence-based by the Substance Abuse and Mental Health Services Administration (SAMHSA, 2012). Unfortunately, many school personnel are reluctant to embrace screening, due to the misconception that raising the topic of suicide with students will increase suicidal thoughts and feelings. Research has indicated that this concern, while widespread, is unfounded (see Miller, 2011). Rather, screening is considered the "most direct, effective, and efficient method" for identifying at-risk students (Miller, 2012, p. 216).

Risk Assessment

Risk assessment is a procedure for estimating students' likelihood of self-harm, with the immediate goal of ensuring safety. A multimethod approach to suicide risk assessment is recommended, with information gathered from a variety of sources and modalities. At a minimum, however, the risk assessment must include a student interview (Miller, 2011). Several standardized self-report instruments with adequate psychometrics (e.g., Children's Depression Inventory [Kovacs, 2004]; Center for Epidemiological Studies Depression Scale for Children [Faulstich, Carey, Ruggiero, Enyart, & Gresham, 1986]) exist to supplement the interview, but they should never replace it (Desrochers & Houck, 2013). Although a standardized instrument is neither necessary nor sufficient, using a structured set of questions to guide the interview may reduce the assessor's anxiety and ensure that pertinent areas are addressed (Miller, 2011). In order to determine whether, and to what degree, students intend to hurt themselves, school-based mental health professionals must inquire about intentions, plans, methods, and previous attempts. They should also gather information on the student's history of mental illness, experience of recent losses, and perceived support system (Desrochers & Houck, 2013). Given the association between suicide and other behaviors, the assessor should differentiate between suicide and nonsuicidal self-injury and determine whether the adolescent it is at risk of harming others in addition to him or herself (Miller, 2011). Questions should be asked in a direct, straightforward, and developmentally appropriate manner, and confidentiality should not be promised to students (Desrochers & Houck, 2013). In addition to student-report, school-based mental health professionals should obtain information from teachers regarding warning signs, as well as information from parents/caregivers regarding family history (Miller, 2011).

Given the documented prevalence rates of internalizing disorders and the noted burden they carry in terms of impairment to quality of life (e.g., academic, social, behavioral, emotional functioning), the next logical question becomes: Are adolescents with these concerns receiving supportive services? Unfortunately, the disheartening answer to this question seems to be "no." Findings dating back 20 years (Burns et al., 1995) revealed that less than half (40.3%) of youth with a psychiatric disorder and experiencing associated impairment were accessing care from any of five human service sectors. Discouragingly, this number has remained remarkably stable over time, as recent contemporary data from the NCS-A (Merikangas et al., 2011) found that only slightly more than a third (36.2%) of adolescents with psychiatric diagnoses received services for their illness. Unfortunately, those with internalizing difficulties are particularly unlikely to seek services (Colognori et al., 2012). Indeed, while those with mood disorders accessed services at a rate close to the overall average (37.7%), less than one in five (17.8%) with an anxiety disorder received support (Merikangas et al., 2011).

The school setting seemingly offers an opportunity for maximized access and an enhanced ability to reach youth by delivering interventions "where they are" (Weist, Evans, & Lever, 2003). Encouragingly, the evidence seems to suggest that school systems are indeed acting as a major provider of services. Burns and colleagues (1995) found that nearly three-quarters of youth "who received services for a mental health problem were seen by providers working within the education sector (mostly guidance counselors and school psychologists)" (p. 152) while Farmer and colleagues (2003) determined that "the education sector was the most common point of entry and provider of services across all age groups" (p. 60).

Whether youth *do* actually receive services through schools can be a complex matter. The current legislation that governs the implementation of special education across all 50 states is the Individuals with Disabilities Education Improvement Act of 2004 (IDEIA, P.L. 108-446). IDEIA is a national special education law that "informs general provisions, funding formulas, and definitions of how states and federally funded public agencies provide early intervention, special education, and related services to children with disabilities" (Sulkowski, Joyce, & Storch, 2012, p. 940). A Federal Register that details the qualifying criteria for the 13 categories of disability in IDEIA has also been disseminated by the Office of Special Education and Rehabilitative Services (OSERS, 2006) of the U.S. Department of Education.

Unfortunately, the parameters guiding the determination of eligibility for such services are vague when it comes to regulating emotions. For instance, neither anxiety disorders nor mood disorders are specifically mentioned in IDEIA or the Federal Register as distinct types of exceptionality classifications. Rather, allusions to internalizing symptomatology (e.g., "fears," "mood of unhappiness") are contained within the definition for an *Emotional Disturbance* (ED). Another category, *Other Health Impairment* (OHI), is intended for acute or chronic health conditions that lead to limitations in alertness in the domain of the educational environment (OSERS, 2006). Anxious or depressed adolescents whose symptoms warrant either of these classifications will be guaranteed services under IDEIA via an individualized education plan (IEP); however, a central criterion for the both the ED and OHI designation is that the condition must be adversely affecting educational performance. This can create problems with being deemed eligible for services, as youth may maintain academic achievement despite experiencing significant psychological suffering; the specific manner in which schools define an adverse effect on educational performance can also be a gray area. For instance, the formerly straight-A student whose grades decline to the B-range as a result of depression can create challenges in terms of identification, as the student continues to perform above average relative to peers.

EVIDENCE-BASED PRACTICE

The American Psychological Association (APA) Presidential Task Force on Evidence-Based Practice (EBP) has defined EBP in psychology as "the integration of the best available research with clinical expertise in the context of patient characteristics, culture, and preferences" (APA, 2006, p. 273). When it comes to internalizing disorders for youth, a significant amount of intervention research has been conducted over the last three decades; in most cases, the development and evaluation of intervention protocols has originated in academic university clinics. Based on the accumulation of findings from outcome studies of these protocols, as well as conclusions reached by reviews (e.g., Horowitz & Garber, 2006; James, Soler, & Weatherall, 2005) of the results produced, cognitive behavioral therapy (CBT) meets established standards to be considered an efficacious treatment for anxiety and depression in youth, and thus should be recommended as the first-line treatment of choice for youth struggling with these problems (Compton et al., 2004).

However, the question of whether such *efficacious* interventions prove to be *effective* when applied within schools is a matter of "transportability," or the degree to which evidence-based treatments work when implemented in community contexts (Schoenwald & Hoagwood, 2001). Encouragingly for school personnel seeking to implement programs, a review conducted by Spence and Shortt (2007) concluded that outcomes "do not appear to be related to the level of mental health training of the person delivering the program" (p. 537). Similarly, a recent meta-analysis by Mychailyszyn and colleagues (2012) of school-based cognitive behavioral interventions for youth anxiety and depression compared protocols delivered by school personnel to those led by research staff and found that "mean summary effect size findings indicated that there was no difference between these implementers in terms of the amount of reduction in symptomatology from baseline to postintervention" (p. 144). Thus, there appears to be a strong evidence base supporting psychosocial interventions for internalizing disorders—when delivered both outside and within schools.

When it comes to providing interventions, services can range from prevention to treatment, with the former being divisible into a continuum of levels depending upon the population of interest. According to the Institute of Medicine (Mrazek & Haggerty, 1994) "universal preventive interventions" are intended for entire population groups and are not based on any identified risk status; "selective preventive interventions" are meant for individuals who possess risk factors (e.g., hereditary, psychological, social) associated with a disorder; and "indicated preventive interventions" seek to help individuals deemed as being high-risk because they exhibit elevated symptoms of mental disorder but do not presently meet sufficient criteria to warrant a clinical diagnosis. Interestingly, many programs for anxiety and depression are fairly similar regardless of the level of intervention, focusing on instruction of psychosocial coping skills to combat internalizing symptomatology. While the literature generally supports the effectiveness of most intervention efforts, the overall magnitude of change (typically measured in terms of effect size) tends to increase as one moves along the continuum from universal prevention to treatment. This is because the former design is inherently subjected to "floor effects," whereas greater initial symptom levels have more room for improvement.

Evidence-Based Prevention Efforts

In terms of school-based suicide prevention programs, a recent review of the literature identified "gatekeeper" programs (e.g., universal interventions such as educational programs whereby students and staff members learn to recognize signs and symptoms of suicide and act as referral sources to school-based mental health professionals) and screening as being among the "most promising" (Robinson et al., 2013, p. 164). The most effective programs emphasize a mental health model of suicide rather than a stress model (i.e., they explain that suicide is linked to mental health disorders rather than to extreme levels of stress), are delivered on a long-term rather than short-term basis (Miller, 2011), and provide opportunities for participants to actively practice skills (SAMHSA, 2012). SAMSHA (2012) provides information on student and staff programs that have been recognized by the National Registry of Evidence-based Prevention Practices (NREPP) or the Best Practices Registry (BPR). School-based mental health professionals are encouraged to consider the culture of their school when adopting a program, and to seek consultation from program developers regarding how to meet the specific needs of their population without sacrificing the integrity of the intervention (SAMHSA, 2012).

Selected school-based suicide prevention programs are designed for students who are not in imminent danger, but are considered to have a higher likelihood than their peers of suicidal behavior based upon specific risk factors, such as symptoms of depression or substance abuse. Such approaches are designed to prevent or reduce students' suicidal behaviors. Desrochers and Houck (2013) and Miller (2011) provide examples of effective school-based programs. According to Miller (2011), most school districts fail to implement any form of suicide prevention but do provide crisis intervention (e.g., conduct a risk assessment) when a student is referred for suicide-related behaviors. Consistent with this practice, SAMHSA (2012) recommends that all schools have interventions in place at the indicated level before establishing interventions at the universal and/or selected levels. Because the latter interventions may increase the number of referrals to school mental health professionals, it is essential that schools have protocols to guide their responses to referrals and to completed suicides.

Evidence-Based Intervention Efforts

Several effective evidence-based practices for internalizing disorders incorporate cognitive behavioral and interpersonal approaches over a range of treatment modalities that can be applied by school mental health professionals. For example, while treating students on an individual basis has advantages in terms of scheduling flexibility and providing individualized care, the school setting also provides an opportunity to treat several students at once through a group-targeted approach (Ruffolo & Fischer, 2009). Though parental participation and support is generally encouraged during treatment for children and adolescents, attending school-based sessions can be difficult for parents due to occupational commitments and scheduling conflicts (Young, Mufson, & Gallop, 2010). Despite these challenges, research demonstrates promising developments for treatment that integrates evidence-based practices into school-based individual, group, and family intervention models.

CBT is the theoretical foundation of the Coping Cat program, an individual-oriented approach to the treatment of youth anxiety (Podell, Mychailyszyn, Edmunds, Puleo, & Kendall, 2010). The Coping Cat utilizes psychoeducation and graduated exposure therapy to develop coping skills and emotional problem-solving abilities that equip youth to confront and manage anxiety-provoking situations. While the *Coping Cat* program was initially developed for and demonstrated efficacy as an individualized intervention, similar reductions in anxiety levels were found when the program was structured to a group-targeted model (Flannery-Schroeder & Kendall, 2000). Though scheduling and time limitations may reflect challenges for implementation, school mental health professionals and trained staff have some flexibility in tailoring individual and group sessions while maintaining treatment consistency.

Though a CBT approach is the foundation of many evidence-based practices for the treatment of internalizing disorders, Interpersonal Psychotherapy-Adolescent Skills Training (IPT-AST), an interpersonal approach used to improve adolescent emotional and social functioning, has also proven to be beneficial in the prevention and treatment of adolescent depression. IPT-AST consists of individual and small group sessions, as well as the planned involvement of parents who attend an individual session, a group session, and a post-group session with the adolescent to provide emotional support and assist with generalization of skills (Young et al., 2010). By fostering communication and socio-emotional functioning of adolescents, positive relationships with peers and family members are promoted to reduce depression while also serving as a buffer for increased depressive symptoms in the future. For instance, Young and colleagues (e.g., see Young, Kranzler, Gallop, & Mufson, 2012; Young, Mufson, & Davies, 2006) have found that adolescents receiving IPT-AST had significantly fewer depression symptoms at post-intervention and follow-up than those receiving usual school counseling, significantly greater improvements in total social functioning and friend functioning during the intervention, and fewer depression diagnoses than those in usual care. While research suggests that IPT-AST can yield significant improvements in school contexts, challenges exist with regard to parent participation, time commitments by parents and students, and the cost of trained clinicians to lead the intervention.

In an effort to modify manual-driven evidence-based intervention programs for different school environments, modular CBT has been proposed to address the issue of treatment flexibility. The modular approach allows experienced clinicians and school mental health professionals to tailor manual-based treatments to relevant issues that are of particular importance to that individual or group (Becker, Becker, & Ginsburg, 2012). One study (Chiu et al., 2013) modified the Building Confidence program, which emphasizes parental involvement in reducing childhood and adolescent anxiety symptoms, into a modular CBT format. During 16 weekly sessions, children develop skills through psychoeducation and exposure therapy to manage anxiety and confront anxiety-provoking situations, while parent sessions provide education on internalizing disorders and ways to continue exposure treatment for the child in the home environment. Though this modular approach to implementing evidence-based practice requires the participation of experienced mental health professionals to select modules appropriately and a time commitment for training, modular CBT approaches may be more feasible in the school environment because of the flexibility of treatment sequence and session duration.

Evidence-based programs utilizing a cognitive behavioral approach have been successful in preventing and treating anxious and depressive symptoms among youth in economically disadvantaged and culturally diverse schools. The Penn Resiliency Program (PRP; Gillham, Reivich, & Jaycox, 2008) is a 12-week program that focuses on cognitive restructuring, goal setting, and conflict management in the prevention of youth depression. This program has been organized to incorporate issues and scenarios that engage and apply to low-income minority populations. Research conducted by Cardemil, Reivich, and Seligman (2002) indicated a decrease in fifth and sixth grade (average age = 11 years old) Latino and African American students' depressive symptoms immediately following treatment and at three and six months post-treatment.

The Cool Kids Program treats anxiety in children and adolescents through learned coping techniques, social skills training, and exposure therapy. The group version of the treatment consists of eight 2-hour sessions for students and two 2-hour sessions for parents, led by school counselors and mental health professionals (McLoone, Hudson, & Rapee, 2006). In order to address economically disadvantaged populations, the program has been organized to focus on issues affecting low-income households. In one evaluation of this program, Mifsud and Rapee (2005) found that, from among 425 students (ages 8–11) across nine low-income schools in Sydney, Australia, children assigned to Cool Kids demonstrated significant reductions in symptoms of anxiety relative to children assigned to waitlist, with differences maintained four months after treatment, according to both self-report and teacher report.

Another school-based program that has received a great deal of support in the research literature (Kataoka et al., 2003; Stein et al. 2003) for the treatment of depression related to trauma in culturally diverse youth is the Cognitive Behavioral Intervention for Trauma in Schools (CBITS) program (Jaycox, 2004). The course of the CBITS program consists of 10 weekly group sessions and at least 1 individual session. Sessions emphasize psychoeducation, coping with traumatic stress, and exposure to individual traumatic memories (Langley, Nadeem, Kataoka, Stein, & Jaycox, 2010). In contrast to other evidence-based programs, CBITS concentrates specifically on treating depression due to trauma in minority and immigrant populations within the school system by establishing community partnerships for additional support (Ngo et al., 2008). Importantly, CBITS has demonstrated efficacy for diverse populations of adolescents, such as American Indians living on a reservation (Morsette et al., 2009).

Guided by an expanding focus on how evidence-based treatments can be efficiently disseminated and implemented, investigators are increasingly exploring new modalities of treatment delivery—most specifically utilizing the computer/Internet. Kendall and colleagues (2011) review some of these efforts, focusing specifically on the Camp Cope-A-Lot (CCAL) program—a translation of the *Coping Cat* program into a computer-assisted format. Feasibility and acceptability of the CCAL was found to be favorable, and an RCT (Khanna & Kendall, 2010) comparing CCAL, CBT, and an education, support, and attention (ESA) control condition indicated higher diagnostic recovery rates in the CCAL compared to the ESA condition. Similar endeavors have also been made in the realm of youth depression. For instance, among 157 adolescent girls (ages 15–16), O'Kearney and colleagues (2009) found significantly faster declines in depressive symptomatology as compared to controls in an evaluation of a self-directed Internet intervention for depression (MoodGYM) delivered as a part of the high school curriculum, while Saulsberry and colleagues (2013) have developed a culturally adapted Internet-based depression prevention program for urban African American and Latino adolescents.

Feasibility of evidence-based practices in schools. The school environment has the potential to provide vital mental health services for students who may lack the emotional, social, and financial resources to effectively cope with a range of mental health concerns (Beidas et al., 2012). While it is feasible within the school setting to provide current evidence-based practices to children and adolescents who struggle with internalizing disorders, several challenges to appropriate implementation exist. One central obstacle involves the degree to which school staff are involved in the actual delivery of such programs. Similar to the role that teachers and school mental health professionals may play in successfully identifying and assisting students with academic learning difficulties, they should also be expected to play a role in supporting students plagued with anxiety and mood disorders.

Though teachers agree that they have a responsibility in terms of fostering the social and emotional development of their students, many teachers receive limited training in mental health (Miller, Short, Garland, & Clark, 2010). Research conducted by Reinke, Stormont, Herman, Puri, and Goel (2011) found that only 4% of teachers reported that they possessed the tools and training required to properly address the mental health needs of their students. Furthermore, teachers' misconceptions about social, emotional, and behavioral difficulties may result in the under-referral of students who could benefit from services, and consequently an escalation in individuals' internalizing symptoms (Cooper & Cefai, 2013). Soles, Bloom, Heath, and Karagiannakis (2008) demonstrated that teacher reports reflected gender stereotypes when asked to rate their female and male students' symptom expression, and, as such, females were identified as expressing more internalizing symptoms than males and were only identified as possessing externalizing symptoms when the presentation was perceived as severe. Therefore, in an effort to improve the identification, prevention, and treatment of emotion regulation difficulties among youth, teachers may benefit from the completion of a formalized training program that emphasizes key mental health aspects.

While many teachers and school mental health professionals support the implementation of structured efforts aimed at improving psychological functioning among students, time constrictions imposed by professional workloads and students' classroom schedules create barriers to the planning and delivery of such services within the school setting (Beidas et al., 2012). Other limitations to feasibility include resistance from school administrators, school mental health professionals, teachers, and parents to participate in and follow the program protocol while employing techniques that are consistent with evidence-based practices (Warner & Fox, 2012). Despite these obstacles, the school environment has the ability to offer services to a number of children and adolescents, and neglecting to assist these individuals in psychological distress will likely cause detriments to their academic performance and future cognitive, social, and emotional functioning (Mychailyszyn et al., 2011).

To address obstacles pertaining to implementation feasibility, relevant school personnel require increased access to formal training in mental health issues and evidence-based practices. Research has shown that a school and community collaborative approach to training school mental health professionals in evidence-based practices may increase the utility of programs within the school setting (Stephan, Connors, Arora, & Brey, 2013). Furthermore, solidifying a network of teachers, school mental health professionals, and community mental health professionals facilitates communication and consultation for employing evidence-based treatments effectively throughout organized programs (Cappella, Jackson, Bilal, Hamre, & Soule, 2011). With appropriate training, school mental health professionals can learn to modify the delivery of evidence-based practices (e.g., shortening sessions, reducing session frequency) to fit the demands of a particular school environment while maintaining treatment fidelity (Warner & Fox, 2012).

Another issue that poses a threat to implementation is the stigma that continues to surround mental health issues. Students may be resistant to participating and engaging in mental health services out of a fear of judgment and ridicule from classmates (Kranke, Floersch, Townsend, & Munson, 2010; Offord, Kraemer, Kazdin, Jensen, & Harrington, 1998). However, research indicates that school mental health services carry less stigma than those offered in the community (Storch & Crisp, 2004). Therefore, school-based initiatives that encourage mental health awareness and understanding may serve to reduce stigma among students, teachers, and parents surrounding the use of mental health services in the school system (Bowers, Manion, Papadopoulos, & Gauvreau, 2013). Though barriers to implementing evidence-based practices may hinder their feasibility in the school system, important advantages may be derived from effective programming, and school professionals should make efforts to overcome these obstacles to ensure the appropriate care and development of their students.

SERVICE DELIVERY MODEL

Sulkowski and colleagues (2012) propose a school-based model for addressing mental health concerns that has excellent application value for adolescent internalizing disorders. With different levels of service intensity, what makes this model particularly relevant in the educational domain is that is constructed to be consistent with the core elements of the Response to Intervention (RtI) framework, a multi-tiered school-based system of academic and behavioral supports. Tier 1 of the model endorses the universal administration of behavioral screening measures whose scores can signal if a student is in the at-risk range for development of problems with emotion regulation. In Tier 2, those students identified by universal screenings would undergo a more comprehensive multimethod assessment involving such tools as interviews, observation, and measures of social, emotional, and/or behavioral functioning. Since students may previously have been receiving some form of class-wide universal intervention, the combination of Tier 1 and Tier 2 assessment reflects the central facet of RtI by examining what benefits, if any, students are experiencing in response to differing levels of service provision. Students deemed to be experiencing significant internalizing distress (and thus not being sufficiently aided by universal programs) would be referred for targeted group-based interventions such as group therapy. Finally, based upon ongoing progress monitoring, students exhibiting a limited response to the above strategies would be eligible for more intensive Tier 3 services, such as individual therapy with a higher frequency of sessions and the availability of other supports.

Regardless of how effective in terms of service provision school mental health is able to be in the future, circumstances will likely always exist in which collaboration with community providers will be necessary. First and foremost, school professionals should consider referring a student elsewhere for services when the appropriate training is absent. Fundamental ethical guidelines require that mental health providers not practice outside their area of expertise. A school provider may seek consultation and supervision from a community professional with advanced knowledge in the area, though in lieu of this, a referral should be made. School providers should also strive to maintain ongoing communication with the medical doctors prescribing medications for students. The fine-tuning of pharmacotherapy regimens requires data about the nature of behavioral and emotional responses and progress, and school personnel attending to the mental health needs of adolescents in schools are uniquely poised to be sources of this information. Community resources should also be accessed when the severity of the problem is extreme. A prime example would be the student experiencing serious suicidal ideation. In such a case, even if intensive interventions are already being implemented in the school, additional services (which could be of varying formats) may be clinically indicated.

One of the most practical remaining issues to consider is the *cost* of providing school-based mental health services. In writing about the utilization, effectiveness, and consent procedures of mental health services in schools, Evans (1999) stated, "In reviewing literature for this article, no studies were identified that examined cost of school-based versus clinic-based services" (p. 166). Unfortunately, relatively little direct work on this topic has been conducted in the area of internalizing disorders for adolescents over the intervening 15 years. While the financial costs of services are recognized as a major challenge, the exact numbers are difficult to determine, are likely to vary widely from district to district, and thus are largely unknown. What *can* be offered at this time is information about potential funding options available for schools to cover these costs. Maag and Katsiyannis (2010) describe federal legislative mandates and initiatives that have funding mechanisms to provide mental health services to children in schools. Citing such sources as Medicaid, the Social Security Act, and the Public Health Service Act, these authors assert that "there are a surprising number of federal funding sources for children to receive mental health services that schools may be unaware of or that are underused" (p. 174).

Research has demonstrated that it is well within the capacity of schools to provide effective programs for adolescents with internalizing disorders. However, a myriad of obstacles hinder their widespread implementation on a day-to-day basis, and, to date, "few school-based mental health services are evidence-based" (Warner & Fox, 2012, p. 193). In order to encourage change on a systems-wide level, all professionals involved in the endeavor of school mental health must become advocates for the advancement of services. Perhaps only when the very *culture* of school systems shifts in such a direction that socio-emotional–behavioral health is universally accepted as being inextricably intertwined with school-based quality of life will the goal of more comprehensive school-based psychological services be fully realized. Until such a time has been reached, however, it remains the work of all relevant parties to continue searching for and evaluating the best models and practices that will achieve this critical end for youth struggling with the regulation of emotions.

RECOMMENDATIONS FOR FUTURE RESEARCH

Research over the last 30 years has been marked by substantial advances in knowledge regarding the successful implementation of evidence-based practice for internalizing disorders within the school context. However, as many of the points above have indicated, there is still a considerable way to go. The first recommendation for future research we would offer is for investigators to develop research designs that more appropriately evaluate prevention. In a meta-analytic review of prevention studies for youth depression, Horowitz and Garber (2006) insightfully remind us that in order for a study's results to be considered a *prevention* effect, the control group must demonstrate an increase in symptomatology while the intervention group must exhibit no such increase or at least an attenuated increase. Based on this definition, these authors concluded that "none of the studies of universal interventions met the criteria to be considered prevention" (p. 410). This is a crucial point. Many so-called prevention studies are thus actually yielding *treatment* effects by producing larger symptom reductions in intervention groups than in control groups. It is difficult to suggest that we are "preventing" the onset of anything if individuals in control groups receiving no treatment demonstrate that the natural symptom trajectory is to remain stable or actually decrease over time.

Another suggestion, which follows from the first, is the need to conduct follow-up evaluations of much longer duration. This is especially pertinent for universal prevention efforts, where we would not expect significant numbers of individuals to experience the onset of disorder in the relatively short span of time (e.g., typically 8–16 weeks) that the study period lasts. Thus, as Spence and Shortt (2007) point out, it may be possible that a "sleeper effect" (p. 534) exists whereby the benefits of learned coping skills may not manifest until many months, or perhaps even years, later, when adolescents encounter more substantial and challenging life stressors.

Finally, researchers need to identify how to make themselves obsolete! This tongue-in-cheek recommendation is made to underscore that if school mental health services focused on regulating emotions are ever to become self-sufficient and sustaining, we must ascertain how schools can eventually implement evidence-based practices independently. Indeed, Warner and Fox (2012) suggest that perhaps the most crucial challenge is "to develop less burdensome methods for detecting anxious and depressed youth that are feasible for schools to execute without researcher support" (p. 195). Thus, investigators must continue working on creating tools that can be practically used by school personnel to effectively identify which adolescents need support, and on determining how those same personnel—be they teachers, counselors, school psychologists, or other professionals—can become proficient in the delivery of evidence-based programs so that schools have their own mental health providers to whom struggling youth can go for help.

REFERENCES

American Psychological Association. (2006). Evidence-based practice in psychology. *American Psychologist, 61*, 271–285.

Auger, R. W. (2004). The accuracy of teacher reports in the identification of middle school students with depressive symptomatology. *Psychology in the Schools, 41*, 379–389.

Becker, E., Becker, K., & Ginsburg, G. (2012). Modular cognitive behavioral therapy for youth with anxiety disorders: A closer look at the use of specific modules and their relation to treatment process and response. *School Mental Health, 4*, 243–253.

Beidas, R., Mychailyszyn, M., Edmunds, J., Khanna, M., Downey, M., & Kendall, P. (2012). Training school mental health providers to deliver cognitive-behavioral therapy. *School Mental Health, 4*, 197–206.

Bowers, H., Manion, I., Papadopoulos, D., & Gauvreau, E. (2013). Stigma in school-based mental health: Perceptions of young people and service providers. *Child and Adolescent Mental Health, 18*, 165–170.

Burns, B. J., Costello, E. J., Angold, A., Tweed, D., Stangl, D., Farmer, E. M. Z., & Erkanli, A. (1995). DataWatch: Children's mental health service use across service sectors. *Health Affairs, 14*, 147–159.

Cappella, E., Jackson, D. R., Bilal, C., Hamre, B. K., & Soulé, C. (2011). Bridging mental health and education in urban elementary schools: Participatory research to inform intervention development. *School Psychology Review, 40*, 486–508.

Cardemil, E. V., Reivich, K. J., & Seligman, M. E. P. (2002). The prevention of depressive symptoms in low-income minority middle school students. *Academy of Child and Adolescent Psychiatry, 34,* 312–331.

Chiu, A. W., Langer, D. A., McLeod, B. D., Har, K., Drahota, A., Galla, B. M., . . . Wood, J. J. (2013). Effectiveness of modular CBT for child anxiety in elementary schools. *School Psychology Quarterly, 28,* 141–153.

Collins, K. A., & Dozois, D. J. A. (2008). What are the active ingredients in preventative interventions for depression? *Clinical Psychology: Science and Practice, 15,* 313–330.

Colognori, D., Esseling, P., Stewart, C., Reiss, P., Lu, F., Case, B., & Masia Warner, C. (2012). Advances and challenges in school-based intervention for anxious and depressed youth: Identifying and addressing issues of sustainability. *School Mental Health, 4,* 193–196.

Comer, J. S., Furr, J. M., Beidas, R. S., Weiner, C. L., & Kendall, P. C. (2008). Children and terrorism-related news: Training parents in coping and media literacy. *Journal of Consulting and Clinical Psychology, 76,* 568–578.

Comer, J. S., & Kendall, P. C. (2007). Terrorism: The psychological impact on youth. *Clinical Psychology: Science and Practice, 14,* 178–212.

Compton, S. N., March, J. S., Brent, D., Albano, A. M., Weersing, V. R., & Curry, J. (2004). Cognitive-behavioral psychotherapy for anxiety and depressive disorders in children and adolescents: An evidence-based medicine review. *Journal of the American Academy of Child and Adolescent Psychiatry, 43,* 930–959.

Cooper, P., & Cefai, C. (2013). Evidence-based approaches to social, emotional, and behavior difficulties in schools. *KEDI Journal of Educational Policy, 10,* 81–101.

Costello, J. E., Egger, H. L., & Angold, A. (2005). 10-year research update review: The epidemiology of child and adolescent psychiatric disorders: I. Methods and public health burden. *Journal of the American Academy of Child and Adolescent Psychiatry, 44,* 972–986.

Desrochers, J. E., & Houck, G. (2013). *Depression in children and adolescents: Guidelines for school-based practice.* Silver Spring, MD: National Association of School Nurses.

Evans, S. W. (1999). Mental health services in schools: Utilization, effectiveness, and consent. *Clinical Psychology Review, 19,* 165–178.

Farmer, E. M. Z., Burns, B. J., Phillips, S. D., Angold, A., & Costello, E. J. (2003). Pathways into and through mental health services for children and adolescents. *Psychiatric Services, 54,* 60–66.

Fauber, R., Forehand, R., Long, N., Burke, M., & Faust, J. (1987). The relationship of young adolescent Children's Depression Inventory (CDI) scores to their social and cognitive functioning. *Journal of Psychopathology and Behavioral Assessment, 9,* 161–172.

Faulstich M. E., Carey, M. P., Ruggiero L., Enyart, P., & Gresham, F. (1986). Assessment of depression in childhood and adolescence: An evaluation of the Center for Epidemiological Studies Depression Scale for Children (CES-DC). *American Journal of Psychiatry, 143,* 1024–1027.

Flannery-Schroeder, E., & Kendall, P. C. (2000). Group and individual cognitive-behavioral treatments for youth with anxiety disorders: A randomized clinical trial. *Cognitive Therapy and Research, 24,* 251–278.

Georgiades, K., Lewinsohn, P. M., Monroe, S. M., & Seeley, J. R. (2006). Major depressive disorder in adolescence: The role of subthreshold symptoms. *Journal of the American Academy of Child & Adolescent Psychiatry, 45,* 936–944.

Gillham, J. E., Reivich, K. J., & Jaycox, L. H. (2008). *The Penn Resiliency Program.* Unpublished manuscript, University of Pennsylvania.

Hammen, C., & Rudolph, R. D. (2003). Childhood mood disorders. In E. J. Mash & R. A. Barkley (Eds.), *Child psychopathology* (2nd ed., pp. 233–278). New York, NY: Guilford Press.

Harris, B. (2008). Befriending the two-headed monster: Personal, social, and emotional development in schools in challenging times. *British Journal of Guidance and Counselling, 36,* 367–383.

Heckel, L., Clarke, A., Barry, R., McCarthy, R., & Selikowitz, M. (2009). The relationship between divorce and the psychological well-being of children with ADHD: Differences in age, gender, and subtype. *Emotional & Behavioural Difficulties, 14,* 49–68.

Horowitz, J. L., & Garber, J. G. (2006). The prevention of depressive symptoms in children and adolescents: A meta-analytic review. *Journal of Consulting and Clinical Psychology, 74,* 401–415.

Ialongo, N., Edelsohn, G., Werthamer-Larsson, L., Crockett, L., & Kellam, S. (1995). The significance of self-reported anxious symptoms in first grade children: Prediction to anxious symptoms and adaptive functioning in fifth grade. *Journal of Child Psychology and Psychiatry, 36,* 427–437.

Individuals with Disabilities Education Improvement Act of 2004. 20 U.S.C. § 1400 et seq.

James, A. A. C. J., Soler, A., & Weatherall, R. R. W. (2005). Cognitive behavioural therapy for anxiety disorders in children and adolescents. *Cochrane Database of Systematic Reviews,* Issue 4, Art. no. CD004690. doi:10.1002/14651858.CD004690.pub2

Jaycox L. H. (2004). *Cognitive Behavioral Intervention for Trauma in Schools.* Longmont, CO: Sopris West Educational Services.

Jaycox, L. H., Stein, B. D., Paddock, S., Miles, J. N. V., Chandra, A., Meredith, L. S., . . . Burnam, A. (2009). Impact of teen depression on academic, social, and physical functioning. *Pediatrics, 124,* e596–e605.

Kataoka, S. H., Stein, B. D., Jaycox, L. H., Wong, M., Escudero, P., Tu, W., . . . Fink, A. (2003). A school-based mental health program for traumatized Latino immigrant children. *Journal of the American Academy of Child and Adolescent Psychiatry, 42,* 311–318.

Kendall, P. C., Khanna, M. S., Edson, A., Cummings, C., & Harris, M. S. (2011). Computers and psychosocial treatment for child anxiety: Recent advances and ongoing efforts. *Depression and Anxiety, 28,* 58–66.

Kendall, P. C., Safford, S., Flannery-Schroeder, E., & Webb, A. (2004). Child anxiety treatment: Outcomes in adolescence and impact on substance abuse and depression at 7.4 year follow-up. *Journal of Consulting and Clinical Psychology, 72,* 276–287.

Khanna, M., & Kendall, P. C. (2010). Computer-assisted cognitive-behavioral therapy for child anxiety: Results of a randomized clinical trial. *Journal of Consulting and Clinical Psychology, 78,* 737–745.

Kovacs, M. (2004). *Children's Depression Inventory 2.* North Tonawanda, NY: Multi-Health Systems

Kranke, D., Floersch, J., Townsend, L., & Munson, M. (2010). Stigma experience among adolescents taking psychiatric medication. *Children and Youth Services Review, 32,* 496–505.

Langley, A. K., Nadeem, E., Kataoka, S. H., Stein, B. D., & Jaycox, L. H. (2010). Evidence-based mental health programs in schools: Barriers and facilitators of successful implementation. *School Mental Health, 2,* 105–113.

Maag, J. W., & Katsiyannis, A. (2010). School-based mental health services: Funding options and issues. *Journal of Disability Policy Studies, 21*, 173–180.

Mazza, J. J., & Reynolds, W. M. (2007). School-wide approaches to the prevention of depression and suicidal behaviors. In E. J. Doll & J. A. Cummings (Eds.), *Transforming school mental health services: Population-based approaches to promoting the competence and wellness of children* (pp. 213–241). Thousand Oaks, CA: National Association of School Psychologists and Corwin.

McGuire, L. C., & Flynn, L. (2003). The Columbia TeenScreen Program: Screening youth for mental illness and suicide. *Trends in Evidence-based Neuropsychiatry, 5*, 56–62.

McLoone, J., Hudson, J. L., & Rapee, R. M. (2006). Treating anxiety disorders in a school setting. *Education and Treatment of Children, 29*, 219–242.

Merikangas, K. R., He, J., Burstein, M., Swanson, S. A., Avenevoli, S., Cui, L., . . . Swendsen, J. (2010). Lifetime prevalence of mental disorders in U.S. adolescents: Results from the National Comorbidity Survey Replication–Adolescent Supplement (NCS-A). *Journal of the American Academy of Child & Adolescent Psychiatry, 49*, 980–989.

Merikangas, K. R., He, J., Burstein, M., Swendsen, J., Avenevoli, S., Case, B., . . . Olfson, M. (2011). Service utilization for lifetime mental disorders in U.S. adolescents: Results of the National Comorbidity Survey–Adolescent Supplement (NCS-A). *Journal of the American Academy of Child & Adolescent Psychiatry, 50*, 32–45.

Messner, S. F., Bjarnason, T., Raffalovich, L. E., & Robinson, B. K. (2006). Nonmarital fertility and the effects of divorce rates on youth suicide rates. *Journal of Marriage and Family, 68*, 1105–1111.

Miller, D. N. (2011). *Child and adolescent suicidal behavior: School-based prevention, assessment, and intervention*. New York, NY: Guilford.

Miller, D. N. (2012). Preventing student suicide. In S. E. Brock & S. R. Jimerson (Eds.), *Best practices in school crisis prevention and intervention* (2nd ed., pp. 203–222). Bethesda, MD: National Association of School Psychologists.

Miller, L. D., Short, C., Garland, J., & Clark, S. (2010). The ABCs of CBT (cognitive behavior therapy): Evidence-based approaches to child anxiety in public school settings. *Journal of Counseling & Development, 88*, 432–439.

Mifsud, C., & Rapee, R. M. (2005). Early intervention for childhood anxiety in a school setting: Outcomes for an economically disadvantages population. *Journal of American Academy of Child and Adolescent Psychiatry, 44*, 996–1004.

Moor, S., Ann, M., Hester, M., Elisabeth, W. J., Robert, E., Robert, W., & Caroline, B. (2007). Improving the recognition of depression in adolescence: Can we teach the teachers? *Journal of Adolescence, 30*, 81–95.

Morsette, A., Swaney, G., Stolle, D., Schuldberg, D., van den Pol, R., & Young, M. (2009). Cognitive Behavioral Intervention for Trauma in Schools (CBITS): School-based treatment on a rural American Indian reservation. *Journal of Behavior Therapy and Experimental Psychiatry, 40*, 169–178.

Mrazek, P. J. & Haggerty, R. J. (Eds.) (1994). *Reducing risks for mental disorders: Frontiers for prevention research*. Washington, DC: National Academy Press.

Muller, B. E., & Erford, B. T. (2012). Choosing assessment instruments for depression outcome research with school-age youth. *Journal of Counseling and Development, 90*, 208–220.

Mychailyszyn, M. P., Beidas, R. S., Benjamin, C. L., Edmunds, J. M., Podell, J. L., Cohen, J. S., & Kendall, P. C. (2011). Assessing and treating child anxiety in schools. *Psychology in the Schools, 48*, 223–232.

Mychailyszyn, M. P., Brodman, D. M., Read, K. L., & Kendall, P. C. (2012). Cognitive-behavioral school-based interventions for anxious and depressed youth: A meta-analysis of outcomes. *Clinical Psychology: Science and Practice, 19*, 129–153.

Mychailyszyn, M. P., Mendez, J. L., & Kendall, P. C. (2010). School functioning in youth with and without anxiety disorders: Comparisons by diagnosis and comorbidity. *School Psychology Review, 39*, 106–121.

Ngo, V., Langley, A., Kataoka, S. H., Nadeem, E., Escudero, P., & Stein, B. D. (2008). Providing evidence-based practice to ethnically diverse youths: Examples from the Cognitive Behavioral Intervention for Trauma in Schools (CBITS) program. *Journal of American Academy of Child and Adolescent Psychiatry, 47*, 858–862.

Office of Special Education and Rehabilitative Services, Department of Education. (2006). Federal Register: Part II Department of Education, 34 CFR Parts 300 and 301, Assistance to states for the education of children with disabilities and preschool grants for children with disabilities; Final rule. Washington, DC: Author.

Offord, D. R., Kraemer, H. C., Kazdin, A. E., Jensen, P. S., & Harrington, R. (1998). Lowering the burden of suffering from child psychiatric disorder: Trade-offs of among clinical, targets, and universal interventions. *Journal of the American Academy of Child and Adolescent Psychiatry, 37*, 686–694.

O'Kearney, R., Kang, K., Christensen, H., & Griffiths, K. (2009). A controlled trial of a school-based Internet program for reducing depressive symptoms in adolescent girls. *Depression and Anxiety, 26*, 65–72.

Podell, J. L., Mychailyszyn, M. P., Edmunds, J., Puleo, C. M., & Kendall, P. C. (2010). The Coping Cat program for anxious youth: The FEAR Plan comes to life. *Cognitive and Behavioral Practice, 17*, 132–141.

Reinke, W. M., Stormon, M., Herman, K. C., Puri, R., & Goel, N. (2011). Supporting children's mental health in schools: Teacher perceptions of needs, roles, and barriers. *School Psychology Quarterly, 26*, 1–13.

Robinson, J., Cox, G., Malone, A., Williamson, M., Baldwin, G., Fletcher, K., & O'Brien, M. (2013). A systematic review of school-based interventions aimed at preventing, treating, and responding to suicide-related behavior in young people. *Crisis, 34*, 164–182.

Ruffolo, M. C., & Fischer, D. (2009). Using an evidence-based CBT group intervention model for adolescents with depressive symptoms: Lessons learned from a school-based adaptation. *Child and Family Social Work, 14*, 189–197.

Saulsberry, A., Corden, M. E., Taylor-Crawford, K., Crawford, T. J., Johnson, M., Froemel, J., . . . Voorhees, B. W. V. (2013). Chicago urban resiliency building (CURB): An Internet-based depression-prevention intervention for urban African-American and Latino adolescents. *Journal of Child and Family Studies, 22*, 150–160.

Schoenwald, S. K., & Hoagwood, K. (2001). Effectiveness, transportability, and dissemination of interventions: What matters when? *Psychiatric Services, 52*, 1190–1197.

Soles, T., Bloom, E., Heath, N., & Karagiannakis, A. (2008). An exploration of teachers' current perceptions of children with emotional and behavioural difficulties. *Emotional and Behavioral Difficulties, 13*, 275–290.

Spence, S. H., & Shortt, A. L. (2007). Research review: Can we justify the widespread dissemination of universal, school-based interventions for the prevention of depression among children and adolescents? *Journal of Child Psychology and Psychiatry, 48*, 526–542.

Stein, B. D., Jaycox, L. H., Kataoka, S. H., Wong, M., Tu, W., Elliott, M. C., & Fink, A. (2003). A mental health intervention for schoolchildren exposed to violence: A randomized controlled trial. *Journal of the American Medical Association, 290*, 603–611.

Stephan, S., Connors, E., Arora, P., & Brey, L. (2013). A learning collaborative approach to training school-based health providers in evidence-based mental health treatment. *Children and Youth Services Review, 35,* 1970–1978.

Storch, E. A., & Crisp, H. L. (2004). Taking it to the schools—Transporting empirically supported treatments for childhood psychopathology to the school setting. *Clinical Child and Family Psychology Review, 7*(4), 191–193.

Strauss, C. C., Frame, C. L., & Forehand, R. (1987). Psychosocial impairment associated with anxiety in children. *Journal of Clinical Child Psychology, 16,* 235–239.

Substance Abuse and Mental Health Services Administration. (2008). National Registry of Evidence-based Programs and Practices: SOS Signs of Suicide Prevention Program. Retrieved from http://www.nrepp.samhsa.gov/ProgramProfile.aspx?id=85

Substance Abuse and Mental Health Services Administration (2012). *Preventing Suicide: A Toolkit for High Schools.* HHS Publication No. SMA-12-4669. Rockville, MD: Center for Mental Health Services, Substance Abuse and Mental Health Services Administration, 2012.

Sulkowski, M.L., Joyce, D.K.,& Storch, E.A. (2012). Treating childhood anxiety in schools: Service delivery in a response to intervention paradigm. Journal of Child & Family Studies, 21, 938–947

U. S. Department of Health and Human Services (HHS) Office of the Surgeon General and National Action Alliance for Suicide Prevention. *2012 national strategy for suicide prevention: Goals and objectives for action.* Washington, DC: HHS, September 2012.

Viken, A. (1985). Psychiatric epidemiology in a sample of 1510 ten-year-old children: 1. Prevalence. *Journal of Child Psychology & Psychiatry, 26,* 55–75.

Weist, M. D., Evans, S. W., & Lever, N. A. (2003). Introduction: Advancing mental health practice and research in schools. In M.D. Weist, S.W. Evans, & N.A. Lever (Eds.), *Handbook of school mental health: Advancing practice and research* (pp. 1–7). New York, NY: Kluwer Academic/Plenum.

Wood, J. (2006). Effect of anxiety reduction on children's school performance and social adjustment. *Developmental Psychology, 42,* 345–349.

Young, J. F., Kranzler, A., Gallop, R., & Mufson, L. (2012). Interpersonal psychotherapy-adolescent skills training: Effects on school and social functioning. *School Mental Health, 4,* 254–264.

Young, J. F., Mufson, L., & Davies, M. (2006). Efficacy of interpersonal psychotherapy-adolescent skills training: An indicated preventive intervention for depression. *Journal of Child Psychology and Psychiatry, 47,* 1254–1262.

Young, J. F., Mufson, L., & Gallop, R. (2010). Preventing depression: A randomized trial of interpersonal psychotherapy-adolescent skills training. *Depression and Anxiety, 27*(5), 426–433.

Warner, C. M., & Fox, J. (2012). Advances and challenges in school-based intervention for anxious and depressed youth: Identifying and addressing issues of sustainability. *School Mental Health, 4,* 193–196.

8

Emotion Regulation and Social Functioning in Adolescence

Conceptualization and Treatment

NORA BUNFORD AND STEVEN W. EVANS ■

Adolescence is a lengthy transition phase during which the individual is no longer a child but not yet an adult. Although adolescents strive for independence, parents, teachers, and social institutions recognize that they are largely unprepared to assume adult responsibilities (Cicchetti, 1984). Thus, adolescence is both a conflicted and a vulnerable period, during which teens undergo significant biological and psychological changes (Cicchetti & Rogosch, 2002), while also experiencing changes in social demands and settings (Feldman & Elliott, 1990; Spear, 2000a, 2000b).

With adolescence being a conflicted and vulnerable period, it is not surprising that, as a developmental phase, it is associated with more psychological turmoil than childhood or adulthood (Resnick et al., 1997). The three central correlates of this turmoil are conflict with parents, emotional problems, and risky behaviors (Arnett, 1999). In this chapter, we focus on the second of these: the development of emotional competencies, with a focus on the development of emotion regulation skills, from childhood through adolescence. In keeping with the literature, we will argue that the acquisition of emotion regulation skills is one of the main developmental tasks of adolescence and consider ways in which the development of such skills can go awry and result in emotion dysregulation (ED). We will further argue that although to some extent, emotional lability (i.e., "involuntary emotional displays of mood that are overly frequent and excessive" [Bolt, 2011, p. 576]) is part of normative adolescent development (Cicchetti & Rogosh, 2002), ED can play an important role in the social impairment youth experience in the home, peer, and school settings. It follows that psychosocial interventions that address ED and social impairment, can be implemented by school mental health professionals, and can be implemented in a manner that results in generalizability to all relevant settings are needed. We will describe one such psychosocial intervention, the Interpersonal Skills Group (ISG), which was designed to target ED and social impairment in adolescents and to generalize to the home, peer, and school settings. Although ISG is applicable to settings beyond schools, we will describe ISG as it is delivered in schools, by school mental health professionals. By delivering ISG in schools, professionals are able to work with adolescents in the setting where they spend the majority of their time. This obviates the need for families to commute to mental health agencies or clinics (which can be costly and time-consuming). In this manner, retention and treatment completion rates can also be increased.

EMOTION REGULATION: A MAJOR DEVELOPMENTAL TASK OF ADOLESCENCE

There are a handful of crucial, stage-salient developmental tasks of adolescence, including establishing psychological autonomy and a cohesive sense of identity, transitioning to secondary school and subsequently to postsecondary education or work, and forming friendships across and within gender (Masten & Coatsworth, 1998). Acquiring emotion regulation competencies and skills is another major developmental task of the adolescent period (Cicchetti, Ganiban, & Barnett, 1991; Dodge, 1989; Kopp, 1989). Yet the developmental literature on emotion regulation is primarily focused on infancy through childhood (e.g., Thompson, 1994). Data on these earlier periods may be helpful for understanding the types of skills youth can be expected to master by the time they reach their teenage years. As such, we next provide a brief review of the literature on the development of emotion regulation competencies and skills across childhood.

Infancy Through Middle Childhood

Early in development, when infants and toddlers experience distress or fear, they exhibit relatively primitive and undifferentiated signals of such emotions—crying, for example. In response, the mother (or other caregiver) notes these signals and soothes the infant or toddler (Bowlby, 1969, 1973). This typical interaction exemplifies that a meaningful portion of emotion regulation is external to the child in infancy and toddlerhood. During the preschool years, however, an increase in adult-child co-regulation is observable (see Cole, Michel, & Teti, 1994 for review) and this co-regulation is accompanied by a differentiation or diversification of emotion signals and emotion regulation skills (Kopp, 1989). A related developmental task of the preschool years is for children to learn to receive feedback from their environment on their emotion reactivity and expression, which they then progressively incorporate into their behavioral repertoire.

By middle childhood, emotion regulation primarily takes the form of child self-regulation (though external regulation still plays a role; see Coyne & Downey, 1991). Changes in cognitive, perceptual, and verbal skills allow for this increase in the degree to which children are able to self-regulate their emotions (Cole et al., 1994). For example, developments in cognitive skills allow children to reflect on their behaviors, emotions, and thoughts. It is during middle childhood that children learn to appreciate the possibility of simultaneously experiencing multiple, sometimes incongruent emotions (Cole et al., 1994). Of import, as children are better able to reflect on their emotions, they also begin to have emotions about their own emotions (i.e., secondary emotions). Developments in perceptual skills (e.g., visuospatial; Cole et al., 1994) aid children in their ability to accurately perceive emotions in others and, consequently, to better understand and respond to social situations. As a final example, developments in verbal skills equip children with alternative ways to express their emotions (see Cole et al., 1994 for review).

Early Adolescence

Effective emotion regulation abilities become linked to critical domains of functioning during early adolescence, as emotion regulation plays a role in decision-making, and risky decisions can have deleterious and/or serious consequences. Typically developing early adolescents are increasingly more reliant on both emotional and rational input into decisions. Yet there may be incongruity between an early adolescent's emotional and rational (i.e., cognitive) development, for while the former—the development of affect, arousal, and motivation regulation—are related to pubertal maturation (Neeman, Hubbard, & Masten, 1995; Udry, 1987), the latter, or cognitive development, has primarily been linked to chronological age (Steinberg, 1987). As a result, an early adolescent's emotional and cognitive development may not be congruous, and such incongruity has implications for decision-making, including about risky behaviors or situations. Although early research indicated that youth engage in risky behaviors because their poor cognitive skills result in poor decisions (Botvin, Botvin, Michela, Baker, & Filazzola, 1991; Tobler, 1986), more recent findings indicate that youth engage in risky behaviors even when they are aware of the consequences and risks involved (Benthin, et al., 1995, Cauffman & Steinberg, 1995; Martin et al., 2002). Thus, the leading perspective today is that early adolescents' decision-making is influenced both by them rationally weighing relative risks and by their emotions (Steinberg, 2004). For these reasons and beyond, beginning to learn how to balance emotional and cognitive input into decisions is important in early adolescence.

Taken together, over the course of development there is a shift from primarily external regulation of emotions, through a combination of external and self-regulation, to primarily self-regulation. Middle childhood ends around puberty, which typically marks the beginning of adolescence. By the time they reach adolescence, typically developing teens are equipped with multiple ways to express and regulate their emotions and are able to receive and integrate feedback on their emotion expression and regulation into their behavioral repertoire.

Adolescence

Adolescence is perhaps the most crucial period for the development of emotion regulation, as it is a time when maturational, social, and temperamental forces come together to lay the foundation for individual differences in emotion regulation observed in adulthood. This crucial period is also a period of heightened vulnerability regarding the development of emotion regulation and, consequently, of ED. The heightened vulnerability regarding emotion regulation and ED is due, in part, to an exacerbation of the incongruity between emotional and cognitive development already present in early adolescence. Specifically, it is during adolescence that the possibility for an asynchronicity among brain development, self-regulatory (behavioral, cognitive, and emotional) skill development, and environmental demands is at its peak (Steinberg, 2005).

First, there can be a disconnect between the development of adolescents' self-regulatory skills and changes in environmental contexts and demands for self-regulation. Although there is an increased need to self-regulate behavior, cognitions, and emotions in a manner that is congruent with long-term goals, this increased need is combined with diminished input from the adults (e.g., parents, teachers) who had previously provided regulatory guidance and structure (Steinberg, 2005).

Second, maturational brain processes continue through adolescence, with some processes maturing earlier than others. Although puberty brings on changes in arousal and motivation, the development of regions and systems associated with regulating these are among the last to develop (e.g., executive functions, frontal lobes; see Steinberg, 2005). This can result in a disjunction between adolescents' emotional experiences (arousal and motivation) and their ability to regulate those experiences (Steinberg, 2005). Thus, although normative adolescent emotional development is characterized by an increase in emotional awareness and in adolescents' ability to respond to emotions strategically (i.e., to exercise effortful control over inner feeling states and the outward expression thereof; Kopp 1992; Southam-Gerow & Kendall 2002), the development of executive functions is a lengthy process, and a fully controlled and coordinated set of executive functions is acquired late in development. As such, the developments of "adolescence may well create a situation in which one is starting an engine without yet having a skilled driver behind the wheel" (Steinberg, 2005, p. 70). In the absence of a "skilled driver", there are increased opportunities for suboptimal developmental trajectories. These suboptimal trajectories can broadly take the form of psychopathology, or specifically take the form of ED, including deficits in the down- or up-regulation of negative and positive emotions (Bunford, Evans, & Wymbs, 2015).

In addition to changes related to emotion regulation, there is also evidence for a relation between pubertal maturation and changes in social information processing. For example, at the time of sexual maturation, a *decrement* in face processing and voice recognition skills is observable (Steinberg, 2005). As such, adolescence is not only a prime time for the development of ED (due to the disjunction between adolescents' emotional experiences and their ability to regulate such experiences), but also for difficulties with social information processing. For this reason, it is not surprising that many teens struggle with emotion regulation and experience impairments in social functioning, both independently from ED and as a result of ED.

ED, SOCIAL IMPAIRMENT, AND ADHD

A variety of emotion-related processes (e.g., emotion recognition in the self and others, emotional lability, ED) are linked to the etiology and manifestation of various internalizing and externalizing disorders and to social impairment (Bunford, Evans, & Wymbs, 2015; Silk, Steinberg, & Morris, 2003). Emotional lability differentiates adolescents who show elevations on internalizing symptoms only, who show elevations on externalizing symptoms only, and who show elevations on either, both, or neither domain (Angold, Costello, Burns, Erkanli, & Farmer, 2000). A large body of research links ED in adolescence to symptoms of anxiety and depression (Wasser, Tyler, McIlhaney, Taplin, & Henderson, 2008; Zeman, Cassano, Perry-Parrish, & Sheri, 2006), to bipolar disorder (Goldstein, Axelson, Birmaher, & Brent, 2007), to oppositional defiant and conduct disorders (Hinshaw, 2003; Nelson-Gray, et al., 2006), and to ADHD (Barkley, 2010; Bunford, Evans, & Langberg, 2014; Bunford et al., 2016; Melnick & Hinshaw, 2000). Indeed, ED is a common dimension of most psychopathologies, and a defining feature of many. For example, avoidance or blunting of emotions, constricted affect, chronic tension or worry, affect that is inappropriate given situational content, unpredictable fluctuations between emotionlessness and elation, dejection or rage, the predominance of one emotion combined with the relative absence of another, or sustained negative emotions are common examples of characteristics redolent of ED that are associated with psychiatric disorders (Cole, Michel, & Teti, 1994).

In addition to an association with psychiatric disorders, emotion-related processes are also related to various aspects of social functioning. For example, emotion recognition is associated with the ability to accurately interpret social situations (Feldman, Philippot, & Custrini, 1992). ED is associated with behaviors relevant for social functioning (e.g., aggression [Calkins, Gill, Johnson, & Smith, 1999; Furlong & Smith, 1994]) and with difficulties in domains of functioning that occur in a social context (e.g., family conflict [Kobak et al., 1993], and marital or romantic relationships [Skowron, 2000; Skowron & Friedlander, 1998]). ED is also directly linked to social impairment (Eisenberg, Fabes, & Losoya, 1997). Taken together, ED is transdiagnostic, and much has been studied about its role in psychiatric disorders and a variety of areas of impairment. Our work to date has primarily focused on the relationship between ED and ADHD. Thus, the remainder of this chapter will be focused on ED, social impairment, and ADHD. In the context of ADHD:

> **Emotion regulation** is an individual's ability to modulate (1) the speed with which and degree to which the physiological, experiential, and behavioral expression of an emotion escalates, (2) the intensity of the physiological, experiential, and behavioral expression of an emotion, and (3) the speed with which and degree to which physiological, experiential, and behavioral expression of an emotion de-escalates in a manner congruent with an optimal level of functioning. (Bunford, Evans, & Wymbs, 2015; p. 188)

> **Emotion dysregulation** is an individual's inability to exercise any or all aspects of the modulatory processes involved in emotion regulation, to such a degree that the inability results in the individual functioning meaningfully below his or her baseline. (Bunford, Evans, & Wymbs, 2015; p. 188)

ED can manifest in multiple ways. In response to emotional stimuli, the emotions and/or behaviors of well-regulated individuals escalate; however, that escalation does not impair the individual's functioning. We have outlined three primary manifestations of ED, when associated with ADHD among adolescents (Bunford, Evans, & Wymbs, 2015). Regarding the first manifestation, the emotions of the individual with ED do not escalate at a different rate from the well-regulated person's, but the degree of the escalation is such that it causes impairment. In addition, when the provoking stimulus has ended or is removed, the individual with ED de-escalates at a rate slower than the individual without ED. As such, the first manifestation of ED mainly involves emotional intensity above the impaired threshold and slow return to baseline. Regarding the second manifestation, the emotions of the person with ED escalate more quickly and with more intensity than the person without ED and into the impaired range. However, this person returns to baseline at a rate similar to the well-regulated individual. Thus, this manifestation is mainly characterized by a magnitude of the response that is dramatically out of proportion relative to the provocation, but not so much by slow return to baseline. The third category of dysfunction involves individuals who experience all difficulties associated with ED, with emotions that (a) escalate more quickly than the well-regulated individual, (b) escalate to a degree of unexpected intensity, and (c) only slowly return to baseline. Thus, this person's ED will be intense and last for extended periods of time (Bunford, Evans, & Wymbs, 2015).

Of import, it is likely that the three manifestations of ED patterns vary across individuals as well as within an individual across development and situations. In addition, an individual's emotional baseline also varies given different settings and different times (Fruzzetti, Shenk, & Hoffman, 2005). As such, when considering the impact of emotion escalation rate and extent and return to baseline, the judgment of impairment is relative to the individual's own level of functioning and not to some population parameter (Bunford, Evans, & Wymbs, 2015).

As we highlighted previously, difficulties with emotion regulation are associated with psychiatric disorders and can interfere with appropriate response to environmental events. It is no different in the case of ADHD; the impairments associated with ED contribute to social difficulties among youth with ADHD, including impairment in peer relationships (Maedgen & Carlson, 2000; Melnick & Hinshaw, 2000) and deficits in prosocial behaviors (Bunford, Evans, & Langberg, 2014, Bunford, Evans, Becker, & Langberg, 2015).

The relatively small empirical literature on the association between emotion-related processes and social impairment among youth with ADHD indicates that problems with both emotion recognition and emotion regulation contribute to social impairment in this population. Emotion recognition and emotion regulation are separate but overlapping constructs, and some have conceptualized the former as a necessary but insufficient precondition for emotion regulation that involves attending to and correctly identifying emotions in the self and others (Bunford, Evans, & Wymbs, 2015). As defined previously, emotion regulation involves modulating the speed with which and degree to which the physiological, experiential, and behavioral expression of an emotion escalates; the intensity of corresponding expressions of an emotion; and the speed with which and degree to which physiological, experiential, and behavioral expression of an emotion de-escalate. Emotion recognition and regulation are both associated with social impairment among youth with ADHD.

For example, children with ADHD make more errors in emotion recognition than children without ADHD, and these errors are associated with social impairment (Singh et al., 1998). Specifically, children with ADHD less often recognize anger correctly; more often confuse anger, sadness, and happiness with fear; and more often confuse anger with sadness (Singh et al., 1998). Youth with ADHD also take longer to react to emotional faces (Kats-Gold, Besser, & Priel, 2007[1]; Serrano, Owens, & Hallowell, 2015) and spend less time viewing relevant areas of emotional images than their typically developing counterparts (Serrano et al., 2015). In turn, deficient emotion recognition is associated with social problems among youth with ADHD (Friedman et al., 2003; Kats-Gold et al., 2007), such as deficits in social skills, including teacher-rated assertiveness, cooperation, and self-control and peer-rated desirability as a play- or study-partner. Similar to emotion recognition, there is a relationship between ED and social impairment among children and adolescents with ADHD. Maedgen and Carlson (2000) found that children with ADHD exhibited ED in the form of heightened intensity and excessive behavioral expressions of negative and positive emotions. These aspects of ED predicted negative peer ratings with regard to desirability as a friend. Similarly, Melnick and Hinshaw (2000) found that emotional accommodation[2] and negative

---

1. Longer reaction time did not correspond to heightened emotion recognition accuracy.

2. "Child cognitively reinterprets the situation to find a tenable way, or sees a bright side, for example, 'Even though I can't finish, the model, I can still have fun.' Alternatively, he makes verbal statements or behaves in a way that indicates acceptance of the given conditions of the task, for example, shrugs shoulders and says 'its okay'" (Melnick & Hinshaw, 2000, p. 77).

emotional responses[3] predicted[4] the parent- and teacher-rated social preference of children with ADHD. Regarding adolescents, our findings indicate that inflexibility/slow return to baseline, low threshold for emotional excitability/impatience, and behavioral dyscontrol in response to strong emotions predict deficits in prosocial behaviors (Bunford et al., 2014). Two of these manifestations, inflexibility/slow return to baseline and low threshold for emotional excitability/impatience, mediated the negative association between ADHD and social skills (Bunford, Evans, Becker, & Langberg, 2015). Together, these findings indicate that among children with ADHD, ED is associated with impaired peer relationships, and that among adolescents with ADHD, it is associated with impaired prosocial behaviors.

INTERVENTION: INTERPERSONAL SKILLS GROUP (ISG)

Empirically supported interventions for ADHD include psychopharmacological and psychosocial interventions (Evans, Owens, & Bunford, 2014). With regard to the former, medications offer little benefit for social impairment (Bagwell, Molina, Pelham, & Hoza, 2001) and are less effective for adolescents than for children with ADHD (Faraone & Buitelaar, 2010). With regard to the latter, only a minority of adolescents with ADHD respond favorably to interventions targeting social functioning (Coie & Krehbiel, 1984; Sadler, Evans, Schultz, & Zoromski, 2011).

One explanation for this may be an overemphasis on cognitive techniques (Pelham & Sams, 1992), which in general have not fared well with youth with ADHD (Abikoff, 1991). As such, there may be a need to enhance and modify current psychosocial interventions targeting social impairment, potentially by incorporating a direct emphasis on ED, given that it is an associated feature of ADHD and a predictor of social impairment (Bunford, Evans, & Wymbs, 2015).

Another explanation for limitations to the benefits of psychosocial interventions targeting social impairment may be that most interventions for adolescents are upward extensions of interventions designed for children. Due to contextual and developmental differences between children and adolescents, this approach is unlikely to be successful. The state of the science is such that the empirically supported psychosocial treatments for children with ADHD all rely on behavior management (Evans et al., 2014) and thus require adults to implement behavior modification techniques, in both the setting where children exhibit problems and the setting where outcomes are measured. Although behavior modification techniques are feasible with children, they are less so with adolescents. First, relative to children, adolescents are often without adult monitoring. Second, it is more difficult to identify salient consequences (i.e., punishment and reinforcements,

3. "Child makes statements or expressions focusing on the negative, threatening, or uncontrollable aspects of the task, for example, blames others or complains he won't win the prize" (Melnick & Hinshaw, 2000, p. 78).

4. Marginally significant finding.

which are necessary components of behavior modification) for adolescents, and the rewards that are desirable to adolescents are often more costly than the ones that are desirable to children. Third, because there is a greater number of adults who interact with adolescents in secondary schools than with children in elementary schools, coordinating across adults for implementing behavior modification is challenging. Together, differences in youth (children vs. adolescents) and settings (elementary vs. secondary schools) make traditional behavior modification less likely to be effective and/or feasible with adolescents than with children. Training interventions are an alternative approach that address some of the limitations of traditional behavior modification. Indeed, training interventions avoid many of the feasibility challenges of traditional behavior management and have demonstrated effectiveness with targeting academic impairment among adolescents (Evans et al., 2016). Training interventions involve teaching skills that are practiced to the extent that they become automatized, overlearned, and/or routine (Evans et al., 2014). Unlike traditional approaches, training interventions do not necessitate contingency management in settings where adolescents exhibit problems or where outcomes are measured.

Taken together, limitations of psychosocial interventions designed for adolescents with ADHD and to target social impairment call for (1) an increased emphasis on ED, as emotion regulation is a crucial developmental task of adolescence and ED is an associated feature of ADHD and a predictor of social impairment; and (2) a shift from traditional behavior modification to an increased reliance on training interventions. One developmentally informed and innovative training intervention, the Interpersonal Skills Group (ISG), was developed as part of the Challenging Horizons Program (Evans, Schultz, DeMars, & Davis, 2011; Evans, Serpell, Schultz, & Pastor, 2007). The most recent iteration of ISG directly targets ED and is designed to target and allow for skills to generalize to three settings: the home, peer, and school settings.

ISG is a group intervention that was originally designed for adolescents with ADHD. ISG targets ED and social impairment (indirectly through ED as well as directly). ISG has been tested with adolescents with emotional and behavioral disorders (Kern et al., 2015) and with detained juvenile offenders with externalizing (and internalizing) disorders in a juvenile detention facility (Bunford & Evans, under review). ISG is being continually refined for applicability to ED and social impairment regardless of diagnostic status. It is based on a model that is distinct from traditional social skills models. In traditional social skills models, youth are taught predetermined skills that purportedly facilitate adaptive social functioning. Evidence suggests that these traditional approaches are not effective for children or adolescents with ADHD. Conversely, in ISG, participants identify ways in which they wish to be perceived (Ideal Self Goals) and identify specific behaviors that may lead to those perceptions by others (operational definitions of Ideal Self Goals). In addition, adolescents learn to attend to overt and subtle feedback from peers and adults as indicators of relative success in achieving the desired perceptions. This approach is consistent with the developmental literature, as by the time children reach adolescence, well-regulated youth are able to receive feedback from their social environment and incorporate such feedback into their behavioral repertoire (Lorch et al., 2004).

The associated social cognitive deficits pertaining to managing one's behavior in relation to how one wishes to be perceived by others is related to limitations in the ability of youth with ADHD to understand cause and effect relationships in social situations (Lorch, Milich, Astrin, & Berthiaume, 2006). This inability is in turn associated with social impairment (Sibley, et al., 2010). If someone cannot accurately interpret the relationship between one's own behavior and the reactions of others, he or she will be unable to effectively modify his or her behavior to achieve goals. These considerations constitute part of the theoretical underpinnings of ISG, wherein behavioral principles are applied to the social cognitive deficits and related behaviors that underlie social impairment experienced by adolescents with ADHD. In particular, one aim of ISG is to train teens to attend to and understand the relationship between their behaviors and others' reactions to such behaviors and others' perceptions of them.

There are three domains of functioning (contexts) that are directly targeted in ISG, and each context has three Phases. The three contexts correspond to the three main social contexts in which adolescents live and spend time. These include peer relations (Context 1), school or classroom functioning (Context 2), and home functioning or relations with parents (Context 3). The three Phases are Psychoeducation (Phase 1), Skill Building (Phase 2), and Generalization (Phase 3). For example, after learning specific vocabulary necessary for each context, adolescents establish goals in a manner that highlights that their goals may be context specific (Phase 1). For example, adolescents may prioritize "hard-working" as a goal for how they wish their teachers to perceive them; however, their priorities with peers may be related to being seen as fun. After establishing goals and defining behaviors that adolescents can exhibit to achieve their goals, they practice in the context of social activities (Phase 2). Consistent with the nature of training interventions, practice is extensive and includes frequent feedback in relation to adolescents' goals. (See below for examples of Phase 3).

Context 1. The first context, peer relations, is addressed in a group format. Group sessions during the first phase (i.e., Phase 1) involve adolescents learning vocabulary terms pertinent to emotions, emotion regulation, and social functioning. It is during this phase that adolescents work with counselors to generate individualized goals to work toward in treatment: Ideal Self Goals. As we began to describe above, Ideal Self Goals are descriptions of the way in which adolescents wish to be considered by others, such as funny or nice. Adolescents also learn about the related concept of Real Self, which is a description of the way in which they are actually perceived by others. Once Ideal Self Goals are developed, adolescents work with counselors to establish a set of operational definitions of behaviors that they can exhibit that will lead their peers to perceive them in a manner consistent with their goals.

Once adolescents have successfully completed tasks associated with Phase 1, they move on to Phase 2. Phase 2 involves practice activities and feedback sessions. The practice activities resemble real-world situations in which adolescents

commonly experience social impairment (e.g., adolescents may engage in recreational activities, board games, or sports). The counselors do not lead or participate in the activities. They may provide games or recreation equipment for
the adolescents to use during practice (e.g., basketball, Jenga), and the adolescents may or may not choose to use the materials. Accordingly, the activities
require competition or cooperation (and thus potentiate frustration). As such,
ISG activities are selected to align with the recommendation that, for youth to
learn emotion regulation skills and become competent at modifying the impact
of their emotions on their behaviors and thoughts, emotion patterns have to be
experienced in treatment (Greenberg & Safran, 1989). During this second phase,
adolescents are briefly pulled individually from group activities at regular intervals for feedback sessions.

Feedback. The feedback sessions begin with adolescents rating their emotional
state (for the previous observation period) on an Emotions Thermometer. First,
the adolescent selects his or her primary emotion (anger/frustration, excitement/
happiness, or disappointment/sadness). Then, the adolescent rates the intensity
of the emotion, on a 0–100 scale, where 0 represents the least intensity and 100
represents maximum intensity.

After the Emotions Thermometer ratings, adolescents (first) and their counselor (second) rate the adolescent's social performance (for the previous observation period), indexed by the relative degree to which the adolescent made progress
toward his or her Ideal Self Goals. Ratings are made on -3 to +3 scale; the numbers
represent the degree to which the adolescent's behaviors were consistent with his
or her Ideal Self Goals. Once both the adolescent and the counselor have rated the
adolescent's performance, the two engage in a brief discussion about the ratings.
In these discussions, the adolescent is asked to explain the rationale for his or
her ratings by citing specific behavioral examples. The counselor does the same.
Throughout, adolescents and counselors focus on attending to and interpreting
others' feedback in response to the adolescent's social behavior. For example, one
of the adolescent's goals may be to be nice, and behaviors identified as enhancing the likelihood that others will perceive of him or her as nice include "giving a
compliment," "offering to help," and "responding when spoken to directly." As an
example, during the group activity that involved tie-dyeing t-shirts, Jensen may
have asked Graham if he needed help with placing rubber bands on his shirt, and
then told Hayley that he liked the colors she picked for her shirt. These behaviors
may have resulted in both Graham and Hayley smiling at Jensen, one peer offering
help in return, and the other complimenting his color choices in return. However,
Jensen may have ignored a third peer, who was asking him a question. In this
example, Jensen may have rated himself as a +2 for his Ideal Self Goal to be nice
and his counselor may have rated him as a +1. Jensen may have listed the above
two positive behaviors as supporting his self-rating. The counselor may have also
recognized these positive behaviors, but may have also noticed the ignoring as
well as a missed opportunity to offer another compliment.

Ratings and information on specific behaviors is next used to inform behavioral changes for the upcoming observation interval. First, the adolescent is

asked to brainstorm examples of behaviors he or she may exhibit that would result in an improved rating (or in the maintenance of a high rating). The counselor helps the adolescent with such brainstorming. For example, the counselor may *encourage*[5] the adolescent to continue exhibiting the two positive behaviors during the next rating period. In addition, the counselor may also *encourage* the adolescent to also exhibit behaviors that are in line with the third aspect of his or her definition: "responding when spoken to directly." Finally, the counselor may *encourage* the adolescent to exercise heightened awareness of his or her environment and attend to opportunities for further complimenting. Alternatively, had a peer rejected an offer of assistance, the discussion may have centered on ways of responding when rejected, anticipating acceptance of offers to help, and interpreting rejection.

At the end of the feedback, the adolescent and counselor discuss the degree to which the adolescent's specific emotion and the relative intensity of that emotion impacted his or her ability to exhibit behaviors congruent with his or her Ideal Self Goal and to attend to feedback from his or her peers. Over time, the counselor aims to help the adolescent identify a pattern (if present) wherein the more intense the adolescent's emotion, the more difficult it is for him or her to exhibit behaviors congruent with his or her Ideal Self Goal, so as to highlight the importance of emotion regulation. The counselor is also to help the adolescent identify a pattern (if present), wherein, despite the intensity of emotions, when the adolescent is able to regulate his or her behavioral responses to the strong emotion, he or she is better able to exhibit behaviors congruent with his or her Ideal Self Goal *and* attend to feedback from his or her peers, so as to further highlight the benefits of emotion regulation. Once the discussion is concluded, the adolescent returns to the activity until the next feedback session. Experienced counselors can competently complete these feedback sessions in less than three minutes. This practice phase is expected to occur at least once each week (twice is notably better), and to continue for at least 7, but ideally 12 or more, weeks before mastery is achieved (Evans et al., 2009).

The goal of Phase 3 is generalization of skills. During this phase, a counselor meets with the adolescent on an individual basis, at least once a week. In these meetings, counselors and adolescents identify a social interaction the teen experienced during the past week. The counselor and adolescent review this event and the adolescent identifies an Ideal Self Goal that pertained to the interaction. This goal may or may not coincide with the adolescent's Ideal Self Goal from Phases 1 and 2. In fact, one aim of the third phase is for youth to learn that their goals may differ across social situations, even with the same people. Of note, it is true of ISG as a whole that goals and the related behaviors thereof are subject to change

---

5. *Encourage* is a key word here. In ISG, adults do not instruct or tell teens what to do and what not to do. Adults mainly offer ideas and suggestions, which the adolescent then may choose to accept or not accept. It has been our clinical experience that teens are more likely to respond to adults when they offer suggestions as opposed to when they issue demands or rules.

throughout the intervention. Adolescents may recognize that their goals are such that, even when they are "accomplishing" them, they realize that they really would prefer to been seen differently by others. This is consistent with the evolving self-identity development that is part of adolescence. Thus, goal revisions are not to be discouraged, but rather considered as part of the progress in ISG and the maturation process. Adolescents may also learn to recognize that in order to achieve their goal (e.g., of being nice), they first need to set another goal (e.g., of being able to regulate one's anger).

Once the goal has been identified for the specific situation being reviewed, the counselor and adolescent discuss the behaviors that could have helped the youth achieve the goal. The two of them then proceed through the feedback process regarding ratings, rationale for ratings, and plans for future similar interactions.

Context 2. The second context, classroom, is addressed in an individual format. In addition to the vocabulary from the first context, adolescents are introduced to the concept of Expected Self as it relates to the expectations of others. In the school context, this primarily pertains to the expectations of teachers and school administrators. Expected Self is a description of what adolescents' teachers expect of them. Expected Self is primarily a function of rules and social norms. During this phase (i.e., Phase I) of Context 2, adolescents work with counselors to generate Ideal Self Goals for the classroom. These may or may not align with their goals for the peer context, and they may or may not align with teachers' Expected Self Goals for them. The purpose of Expected Self is to ensure that adolescents consider what is going to be expected in a social context while they develop their Ideal Self Goals. Counselors do not encourage concordance between Ideal Self and Expected Self Goals, but they do make sure that the adolescent is aware of various social expectations. Once youth are introduced to the concept of Expected Self and create their Ideal Self Goals, they begin Phase 2 in the classroom, which involves standard classroom participation.

Feedback. Ratings in the second context involve teacher ratings and youth self-ratings. Teachers rate students on two measures. First, teachers receive a list of common Ideal Self Goals and rate each teen on those. This list includes the goals of the teens in ISG, but teachers are not aware of which goal belongs to which student. Second, teachers also rate youth on a measure of academic performance and classroom behavior that constitute the Expected Self in this context. The adolescents rate themselves on the same measures, and ratings are collected once a month.

The guiding principle for the classroom context is similar to that underlying self-management interventions. The goal is for the adolescent to be able to match his or her teacher's ratings on the measure of Expected Self and to receive high scores and match the teacher on the rating of Ideal Self. Thus, the student is trained to consider his or her own behavior in relation to expectations in a manner similar to the teacher. The student is also trained to exhibit behavior consistent with his or her Ideal Self Goals, and thus these ratings will be high and convergent between the two raters. It is possible that an Ideal Self Goal will be incongruent with an Expected Self Goal, and this can lead to problems in the classroom. In

ISG the adolescent is made aware of this incongruence and the problems it may be causing; however, the choice of Ideal Self Goals that are congruent with the expectations of others belongs to the adolescent. In settings where Ideal Self Goals and Expected Self Goals are similar, adolescents are likely to be most successful across behavioral, performance, and social indices. When multiple consecutive ratings between teachers and the student are equivalent, the frequency of ratings is gradually faded. The fading phase constitutes Phase 3 of the classroom context.

Context 3. The third context, home or relations with parents, is addressed in an individual format. During the first phase, adolescents are introduced to the concept of Expected Self as it relates to parental expectations. Specifically, Expected Self is a description of what adolescents' parents expect from them. During this phase (i.e., Phase I) of Context 3, adolescents work with counselors to generate Ideal Self Goals for their home. The counselors also discuss this process with parents and work with them to identify a set of expectations that can be stated as Expected Self Goals. The adolescent's Ideal Self Goals may or may not align with their goals for the peer or the classroom contexts, and they may or may not align with parent Expected Self Goals. Once students create their Ideal Self Goals for this context, they begin Phase 2 in the home.

Feedback. Similar to the classroom context, ratings for the home context involve monthly parent ratings and youth self-ratings. Parents rate their children on a set of anonymous Ideal Self Goals and their Expected Self Goals. Adolescents rate themselves on the same measures. The feedback sessions are similar to those described above regarding classroom behavior. Incongruence between Ideal and Expected Self Goals are noticed, along with the potential consequences, but the adolescent has complete autonomy in deciding his or her own Ideal Self Goals. Similar fading procedures as noted above are also followed.

Ideal Self, Real Self, and Expected Self. There are some important notions to consider regarding the three selves and what adolescents are expected to take away from the corresponding model. First, there is often a disconnect between the Ideal Self and the Real Self of teens with social impairment, in part because they don't attend to feedback from the environment or comprehend the cause and effect relationship between their behavior and such feedback. If the teen's perceptions about him or herself (his or her *assumed* Real Self) aligns with the perceptions of others (his or her *actual* Real Self), it will be easier to improve the Real Self to become congruent with the Ideal Self or with selves expected by his or her teachers and parents. Adolescents familiar with these terms who can accurately observe how they operate in the environment have a greater opportunity to be socially competent than those who do not.

Second, as noted above, the Ideal and Expected Selves may be congruent or incongruent, depending on the adolescent or the situation. For example, for Jensen, his Ideal and Expected Self may usually be congruent; however, his Ideal Self Goals may include that he wants to be seen as independent. From his perspective, achieving this goal may include rejecting offers of assistance from others. His teacher may see this rejection as Jensen not caring how he does in school and thus criticize him for being lazy. In ISG, Jensen would be free to maintain his behavior of rejecting offers of assistance in order to achieve his goal; however, his counselor would make it clear to him that competing goals are possibly leading to a problem (i.e., the teacher seeing Jensen as not caring about how he does in school). Jensen's counselor may also brainstorm with him about ways in which he could modify his behavior (if he wishes) and still ultimately achieve his Ideal Self Goal. Given the developmental importance of adolescents learning autonomy, self-reliance, and identity formation, Jensen will have the final say regarding his Ideal Self Goals, and his ISG counselor will consistently communicate respect for his choices.

Relatedly, counselors may help teens seek out, to the extent possible, situations wherein both the Ideal and the Expected Selves can thrive because of their congruence. Alternatively, it may be best for adolescents to avoid, to the extent possible, situations wherein incongruence between the Ideal and Expected Selves might occur. As there are limitations on the degree to which adolescents can make choices about avoiding situations of potential incongruence (e.g., they cannot choose to avoid school), social, recreational, and vocational opportunities provide a good starting point for learning how to make such choices. When situations that include incongruent goals and expectations cannot be avoided, it is important for teens to learn (1) to recognize these situations and the specific aspects of the incongruence, and (2) to prioritize in a manner that is most consistent with long-term goals.

In the explanation of Real Self, youth learn that changes in how others perceive them may be slower than changes in their behavior. This is because others' impressions are subject to a "reputation bias." People form impressions of others based on experience. To change these perceptions, one must consistently demonstrate significantly different behavior for a sustained period of time so that others' old memories can be replaced with new information. This time period, when others' impressions of us are changing slower than we are changing our behaviors, can be conceptualized as a "vulnerability period." Changing behaviors can be difficult, and sustaining changed behaviors in the absence of clear external reinforcers can be even more difficult. Thus, it is often the case that during the vulnerability period individuals revert to old behaviors when under stress, because the old behaviors are "what they know" and are what they are comfortable with. It is thus a further important skill for youth to learn (1) what to do when others' perceptions are not "following suit" with their behavioral changes, and (2) what to do when one is working genuinely and hard on changing his or her behaviors but others are not noticing these efforts or are doubting that he or she is making an effort or can succeed.

Emotion regulation in ISG. As discussed above, some adolescents with ADHD experience heightened reactivity to emotionally charged events, exhibit overreactivity to emotions (Erhardt & Hinshaw, 1994; Saunders & Chambers, 1996) and have deficiencies in behavioral inhibition when experiencing strong emotions (Bunford, et al., 2014). In addition to adolescents rating their emotions on the Emotions Thermometer and linking the intensity of such emotions to the relative ease versus difficulty of achieving their Ideal Self Goals, there are two additional elements of ISG that address ED. Choosing Ideal Self Goals relevant to emotion regulation and mindfulness meditation are effective adjuncts for teens who exhibit ED.

Choosing Ideal Self Goals relevant to emotion regulation. On an as-needed basis, some adolescents may choose an Ideal Self Goal that is specifically related to emotion regulation (e.g., calm, even-tempered, patient, slow to anger) or define one or more of their goals with behaviors that are specifically related to emotion regulation (e.g., "I continue to talk in a friendly tone and normal pace even when others are excited," "I express my emotions in an assertive manner, by making a respectful statement about them"). As noted above, in ISG, adolescents learn that their goals may differ across situations, and teens may learn to recognize that in order to achieve one of their social goals, they first need to set an emotion regulation goal.

Mindfulness meditation. Mindfulness meditation as an independent practice involves intentionally shifting one's attention toward one's thoughts, feelings, and bodily states (while adopting an observant and nonjudgmental stance) (Bishop et al., 2004). Mindfulness meditation is associated with decreased emotional reactivity and improvements in an individuals' ability to experience negative emotions and stress without acting impulsively to self-sooth (cf. Brown, Ryan, & Creswell, 2007). According to a recent review (Cassone, 2015), mindfulness meditation is associated with improvements in attention, ADHD symptoms, and anxiety and depression, as well as with reductions in behavior problems and peer relationship problems among youth with ADHD. Youth for whom mindfulness meditation is prescribed as an adjunct to ISG are introduced to various mindfulness techniques (e.g., sitting mediation, walking meditation). Counselors can integrate the training and practice of mindfulness techniques with the procedures of ISG to effectively address social impairment associated with ED.

CONCLUSION

Emotion regulation is a key developmental task of adolescence. Well-regulated adolescents have a variety of emotion regulation skills and are able to rely on self-regulation. Yet acquiring adaptive and socially appropriate emotion regulation skills can be problematic due to a mismatch between the development of various systems, including between adolescents' ability to self-regulate and environmental demands, as well as among brain, cognitive, emotional, and pubertal development during the teenage years. Emotional lability is, to some extent, part of normative adolescent development, but ED is associated with social impairment among youth in general, and among teens with ADHD in particular. It was for teens with ADHD and social impairment that a developmentally informed, novel intervention, the ISG, was developed. Recent iterations of ISG include emotion regulation adjuncts (Emotions Thermometer, Ideal Self Goals or definitions specific to emotion regulation, and mindfulness mediation) and target functioning in the three primary domains of functioning of adolescence: the home, peer, and school settings.

ISG is a promising training intervention not only for youth with ADHD and social impairment, but also for teens in general who exhibit ED and experience social impairment (as a result of or independent from ED). Specifically, ISG (as a part of the Challenging Horizons Program) was evaluated in two large randomized trials, and ISG and efficacy data are encouraging. ISG with the emotion regulation adjuncts (Emotions Thermometer, Ideal Self Goals or definitions specific to emotion regulation, and mindfulness mediation) was recently evaluated in a waitlist-controlled pilot feasibility and efficacy trial (Bunford & Evans, under review) and the most recent iteration of ISG with the emotion regulation adjuncts and the three contexts is currently being evaluated in a large randomized clinical trial. All of the development work with ISG has been done in middle or high schools and a juvenile detention facility. Although the procedures are extensive, we believe that they are necessary to meaningfully impact the social impairment often associated with ADHD among adolescents. Even with these time-demanding procedures, ISG has successfully been implemented in these settings. Continued research and development on ISG and related ED adjuncts is sorely needed, as social impairment and ED are costly and problematic for teens with ADHD.

REFERENCES

Abikoff, H. (1991). Cognitive training in ADHD children: Less to it than meets the eye. *Journal of Learning Disabilities, 24*(4), 205–209.

Angold, A., Costello, E. J., Burns, B. J., Erkanli, A., & Farmer, E. M. (2000). Effectiveness of nonresidential specialty mental health services for children and adolescents in the "real world." *Journal of the American Academy of Child & Adolescent Psychiatry, 39*(2), 154–160.

Arnett, J. J. (1999). Adolescent storm and stress, reconsidered. *American Psychologist, 54*(5), 317–326.

Bagwell, C. L., Molina, B. S., Pelham, W. E., & Hoza, B. (2001). Attention-deficit hyperactivity disorder and problems in peer relations: Predictions from childhood to adolescence. *Journal of the American Academy of Child & Adolescent Psychiatry, 40*(11), 1285–1292.

Barkley, R. A. (2010). Deficient emotional self-regulation: A core component of attention-deficit/hyperactivity disorder. *Journal of ADHD and Related Disorders, 1*, 5–37.

Benthin, A., Slovic, P., Moran, P., Severson, H., Mertz, C. K., & Gerrard, M. (1995). Adolescent health-threatening and health-enhancing behaviors: A study of word association and imagery. *Journal of Adolescent Health, 17*(3), 143–152.

Bishop, S. R., Lau, M., Shapiro, S., Carlson, L., Anderson, N. D., Carmody, J., ... & Devins, G. (2004). Mindfulness: A proposed operational definition. *Clinical Psychology: Science and Practice, 11*(3), 230–241.

Bolt, N. (2011). Emotional lability. In S. Goldstein & J. A. Naglieri (Eds.), *Encyclopedia of child behavior and development* (p. 576). New York, NY: Springer.

Botvin, E. M., Botvin, G. J., Michela, J. L., Baker, E., & Filazzola, A. D. (1991). Adolescent smoking behavior and the recognition of cigarette advertisements. *Journal of Applied Social Psychology, 21*(11), 919–932.

Bowlby, J. (1969). *Attachment and loss: Vol. 1. Attachment.* New York: Basic Books.

Bowlby, J. (1973). *Attachment and loss: Vol. 2. Separation, anxiety and anger.* New York: Basic Books.

Brown, K. W., Ryan, R. M., & Creswell, J. D. (2007). Mindfulness: Theoretical foundations and evidence for its salutary effects. *Psychological Inquiry, 18*(4), 211–237.

Bunford, N., & Evans, S. W. (under review). Interpersonal Skills Group—Corrections modified for detained juvenile offenders with externalizing disorders: A controlled pilot clinical trial.

Bunford, N., Evans, S. W., Zoccola, P. M., Owens, J. S., Flory, K., & Spiel, C. F. (2016). Correspondence between Heart Rate Variability and Emotion Dysregulation in Children, Including Children with ADHD. *Journal of Abnormal Child Psychology,* doi:10.1007/s10802-016-0257-2

Bunford, N., Evans, S. W., Becker, S. P., & Langberg, J. M. (2015). Attention-deficit/hyperactivity disorder and social skills in youth: A moderated mediation model of emotion dysregulation and depression. *Journal of Abnormal Child Psychology, 43*(2), 283–296.

Bunford, N., Evans, S. W., & Langberg, J. M. (2014). Emotion dysregulation is associated with social impairment among young adolescents with ADHD. *Journal of Attention Disorders* Advance online publication. doi:10.1177/1087054714527793

Bunford, N., Evans, S. W., & Wymbs, F. (2015). ADHD and emotion dysregulation among children and adolescents. *Clinical Child and Family Psychology Review, 18,* 185–217.

Calkins, S. D., Gill, K. L., Johnson, M. C., & Smith, C. L. (1999). Emotional reactivity and emotional regulation strategies as predictors of social behavior with peers during toddlerhood. *Social Development, 8*(3), 310–334.

Cassone, A. R. (2015). Mindfulness training as an adjunct to evidence-based treatment for ADHD within families. *Journal of Attention Disorders, 19*(2), 145–157. doi:1087054713488438

Cauffman, E., & Steinberg, L. (1995) The cognitive and affective influences on adolescent decision-making. *Temple Law Review, 68,* 1763–1789.

Cicchetti, D. (1984). The emergence of developmental psychopathology. *Child Development, 55,* 1–7.

Cicchetti, D., Ganiban, J., & Barnett, D. (1991). Contributions from the study of high-risk populations to understanding the development of emotion regulation. In J. Garber & K. A. Dodge (Eds.), *The development of emotion regulation and dysregulation* (pp. 15–48). New York, NY: Cambridge University Press.

Cicchetti, D., & Rogosch, F. A. (2002). A developmental psychopathology perspective on adolescence. *Journal of Consulting and Clinical Psychology, 70*(1), 6–20.

Coie, J. D, & Krehbiel, G. (1984). Effects of academic tutoring on the social status of low-achieving, socially rejected children. *Child Development, 55,* 1465–1478.

Cole, P. M., Michel, M. K., & Teti, L. O. D. (1994). The development of emotion regulation and dysregulation: A clinical perspective. *Monographs of the Society for Research in Child Development, 59*(2–3), 73–102.

Coyne, J. C., & Downey, G. (1991). Social factors and psychopathology: Stress, social support, and coping processes. *Annual Review of Psychology, 42*(1), 401–425.

Dodge, K. A., Asher, S. R., & Parkhurst, J. T. (1989). Social life as a goal-coordination task. *Research on Motivation in Education, 3,* 107–135.

Eisenberg, N., Fabes, R. A., & Losoya, S. (1997). Emotional responding: Regulation, social correlates, and socialization. In P. Salovey & D. J. Sluyter (Eds.), *Emotional development and emotional intelligence: Educational implications* (pp. 129–163). New York, NY: Basic Books.

Erhardt, D., & Hinshaw, S. P. (1994). Initial sociometric impressions of attention-deficit hyperactivity disorder and comparison boys: Predictions from social behaviors and from nonbehavioral variables. *Journal of Consulting and Clinical Psychology, 62*(4), 833.

Evans, S. W., Langberg, J. M., Schultz, B. K., Vaughn, A., Altaye, M., Marshall, S. A. & Zoromski, A. K., (2016). Evaluation of a school-based treatment program for young adolescents with ADHD. *Journal of Consulting and Clinical Psychology, 84*, 15–30.

Evans, S. W., Owens, J. S., & Bunford, N. (2014). Evidence-based psychosocial treatments for children and adolescents with attention-deficit/hyperactivity disorder. *Journal of Clinical Child & Adolescent Psychology, 43*(4), 527–551.

Evans, S. W., Schultz, B. K., DeMars, C. E., & Davis, H. (2011). Effectiveness of the Challenging Horizons after-school program for young adolescents with ADHD. *Behavior Therapy, 42*, 462–474.

Evans, S. W., Serpell, Z. N., Schultz, B. K., & Pastor, D. A. (2007). Cumulative benefits of secondary school-based treatment of students with attention deficit hyperactivity disorder. *School Psychology Review, 36*(2), 256–273.

Faraone, S. V., & Buitelaar, J. (2010). Comparing the efficacy of stimulants for ADHD in children and adolescents using meta-analysis. *European Child & Adolescent Psychiatry, 19*(4), 353–364.

Feldman, S. S., & Elliott, G. R. (Eds.). (1990). *At the threshold: The developing adolescent.* Cambridge, MA: Harvard University Press.

Feldman, R. S., Philippot, P., & Custrini, R. J. (1992). Social competence and nonverbal behavior. In R. S. Feldman & B. Rime (Eds.), *Fundamentals of nonverbal behavior* (pp. 329–350). New York, NY: Cambridge University Press.

Friedman, S. R., Rapport, L. J., Lumley, M., Tzelepis, A., VanVoorhis, A., Stettner, L., & Kakaati, L. (2003). Aspects of social and emotional competence in adult attention-deficit/hyperactivity disorder. *Neuropsychology, 17*(1), 50–58.

Fruzzetti, A. E., Shenk, C., & Hoffman, P. D. (2005). Family interaction and the development of borderline personality disorder: A transactional model. *Development and Psychopathology, 17*(4), 1007–1030.

Furlong, M. J., & Smith, D. C. (1994). *Anger, Hostility, and Aggression: Assessment, Prevention, and Intervention Strategies for Youth.* Clinical Psychology Publishing Company, Inc., 4 Conant Square, Brandon, Vermont 05733.

Goldstein, T. R., Axelson, D. A., Birmaher, B., & Brent, D. A. (2007). Dialectical behavior therapy for adolescents with bipolar disorder: A 1-year open trial. *American Academy of Child and Adolescent Psychiatry, 46*, 820–830.

Greenberg, L. S., & Safran, J. D. (1989). Emotion in psychotherapy. *American Psychologist, 44*(1), 19–29.

Hinshaw, S. P. (2003). Impulsivity, emotion regulation, and developmental psychopathology: Specificity versus generality of linkages. *Annals of the New York Academy of Sciences, 1008*, 149–159.

Kats-Gold, I., Besser, A., & Priel, B. (2007). The role of simple emotion recognition skills among school aged boys at risk of ADHD. *Journal of Abnormal Child Psychology, 35*, 363–378.

Kern, L., Evans, S. W., Lewis, T. J., State, T. M., Weist, M. D., & Wills, H. P. (2015). CARS Comprehensive Intervention for Secondary Students With Emotional and Behavioral Problems: Conceptualization and Development. *Journal of Emotional and Behavioral Disorders*, DOI: 10.1177/1063426615578173

Kobak, R. R., Cole, H. E., Ferenz-Gillies, R., Fleming, W. S., & Gamble, W. (1993). Attachment and emotion regulation during mother-teen problem solving: A control theory analysis. *Child Development, 64*, 231–245.

Kopp, C. B. (1989). Regulation of distress and negative emotions: A developmental view. *Developmental Psychology, 25*(3), 343–354.

Kopp, C. B. (1992). Emotional distress and control in young children. *New Directions for Child and Adolescent Development, 1992*, 41–56.

Lorch, E. P., Eastham, D., Milich, R., Lemberger, R. P., Sanchez, R. P., & Welsh, R. (2004). Difficulties in comprehending causal relations among children with ADHD: The role of cognitive engagement. *Journal of Abnormal Psychology, 113*, 56–63.

Lorch, E. P., Milich, R., Astrin, C. C., & Berthiaume, K. S. (2006). Cognitive engagement and story comprehension in typically developing children and children with ADHD from preschool through elementary school. *Developmental Psychology, 42*(6), 1206–1219.

Maedgen, J. W., & Carlson, C. L. (2000). Social functioning and emotional regulation in the attention deficit hyperactivity disorder subtypes. *Journal of Clinical Child Psychology, 29*, 30–42.

Martin, C. A., Kelly, T. H., Brogli, B. R., Brenzel, A., Smith, W. J., & Omar, H. A. (2002). Sensation seeking, puberty and nicotine, alcohol and marijuana use in adolescence. *Journal of the American Academy of Child and Adolescent Psychiatry, 41*, 1495–1502.

Masten, A. S., & Coatsworth, J. D. (1998). The development of competence in favorable and unfavorable environments: Lessons from research on successful children. *American Psychologist, 53*(2), 205–220.

Melnick, S. M., & Hinshaw, S. P. (2000). Emotion regulation and parenting in AD/HD and comparison boys: Linkages with social behaviors and peer preference. *Journal of Abnormal Child Psychology, 28*, 73–86.

Neeman, J., Hubbard, J., & Masten, A. S. (1995). The changing importance of romantic relationship involvement to competence from late childhood to late adolescence. *Development and Psychopathology, 7*, 727–750.

Nelson-Gray, R., Keane, S., Hurst, R., Mitchell, J., Warburton, J., Chok, J., & Cobb, A. (2006). A modified DBT skills training for oppositional defiant adolescents: Promising preliminary findings. *Behavior Research and Therapy, 44*, 1811–1820.

Pelham, W. E., & Sams, S. E. (1992). Behavior modification. *Child and Adolescent Psychiatric Clinics of North America, 1*, 505–918.

Resnick, M. D., Bearman, P. S., Blum, R. W., Bauman, K. E., Harris, K. M., Jones, J., . . . Udry, J. R. (1997). Protecting adolescents from harm: Findings from the National Longitudinal Study on Adolescent Health. *JAMA, 278*(10), 823–832.

Sadler, J. M., Evans, S. W., Schultz, B. K., & Zoromski, A. Z. (2011). Potential mechanisms of action in the treatment of social impairment and disorganization in adolescents with ADHD. *School Mental Health, 3*, 156–168.

Saunders, B., & Chambers, S. M. (1996). A review of the literature on Attention-Deficit Hyperactivity Disorder children: Peer interactions and collaborative learning. *Psychology in the Schools, 33*(4), 333–340.

Serrano, V. J., Owens, J. S. & Hallowell, B. (2015). Where children with ADHD direct visual attention during emotion knowledge tasks: Relationships to accuracy, response time, and ADHD symptoms. *Journal of Attention Disorders*. Advance online publication. doi:10.1177/1087054715593632

Sibley, M. H., Evans, S. W., & Serpell, Z. N. (2010). Social cognition and interpersonal impairment in young adolescents with ADHD. *Journal of Psychopathology and Behavioral Assessment, 32*(2), 193–202.

Silk, J. S., Steinberg, L., & Morris, A. S. (2003). Adolescents' emotion regulation in daily life: Links to depressive symptoms and problem behavior. *Child Development, 74*, 1869–1880.

Singh, S. D., Ellis, C. R., Winton, A. S., Singh, N. N., Leung, J. P., & Oswald, D. P. (1998). Recognition of facial expressions of emotion by children with attention-deficit hyperactivity disorder. *Behavior Modification, 22*(2), 128–142.

Skowron, E. A. (2000). The role of differentiation of self in marital adjustment. *Journal of Counseling Psychology, 47*, 229–237.

Skowron, E. A., & Friedlander, M. L. (1998). The differentiation of self inventory: Development and initial validation. *Journal of Counseling Psychology, 45*, 235–246.

Southam-Gerow, M. A., & Kendall, P. C. (2002). Emotion regulation and understanding: Implications for child psychopathology and therapy. *Clinical Psychology Review, 22*, 189–222.

Spear, L. P. (2000a). The adolescent brain and age-related behavioral manifestations. *Neuroscience & Biobehavioral Reviews, 24*(4), 417–463.

Spear, L. P. (2000b). Neurobehavioral changes in adolescence. *Current Directions in Psychological Science, 9*(4), 111–114.

Steinberg, L. (1987). The impact of puberty on family relations: Effects of pubertal status and pubertal timing. *Development and Psychopathology, 23*, 451–460.

Steinberg, L. (2004) Risk-taking in adolescence: What changes, and why? *Annals of the New York Academy of Sciences, 1021*, 51–58.

Steinberg, L. (2005). Cognitive and affective development in adolescence. *Trends in Cognitive Science, 9*, 69–74.

Thompson, R. A. (1994). Emotion regulation: A theme in search of definition. *Monographs of the Society for Research in Child Development, 59*(2–3), 25–52.

Tobler, N. (1986). Meta-analysis of 143 adolescent prevention programs: Quantitative outcome results of program participants compared to a control or comparison group. *Journal of Drug Issues, 16*, 537–567.

Udry, J. (1987). Hormonal and social determinants of adolescent sexual initiation. In J. Bancroft (Ed.), *Adolescence and puberty* (pp. 70–87). New York, NY: Oxford University Press.

Wasser, T., Tyler, R., McIlhaney, K., Taplin, R., & Henderson, L. (2008). Effectiveness of dialectical behavior therapy (DBT) versus standard therapeutic milieu (STM) in a cohort of adolescents receiving residential treatment. *Best Practices in Mental Health, 4*(2), 114–126.

Zeman, J., Cassano, M., Perry-Parrish, C., & Sheri, S. (2006). Emotion regulation in children and adolescents. *Journal of Developmental and Behavioral Pediatrics, 27*, 155–168.

9

Working with Adolescents with Autism Spectrum Disorder

LYNN KERN KOEGEL, SUNNY KIM, AND ROBERT L. KOEGEL ■

This chapter discusses issues related to the identification and treatment of autism spectrum disorders. Changes in the diagnostic criteria are described in relation to the effects these may have on school personnel who develop intervention plans for students with autism. We also discuss evidence-based treatments as well as prevention strategies that are effective in improving core and secondary characteristics of adolescents with autism spectrum disorders in school settings. Finally, a variety of general issues related to service delivery are presented.

ISSUES RELATED TO IDENTIFICATION AND REFERRAL FOR TREATMENT IN SCHOOLS

There are several important issues relating to identification and treatment of adolescents with pervasive developmental disorder in schools. In regard to the history of autism, Leo Kanner first described 11 children in a 1943 paper titled "Autistic Disturbances of Affective Contact" whose characteristics were markedly distinct; all were described as having social, communicative, and behavior issues. These three categories remained relatively stable as diagnostic criteria until May 2013, when the diagnostic criteria for autism spectrum disorder (ASD) were changed, which may affect the diagnosis, referral, and treatment process. In this section we will discuss the history and changes in the diagnostic criteria, implications for practitioners, and assessment issues in relation to identification and referral.

To provide a little background, the *DSM-III* (released in 1980) was the first to describe the general category of Pervasive Developmental Disorders (PDD), which included Childhood Onset PDD, Infantile Autism, and Atypical Autism (prior to 1980, children exhibiting these characteristics were diagnosed with schizophrenia) (*DSM-I*, 1952; *DSM-II*, 1968). In 1987 the *DSM-III* was revised to include only Pervasive Developmental Disorders-Not Otherwise Specified (PDD-NOS) and Autistic Disorder and was published as the *DSM-III-R*. Then, in 1994, additional categories were added to the *DSM-IV*, including Asperger's Disorder, Childhood Disintegrative Disorder, Rett Syndrome, and PDD-NOS, such that PDD included five different diagnostic categories. Aligned with Kanner's (1943) description, the diagnosis of autism required that an individual exhibit behaviors in three distinct areas: (1) impairment in social interaction; (2) impairments in communication; and (3) restricted repetitive and stereotyped patterns of behavior, interests, and activities. These three categories remained stable for many decades until May of 2013, when the *DSM-5* combined the social and communication category. Along with that change, Autism Spectrum Disorder (ASD) was included as a single diagnosis, and Asperger's Disorder (also referred to as Asperger's Syndrome or AS), Childhood Disintegrative Disorder, Rett Syndrome, and PDD-NOS were eliminated. Another change in the *DSM-5* is that, for diagnostic purposes, children are assigned "levels," or scores, in regard to severity in each of the two categories (social communication and restricted repetitive behaviors). The severity ratings range from "Requiring Support" (Level 1) to "Requiring Very Substantial Support" (Level 3). Further, a new category, "Social (Pragmatic) Communication Disorder" (SCD), was added, which resembles some of the more mild forms of what was previously classified under ASD, such as PDD-NOS or AS. Individuals with average or above average vocabulary, structural language development, and intellectual functioning, but with deficits in the social use of language who do not exhibit restricted and repetitive behaviors, fall into this new category.

There are several issues that are important for school practitioners in regard to these changes. First, if a student received an ASD diagnosis prior to the 2013 change, practitioners and diagnosticians are not required to change the ASD diagnosis or rediagnose the students, despite the fact that many categories of ASD (and diagnostic labels) no longer exist. Therefore, two individuals demonstrating the exact same characteristics may have different diagnoses depending on the year in which they were diagnosed. This does not necessarily change the need for intervention, but it may change the level of support that is provided, as autism spectrum disorder is considered a severe disability, while language disorders often are not. Thus, many feel that the changes in the *DSM* will negatively affect the ability of some individuals, particularly those with fewer support needs, to obtain important intervention services (McPartland, Reichow, & Volkmar, 2012). In addition, research studies that have previously used diagnostic labels that no longer exist may make the applicability of described interventions more difficult to determine. But what does this mean for adolescents in the schools?

While most individuals with ASD will have received a diagnosis and have individualized educational programs (IEPs) in place well before their adolescent years, milder forms of ASD (such as AS) are often not diagnosed until late childhood or early adolescence (Matson & Nebel-Schwalm, 2007). These students also need an assessment and specialized programs for social difficulties. In regard to prognosis for those with ASD, the literature has been consistent over many years, suggesting that higher tested intelligence quotients along with better language and social communication skills in childhood are correlated with improved outcomes in adolescence and adulthood (Koegel, Koegel, Shoshan, & McNerney, 1999; Nordin & Gillberg, 1998). However, children with the more mild forms of the disability may no longer qualify for an ASD diagnosis, and despite their potential for good outcomes, they may not receive needed social interventions and comprehensive programs. Consequently, they may develop more serious symptoms as well as comorbid disabilities.

Comorbid disorders may develop before or during adolescence, and the presence of at least one comorbid psychiatric disorder may be present in as many as 80% of individuals on the autism spectrum (de Bruin, Ferdinand, Meester, de Nijs, & Verheil, 2007). In addition, some may also develop aggression or self-injury (Smith & Matson, 2010), anxiety (Wood et al., 2008; Wood & Gadow, 2010), depression (Lainhart 1999; Stewart, Barnard, Pearson, Hasan, & O'Brien, 2006), attention-deficit/hyperactivity disorder (ADHD; Simonoff et al., 2008), eating disorders (Huke, Turk, Saeidi, Kent, & Morgan, 2013; Rastam, 2008), phobias (Leyfer, et al., 2006), and/or obsessive com-pulsive disorder (OCD; Lainhart, 1999). Depression and anxiety may be difficult to measure among this population, as the diagnosis depends to some extent on intact verbal and communication skills. Therefore, the incidence may be even higher than estimated using standardized measures, and because instrumentation differs there is a range in reported comorbidity (Leyfer et al., 2006). For example, depression can range from 17% to 84% depending on the study. The presence of these comorbid dis-orders should not be taken lightly, as some research indicates that these may put the person at risk for suicide, greater levels of withdrawal, noncompliance, and aggres-sion (Matson & Nebel-Schwalm, 2007). In addition, these comorbidities can increase already high levels of family stress and conflict, which may present even more chaos and discomfort in the adolescent with ASD's life. Overall well-being- such as aca-demic achievement, psychological health, community involvement, and employ-ment, are likely to be affected if an individual (such as an adolescent with AS) does not receive services (Koegel, Ashbaugh, Koegel, Detar, & Register, 2013).

In addition to mental health, other physical health problems more common in individuals with ASD include seizures (Ballaban-Gil & Tuchman, 2000), and early or late (more frequently) onset of puberty is reported for over 20% of chil-dren with ASD. This population also has an increased likelihood of accidents that lead to an early death in 4% to 7%. It is reported that about 17% of individuals with ASD have a clear setback during adolescence, with close to half of those chil-dren never fully recovering (Billstedt, Gillberg, & Gillberg, 2005). How can school practitioners address these issues?

Assessment

In terms of assessing the needs of these individuals, while standardized measures are available, they often do not reflect an individual's behaviors in the school set-ting. Behavioral assessments can be systematically implemented so that certain areas, such as social isolation, can be quantified. Also, specific counts of the type of verbal interactions that are occurring between the adolescent with ASD and his or her typical peers can be analyzed through language samples. Comparing the type and number of responses during social interactions with typically developing peers provides an indication of how the adolescent is performing relative to typically developing students, and also provides suggestions for intervention. Pragmatic areas, including inappropriate body language, difficulties with intonation, poor social reciprocity, difficulties expressing empathy, and so on, which are often a problem, can also be analyzed and targeted.

Another important area to assess relates to bullying and victimization. While many typically developing adolescents report some bullying experiences (Salmivalli & Peets, 2009), these experiences are four times more likely to occur among students with ASD (Humphrey & Symes, 2010; Little, 2002; Roekel, Scholte, & Didden, 2010; Symes & Humphrey, 2010). Especially troubling is that more than half are considered victimized (repeated bullying) by their peers, particularly with students who exhibit social and communicative difficulties (Cappadocia, Weiss, & Pepler, 2012; Carter, O'Rourke, Sisco, & Pelsue, 2009). Students who are bullied are more likely to exhibit mental health problems, including poor social and emotional development, depression, and anxiety (Grills & Ollendick, 2003; White & Schry, 2011). For this reason, it is critical that school interventions focus on improving socialization, peer acceptance, and incorporation of typically developing peers in the process, and if students have been bullied, some interventions to address this may be necessary. Unfortunately, special education staff members are often overworked (Giangreco, 2003; Giangreco & Broer, 2005) and may neglect students who are socially isolated but do not exhibit any disruptive behaviors (which are often addressed immediately). Similarly, general education teachers are also often unaware of the lack of social skills students with ASD exhibit during nonacademic periods (e.g., lunchtime), as they are not with their students at these times. Attention to social issues and proper assessment may greatly improve the outcome of a student with ASD.

Evidence-Based Practices

Training and education of teachers and paraprofessionals. Along with assessment, identification, and referral, evidence-based treatments (EBTs) become relevant. That is, ASD is the fastest-growing disability category, but most general and special education teachers face challenges to which they are unaccustomed while educating these students. Research shows that the level of preparation and training that general education teachers receive for implementing EBTs for students with ASD is greatly lacking (Dybvik, 2004). Specifically, less than 5% of special education teachers and only about 4% of general education teachers are trained to implement appropriate EBTs for students with ASD (Loiacono & Valenti, 2010).In addition, more than 50% of teachers use ineffective treatments with these students (Hess, Morrier, Heflin, & Ivey, 2008). The National Research

Council (2001) reports that most educators complete their graduate programs receiving minimal training in EBTs for teaching students diagnosed with ASD. These studies indicate that there is a clear problem with the currently accepted training models for special education teachers, and that graduate-level courses and in-services at the school sites need to emphasize the importance of using EBTs, such as behavioral treatment methodologies (Loiacono & Valenti, 2010; Dybvik, 2004). In addition, there is a need for special and general education teachers to collaborate and work as partners in order to provide a meaningful inclusive education for students with ASD.

Schools' increased use of and reliance upon paraprofessionals adds another complex dimension. Special education teachers report that they spend an average of only 34% of their time instructing their students, while paraprofessionals report that they spend an average of 50% of their time instructing students (Morrier, Hess, & Helfin, 2011). In fact, paraprofessionals express concerns about being the primary instructor for students with disabilities, and this large responsibility often leaves paraprofessionals feeling a lack of appreciation and respect from educators and administrators, a desire for more training and clearer job descriptions, and a desire for quality supervision (Patterson, 2006; Riggs & Mueller, 2001). The reason for this shift in teaching responsibility is unknown, but some suggest that special education teachers are getting increasingly larger caseloads, which results in less time to provide specialized instruction for students with disabilities (French, 2001; Giangreco, Doyle, Halvorsen, & Broer, 2004; Suter & Giangreco, 2009). Furthermore, although there is a heavy reliance on paraprofessionals, special and general education teachers do not necessarily receive training on how to train and supervise them (French, 2001; French & Pickett, 1997; Scheuermann, Webber, Boutot, & Goodwin, 2003). Currently, the most common training method for paraprofessionals is required attendance at either half- or full-day workshops, followed by hands-on training and self-taught methods (Morrier, Hess, & Helfin, 2011), but these methods are infrequent, inadequate, and unsystematic. In reality, paraprofessionals are often left to make key educational decisions on their own (Downing, Ryndak, & Clark, 2000), and most report that they have to teach themselves how to work with their assigned students by reading, observing others, and recalling past experiences. Additionally, paraprofessionals receive little to no guidance on appropriately intervening when students exhibit inappropriate behaviors (Downing et al., 2000).

Most paraprofessionals are not properly trained in systematic prompt fading relevant to student proximity, and they therefore are unable to teach the student and then systemically fade their presence. Thus, they tend to either not engage with the child or to "hover." Interestingly, when asked, paraprofessionals generally do not view hovering, or being in too close proximity, to their assigned student as a concern (Giangreco & Broer, 2005), and they view their assigned students as "a friend." It is not surprising, therefore, that research shows that this close proximity negatively impacts the students' social interactions with typical peers (Malmgren & Cauriston-Theoharis, 2006). Elucidating this unhealthy relationship is the fact that many students view having a paraprofessional as necessary for inclusion and socialization despite the fact that having a paraprofessional actually tends to compromise their social relationships with typically developing peers (Tews & Lupart, 2008). Furthermore, when paraprofessionals provide one-on-one support, the teacher-student relationship diminishes (Giangreco, Broer, & Edelman, 2001). In contrast, when the paraprofessionals' service delivery model is program-based, with paraprofessionals assisting the teacher and having a collaborative role, the student-teacher relationship is not negatively affected. Thus, when paraprofessionals' primary roles in the classroom are less instructional in nature and involve providing assistance to the teacher in such ways as making modifications to the student's work or making sure the student is on task, the teacher-student relationship is not hindered (Robertson, Chamberlain, & Kasari, 2003).

Overall, this lack of training will affect the education of students with ASD. Once special and general education teachers are properly trained in EBPs, they may coordinate with and train paraprofessionals. It is important, therefore, for educators, researchers, and policymakers to work collaboratively in order to change the current standards in this regard. General and special education teachers and school staff should benefit from in-services on autism and behavior management, as well as learning to implement "practice with feedback" to assure that fidelity of implementation of EBPs is being met (Koegel & Koegel, 2013).

In the next sections, we will discuss intervention and prevention EBPs that have been successful with students with ASD.

Interventions

Self-management. Self-management is an ideal intervention to use with adolescents in school settings, as the procedures are designed to decrease the need for constant vigilance by a teacher, paraprofessional, or special education staff member. Self-management is accomplished by having the individual with ASD independently engage in, evaluate, monitor, and self-reward (when possible) the occurrence or absence of his or her own target behavior. It can be implemented using event recording or an interval system. The general self-management steps involve defining and measuring a target behavior and then teaching the individual to identify and record the occurrence or absence of that behavior. It is important that the intervals or number of responses are developed from the baseline data and are small enough so that the individual experiences success and receives frequent rewards initially for engaging in the desired behaviors. Eventually, the intervals or number of responses required for a reward can be gradually and systematically increased, so that fading is programmed into the intervention, which creates independence. Self-management can be used for a wide variety of behaviors. For example, adolescents have learned to improve their responsiveness to social conversation using self-management (Koegel, Koegel, Hurley, & Frea, 1992). The students, who only responded about half the time, were given small wrist counters that resembled a watch and taught to give themselves a point (by pressing the wrist counter) every time they immediately responded to a conversational partner's question. All students improved their responsiveness, and the self-management was programmed to occur in natural community settings, where improvements were also noted in the absence of an interventionist. Other important pragmatic behaviors, such as eye contact, appropriate motor behavior, voice volume, topic maintenance, and so on, have been improved through self-management using time intervals, which can gradually and systematically be increased (Koegel & Frea, 1993). Interestingly, researchers have found that pragmatic behaviors tend to function as a response class, so that when one or a small number of behaviors is targeted, generalization to untreated pragmatic areas occurs (Koegel & Frea, 1993). Thus, self-management may be a particularly effective intervention when addressing multiple social and pragmatic areas in adolescents with ASD.

Video modeling. Many studies have shown that students can effectively respond to video modeling in school settings for a variety of different behaviors (Hitchcock, Dowrick, & Prater, 2003), but few have focused on using the procedure with individuals with ASD, particularly adolescents. While the studies that exist suggest that video modeling may be effective with individuals with ASD (de Bruin, Deppeler, Moore, & Diamond, 2013), it appears as though the individual must be able to attend to a model in order to engage in the observational learning required in the procedure. Also, the individual's willingness to engage in role-play of the target behavior is helpful (Bellini & Akkullian, 2007). It has been noted that those individuals with ASD who prefer watching videos over engaging in human interaction are likely to respond more favorably to video modeling than in vivo intervention (Charlop-Christy, Le, & Freeman, 2000).

Video modeling can be implemented in a different ways, such as videotaping the adolescent and having him or her watch the clips while providing feedback (i.e., self as a model). Several good examples can be embedded in between "needs improvement" examples. After watching and discussing the video clips, the student can practice the appropriate behavior while videotaping for the next session. As such, the adolescent has an opportunity to view both positive examples and examples of the absence or excess of the target behavior. Other studies have clipped together examples of the individual's successful use of the target behavior prior to viewing the clips. Finally, some interventions videotape another person engaging in the desired behavior, have the student watch these examples, and then have the student practice the behavior. While there is still research that needs to be conducted to better understand the procedure, the general consensus is that the more similar the model is to the target individual (in terms of physical characteristics, age, group affiliation, and ethnicity, as well as perceived competence of the individual), the more likely the individual will attend to the model (Bellini & Akkullian, 2007). Effective self-modeling programs have been demonstrated in school settings with adolescents using a number of different target behaviors, including functional skills and social communication (Haring, Kennedy, Adams, & Pitts-Conway, 1987), conversational skills (Charlop & Milstein, 1989), academics (Delano, 2007), and social conversation (Detar, 2013). While additional research is needed, video modeling appears to be a promising intervention for adolescents.

Functional behavior assessment. In regard to problem behaviors, analyzing the setting events, antecedent stimuli, consequences, and environmental factors that may contribute to problem behaviors helps us to make environmental manipulations that reduce disruptive behaviors and/or teach replacement behaviors that serve the same function as the disruptive behavior. Setting events (also called establishing operations) are events that occur prior to the teacher's instruction, social demand, or other event. Setting events alter the value of the consequence, so that the adolescent responds differently than usual. For example if an adolescent has premenstrual symptoms, feels ill, is tired, or is hungry, she may exhibit disruptive behavior when people attempt to interact with her in ways that previously were positive. If school staff are unaware of the setting event, the behavior may be viewed by as erratic or unpredictable. Understanding these situations helps to develop plans wherein the environment is manipulated to take the context (setting events) into consideration in order to avoid such situations in the future.

In cases where disruptive behavior is serving the common function of avoidance, escape, or attention (Wacker, et. al, 1990), replacement behaviors that serve the same communicative function can be taught (Durand & Crimmins, 1988). For example, if an adolescent engages in disruptive behavior every time the teacher asks him to engage in challenging academics, he could be taught to raise his hand and ask for "help" as a replacement behavior. Similarly, if a student is engaging in disruptive behaviors to gain social attention, teaching her how to engage in successful and appropriate social interactions will reduce the disruptive behavior. Importantly, when replacement behaviors are being taught, the disruptive behaviors need to be ignored so that they become inefficient and ineffective. A partial reinforcement schedule, when adults or peers inadvertently reward the problem behavior on some occasions, may function to maintain and strengthen the disruptive behaviors; therefore consistency in implementing the intervention is important. Also, when extinguishing a problem behavior, it is important that all those involved are aware of a possible extinction burst, so that a temporary rise in the problem behavior is not viewed as an ineffective intervention. Finally, it is important to teach the replacement behaviors at times when the disruptive behavior is not occurring. That is, teaching and practicing the replacement behavior when the individual is calm, and then subsequently prompting it in contexts where disruptive behavior occurs is recommended to minimize disruptive behavior. Once the individual has learned the functionally equivalent replacement behavior, durable decreases in disruptive behaviors are likely.

Cognitive behavioral therapy (CBT). As mentioned previously, the frequent development or occurrence of comorbid disorders in adolescents with ASD has been increasingly discussed in the literature (Simonoff et al., 2008), and studies suggest that among verbal adolescents with autism, anxiety and depression are at high levels and are often a direct result of their social communication challenges (Koegel & LaZebnik, 2009). CBT, which is generally implemented by the school psychologist, can be helpful with comorbidity, but is generally more effective if the student has intact language skills, as most programs require dialog between the student and interventionist. As described by Fujii et al. (2013), when implementing a CBT program, the student generally provides detailed descriptions of when problems do and do not occur. For example, a hierarchy of feared situations may be described from the least to the most distressing. Students systematically work their way up through the hierarchy for gradual and systematic exposure to increasingly feared situations. This type of hierarchical exposure is generally combined with skill training, such as social conversation. In addition, the students are often taught to "rethink" the situation. For example, the interventionist may say to the student who does not socially interact, "If you offer to share your snacks with your friends, how might they feel about you?" Helping the student to rethink the situation can reduce self-imposed anxieties by creating an awareness of another person's point of view, which is often challenging for individuals with ASD. For example, when entering a social situation, replacing thoughts such as "What if no one likes me?" with "People will enjoy being around me if I give them compliments and ask questions," can lead to prosocial behavior and reduce anxiety. Often school CBT programs partner with parents (and teachers) to practice specific target areas and monitor progress across settings. Learning to change negative thoughts to positive thoughts, coupled with other programs, can reduce fears, anxieties, repetitive behaviors, and depression that result from difficulties with socialization. While more studies are important to determine the relative strength of various components used in CBT programs, there are some promising results suggesting that this may be a helpful intervention for adolescents with ASD in the schools.

Prevention

While the implementation of many programs is necessary when areas need to be addressed after they have already become problems, antecedent interventions that prevent problem behaviors are preferable. Below we discuss several such interventions.

Social groups/clubs. Students with ASD often spend their lunch and other free periods alone (Locke, Ishijima, Kasari, & London, 2010). Some of these students exhibit restricted interests that have developed into a large amount of accumulated information about a particular topic (Klin, Danovitch, Merz, & Volkmar, 2007), and they spend virtually all their free time engaged in related activities. In the past, it appeared as if there were a dilemma between choosing to let these students remain isolated and involved in the restricted interest, or to not allow the restricted interest behaviors to occur, and then have problem behaviors when they are removed or redirected from this very reinforcing activity. However, recent research has shown that using these restricted interests as the theme of social clubs results in improved verbal and social interactions among adolescents (Koegel, Fredeen, Koegel, & Lin, 2011; Koegel, Kim, Schwartzman, & Koegel, 2013), without the occurrence of problem behaviors. Specifically, the highly focused interest of the adolescent with autism is assessed through student, teacher, and/or parent interviews, and activities are then developed that incorporate the particular interest into a group activity that is engaging for both the student with ASD and typically developing peers. The data show that these clubs can provide a context for adolescents with ASD to feel socially confident and come to be viewed as a valued club member because of their expertise on the club theme (Koegel et al., 2011; Koegel et al., 2013). In addition, these interactions can provide a common ground upon which friendships can be formed with typically developing peers who share related interests (Feld, 1982; Cohen, 1977). Furthermore, their peers have a context for positive interactions with the adolescent with ASD, which, in this context, helps prevent bullying and teasing. Research also shows that if a similar club exists on the middle or high school campus, these gains are maintained, even after the specialized intervention has concluded (Koegel et al., 2013). Again, these clubs have the potential to benefit all of the students while improving peer socialization and mental health.

Priming. Priming, or previewing activities before they occur in daily life, has been shown to reduce behavior problems and improve academic and social behavior. For example, exposing adolescents to academic material at home the evening before it is presented in class reduces disruptive behavior and improves academic responding (Koegel, Koegel, Frea, & Green-Hopkins, 2003). In addition, priming for social activities has been very effective in improving peer interaction during recess in elementary school students (Gengoux, 2009) and should also be helpful for adolescents. This can be accomplished with priming of greetings, question asking, and enjoyable games and activities. Theoretically, priming these activities in a pleasant context before they are likely to arise in natural settings will decrease avoidance and escape-motivated behavior, thereby improving engagement with peers. While information relating to the specific way in which the priming is presented has not been well researched, the general procedure recommends that the materials or activities be presented with a calm and nondemanding demeanor. This may result in not only producing some degree of competency in the activity, but also in reducing any negative aspect to the activity so that it is not likely to be avoided. Priming can be implemented by school staff (speech-language pathologist, teacher, resource specialist, psychologist, paraprofessional, etc.) during after school programs, or in the evening by the parents.

Peer-mediated interventions. The use of peers to assist in the intervention process is efficient and provides increased social interactions between students with disabilities and their typical peers. Harper, Simon, and Frea (2008) investigated the effectiveness of training peers to implement motivational components of Pivotal Response Treatment (PRT) during recess in order to improve social play during indoor (e.g., beanbag toss, ring toss) and outdoor (e.g., jump rope, basketball, swings) sport activities. The authors found that the peers were able to implement motivational components of PRT with high fidelity when working with students with ASD, and consequently the students were able to improve their respective social goals. Kasari, Rotheram-Fuller, Locke, and Gulsrud (2012) compared two different intervention approaches: peer-mediated intervention, in which peers led social activities, and another approach in which adults instructed students with ASD on how to socially interact with peers. The authors found that the peer-mediated approach led to a greater improvement in the student with ASD's social network salience, number of friendship nominations, teacher report of social skills in the classroom, and decreased isolation during outdoor periods as compared to the student-assisted approach. Similarly, Shukla, Kennedy, and Cushing (1999) investigated the effectiveness of using peer-mediated intervention approaches in order to improve social interactions for students with severe disabilities in junior high school. Similar to Harper et al. (2008) and Kasari et al. (2012), these authors found that peers were able to provide appropriate social support, which resulted in more frequent and longer social interactions between students with severe disabilities and typically developing peers. While many of the peer intervention studies have been implemented with younger students, several studies have shown that peers can be a great support system and can readily and easily learn procedures to assist with adolescents with ASD (Haring & Breen, 1992). These studies suggest that properly trained peers can be a viable alternative resource to paraprofessionals for helping students with ASD. Additional research in using typically developing peers as adjuncts in the habilitation process will undoubtedly be areas of future exploration.

Service Delivery Issues

Proper training and data collection are critical, as interventions that are not implemented correctly are at minimum ineffective, and may even worsen behavior issues. Furthermore, without systematic and frequent data collection, programs cannot be adjusted accordingly. As mentioned above, paraprofessionals often spend the most time with students with ASD, and there has been some positive movement toward the development of appropriate training for effectively utilizing paraprofessionals in schools. Paraprofessionals can learn to implement EBTs, and monitoring of students' skills, as well as their responsiveness to the intervention, is critical. For example, Quilty (2007) showed that after a short training, paraprofessionals were able to effectively write and implement Social Stories with preadolescents, which resulted in a decrease in the students' disruptive behavior. Other studies have shown that paraprofessionals can be effectively trained to provide and facilitate appropriate social interactions between students with disabilities and their typically developing peers (Causton-Theoharis & Malmgren, 2005; Licciardello, Harchik, & Luiselli, 2008; Mazurik-Charles & Stefanou, 2010; Storey, Smith, & Strain, 1993). Other researchers have trained paraprofessionals to implement a combination of behavioral interventions such as Pivotal Response Treatment (PRT), Discrete Trial Teaching (DTT), and Picture Exchange Communication System (PECS) (Hall, Grundon, Pope, & Romero, 2010). Training consisted of attending a workshop and subsequent ongoing performance feedback from a supervising teacher or specialist to effectively implement targeted goals. Bolton and Mayer (2008) taught paraprofessionals to use a behavior intervention approach, which consisted of a didactic instructional model, demonstration, general case instruction, and practice with feedback. The authors found that, after the training, the paraprofessionals were able to accurately implement behavioral procedures and could generalize their newly acquired skills across settings.

Robinson (2011) used a different approach when training paraprofessionals to implement the motivational procedures of PRT (e.g., child choice, shared control, clear opportunities, and natural/contingent reinforcement) to improve social interaction between students with ASD and typically developing peers. While previous paraprofessional training studies had taught these school personnel via live feedback, this study trained the paraprofessionals via video feedback. That is, paraprofessionals videotaped themselves and later met with a specialist to discuss their implementation of the procedures. As a result, the paraprofessionals' implementation of PRT increased while their hovering and/or lack of involvement with their assigned student decreased. In addition, the students all made positive gains on their individualized target goals and demonstrated either maintained or improved affect. The study found large and rapid improvement in paraprofessionals' performance, and the author noted that this fast learning curve might be a result of the off-site feedback provided to the professionals while they were working with students in their natural environment (which were videotaped). As technology becomes more readily available, exploring the use of training paraprofessionals via video feedback is highly warranted, as it is both time- and cost-efficient, as opposed to having a specialist provide in vivo feedback, which can be very time-consuming. The use of video technology will likely receive attention in future research.

Although these studies have successfully demonstrated that paraprofessionals can be trained to implement the various intervention strategies with high fidelity of implementation, there is still a need for the development of a more unified comprehensive training model (Blalock, 1991; Causton-Theoharis, Giangreco, Doyle, & Vadasy, 2007; Giangreco & Doyle, 2002). Some have suggested four interrelated best-practice categories when working with paraprofessionals (Causton-Theoharis et al., 2007). The first category relates to welcoming and acknowledging paraprofessionals, such as introducing the paraprofessional as part of the teaching team. The second relates to orienting the paraprofessionals to the school by giving them a tour and reviewing the school policies and expectations. The third category relates to planning for paraprofessionals' weekly schedules, and the last category involves regular and ongoing communication with paraprofessionals. In this last category, the authors recommend clarifying the paraprofessionals' roles and responsibilities and developing a standard communication method. Other recommendations include using paraprofessionals for supplemental support, training paraprofessionals explicitly and extensively in behavior management, and providing ongoing feedback. Blalock (1991) emphasized the importance of clearly outlining the paraprofessionals' roles and responsibilities, meeting on a regular basis, and acknowledging paraprofessionals' contributions to the students' progress. A comprehensive model involving all of these areas is likely to decrease the common problem of attrition and burnout by making the paraprofessional feel welcome and part of a team, as well as improving the training, monitoring, and feedback provided to the paraprofessional.

In addition to the influx of students with disabilities into the public school system, schools are becoming more ethnically and linguistically diverse (Aud et al., 2012; Ford, 2012), and researchers have begun investigating the effectiveness of traditional intervention approaches with multicultural students with ASD (Wilder, Dyches, Okiakor, & Algozzine, 2004). To make the educational experience more meaningful for students with disabilities from diverse cultural backgrounds, it is helpful to understand key aspects of ecocultural theory. From an ecocultural perspective, culture plays a pivotal role in a student's development (Weisner, 2002). Ecocultural theory states that it is important to take the family's perspective into account when developing goals and agendas (Bernheimer, Gallimore, & Weisner, 1990; Gallimore, Weisner, Kaufman, & Bernheimer, 1989). According to Bernheimer et al. (1990), there are several key components involved. First, ecocultural theory requires understanding the student's disability as it is perceived by the student's family (in terms of the family's values, goals, and needs). Second, an important unit of analysis in ecocultural theory is the family's daily routines, as these routines mediate the ecocultural effects of interactions with other pertinent individuals. Another aspect of ecocultural theory is the applicability to families of all cultures. Ecocultural theory also posits that a student's outcomes should be meaningful as they relate to the family's values and beliefs, congruent to the student's characteristics, and sustainable across conditions. Because students with ASD respond best when a consistent and comprehensive intervention is implemented across settings, a necessary part of the intervention is the inclusion of families. To do this, careful consideration of the cultural values and practices in everyday life is critical. In regard to cultural considerations at the school site, researchers have recently begun to investigate how key components of ecocultural theory are being incorporated in practice by paraprofessionals in the school setting.

For example, Chopra, Sandoval-Lucero, Aragon, De Balderas, and Carroll (2004) assessed whether paraprofessionals served as connectors between the home and school environment. They conducted focus group interviews with 49 paraprofessionals who worked with a diverse population of students, including students with disabilities, and asked them about their relationships with students and their families, and about their roles in representing the community to the school and vice versa. The researchers found that, in general, paraprofessionals had closer relationships with families from diverse cultural and ethnic backgrounds than teachers did. They also noted that, in most cases, parents felt more comfortable communicating with paraprofessionals, because they were more available than teachers, often spoke the same foreign language, and occasionally even lived in the same neighborhood. In some cases, paraprofessionals reported that parents relied on them for help outside of the school setting, such as to obtain information about the community and resources available to their child. The authors also found that when paraprofessionals share a similar cultural background with the students with whom they work, they are able to provide cultural and linguistic continuity for these students.

Similarly, Ernst-Slavit and Wenger (2006) investigated how paraprofessionals play a pivotal role in educating minority students and how these school personnel can help reveal the "funds of knowledge" of these students. The study found that when paraprofessionals share similar cultural and ethnic backgrounds with the minority students, they are better able to understand the educational difficulties that these students encounter. These may include problems such as dealing with racist comments, absences, or relevant multicultural literature that may be more motivating to minority students. The authors also suggest that when the paraprofessionals and the minority students share similar backgrounds, they are in a unique position to make the educational experience more meaningful and are perhaps more capable of incorporating culturally relevant pedagogy when working with these diverse students.

Although schools have historically tended to hire culturally diverse paraprofessionals in order to better serve minority students, schools do not utilize these paraprofessionals to gain access to students' cultural and community knowledge so that they can develop a culturally based education for these students (Ernst-Slavit & Wenger, 2006; Rueda & Monzo, 2002). While the majority of research on multiculturalism has focused on English language learners (ELLs), the National Research Council (2001) urges service providers of students with ASD to be culturally sensitive, and suggests a need for further research investigating culturally and ethnically diverse students with ASD. For example, in many Asian cultures it is common for students to avoid making eye contact with an adult and to silently respond to a teacher's question (Lian, 1996), and these areas are often targeted for intervention. This example emphasizes the importance of having school personnel consider cultural variables when classifying and developing IEP goals for ethnically and culturally diverse students with ASD. Similarly, Welterlin and LaRue (2007) published an article about the importance of incorporating key aspects of ecocultural theory when developing treatment plans for immigrant families of students with ASD. As the educational and treatment approaches used in America mainly reflect one ideology, educators and service providers who work with culturally and ethnically diverse students with ASD need to be open to different ideologies and beliefs about effective intervention approaches. Educators who share a similar ethnic and cultural background with diverse families may be ideal candidates for educating these families about accepted evidence-based interventions, since they are in a unique position to reference shared cultural values.

SERVICE DELIVERY MODELS FOR ASD

Adolescents with ASD need comprehensive intervention plans that include social, academic, and behavioral goals that are combined with their families' beliefs and values so that seamless, coordinated, and consistent interventions can be implemented. Thus, given the current state of knowledge, an ideal service delivery model would include, at minimum, the following components:

1. *Appropriate diagnosis.* The changing *DSM* criteria for ASD may mean that some adolescents who would greatly benefit from intervention no

longer qualify for services (McPartland, Reichow, & Volkmar, 2012). School personnel need to be especially vigilant in identifying adolescents that would benefit from social interventions. Such interventions are likely to decrease comorbid difficulties that could potentially result in serious long-term challenges. This requires assessment beyond the traditional in-office standardized testing, such as the use of behavioral observations in natural settings, sharing of information with parents and significant others, and consideration of how the adolescent interacts within the peer network.

2. *Training.* Ongoing training of regular and special education teachers, specialists, paraprofessionals, and others who interact with the student is critical (Koegel & LaZebnik, 2004, 2014). Studies repeatedly show that there is inadequate training both at the preservice and the school level. Once teachers and school specialists are properly trained to implement EBPs, they need to learn how to provide appropriate instruction to paraprofessionals. Without this training, it is unlikely that adolescents with ASD will receive suitable and effective interventions.

3. *Peer training and recruitment.* There is often a disconnect between adolescents with ASD and their typical peers. Consequently, high levels of bullying and victimization occur. Typical peers should be both trained in regard to symptoms of ASD and recruited to assist with interventions and serve as positive role models. When recruiting the typical peers, it is important to carefully select the peers to create more stable and salient relationships and higher friendship qualities (Locke, Rotheram-Fuller, & Kasari, 2012). Recruiting and systematically training typically developing peers can provide a cost-effective intervention and improve the skills and quality of life for the adolescent with ASD.

4. *Evidence-based interventions and data collection.* Tragically, effective interventions are not regularly implemented with adolescents with ASD in the schools (cf. Simpson, 2005). The research contains many effective and appropriate interventions for adolescents that can be used to reduce and prevent unwanted behaviors and encourage prosocial behaviors. Additionally, many effective interventions for younger students can be helpful with older students (cf. National Autism Center, 2009; National Research Council, 2001). Data collection at regular intervals is important to assess the adolescent's response to intervention and to make programmatic adjustments when necessary.

5. *Coordinated, consistent, and comprehensive programs.* There is no single intervention program that completely eliminates the core symptoms of ASD or disruptive behavior, so it is critical that adolescents receive a combination of programs implemented simultaneously. For maximal benefit, programs should be consistent across individuals with whom the adolescent interacts and across settings. Programs that are inconsistently or incorrectly implemented may result in an increase in unwanted behaviors (Koegel, Egel, & Williams, 1980). Careful and precise

implementation of interventions across all settings will yield the best outcomes.

6. *Cultural and individual considerations.* Considering the individual's specific learning style and cultural variables that may influence the implementation of goals, as well as the acceptability of goals and intervention programs, is important. Whenever possible, using staff with similar cultural backgrounds helps bridge that gap.

In conclusion, conflict is minimized when clear goals are developed with the family and appropriate and effective interventions are implemented to address those goals with competent school staff (Etscheidt, 2005). The literature is consistent in stating that proper training with empirically validated models and comprehensive programming will provide the greatest outcomes for adolescents with ASD.

REFERENCES

American Psychiatric Association (Ed.). (2000). Diagnostic and statistical manual of mental disorders: DSM-IV-TR®. Arlington, VA: Author

Aud, S., Hussar, W., Johnson, F., Kena, G., Roth, E., Manning, E., . . . Zhang, J. (2012). The condition of education 2012 (NCES 2012-045). Washington, DC: U.S. Department of Education, National Center for Education Statistics.

Ballaban-Gil, K., & Tuchman, R. (2000). Epilepsy and epileptiform EEG: Association with autism and language disorders. Mental Retardation and Developmental Disabilities Research Reviews, 6(4), 300–308.

Bellini, S., & Akullian, J. (2007). A meta-analysis of video modeling and video self-modeling interventions for children and adolescents with autism spectrum disorders. Exceptional Children, 73(3), 264–287.

Bernheimer, L.P., Gallimore, R., & Weisner, T.S. (1990). Ecocultural theory as a context for the individual family service plan. Journal of Early Intervention, 14(3), 219–233.

Billstedt, E., Gillberg, C., & Gillberg, C. (2005). Autism after adolescence: Population-based 13 to 22-year follow-up study of 120 individuals with autism diagnosed in childhood. Journal of Autism and Developmental Disorders, 35(3), 351–360.

Blalock, G. (1991). Paraprofessionals: Critical team members in our special education programs. Intervention in School and Clinic, 26(4), 200–214.

Bolton, J., & Mayer, M. D. (2008). Promoting the generalization of paraprofessional discrete trial teaching skills. Focus on Autism and Other Developmental Disabilities, 23(2), 103–111.

Cappadocia, M. C., Weiss, J. A., & Pepler, D. (2012). Bullying experiences among children and youth with autism spectrum disorders. Journal of Autism and Developmental Disorders, 42(2), 266–277.

Carter, W., O'Rourke, L., Sisco, L. G., & Pelsue, D. (2009). Knowledge, responsibilities, and training needs of paraprofessionals in elementary and secondary schools. Remedial and Special Education, 30(6), 344–359.

Causton-Theoharis, J. N., Giangreco, M. F., Doyle, M. B., & Vadasy, P. E. (2007). Paraprofessionals: The "sous-chefs" of literacy instruction." Teaching Exceptional Children, 40(1), 56–62.

Causton-Theoharis, J. N., & Malmgren, K. W. (2005). Increasing peer interactions for students with severe disabilities via paraprofessional training. Exceptional Children, 71(4), 431–444.

Charlop, M. H., & Milstein, J. P. (1989). Teaching autistic children conversational speech using video modeling. Journal of Applied Behavior Analysis, 22(3), 275–285.

Charlop-Christy, M. H., Le, L., & Freeman, K. A. (2000). A comparison of video modeling with in vivo modeling for teaching children with autism. Journal of Autism and Developmental Disorders, 30(6), 537–552.

Chopra, R. V., Sandoval-Lucero, E., Aragon, L., Bernal, C., De Balderas, H. B., & Carroll, D. (2004). The paraprofessional role as connector. Remedial and Special Education, 25(4), 219–231.

de Bruin, C. L., Deppeler, J. M., Moore, D. W., & Diamond, N. T. (2013). Public school-based interventions for adolescents and young adults with an autism spectrum disorder: A meta-analysis. Review of Educational Research, 83(4), 521–550.

de Bruin, E. I., Ferdinand, R. F., Meester, S., de Nijs, P. F., & Verheij, F. (2007). High rates of psychiatric co-morbidity in PDD-NOS. Journal of Autism and Developmental Disorders, 37(5), 877–886.

Detar, W. J. (2013). *Targeting question-asking initiations through video-feedback to improve social conversation in college students with autism spectrum disorders.* Santa Barbara: University of California, Santa Barbara.

Downing, J. E., Ryndak, D. L., & Clark, D. (2000). Paraeducators in inclusive classrooms: Their own perceptions. Remedial and Special Education, 21(3), 171–181.

Durand, V. M., & Crimmins, D. B. (1988). Identifying the variables maintaining self-injurious behavior. Journal of Autism and Developmental Disorders, 18(1), 99–117.

Dybvik, A. C. (2004). Autism and the inclusion mandate. Education Next, 4(1), 43–49.

Ernst-Slavit, G., & Wenger, K.J. (2006). Teaching in the margins. Anthropology and Education Quarterly, 37(1), 62–82.

Etscheidt, S. (2005). Paraprofessional services for students with disabilities: A legal analysis of issues. Research and Practice for Persons with Severe Disabilities, 30(2), 60–80.

Ford, D. Y. (2012). Culturally different students in special education: Looking backward to move forward. Exceptional Children, 78(4), 391–405.

French, N. K. (2001). Supervising paraprofessionals: A survey of teacher practices. Journal of Special Education, 35(1), 41–53.

French, N. K., & Pickett, A. L. (1997). Paraprofessionals in special education: Issues for teacher educators. *Teacher Education and Special Education: The Journal of the Teacher Education Division of the Council for Exceptional Children,* 20(1), 61–73.

Fujii, C., Renno, P., McLeod, B. D., Decker, K., Lin, C. E., Zielinski, K., & Wood, J. J. (2013). Intensive cognitive behavioral therapy for anxiety disorders in school-aged children with autism: A preliminary comparison with treatment-as-usual. *School Mental Health, 5,* 25–37.

Gallimore, R., Weisner, T. S., Kaufman, S. Z., & Bernheimer, L. P. (1989). The social construct of ecocultural niches: Family accommodation of developmentally delayed children. American Journal on Mental Retardation, 94(3), 216–230.

Giangreco, M. F. (2003). Working with paraprofessionals. Educational Leadership, 61(2), 50–53.

Giangreco, M. F., & Broer, S. M. (2005). Questionable utilization of paraprofessionals in inclusive schools: Are we addressing symptoms or causes? Focus on Autism and Other Developmental Disabilities, 20(1), 10–26.

Giangreco, M. F., Broer, S. M., & Edelman, S. W. (2001). Teacher engagement with students with disabilities: Differences based on paraprofessional service delivery models. Journal of the Association for Persons with Severe Handicaps, 26(2), 75–86.

Giangreco, M. F., & Doyle, M. B. (2002). Students with disabilities and paraprofessional supports: Benefits, balance, and band-aids. Focus on Exceptional Children, 34(7), 1–12.

Giangreco, M. F., Doyle, M. B., Halvorsen, A. T., & Broer, S. M. (2004). Alternatives to overreliance on paraprofessionals in inclusive schools. Journal of Special Education Leadership, 17(2), 82–90.

Grills, A. E., & Ollendick, T. H. (2003). Multiple informant agreement and the anxiety disorders interview schedule for parents and children. Journal of the American Academy of Child & Adolescent Psychiatry, 42(1), 30–40.

Hall L. J., Grundon, G. S., Pope, C., & Romero, A. B. (2010). Training paraprofessionals to use behavioral strategies when educating learners with autism spectrum disorders across environments. Behavioral Interventions, 25(1), 37–51.

Haring, T. G., & Breen, C. G. (1992). A peer-mediated social network intervention to enhance the social integration of persons with moderate and severe disabilities. Journal of Applied Behavior Analysis, 25(2), 319–333.

Haring, T. G., Kennedy, C. H., Adams, M. J., & Pitts-Conway, V. (1987). Teaching generalization of purchasing skills across community settings to autistic youth using videotape modeling. Journal of Applied Behavior Analysis, 20(1), 89–96.

Harper, C. B., Symon, J. B. G., & Frea, W. D. (2008). Recess is time-in: Using peers to improve social skills of children with autism. Journal of Autism and Developmental Disorders, 38(5), 815–826.

Hess, K. L., Morrier, M. J., Heflin, L. J. & Ivey, M. L. (2008). Autism treatment survey: Services received by children with autism spectrum disorders in public school classrooms. Journal of Autism Developmental Disorders, 38(5), 961–971.

Hitchcock, C. H., Dowrick, P. W., & Prater, M. A. (2003). Video self-modeling intervention in school-based settings: A review. Remedial and Special Education, 24(1), 36–45.

Huke, V., Turk, J., Saeidi, S., Kent, A., & Morgan, J. F. (2013). Autism spectrum disorders in eating disorder populations: A systematic review. European Eating Disorders Review, 21(5), 345–351.

Humphrey, N., & Symes, W. (2010). Perceptions of social support and experience of bullying among pupils with autistic spectrum disorders in mainstream secondary schools. European Journal of Special Needs Education, 25(1), 77–91.

Kanner, L. (1943). Autistic disturbances of affective contact. Nervous Child, 2(3), 217–250.

Kasari, C., Rotheram-Fuller, E., Locke, J., & Gulsrud, A. (2012). Making the connection: Randomized controlled trial of social skills at school for children with autism spectrum disorders. Journal of Child Psychology and Psychiatry, 53(4), 431–439.

Klin, A., Danovitch, J., Merz, A. B., & Volkmar, F. R. (2007). Circumscribed interests in higher functioning individuals with autism spectrum disorders: An exploratory study. Research and Practice for Persons with Severe Disabilities, 32(2) 89–100.

Koegel, L. K., Ashbaugh., K., Koegel, R. L., Detar, W. J., & Register, A. (2013). Increasing socialization in adults with Asperger's syndrome. Psychology in the Schools, 50(9), 899–909.

Koegel, L. K., Fredeen, R., Koegel, R. L. & Lin, E. (2011). Relationships, independence, and communication in autism and Asperger's disorder. In D. Amaral, D. Geshwind, & G. Dawson (Eds.), Autism spectrum disorders. Oxford, England: Oxford University Press.

Koegel, L. K., Koegel, R. L., Frea, W., & Green-Hopkins, I. (2003) Priming as a method of coordinating educational services for students with autism. Language, Speech, and Hearing Services in Schools, 34, 228–235.

Koegel, L. K., Koegel, R. L., Hurley, C., & Frea, W. D. (1992). Improving pragmatic skills and disruptive behavior in children with autism through self-management. Journal of Applied Behavior Analysis, 25(2), 341–353.

Koegel, L. K., Koegel, R. L. Shoshan, & McNerney, E. (1999). Pivotal response intervention II: Preliminary long-term outcome data. Journal of the Association for Persons with Severe Handicaps, 24(3), 186–198.

Koegel, L. K., & LaZebnik, C. (2004). Overcoming autism. New York, NY: Viking Penguin.

Koegel, L. K., & LaZebnik, C. (2009). Growing up on the spectrum: A guide to life, love, and learning for teens and young adults with autism and Asperger's. New York, NY: Viking Penguin.

Koegel, R. L., Egel, A., & Williams, J. (1980). Behavioral contrast and generalization across settings in the treatment of autistic children. Journal of Experimental Child Psychology, 30 (3), 422–437.

Koegel, R. L., & Frea, W. D. (1993). Treatment of social behavior in autism through the modification of pivotal social skills. Journal of Applied Behavior Analysis, 26(3), 369–377.

Koegel, R. L., and Koegel L. K. (2012). The PRT pocket guide: Pivotal Response Treatment for autism spectrum disorders. Baltimore, MD: Brookes.

Lainhart, J. (1999). Psychiatric problems in individuals with autism, their parents and siblings. International Review of Psychiatry, 11(4), 279–298.

Leyfer, O. T., Folstein, S. E., Bacalman, S., Davis, N. O., Dinh, E., Morgan, J., . . . Lainhart, J. E. (2006). Comorbid psychiatric disorders in children with autism: Interview development and rates of disorders. Journal of Autism and Developmental Disorders, 36(7), 849–861.

Lian, M. J. (1996). Teaching Asian American children. In E. Duran (Ed.), Teaching student with moderate/severe disabilities, including autism: Strategies for second language learners in inclusive settings (pp. 239–253). Springfield, IL: Charles C. Thomas.

Licciardello, C. C., Harchik, A. E., & Luiselli, J. K. (2008). Social skills intervention for children with autism during interactive play at a public elementary school. Education and Treatment of Children, 31(1), 27–37.

Little, C. (2002). Which is it? Asperger's syndrome or giftedness? Defining the differences. Gifted Child Today, 25(1), 58–63.

Locke, J., Ishijima, E. H., Kasari, C., & London, N. (2010). Loneliness, friendship quality and the social networks of adolescents with high-functioning autism in an inclusive school setting. Journal of Research in Special Educational Needs, 10(2), 74–81

Locke, J., Rotheram-Fuller, E., & Kasari, C. (2012). Exploring the social impact of being a typical peer model for included children with autism spectrum disorder. Journal of Autism and Developmental Disorders, 42(9), 1895–1905.

Loiacono, V., & Valenti, V. (2010). General education teachers need to be prepared to co-teach the increasing number of children with autism in inclusive settings. International Journal of Special Education, 25(3), 24–32.

Malmgren, K. W., & Causton-Theoharis, J. N. (2006). Boy in the bubble: Effects of para-professional proximity and other pedagogical decision on the interactions of a student with behavioral disorders. Journal of Research in Childhood Education, 20(4), 301–312.

Matson, J. L., & Nebel-Schwalm, M. S. (2007). Comorbid psychopathology with autism spectrum disorder in children: An overview. Research in developmental disabilities, 28(4), 341–352.

Mazurik-Charles, R. & Stefanou, S. (2010). Using paraprofessionals to teach social skills to children with autism spectrum disorders in the general education classroom. Journal of Instructional Psychology, 37(2), 161–169.

McPartland, J. C., Reichow, B., & Volkmar, F. R. (2012). Sensitivity and specificity of proposed DSM-5 diagnostic criteria for autism spectrum disorder. Journal of the American Academy of Child & Adolescent Psychiatry, 51(4), 368–383.

Morrier, M. J., Hess, K. L., & Heflin, J. (2011). Teacher training for implementation of teaching strategies for students with autism spectrum disorders. Teacher Education and Special Education: The Journal of the Teacher Education Division of the Council for Exceptional Children, 34(2), 119–132.

National Autism Center. (2009). National standards report. Randolph, MA: Author.

National Research Council. (2001). Educating children with autism. Committee on Educational Interventions for Children with Autism. Division of Behavioral and Social Sciences and Education. Washington, DC: National Academy Press.

Nordin, V., & Gillberg, C. (1998). The long-term course of autistic disorders: Update on follow up studies. Acta Psychiatrica Scandinavica, 97, 99–108.

Patterson, K. B. (2006). Roles and responsibilities of paraprofessionals: In their own words. Teaching Exceptional Children Plus, 2(5), 1–13.

Quilty, K. M. (2007). Teaching paraprofessionals how to write and implement social stories for students with autism spectrum disorders. Remedial and Special Education, 28(3), 182–189.

Rastam, M. (2008). Eating disturbances in autism spectrum disorders with focus on adolescent and adult years. Clinical Neuropsychiatry, 5(1), 31–42.

Riggs, C. G., & Mueller, P. H. (2001). Employment and utilization of paraeducators in inclusive settings. Journal of Special Education, 35(1), 54–62.

Robertson, K., Chamberlain, B., & Kasari, C. (2003). General education teachers' relationships with included students with autism. Journal of Autism and Developmental Disorders, 33(2), 123–130.

Robinson, S. E. (2011). Teaching paraprofessionals of students with autism to implement pivotal response treatment in inclusive school settings using a brief video feedback training package. Focus on Autism and Other Developmental Disabilities, 26(5), 105–118.

Roekel, E. V., Scholte, R. H. J., & Didden, R. (2010). Bullying among adolescents with autism spectrum disorders: Prevalence and perception. Journal of Autism and Developmental Disorders, 40, 63–73.

Rueda, R., & Monzo, L. (2002). Apprenticeship for teaching: Professional development issues surrounding the collaborative relationship between teachers and paraeducators. Teaching & Teacher Education, 18(5), 503–521.

Salmivalli, C., & Peets, K. (2009). Bullies, victims, and bully-victim relationships in middle childhood and early adolescence. In K. H. Rubin, W. M. Bukowski, & B. Laursen (Eds.), Handbook of peer interactions, relationships, and groups (pp. 322–360). New York: Guilford.

Scheuermann, B., Webber, J., Boutot, E. A., &Goodwin, M. (2003). Problems with personnel preparation in autism spectrum disorders. Focus on Autism and Other Developmental Disabilities, 18(3), 197–206.

Simonoff, E., Pickles A., Charman, T., Chandler, S., Loucas, R., & Baird, G. (2008). Psychiatric disorders in children with autism spectrum disorders: Prevalence, comorbidity, and associated factors in a population-derived sample. Journal of the American Academy of Child and Adolescent Psychiatry, 47(8), 921–929.

Simpson, R. L. (2005). Evidence-based practices and students with autism spectrum disorders. Focus on Autism and Other Developmental Disabilities, 20(3), 140–149.

Shukla, S., Kennedy, C. H., & Cushing, L. S. (1999). Intermediate school students with severe disabilities: Supporting their social participating in general education classrooms. Journal of Positive Behavior Interventions, 1(3), 130–140.

Smith, K. R. M., & Matson, J. L. (2010). Behavior problems: Differences among intellectually disabled adults with co-morbid autism spectrum disorders and epilepsy. Research in Developmental Disabilities, 31(5) 1062–1069.

Stewart, M. E., Barnard, L., Pearson, J., Hasan, R., & O'Brien, G. (2006). Presentation of depression in autism and Asperger syndrome: A review. Autism, 10(1), 103–116.

Storey, K., Smith, D. J., & Strain, P. S. (1993). Use of classroom assistants and peer-mediated intervention to increase integration in preschool settings. Exceptionality, 4(1), 1–16.

Suter, F. C., & Giangreco, M. F. (2009). Numbers that count: Exploring special education and paraprofessional service delivery in inclusion-oriented schools. Journal of Special Education, 43(2), 81–93.

Symes, W., & Humphrey, N. (2010). Peer-group indicators of social inclusion among pupils with autistic spectrum disorders (ASD) in mainstream secondary schools: A comparative study. School Psychology International, 31(5), 478–494.

Tews, L., & Lupart, J. (2008). Students with disabilities' perspectives of the role and impact of paraprofessionals in inclusive education settings. Journal of Policy and Practice in Intellectual Disabilities, 5(1), 39–46.

Wacker, D. P., Steege, M. W., Northup, J., Sasso, G., Berg, W., Reimers, T., . . . Donn, L. (1990). A component analysis of functional communication training across three topographies of severe behavior problems. Journal of Applied Behavior Analysis, 23(4), 417–429.

Weisner, T. S. (2002). Ecocultural understanding of children's developmental pathways. Human Development, 45(4), 275–281.

Welterlin, A., & LaRue, R. H. (2007). Serving the needs of immigrant families of children with autism. Disability & Society, 22(7), 747–760.

White, S. W., & Schry, A. R. (2011). Social anxiety in adolescents on the autism spectrum. In C. A. Alfano & D. C. Beidel (Eds.), Social anxiety in adolescents and young *adults: Translating developmental science into practice* (pp. 183–201). Washington, DC: American Psychological Association.

Wilder, L. K., Dyches, T. T., Obiakor, F. E., & Algozzine, B. (2004). Multicultural perspectives on teaching students with autism. Focus on Autism and Other Developmental Disabilities, 19(2), 105–113.

Wood, J. J., Drahota, A., Sze, K., Har, K., Chiu, A., & Langer, D.A. (2008). Cognitive behavioral therapy for anxiety in children with autism spectrum disorders: A randomized, controlled trial. Journal of Child Psychology and Psychiatry, 50(3), 224–234.

Wood, J. J., & Gadow, K. D. (2010). Exploring the nature and function of anxiety in youth with autism spectrum disorders. Clinical Psychology: Science and Practice, 17(4), 281–292.

10

Addressing Adolescent Drug Abuse

KEN C. WINTERS, ERIC WAGNER,
AND WALKER KREPPS ■

Drug[1] use among adolescents, including alcohol consumption, has been a public health concern for decades (Chung & Martin, 2011). Although drug use trends have waxed and waned over the years, recent research continues to show relatively high rates of alcohol and other drug use. The University of Michigan annually surveys adolescents nationwide in grades 8, 10, and 12 as part of its Monitoring the Future Study to determine trends in tobacco, alcohol, and other drug use. The 2016 survey indicated that annual prevalence of marijuana use among high school seniors is still quite elevated —36% of twelfth graders reported using marijuana during 2016(Johnston, O'Malley, Miech, Bachman, Schulenberg, 2016). Daily marijuana use among adolescents at all three grade points surpassed daily tobacco use, which has been on the decline. Although alcohol use declined slightly in comparison with previous years, nearly –half of high school seniors and nearly –10% of eighth graders reported having been drunk at least once in their life (Johnston et al., 2016).

Furthermore, most youth who are reporting either abuse, dependence, or recent binge drinking, which is estimated to account for about 20% of 12–18-year-olds (Winters, Leitten, Wagner, & O'Leary Tevyaw, 2007), are not receiving intervention or treatment. Only about 10% of adolescents who meet these criteria currently receive it (Substance Abuse and Mental Health Services Administration [SAMHSA], 2012).

The public health impact of drug use by adolescents extends beyond the direct and acute effects of the drug on a person's physical health. Onset of drug use during the teenage years has been linked to an increased risk of later development of

---

1. For the sake of parsimony, the term "drugs" refers to alcohol and other drugs.

a substance use disorder (SUD) (Chen, O'Brien, & Anthony, 2005). Also, adolescent drug use is associated with a wide range of social and psychological consequences, including legal problems (e.g., selling drugs and violence-related charges) (Rockholz, 2011), driving under the influence of a substance (SAMHSA, 2004), physical, sexual, and emotional abuse (Hoffman, Abrantes, & Anton, 2003), and poor school performance (DuPont, Caldeira, DuPont, Vincent, Shea, & Arria, 2013). Regarding the latter issue, it is worth emphasizing that the link between drug use and poor school performance is *bidirectional*. Whereas it is generally accepted that poor school connectedness and performance is a risk factor for drug use, there is support for the case that adolescent drug use plays a substantial role in academic failure (DuPont et al., 2013).

In this chapter we will address adolescent drug use, focusing on four issues relevant to school settings: (1) Neurodevelopment and implications when addressing adolescent drug use, (2) prevention programs, (3) intervention strategies, and (4) the value of a clinical program adapted for schools.

NEURODEVELOPMENTAL ISSUES

Adolescent brain research suggests that the prefrontal cortex—which monitors impulsivity, goal setting, reasoning, and judgment—is maturing during adolescence at a slower rate than the limbic brain regions, which are associated with emotionality, motivation, and reward-seeking behaviors (Winters, 2004). This pattern of brain development may impact decision-making such that the teenage years may be a time when acting impulsively and taking more risks in the face of negative consequences is relatively more prevalent (Steinberg, 2004).

There is a growing body of evidence that the developing brain may be particularly vulnerable to the effects of drugs. Epidemiological data suggest that youth become addicted to drugs more rapidly than adults (Brown et al., 2008), and learning impairments have been cited among youth with a history of heavy drinking (Tapert & Schweinsburg, 2005) and cannabis use (Meier et al., 2012). These findings on the effects of drugs on the brain suggest that the developing brain may be more sensitive to the toxicity of exposure to drugs, compared to a fully mature brain, and raises the strong possibility that using drugs during adolescence can interfere with healthy brain development and may cause significant alterations of normal processes (National Institute on Drug Abuse, 2013).

Prevention and intervention programs can be informed by the science of brain development. First, we favor the idea of teaching youth about this emerging knowledge base. There are now a handful of resources for the classroom that guide teachers and students through the various topics of brain development and its implications on teenage health, including how drugs can be particularly harmful to the adolescent's ability to learn (e.g., http://www.drugfree.org/why-do-teens-act-this-way/; Winters, Lee, & Winters, 2010).

Another entry point for neurodevelopment into school-based services and programs is to educate youth about risk-taking. It is the view of experts that

Table 10.1. Characteristics of Four Principles of Motivational Interviewing

Interviewing Style	Characteristics
Express Empathy	Listen rather than talk; communicate respect for and acceptance of client
Roll With Resistance	Divert or direct the client toward positive change; listen carefully
Develop Discrepancy	Promote the client's awareness of consequences of continued use; clarify how present behavior is in conflict with important goals
Support Self-Efficacy	Elicit and support hope; encourage the client's capacity to reach their goals

adolescents understand the harm associated with taking risks, but that they exhibit risk largely because of an inability to resist contextual influences from the presence of peers and arousing situations. Thus, to simply educate youth about the dangers of risk-taking would be relatively ineffective. Rather, teaching adolescents impulse control skills presents a more promising approach. Such skills would include attention regulation, minimizing arousal, anger management, and how to take healthy, socially appropriate, risks.

A third point related to this issue is the importance of utilizing motivational interviewing (Miller & Rollnick, 2012) when delivering counseling services to adolescents. As summarized in Table 10.1, the four main motivational interviewing styles are the following: expressing empathy, rolling with resistance, developing discrepancy, and supporting self-efficacy (Miller & Rollnick, 2012). In general, the style of the counselor is empathetic, encouraging, and collaborative, rather than confrontational and authoritarian. Specifically, this interviewing approach promotes the notion that responsibility for change lies with the student, raises awareness of the client's problems, and provides a framework for identifying a menu of options or strategies for behavior change (see Table 10.1).

PREVENTION

Prevention programs can be categorized based on their target group. Weisz, Sandler, Durlak, and Anton's (2005) classification system describes five types of programs: (1) health promotion/positive youth development strategies, targeted to enhance protective factors, or increase prospects for positive development, for an entire population; (2) universal prevention strategies, targeted to address risk factors for an entire population; (3) selective prevention strategies, targeted to address risk factors among specific subgroups at elevated risk for a disorder; (4) indicated prevention strategies, targeted to individuals with significant symptoms of a disorder, but not meeting diagnostic criteria for that disorder; and (5) treatment interventions, targeted to those presenting with diagnosable disorders. Weisz and colleagues define each program level by the specific (and increasingly narrow) subgroups for which they are appropriate. They also distinguish between selected prevention strategies and indicated prevention strategies; such strategies have smaller subgroup targets than do health promotion/positive development or universal prevention strategies, and larger subgroup targets than do treatment interventions. Moreover, primary targets for change are risk factors for disorder in selected prevention strategies, versus symptoms of disorder in indicated prevention strategies.

In general, universal programs create smaller effects over a broader spectrum of participants, while selected and indicated programs create stronger effects, but among a more limited number of participants. While well-intentioned, most universal prevention programs have not fared well when subjected to rigorous evaluation. To date, the only universal programs showing any promise in preventing adolescent drug use are multifaceted, multiyear, school-based programs that involve skills training for teachers, parents, and young (preteen) children, and that require ongoing professional and peer support (Conrod, Stewart, Comeau, & Maclean, 2006).

Nonetheless, schools provide a cost-effective and convenient platform for universal and targeted prevention programs (selected and indicated), given the ready access to adolescents, their peers and parents, and the opportunity to impact multiple grades.

Elements of Effective Prevention

Prevention program design and execution varies greatly. However, some program characteristics are emerging that, when executed with fidelity, can produce statistically meaningful and sustained results in terms of prevention outcomes, such as reducing the use of drugs and delaying the onset of use. In a review of 100 drug abuse preventive programs that were denoted as exemplary, Winters, Fawkes, Fahnhorst, Botzet, and August (2007) identified 10 characteristics that typified these programs. A summary of them are provided below.

1. Prevention curriculum and activities were aimed at altering psychosocial factors believed to be associated with drug use (e.g., aggression, delinquency, parent relationships, and school affiliation).
2. Programs tended to focus on the two drug most abuse by youth—alcohol and tobacco.
3. Multiple influences and settings were targeted. Extending prevention activities to address the major influences on the youth, particularly peers and parents, and utilizing a variety of settings, such as school, home, and the local neighborhood (Kumpfer, 1998).
4. Program curriculum spanned multiple grades and extended several developmental periods. In general, most exemplary programs had developmentally adjusted versions that provide curricula that span all the school years.

5. Activities and curricula were developmentally and socioculturally sensitive. Developmental adjustments included operational ones, such as consideration of reading level, curricula tailored to the concrete thinking needs of youth rather than abstract thinking, and social and cognitive development. Effective programs also adapted their goals for age relevance.

6. Programs expend a meaningful degree of resources in engaging the target population. Effective programs placed a high priority on developing strategies to promote youth and family engagement and to reduce barriers to participation.

7. Program curricula focused on developing and promoting these social skills: developing general interpersonal social skills to increase positive and prosocial experiences in social settings; building coping skills to address peer pressure to use drugs; and socializing the young person to engage in social activities not involving drug use and related delinquent activities.

8. Programs include a parent component, which is prominent in programs for children, focused on improving parenting skills related to discipline and support.

9. The structure and philosophy of the programs encouraged broad-based involvement in decision-making related to their organizational structure. Examples of this element include shared decision-making on issues pertaining to staffing (e.g., hiring and supervision), financial management and accounting, maximizing program participation, and planning for program sustainability.

10. The programs include several features and activities to promote their sustainability: they follow a structured and logical organizational plan that begins with a needs assessment and continues with a realistic program plan; implementation of the plan occurs with fidelity; and periodic evaluations are conducted that easily communicate program progress and effectiveness to stakeholders and provide a basis for curriculum refinement and adjustment to program staff.

Preventive Programs in Elementary Schools

By the time that students are in their final year of middle school, many have already experimented with drugs. Among eighth graders, 27.8% have used alcohol and 20.3% have tried drugs other than alcohol (Johnston et al., 2013). In other words, one out of four eighth graders have tried alcohol and one out of five have tried other drugs. Prevention efforts beginning in elementary schools, before students begin using substances, can provide a strong foundation for increased prevention efforts in middle school (Donovan, 2007; Nation et al., 2003; Pasch, Perry, Stigler, & Komro, 2009; Centers for Disease Control and Prevention, 1994). Elementary age students present a receptive audience during a time when protective factors can be effectively strengthened in anticipation of students entering secondary schools, where and when the risk for initiating drug use increases dramatically. In part, this increased risk is the result of the rise from middle childhood to adolescence in the degree to which peer influence shapes students' behaviors, including drug involvement. Engaging in preventive efforts during elementary school has the advantages of addressing protective (and risk) factors (a) before the emergence of drug use, (b) during a developmental period when adult influence remains strong, and (c) when these factors are still relatively malleable.

The majority of elementary schools administer a substance use prevention curriculum, but far fewer utilize an evidence-based program. A national survey of elementary schools found that 72% of districts incorporate a substance use curricula for elementary students, but only 35% are using evidence-based curricula and only 14% are using evidence-based programs more than any other prevention efforts (Hanley et al., 2010). This study used a list of nine school-based substance use curricula that were identified as evidence-based on two national registries.

Effective prevention programs for elementary school children target improving academic and social-emotional learning to address developmentally appropriate risk factors for drug abuse, such as early aggression and academic failure. Training and education for this age group typically focuses on improving self-control, emotional awareness, communication, social problem solving, and academics (Conduct Problems Prevention Research Group, 2002; Ialongo, Poduska, Werthamer, & Kellam, 2001; Riggs, Greenberg, Kusche, & Pentz, 2006; Kellam et al., 2008; Beets et al., 2009). These skills can have benefits beyond the prevention of drug use, such as a reduction in violence and mental health problems. Some early-school prevention programs have shown effectiveness long after the program has ended. For example, The Good Behavior Game is a classroom behavior management approach for five-to-seven-year-old students. Positive outcomes for this program have been reported 15 years after the intervention when students were 20 to 21 years old (Strang et al., 2012).

Preventive Programs in Middle School

The middle school years represent an intersection of greater risk-taking as well as receptivity to prevention curricula. Because of this vulnerable time, more middle schools offer drug prevention programs than either elementary schools or high schools. The U.S. Department of Education reported that 90% middle schools implemented prevention efforts during the 2004–2005 school year (Crosse et al., 2011). Middle school prevention programs typically focus on increasing social skills, emphasizing school affiliation, reinforcing anti-drug attitudes, and strengthening personal commitments against drug abuse (Botvin, Baker, Dusenbury, Botvin, & Diaz, 1995; Eisen, Zellman, & Murray, 2003; Haggerty, Skinner, MacKenzie, & Catalano, 2007; Scheier, Botvin, Diaz, & Griffin, 1999).

Preventive Programs in High School

Fewer school systems implement programs for high school students, even though drug use initiation is still increasing rapidly in these grades (Ringwalt et al., 2008). Only 56% of high school districts administered any substance use prevention program (Ringwalt et al., 2008). Programs for high school students typically address peer pressure, using free time wisely, and the importance for thoughtful, health-promoting decision–making/

The Effect of Federal Policy and Funding on School-Based Drug Prevention

Beginning in 1998, the government's financial support and advocacy for evidence based prevention programs precipitated an upsurge in both the creation and implementation of effective prevention programs in schools. For example, the prevalence of middle schools that used evidence-based curricula increased from 34% in 1999 to 47% in 2008 (Ringwalt, Vincus, Hanley, Ennett, Bowling, & Haws, 2011). The results from these programs, in the form of reduced drug and alcohol use by adolescents, are also apparent. Before increased support for evidence-based program funding, lifetime prevalence of use of any illicit drug grew from 30.4% in 1991 to 41.9% in 1999 for grades 8, 10 and 12 (Johnston et al., 2013). As adoption of effective programs grew, the percentage of (lifetime) drug use dropped from 41% in 2000 to a low of 32.5% in 2008 (Johnston et al., 2013). But in recent years, federal funding has been reduced, and lifetime drug use has been increasing each year (33.2% in 2009 to 35.8% in 2013; Johnston et al., 2013). Current government funding has shown a shift toward selective schools where the need is perceived to be the greatest (Ringwalt et al., 2011).

Interventions

Prevention moves to intervention when a school-based drug program's focus is on curbing identified students' problems with alcohol or other drugs. Typically, such students are in the early stages of problematic substance use; adolescents with more severe drug problems often are truant or have dropped out. Moreover, adolescents with more severe problems require more intensive treatments than most schools can or should provide. In a recent meta-analysis of brief alcohol interventions (Tanner-Smith & Lipsey, 2015), 185 experimental and quasi-experimental studies were examined for the effects on alcohol-related outcomes among non-treatment-seeking adolescents and young adults. The meta-analysis includes a large number of studies and utilizes statistical techniques that permitted inclusion of multiple effect sizes from each study. Several findings with research and practice implications are noteworthy. One is that modest but statistically significant post-intervention reductions were observed in alcohol consumption outcome for brief interventions with up to five hours of total contact time. Adolescents experienced larger effects than young adults (.27 and .17 standard deviation reductions in alcohol use, respectively). A similar pattern was found for alcohol-related problem outcomes. Another finding is that for studies that had extended follow-up data, the effects of the brief interventions persist for up to a year after the end of the interventions. But among those few studies that have followed their sample for a longer period, the effects generally dissipated by two years post-intervention.

Then there are the results of the analysis that looked at what were the most effective interventions for adolescents. The authors used statistical projections to identify the profile of characteristics likely to produce the most and least effective intervention effects. Based on the statistical model, the most effective interventions for adolescents would consist of the following: motivational interviewing/motivational enhancement techniques in a single session of more than 15 minutes; and therapeutic components such as decisional balance, goal-setting, and norm referencing. Not included would be blood alcohol content information, basic education/information, or personalized feedback. Therapeutic processes (e.g., changing distorted perceptions about drinking or drugging norms, increasing self-confidence to resist substance use, increasing motivation to change), rather than increased knowledge, are responsible for preventive effects.

In regard to more intensive interventions, Becker and Curry (2008) conducted a quality of evidence review and found only three intervention models to be efficacious: ecological family therapy (EFT); brief motivational intervention (BMI); and cognitive behavioral therapy (CBT). At present, there are several evidence-based EFTs available, including Brief Strategic Family Therapy (Robbins, Feaster, Horigan, Puccinelli, Henderson, & Szapocznik, 2011), Contingency Management with Family Engagement Strategies (Henggeler, McCart, Cunningham, & Chapman, 2012), Ecologically Based Family Therapy (Slesnick, Erdem, Bartle-Haring, & Brigham, 2013), Multidimensional Family Therapy (Liddle, Rowe, Dakof, Henderson, & Greenbaum, 2009), and Multisystemic Therapy (Borduin, Schaeffer, & Heiblum, 2009). As noted earlier, there is large support for the effectiveness of BMI; there also is large support for the effectiveness of CBT for reducing adolescent drug and related problems (Kaminer & Waldron, 2006; Magill & Ray, 2009).

Despite their clinical effectiveness, EFTs are not well-suited to most educational settings. EFTs require trained family therapists, face-to-face involvement with families, and sufficient time and space for providing a full course of treatment; these things are exceedingly rare in schools. BMIs and CBTs likely are better choices for school-based adolescent drug intervention programs, and several good choices are currently available (see http://store.samhsa.gov/facet/ Treatment-Prevention-Recovery/term/Cognitive-Behavioral-Therapy).   There are also combined BMI/CBT interventions, such as Guided Self-Change (GSC; Sobell & Sobell, 2005), which employs (a) a motivational client-therapist interactional style; (b) a cognitive behavioral approach to planning, implementing, and maintaining changes in alcohol and other drug (AOD) behaviors; and (c) a harm-reduction perspective for the treatment of addictive behaviors. Originally developed for adult clinical settings, several recent studies have supported the efficacy of GFC as a school-based intervention with English- and Spanish-speaking teenagers (Gil, Wagner, & Tubman, 2004; Martínez Martínez, Pedroza Cabrera, de los ÁngelesVacío Muro, Jiménez Pérez, & Salazar Garza, 2008; Wagner, Hospital, Graziano, Gil, & Morris, 2014).

SUGGESTED SCHOOL-BASED MODEL TO ADDRESS DRUG USE: THE ADOLESCENT SBIRT

We describe here a model for clinical services that is accommodating to school settings. Known as SBIRT (screening, brief intervention, referral to treatment), this integrated, public health approach provides a framework for the delivery of early intervention and additional services for persons with early-stage drug problems (National Institute on Alcohol Abuse and Alcoholism, 2011; Whitlock, Polen, Green, Orleans, & Klein, 2004). The *screening* component quickly and efficiently assesses for the presence of risky substance use; further assessment is needed for those who show severe substance use disorder. But for those with a mild or moderate substance use disorder or other features suggestive of harmful drug use (e.g., regular binge drinking), a *brief intervention* is recommended. The *referral to treatment* services provide those identified as needing more extensive treatment with access to specialty care.

The SBIRT model provides a framework for matching clinical response to level of substance use involvement. Consider the public health triage model in Figure 10.1. If we consider a cross-section of teenagers, a large proportion of them report no or nonrisky infrequent substance use (e.g., an occasional beer) in the past

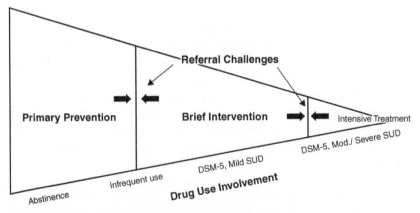

Figure 10.1 Response options within a SBIRT model.
NOTE: Adapted from the public health triage model provided in *Broadening the Base of Treatment for Alcohol Problems* (Institute of Medicine, 1990).

year; for them, prevention is relevant. As severity of use increases, there are correspondingly fewer individuals. As one moves toward the right of the triangle, these youth are experiencing mild-to-moderate drug involvement, and a brief intervention is relevant. The smallest number of teenagers meet criteria for a *DSM-5* (American Psychiatric Association, 2013) Substance Use Disorder, Severe, and for them specialized treatment is appropriate. Screening can assist in identifying where a teenager is located in the triangle.

The application of SBIRT for drug-abusing adolescents is beginning to be applied in health settings, and early efficacy data are promising (Mitchell, Gryczynski, O'Grady, & Schwartz, 2013; Winters, 2016). The authors contend that SBIRT models for adolescent are in their infancy stage, and that more work is needed to shape them to be more developmentally appropriate. For example, extant SBIRT models do not take into account the presence of clinical problems that typically co-occur with drug problems. Perhaps even more so than with adults, adolescent drug problems frequently co-occur with mild to severe mental health and other psychosocial problems; *co-occurring* drug and mental health problems are now commonly understood to be the rule rather than the exception for adolescents (Diaz et al., 2011; Wu, Gersing, Burchett, Woody, & Blazer, 2011), and both types of conditions can complicate treatment and result in poorer outcomes (Rowe, Liddle, Greenbaum, & Henderson, 2004). A Kaiser study of adolescent drug treatment intakes found that over half of them had at least one psychiatric diagnosis, with significantly higher rates of depression, anxiety and neurotic disorders, major psychoses, and eating disorders than a group of matched controls without drug problems (Sterling & Weisner, 2005). Below we describe the core features of a proposed adolescent SBIRT model.

Screening

Requirements for screening are that the tool is brief, easy to use, accurate, and that it screens for drug abuse. Screening determines the need for a comprehensive assessment; it does not establish definitive information about diagnosis and possible treatment needs. A screening should take no longer than 10 minutes; screening questions may inquire about recent drug use quantity and frequency (e.g., How often did you use drugs in the past 6 months?), the presence of adverse consequences of use (e.g., Has your drug use led to problems with your parents?), and contextual factors (e.g., Do your friends use alcohol or other drugs?).

We suggest the six-item CRAFFT as the preferred tool to screen for drug involvement. Each letter in CRAFFT represents the key word for that particular question (e.g., C is for "Have you ever ridden in a **CAR** driven by someone (including yourself) who was 'high' or had been using alcohol or drugs?"). This screener is associated with very favorable psychometric properties (Knight, Sherritt, Harris, Gates, & Chang, 2003) and it is a standard in the field. Box 10.1 provides the six items of the CRAFFT.

Box 10.1

CRAFFT ITEMS

C   Have you ever ridden in a **CAR** driven by someone (including yourself) who was "high" or had been using alcohol or drugs?

R   Do you ever use alcohol or drugs to **RELAX**, feel better about yourself, or fit in?

A   Do you ever use alcohol/drugs while you are by yourself, **ALONE**?

F   Do your **FAMILY** or **FRIENDS** ever tell you that you should cut down on your drinking or drug use?

F   Do you ever **FORGET** things you did while using alcohol or drugs?

T   Have you gotten into **TROUBLE** while you were using alcohol or drugs?

Brief Intervention (BI)

BIs are intended for teenagers who are displaying or exhibiting mild or moderate problems associated with alcohol or other drug use. Such early-stage users often meet *DSM-5* (American Psychiatric Association, 2013) formal criteria for a substance use disorder at a mild or moderate level. That is, these youth show harmful or hazardous consequences from their drug use and may begin to show some signs of dependence (e.g., preoccupied with use). For example, the youth may be experiencing problems at school resulting from drug use, or may be getting into arguments with his or her parents and friends as a result of drug use. Teenagers who are showing loss of control of their drug use and have developed significant tolerance of drug use may need more intensive treatment than is offered by a BI.

Also, there is growing consensus as to the essential features of evidence-based BIs (Tanner-Smith & Lipsey, 2015; Winters, Botzet, Fahnhorst, Stinchfield, & Koskey, 2009). The most effective brief interventions for adolescents consist of the following: motivational interviewing technique as counseling style, emphasizing that the responsibility for change is with the adolescent, negotiating realistic goals, and decisional balance exercise (i.e., the client is asked to weigh the benefits of using against the negatives of using). We contend that an ideal BI program consists of at least two sessions with the student and at least two with both the parent and the teenager, but even a single session with the student has been shown to yield positive results (Tanner-Smith & Lipsey, 2015). Provided in Table 10.2 is a brief overview of the goals of each session.

Table 10.2. Proposed Structure and Content for
a Proposed 4-Session Brief Intervention

Session 1: Adolescent
  Focus: increase problem recognition, explore role of drugs in teen's life
  Activities: pros and cons, exploring ambivalence; establish initial goals

Session 2: Adolescent
  Focus: seek commitment for realistic goals, identify prosocial alternatives to drugs and other risk behaviors
  Activities: skills for coping with triggers and cravings; dealing with peer pressure; review progress with goals

Session 3: Parent
  Focus: increase awareness of parenting skills; understanding current adolescent stressors, risk factors
  Activities: parent communication; household rules about drug use; education on organizational and community resources for adolescents and parents

Session 4: Joint Parent and Adolescent
  Focus: finalize goals; next steps
  Activities: review goals; role of supporting parents; referral needs

Referral to Treatment

The final component of the SBIRT model provides a framework for next steps. For youth who show a favorable change at the conclusion of a BI program (e.g., reduced or no drug use is achieved; favorable progress with the goals), the counselor will want to support the adolescent's progress. No additional services are needed in this instance. But there may be less than a favorable response to the program—as evidenced, for example, by no change in drug involvement or no progress with goals. Here are two recommendations for the counselor or therapist in the face of less than favorable progress: (1) if minimal change: consider booster session(s) revisiting components of the BI (e.g., review progress with goals, troubleshoot barriers to progress); (2) if no change or the problem worsens: consider a *referral* to a specialized drug treatment program.

Essentially, this referral step represents moving from school-based early intervention to clinic-based assessment and treatment. In order to do this in an ethical and informed manner, school counselors and psychologists need to be familiar with adolescent drug treatment options in their community. Optimally, adolescents should be referred to treatment programs that have these features: the program is developmentally appropriate; service providers have specialized training in adolescent treatment approaches; the assessment process is comprehensive and is based on adolescent standardized instruments; the program's outpatient treatment is independent from adult treatment; there is a therapy approach that utilizes motivational enhancement interviewing, cognitive behavioral therapy, and

Table 10.3. REFERRAL OPTIONS WORKSHEET

Client Progress	Response
FAVORABLE • engaged during sessions • worked on the goals • made good progress with goals • expressed intent to continue behavior change	No additional services; support progress; reinforce importance of working on goals; offer future services if needed
MINIMAL CHANGE • mixed engagement during sessions • little or mixed progress with homework assignments • signs of intent to continue behavior change	Booster session(s). Seek interest in additional sessions; consider 1–2 more sessions across the next 4–6 weeks; options include youth alone, parent alone, or family session(s)
NO CHANGE OR WORSENING • no engagement during sessions • no progress with behavior change goals • poor problem recognition	Refer for specialized services; additional drug abuse and/or mental health services may be needed; consider services that have good reputation working with youth and families

Record client progress and referral response:_____

_____

_____

family-based strategies; and the program has an aftercare component (National Institute on Drug Abuse, 2013).

Moreover, school counselors and psychologists need to inform the adolescent and his caregivers of the reasons for the referral in a nonjudgmental, cautiously optimistic, and clear and concise manner. The adolescent and his family should be given the opportunity to ask questions about the referral, and, if possible, a call to the treatment provider to set up the first assessment appointment should be made during this meeting. A brief follow-up contact a few days later with the adolescent and his family to ensure they have followed through on the referral is also advised. We provide in Table 10.3 a worksheet that can guide the referral decision based on the client's response to the BI.

SUMMARY

There is a sizeable unmet need in this country with respect to addressing adolescent drug abuse. School-based settings, supported by provisions in the Mental Health Parity Act and the Affordable Care Act, provide opportunity to offer a range of prevention and intervention services to address the onset, maintenance, and progression of adolescent drug involvement. Evidence-based, universal drug prevention programs are more multi-dimensional and developmentally adjusted than ever before, and the most comprehensive ones are making real impacts in terms of increasing personal and environmental assets and delaying the onset of drug use. But these programs are not likely to have an impact on students who are already using or abusing drugs (Catalano et al., 2012). National data suggest that there is a large proportion of adolescents who are not revealing detectable signs or symptoms of a severe substance use disorder (Winters, Leitten, et al., 2007), and it is these youth for whom we see value in preventive, brief interventions.

Implementing prevention and intervention services in a school setting poses many challenges, including practical, conceptual, and clinical ones. School-based settings offer a great opportunity to address adolescent drug abuse for those for whom prevention is appropriate, as well as for those whose use is already escalating toward dependence and who need more focused services. Furthermore, much progress has occurred to better understand what components are necessary for exemplary drug prevention and intervention programs for adolescents. Schools benefit from the growing number of existing evidence-based programs.

Yet innovation in program development and implementation is still necessary in order to optimize effectiveness and affordability. Program development is needed to address diverse communities and for youth with coexisting disorders, and there are still large knowledge gaps as to the key ingredients for program implementation.

REFERENCES

American Psychiatric Association. (2013). *Diagnostic and statistical manual of mental disorders* (5th ed.). Arlington, VA: American Psychiatric Publishing.

Becker, S. J., & Curry, J. F. (2008). Outpatient interventions for adolescent substance abuse: A quality of evidence review. *Journal Consulting and Clinical Psychology, 76*(4), 531–543.

Beets, M. W., Flay, B. R., Vuchinich, S., Snyder, F. J., Acock, A., Li, K-K., Burns, K., Washburn, I. J., & Durlak, J. (2009). Use of a social and character development program to prevent substance use, violent behaviors, and sexual activity among elementary-school students in Hawaii. *American Journal of Public Health, 99*(8), 1438–1445.

Botvin, G., Baker, E., Dusenbury, L., Botvin, E., & Diaz, T. (1995). Long-term follow-up results of a randomized drug-abuse prevention trial in a white middle class population. *JAMA, 273*, 1106–1112.

Borduin, C. M., Schaeffer, C. M., & Heiblum, N. (2009). A randomized clinical trial of Multisystemic Therapy with juvenile sexual offenders: Effects on youth social ecology and criminal activity. *Journal of Consulting and Clinical Psychology, 77*, 26–37.

Brown, S. A., McGue, M., Maggs, J., Schulenberg, J., Sher, K., Winters, K. C., & Lowman, C. (2008). A developmental perspective on alcohol and youth ages 16–20. *Pediatrics, 121*, S290–S310.

Catalano, R. F., Fagan, A. A., Gavin, L. E., Greenberg, M. T., Charles, E. I., Ross, D. A., & Shek, D. T. L. (2012). Worldwide application of prevention science in adolescent health. *Lancet, 379*, 1653–1664.

Centers for Disease Control and Prevention. (1994). Guidelines for school health programs to prevent tobacco use and addiction. *Morbidity and Mortality Weekly Report,*
43(RR-2), 1–18.

Chen, C. Y., O'Brien, M. S., & Anthony, J. C. (2005). Who becomes cannabis dependent
soon after onset of use? Epidemiological evidence from the United States: 2000–2001.
Drug and Alcohol Dependence, 79(1), 11–22.

Chung, T., & Martin, C. S. (2011). Prevalence and clinical course of adolescent substance
use and substance use disorders. In Y. Kaminer & K. C. Winters (Eds.), *Clinical manual of adolescent substance abuse treatments* (pp. 1–23). Washington, DC: American
Psychiatric Association.

Conduct Problems Prevention Research Group. (2002). Predictor variables associated
with positive Fast Track outcomes at the end of third grade. *Journal of Abnormal Child
Psychology, 30*(1), 37–52.

Conrod, P. J., Stewart, S. H., Comeau, N., & Maclean, A. M. (2006). Efficacy of cognitive-
behavioral interventions targeting personality risk factors for youth alcohol misuse.
Journal of Clinical Child and Adolescent Psychology, 35(4), 550–563.

Crosse, S., Williams, B., Hagen, C., Harmon, M., Ristow, L., DiGaetano, R., . . . Derzon,
J. (2011). Prevalence and implementation fidelity of research-based prevention
programs in public schools: Final report. Washington, DC: U.S. Department of
Education. Retrieved from http://www2.ed.gov/rschstat/eval/other/research-based-
prevention.pdf

Diaz, R., Goti, J., Garcia, M., Gual, A., Serrano, L., Gonzalez, L., Calvo, R., & Castro-
Fornieles, J. (2011). Patterns of substance use in adolescents attending a mental health
department. *European Child & Adolescent Psychiatry, 20,* 279–289.

Donovan, J. (2007). Really underage drinkers: The epidemiology of children's alcohol
use in the United States. *Prevention Science, 8*(3), 192–205.

DuPont, R. L., Caldeira, K. M., DuPont, H. S., Vincent, K. B., Shea, C. L., & Arria, A. M.
(2013). *America's dropout crisis: The unrecognized connection to adolescent substance
use.* Rockville, MD: Institute for Behavior and Health, Inc. Retrieved from http://
www.preventteendruguse.org/pdfs/AmerDropoutCrisis.pdf

Eisen, M., Zellman, G. L., & Murray, D. M. (2003). Evaluating the Lions-Quest "Skills
for Adolescence" drug education program: Second-year behavior outcomes. *Addictive
Behaviors, 28*(5), 883–897.

Gil, A. G., Wagner, E. F., & Tubman, J. G. (2004). Culturally sensitive substance abuse
intervention for Hispanic and African American adolescents: Empirical examples
from the Alcohol Treatment Targeting Adolescents in Need (ATTAIN) Project.
Addiction, 99(S2), 140–150.

Haggerty, K. P., Skinner, M. L., MacKenzie, E. P., & Catalano, R. F. A. (2007). Randomized
trial of Parents who Care: Effects on key outcomes at 24-month follow-up. *Prevention
Science, 8,* 249–260.

Hanley, S., Ringwalt, C., Ennett, S., Vincus, A., Bowling, J. M., Haws, S., & Rohrbach, L.
(2010). The prevalence of evidence-based substance use prevention curricula in the
nation's elementary schools. *Journal of Drug Education, 40*(1), 51–60.

Henggeler S. W., McCart, M. R., Cunningham, P.B., & Chapman J. E. (2012). Enhancing
the effectiveness of juvenile drug courts by integrating evidence-based practices.
Journal of Consulting and Clinical Psychology, 80(2), 264–275.

Hoffman, N. G., Abrantes, A. M., & Anton, R. (2003). Problems identified by the
Practical Adolescent Dual Diagnosis Interview (PADDI) in a juvenile detention

center population. *Offender Substance Abuse Report*, 3(5), 65–70. Retrieved from http://www.civicresearchinstitute.com/online/article_abstract.php?pid=16&aid=5413&iid=815&page=1

Ialongo, N., Poduska, J., Werthamer, L., & Kellam, S. (2001). The distal impact of two first-grade preventive interventions on conduct problems and disorder in early adolescence. *Journal of Emotional and Behavioral Disorders*, 9, 146–160.

Institute of Medicine. (1990). *Broadening the base of treatment for alcohol problems*. Washington, DC: National Academy Press.

Johnston, L. D., O'Malley, P. M., Miech, R. A., Bachman, J. G., & Schulenberg, J. E. (2015). *Monitoring the Future national results on drug use: 1975-2016: 2016 Overview: Key findings on adolescent drug use*. Ann Arbor, MI: Institute for Social Research, University of Michigan. Retrieved from http://monitoringthefuture.org/pubs/monographs/mtf-overview2016.pdf

Kaminer Y., & Waldron, H. B. (2006). Evidence-based cognitive-behavioral therapies for adolescent substance use disorders: Applications and challenges. In H. A. Liddle & C. L. Rowe (Eds.), *Adolescent substance abuse: Research and clinical advances* (pp. 396–419). New York, NY: Cambridge University Press.

Kellam, S. G., Brown, C. H., Poduska, J., Ialongo, N., Wang, W., Toyinbo, P., . . .Wilcox, H. C. (2008). Effects of a universal classroom behavior management program in first and second grades on young adult behavioral, psychiatric, and social outcomes. *Drug and Alcohol Dependence*, 95(Suppl. 1), S5–S28.

Knight, J. R., Sherritt, L., Harris, S. K., Gates, E. C., & Chang, G. (2003). Validity of brief alcohol screening tests among adolescents: A comparison of the AUDIT, POSIT, CAGE, and CRAFFT. *Alcoholism: Clinical and Experimental Research*, 27(1), 67–73.

Kumpfer, K. (1998). Selective prevention interventions: The Strengthening Families Program. In R. Ashery, E. Robertson, & K. Kumpfer (Eds.), *Drug abuse prevention through family interventions* (pp. 160–207). Rockville, MD: National Institutes of Health.

Liddle, H. A., Rowe, C. L., Dakof, G. A., Henderson, C. E., & Greenbaum P. E. (2009). Multidimensional family therapy for young adolescent substance abuse: Twelve-month outcomes of a randomized controlled trial. *Journal of Consulting and Clinical Psychology*, 77(1), 12–25.

Magill, M., & Ray L. A. (2009). Cognitive-behavioral treatment with adult alcohol and illicit drug users: A meta-analysis of randomized controlled trials. *Journal of Studies on Alcohol and Drugs*, 70(4), 516–527.

Martínez Martinez, K. I., Pedroza Cabrera, F.J., de los Ángeles Vacío Muro, M., Jiménez Pérez, A. L., & Salazar Garza, M. L. (2008). School-based brief counseling for teenage drinkers. *Revista Mexicana de Análisis de la Conducta*, 34(2), 247–264.

Meier, M. H., Caspi, A., Ambler, A., Harrington, H., Houts, R., Keefe, R. S. E., . . . Moffitt, T. (2012). Persistent cannabis users show neuropsychological decline from childhood to midlife. *Proceedings of the National Academy of Sciences, 109*(40), E2657–E2664.

Miller, W., & Rollnick, S. (2012). *Motivational interviewing: Helping people change* (3rd ed.). New York, NY: Guildford.

Mitchell, S. G., Gryczynski, J., O'Grady, K. E., & Schwartz, R. P. (2013). SBIRT for adolescent drug and alcohol use: Current status and future directions. *Journal of Substance Abuse Treatment*, 44(5), 463–472.

Nation, M., Crusto, C., Wandersman, A., Kumpfer, K. L., Seybolt, D., Morrissey-Kane, E., & Davino, K. (2003). What works in prevention: Principles of effective prevention programs. *The American Psychologist, 58*(6–7), 449–456.

National Institute on Alcohol Abuse and Alcoholism. (2011). *Alcohol screening and brief intervention for youth: A practitioner's guide*. NIH Pub. No. 11-7805. Rockville, MD: Author. Retrieved from https://www.niaaa.nih.gov/publications/clinical-guides-and-manuals/alcohol-screening-and-brief-intervention-youth

National Institute on Drug Abuse. (2013). *Principles of adolescent substance use disorder treatment: A research-based guide*. Bethesda, MD: Author.

Pasch, K. E., Perry, C. L., Stigler, M. H., & Komro, K. A. (2009). Sixth grade students who use alcohol: Do we need primary prevention programs for "tweens"? *Health Education & Behavior, 36*(4), 673–695.

Riggs, N. R., Greenberg, M. T., Kusche, C. A., & Pentz, M. A. (2006). The mediational role of neurocognition in the behavioral outcomes of a social-emotional prevention program in elementary school students: Effects of the PATHS curriculum. *Prevention Science, 7*(1), 91–102.

Ringwalt, C., Hanley, S., Vincus, A., Ennett, S., Rohrbach, L., & Bowling, M. (2008). The prevalence of effective substance use prevention curricula in the nation's high schools. *Journal of Primary Prevention, 29*(6), 479–488.

Ringwalt, C., Vincus, A., Hanley, S., Ennett, S., Bowling, M., & Haws, S. (2011). The prevalence of evidence-based drug use prevention curricula in U.S. middle schools in 2008. *Prevention Science, 12*(1), 63–69.

Robbins, M. S., Feaster, D. J., Horigian, V. E., Puccinelli, M. J., Henderson, C., & Szapocznik, J. (2011). Therapist adherence in brief strategic family therapy for adolescent drug abusers. *Journal of Consulting and Clinical Psychology, 79*(1), 43–53.

Rockholz, P. B. (2011). Management of youth with substance use disorders in the juvenile justice system. In: Kaminer, Y., & Winters, K. C., (Eds.), *Clinical manual of adolescent substance abuse treatments* (pp. 415–449). Arlington, VA: American Psychiatric Association Press.

Rowe, C. L., Liddle, H. A., Greenbaum, P. E., & Henderson, C. E. (2004). Impact of psychiatric comorbidity on treatment of adolescent drug abusers. *Journal of Substance Abuse Treatment, 26*, 129–140.

Scheier, L., Botvin, G., Diaz, T., & Griffin, K. (1999). Social skills, competence, and drug refusal efficacy as predictors of adolescent alcohol use. *Journal of Drug Education, 29*(3), 251–278.

Slesnick, N., Erdem G., Bartle-Haring S., & Brigham G. S. (2013). Intervention with substance-abusing runaway adolescents and their families: results of a randomized clinical trial. *Journal of Consulting and Clinical Psychology, 81*(4), 600–614.

Sobell, M. B., & Sobell, L. C. (2005). Guided self-change treatment for substance abusers. *Journal of Cognitive Psychotherapy, 19*, 199–210.

Steinberg, L. (2004). Risk taking in adolescence: What changes and why? *Annals of the New York Academy of Sciences, 1021*, 51–58.

Sterling, S., & Weisner, C. (2005). Chemical dependency and psychiatric services for adolescents in private managed care: Implications for outcomes. *Alcoholism: Clinical and Experimental Research, 29*, 801–809.

Strang, J., Babor, T., Caulkins, J., Fischer, B., Foxcroft, D. & Humphreys, K. (2012). Drug policy and the public good: evidence for effective interventions. *Lancet, 379*, 71–83.

Substance Abuse and Mental Health Services Administration. (2004). *Overview of findings from the 2003 National Survey on Drug Use and Health*. Retrieved from http://www.samhsa.gov/data/NSDUH/2003SummNatFindDetTables/Index.aspx

Substance Abuse and Mental Health Services Administration (2012). *Results from the 2011 National Survey on Drug Use and Health: Summary of National Findings.* Retrieved from http://www.samhsa.gov/data/NSDUH/2011SummNatFindDetTables/Index.aspx.pdf

Tanner-Smith, E. E., & Lipsey, M. W. (2015). Brief alcohol interventions for adolescents and young adults: A systematic review and meta-analysis. *Journal of Substance Abuse Treatment, 51*(2), 1–18.

Tapert, S. & Schweinsburg, A. D. (2005). The human adolescent brain and alcohol use disorders. In M. Galanter (Ed.), *Recent developments in alcoholism* (Vol. 17, pp. 177–197). Washington D.C.: American Psychiatric Press.

Wagner, E. F., Hospital, M., Graziano, J. N., Gil, A., & Morris, S. L. (2014). A randomized controlled trial of guided self-change with minority adolescents. *Journal of Consulting and Clinical Psychology, 82*(6), 1128–1139.

Weisz, J. R., Sandler, I. N., Durlak, J. A., & Anton, B. S. (2005). Promoting and protecting youth mental health through evidence-based prevention and treatment. *American Psychologist, 60*(6), 628–648.

Whitlock, E. P., Polen, M. R., Green, C. A., Orleans, T., & Klein, J. (2004). Behavioral counselling interventions in primary care to reduce risky/harmful alcohol use by adults: A summary of the evidence for the US Preventative Services Task Force. *Annals of Internal Medicine, 140*(7), 557–68.

Winters, K. C. (2004). *Adolescent brain development and drug use.* Retrieved from http://www.mentorfoundation.org/uploads/Adolescent_Brain_Booklet.pdf

Winters, K.C. (2016). Adolescent brief interventions. *Journal of Drug Abuse, 2,* 1–3.

Winters, K. C., Botzet, A. M., Fahnhorst, T., Stinchfield, R., & Koskey, R. (2009). Adolescent substance abuse treatment: A review of evidence-based research. In C. Leukefeld, T. Gullotta, & M. Staton Tindall (Eds.), *Adolescent substance abuse: Evidence-based approaches to prevention and treatment* (pp. 73–96). New York, NY: Springer Science+Business Media.

Winters, K.C., Fawkes, T., Fahnhorst, T., Botzet, A., & August, G.J. (2007). A synthesis review of exemplary drug abuse prevention programs in the United States. *Journal of Substance Abuse Treatment, 32,* 371–380.

Winters, K. C., Lee, J., & Winters, M. K. (2010). *Drugs and the developing brain: The science behind young people's substance use.* Center City, MN: Hazelden Press.

Winters, K. C., Leitten, W., Wagner, E., & O'Leary Tevyaw, T. (2007). Use of brief interventions in a middle and high school setting. *Journal of School Health, 77,* 196–206.

Wu, L. T., Gersing, K., Burchett, B., Woody, G. E., & Blazer, D. G. (2011). Substance use disorders and comorbid Axis I and II psychiatric disorders among young psychiatric patients: findings from a large electronic health records database. *Journal of Psychiatric Research, 45,* 1453–1462.

11

Managing Chronic Health Concerns

CHRISTY M. WALCOTT AND JENNIFER S. KAZMERSKI ■

Approximately 14% of adolescents in the United States have chronic health conditions (National Survey of Children's Health, 2007), defined as those having debilitating or ongoing symptoms that last for more than three months per year (Thompson & Gustafson, 1996). Prior to the 1990s, chronic health concerns were defined by the presence of specific medical conditions, such as asthma, diabetes, or epilepsy; however, this "categorical" approach did not lend itself well to research, policy, and program development, particularly for those interested in psychological and social outcomes of chronic illness (Perrin et al., 1993). As a result, researchers pushed for a more appropriate way to conceptualize chronic illness from a "noncategorical" perspective. As the definition above suggests, chronic health concerns are no longer defined as having a specific disease or condition, but rather as having functional impairments (e.g., mobility, sensory, cognitive, emotional) that require ongoing medical care (Perrin et al., 1993). Frequent health conditions present during adolescence include asthma, obesity, diabetes, depression, and attention-deficit/hyperactivity disorder (ADHD), but some chronic health concerns will elude traditional labels despite the presence of ongoing functional impairment.

Importantly, not all youth experience the same standard of care. A recent review of the literature noted significant racial disparities in youth health outcomes. Berry, Bloom, Foley, and Palfrey (2010) reviewed the pediatric literature for the prognosis of various chronic health concerns, such as asthma, ADHD, cystic fibrosis, diabetes mellitus, HIV/AIDS, and sickle cell anemia, and found that racial and cultural differences were noted consistently across conditions. Evident were increases in diagnosis among minority groups for certain chronic conditions, higher mortality rates for other conditions, and poorer control of symptom management overall (Berry, Bloom, Foley, & Palfrey, 2010). Thus, despite medical advances in the management of chronic conditions, such as those listed above, not all youth populations experience better outcomes. Additionally, there exists disjointed delivery of healthcare for all youth and poor communication across providers, all of which contributes to a lack of identification, prevention, and management of symptoms across populations (National Alliance on Mental Illness, 2011). Because schools are a central context for almost all youth, school-based services for chronically ill adolescents are crucial to a quality continuum of care.

Health psychology is dedicated to understanding the scientific relations among psychological, social-behavioral, and biological factors that influence health and illness. In recent years, a subspecialty of school psychology has focused on pediatric issues by considering promotion of health and development via coordination of services across school and other care systems (e.g., Power & Bradley-Klug, 2013), as well as by applying pediatric psychology principles to school psychology practices (e.g., Shaw, 2003). The rise of these subspecialties is due, in part, to prevalence data suggesting that increasingly more students with chronic illnesses and behavioral/mental health problems are attending K-12 schools. Working with chronically ill students requires school personnel to have a greater awareness of biopsychosocial influences on learning and behavior. It also calls for better service delivery models within schools to address the myriad issues surrounding the education of chronically ill students. The purpose of this chapter is to increase awareness of such issues and present potential interventions and service models targeting chronically ill youth.

Estimates of the prevalence of chronic illnesses among students vary based on what conditions are included within the estimates. For example, many chronic illnesses are widespread and largely preventable, such as obesity, which affects nearly 21% of adolescents aged 12–19 in the United States. (Ogden, Carroll, Kit, & Flegal, 2014). Chronic illnesses originating from birth defects and developmental disabilities, such as spina bifida, cerebral palsy, or Down syndrome, occur in approximately 16% of children in the United States. (Boyle et al., 2011) and often continue to impact affected children throughout their lives. Asthma occurs in approximately 9% of school-aged children (Agency for Healthcare Research & Quality, 2013), while childhood cancers and brain tumors are much more rare, occurring in <1% of school-aged children (U.S. Cancer Statistics Working Group, 2013). No matter how broadly one defines chronic illness, it is clear that public schools see many students who suffer physical, academic, social-behavioral, and/ or emotional impairments due to health-related problems.

In addition to the more obvious physical effects of illness, there is a link between chronic health concerns and psychological problems, relative to peers who are healthy (Pinquart & Teubert, 2012). Although the emotional stress of coping with a chronic illness is one obvious challenge for students, studies have documented that other academic, physical, and social-behavioral difficulties are associated with chronic illness in general (e.g., Martinez & Erickan, 2009; Pinquart & Teubert, 2012; Taras & Potts-Datema, 2005) and with specific medical conditions, such as pediatric HIV (Walsh & Chenneville, 2013), sickle cell disease (Smith, Patterson, Szabo, Tarazi, & Barakat, 2013), and childhood cancer

(Roberts, Robins, Gannoni, & Tapp, 2013). Although functional impairments due to chronic illness will vary by illness type and severity, common problems include fatigue, medication and other treatment side effects, academic functioning (exacerbated by frequent absences), peer relationship issues, behavioral problems, stress, and metacognitive problems (particularly with illnesses that affect the central nervous system, such as seizure disorder, TBI, and sickle cell–related strokes). Pinquart and Teubert (2012) posit several reasons for such health-related impairments, including the fact that a chronic illness may limit one's exposure to and contact with peers, school, and other activities (e.g., sports). Likewise, side effects of medical interventions can directly impact cognitive and academic functioning. Importantly, the reactions of parents, teachers, and peers can either help or hinder one's adjustment to living with a chronic illness (e.g., overprotective parenting, teasing or bullying by peers). Clearly, supports are needed within schools and across settings to proactively address issues for which students with chronic illnesses are at risk. This is important to engender positive and supportive learning environments for chronically ill students and their families, as well as to identify and treat specific academic and emotional/behavioral problems that arise.

IDENTIFYING STUDENTS WITH CHRONIC ILLNESS IN THE SCHOOL SETTING

Medical diagnoses and health-related information are subject to the Health Insurance Portability and Accountability Act (HIPAA) Privacy Rule, which protects the privacy of individually identifiable health information. Thus, unless the medical condition is obvious, the school is dependent upon parents or students to share specific medical diagnoses and conditions affecting them. Parents may initially tell the school nurse, because of the need for medical monitoring or medication administration during school hours. Alternatively, parents may inform school administration of a chronic illness so that proactive measures can be put into place to address potential sequelae.

Once the school administration is aware of a student's chronic health impairment, it is imperative that parents communicate often to keep the school abreast of any changes in how the illness is affecting their child. Health conditions may result in varied symptoms and differences in functioning day-to-day or week-to-week, depending on the course of a disease and treatments involved. Thus, what works for a chronically ill student at one time point may not provide enough support at a different time point. Communication between the family and the school is key, and early efforts should delineate who the family's main contact person will be, how communications should occur (e.g., regular meetings, email, phone contacts), and exactly what privacy-protected health information the administration is authorized to relay to teachers and/or the broader school population. As will be described later, the school nurse may lead an effort to draft an individualized healthcare plan to outline specific medical needs and responses required of school staff in the event of a medical emergency (National Association of School Nurses, 2013).

TYPICAL SUPPORT MECHANISMS
IN SCHOOL SETTINGS

As medical advances increase, the need for schools to engage and accommodate students with chronic illnesses also increases. It is clear from the research
mentioned earlier (e.g., Pinquart & Teubert, 2012) that chronic medical conditions can negatively impact the educational and social-behavioral functioning of
school-aged students and create unique barriers to learning and development.
Moreover, there will be heterogeneous responses to chronic illness, in that adolescents with similar medical conditions will have different patterns of adjustment
and functioning based on mediating variables. These include the student's cognitive and social-emotional levels of development, basic resources available to the
family, family functioning and community supports, and coping skills, among
others (e.g., Meijer, Sinnema, Bijstra, Mellenbergh, & Wolters, 2002). So it will
not suffice to have one set of conditions to apply to all students with a particular
medical condition, such as diabetes or cancer.

To complicate matters, the various parties involved in serving a student with
chronic illness will have different reactions to and understandings of how the illness is impacting the child, as well as different conceptions of what their role is
in supporting learning and development. This calls for innovative programs of
service delivery and collaboration across systems of care that allow for tailored
services for students with chronic illness based on their individual strengths and
needs (Power & Bradley-Klug, 2013). Although school-based services may occur,
in part, through the development of an individual education plan (IEP) via special
education eligibility, it may not necessarily require this formal designation. Indeed,
for many students with chronic illness, their barriers to learning and development
may not specifically require differently designed instruction (a prerequisite for
special education eligibility), despite the fact that the issues are problematic and
deserving of intervention. Below, three common approaches to addressing significant health impairments are presented, the individualized healthcare plan, the
individualized education plan, and the 504 accommodation plan.

Individualized Healthcare Plan (IHP)

An individualized healthcare plan (IHP) is a formal agreement outlining medical needs and a plan for addressing those needs. It is designed to address medical
issues that do not necessarily impact the student's learning (National Association
of School Nurses, 2013). Ideally, parents, the student, the student's healthcare provider, and a multidisciplinary team of school staff work together to develop the
IHP. Although the IHP format varies from state to state, and often from district
to district, most have common elements, including specific documentation of the
roles and responsibilities of the student, the family, and the school. For example,
it may clarify how medication will be administered, how the student's health status will be monitored, the location where care will be provided, and who will be

providing the care. When necessary, the IHP should provide for staff training and specify who will provide that training (National Association of School Nurses, 2013). Although there are no formal re-evaluation requirements, review dates should be written into the plan to ensure it remains current.

Individualized Education Plan (IEP)

If the chronic illness begins to negatively affect the student's academic performance, a multidisciplinary team of professionals, including the parents and school administrators, might consider eligibility for special education services due to Other Health Impairment (OHI). The federal definition of OHI, from the Individuals with Disabilities Education Improvement Act of 2004, §300.8I(9), is as follows:

> Other health impairment means having limited strength, vitality, or alertness, including a heightened alertness to environmental stimuli, that results in limited alertness with respect to the educational environment, that—(i) Is due to chronic or acute health problems such as asthma, attention deficit disorder or attention deficit hyperactivity disorder, diabetes, epilepsy, a heart condition, hemophilia, lead poisoning, leukemia, nephritis, rheumatic fever, sickle cell anemia, and Tourette syndrome; and (ii) Adversely affects a child's educational performance.

However, merely having one of the listed health conditions does not alone suggest the need or eligibility for special education. There must be evidence that the student's health impairment is significantly and negatively affecting the student's educational performance (see point ii in the definition above), and that the student's learning needs require specially designed instructional approaches different from or in addition to those provided in the general education curriculum. Although special education services may be necessary for some adolescents with chronic health problems, such services may be provided in a more restrictive educational environment that reduces a student's access to typical peers. As such, less restrictive intervention approaches should be considered when appropriate.

504 Accommodation Plan

Another typical avenue for schools to document chronic health impairments and resulting accommodations is a Section 504 accommodation plan. Section 504 of the Rehabilitation Act of 1973, as amended in 2008, is a civil rights law that protects individuals with disabilities within any program or activity that receives federal funds, including schools. If a student has an impairment that significantly limits major life activities, they may be eligible for a Section 504 plan. According to Section 504:

No otherwise qualified individual with a disability in the United States . . . shall, solely by reason of her or his disability, be excluded from the participation in, be denied the benefits of, or be subjected to discrimination under any program or activity receiving Federal financial assistance.

As with special education eligibility, a medical diagnosis of an illness does not automatically qualify a student under Section 504. The illness must cause a substantial limitation in the student's ability to learn or in another major life activity. If a student's chronic illness does not limit his or her ability in these ways, special accommodations may be unnecessary. Accommodations delivered under a 504 plan typically assist students in accessing the general education curriculum while addressing health-related limitations in functioning. Examples include allowing students extra time to take tests, using technology to help a chronically ill student stay connected and access learning materials, or thinking creatively about attendance so as not to penalize a child with a law that is intended to deter truancy. For example, if through self-study an adolescent can demonstrate competency in particular course content, there is no reason for schools to withhold credit for classes because attendance is poor due to medical reasons. Whatever services are deemed appropriate for a student with chronic illness, best practices dictate that schools work collaboratively with families, medical professionals, and relevant community professionals to best support academic performance and overall school functioning (Grier & Bradley-Klug, 2011; Power & Bradley-Klug, 2013).

EVIDENCE-BASED PRACTICE

Evidence-based practice (EBP) refers to the use of the most current research available combined with clinical expertise that best fits the needs of the student based on individual characteristics, cultural differences, and preferences (American Psychological Association Presidential Task Force on Evidence-Based Practice, 2006). Within the field of pediatric psychology, there is much debate over the use of EBPs, with concerns for the current science-practice gap. Specifically, clinicians may not employ EBPs due to practicality of clinical work, lack of progress monitoring data, and limited research base for many techniques (Nelson & Steele, 2009). As a result of this disconnect, researchers have made better efforts toward wider dissemination of research findings and more training in how to adapt EBPs to individual differences. EBPs have evolved and been applied to a variety of chronic and mental health concerns across a variety of settings. Many of the EBPs that are used within school settings are built and implemented within a multi-tiered service delivery model that allows for universal, selective, and indicated prevention. This service delivery model allows for school personnel to consult and collaborate with internal and external professionals addressing the medical, academic, social, and behavioral needs of the child.

Several treatments that address behavioral and emotional concerns with children and adolescents use this multi-tiered delivery system and have recently been adapted to address specific medical concerns. A prime example of this adaptation is in the area of behavioral parent training, which is a widely used intervention with an extensive research base. Specifically, behavioral parent training programs, such as *Parent-Child Interaction Therapy* (Hembree-Kigin & McNeil, 2011), *Helping the Noncompliant Child* (McMahon & Forehand, 2003), *Defiant Children* (Barkley, 2013), and the *Incredible Years* (Webster-Stratton, 2011), have shown success in decreasing disruptive behavior among adolescents, improving parent-child or teacher-child relationships, and in the generalization of skills across settings. Recent evaluations have included the extension of these interventions to address behavioral health concerns at both the family and classroom level. A more extensive multi-tiered approach is that of *Triple P-Positive Parenting Program* (Sanders, 1999), which includes systems allowing for prevention, early intervention and targeted intervention services for chronic behavioral concerns, with the inclusion of the medical team, schools, and the home. The inclusion of the medical team allows for Triple P to extend the use of the intervention to adolescents with specific chronic medical concerns, as well as early identification of those who are at risk.

Parent-child interactions are bidirectional and reciprocal, which can maintain coercive patterns of family interactions. Long term, these impaired family interactions damage the family relationship and are predictive of future antisocial behavior in youth (Patterson et al., 1982). Triple P is designed to prevent significant emotional and behavioral concerns by incorporating multiple levels of intervention and collaboration across multiple professional domains. Establishment of appropriate parenting skills and positive parent-child and peer-child relationships for chronically ill youth has a significant impact on academic, social, and emotional outcomes. Additionally, for children with chronic health concerns, positive relationships impact treatment adherence and other risk factors (Doherty, Calam, & Sanders, 2013).

Triple P uses a multi-tiered system of intervention that is implemented at specific levels based on the need of the individual child and family. The levels of intervention consist of Universal Triple P, Selective Triple P, Primary Care Triple P, Standard Triple P, and Enhanced Triple P. Universal Triple P refers to preventative care that may be provided in an individual, group, or mass media format. Within Selective Triple P, recommendations are made for specific concerns and may be provided in a phone, individual, or group session. Primary Care Triple P consists of brief short-term therapy that incorporates modeling and performance feedback of specific targeted skills. Standard Triple P refers to intensive therapy that includes generalization strategies provided in individual therapy, group therapy, and phone contacts. Enhanced Triple P is a level of service that includes intensive therapy building upon previous levels and including the addition of home visits to increase generalization and provide additional support to the family.

These levels of intervention have been shown to be highly effective in decreasing disruptive behavior in children and adolescents across settings. By addressing parenting skills deficits with the use of Triple P, generalization of appropriate behaviors acquired by the adolescent has been demonstrated across settings. Additionally, the incorporation of school and medical professionals in the implementation of Triple P has shown even greater improvement in youth functioning (Sanders, Markie-Dadds, & Turner, 2012). Concerns have been noted within recent evaluations of Triple P (Wilson et al., 2012; Coyne & Kwakkenbos, 2013) regarding the methodology used to evaluate and generalize the findings of the program; however, further evaluation is needed to substantiate these claims.

As an example of this intervention with chronically ill youth, Doherty and colleagues (2013) used Triple P to manage glycemic control in adolescents with Type 1 diabetes. Multisystemic interventions, such as Triple P, fit within the tiered framework of mental health service delivery that is recommended within the school system. Specifically, Triple P was used as part of a positive behavior intervention support (PBIS) framework to address overall behavioral concerns while also introducing specific aims and measures to address concerns that were specific to the chronic health concerns. Adolescents that present with chronic health concerns often present with additional externalizing and internalizing concerns that could be remediated with such programs.

Interventions for Specific Chronic Health Concerns

Chronic pediatric health concerns are impacting the educational, social, and emotional functioning of adolescents, as previously discussed. Reported rates of pediatric obesity and asthma indicate that they are, in fact, commonly present within school-aged populations. However, given the previously noted lack of communication and intervention efforts across school and medical systems, these commonly occurring conditions are often under-identified within school systems, resulting in limited prevention and intervention availability. Due to relatively high prevalence rates, chronic prognosis, and concerns for significant impairment if left untreated, the following specific health conditions are highlighted below: pediatric asthma, diabetes mellitus, and pediatric obesity.

Pediatric Asthma. Asthma is a chronic inflammatory disorder that includes periods of airway obstruction. Current research has estimated that 9.4% of children in the United States are diagnosed with pediatric asthma (Bloom & Cohen, 2007). Associated symptoms include chronic inflammation, bronchoconstriction, swelling and hyper-responsiveness of airways, and an increase in mucus production. Asthmatic symptoms are often exacerbated by a variety of triggers, such as cigarette smoke, perfumes, pollen, and dust. These triggers increase swelling of airways, constriction of muscles, and mucus production, obstructing airways and making it difficult for the individual to breathe. The prognosis of pediatric asthma is generally positive, with low asthma-related fatalities, but there is a disproportionate number of fatalities and poor management of symptoms associated with minority and low-income populations (Bray, Kehle, Grigerick, Loftus, & Nicholson, 2008).

Management and reduction of asthmatic symptoms primarily relies on the management of antecedents known to exacerbate the constriction of airways, including stress. Adolescents diagnosed with asthma are more likely to also have comorbid diagnoses of internalizing and externalizing disorders. Having difficulty managing stress or avoidance of particular stimuli are known to exacerbate symptoms or significantly impact social functioning, also impacting stress levels, and are common in those diagnosed with an internalizing disorder, such as anxiety. Additionally, those also presenting with externalizing concerns are more likely to be nonadherent to their treatment regimen, including the management of external antecedents (e.g., smoking), which exacerbates symptoms (McQuaid & Abramson, 2009).

Established medical treatments are often used when asthmatic symptoms are presented (Bray et al., 2008; McQuaid & Abramson, 2009); however, an interdisciplinary approach is recommended to address additional concerns at home and school that impact youth outcomes. Fitting within a school-based mental health model, with the emphasis on selective and indicated prevention, both school-based and clinic-based psychologists can help the student, family, and school personnel by providing education regarding asthma symptoms and self-management. Educational programs that include the use of self-management have shown the most positive outcomes by reducing the number of medical appointments and emergency room visits (DePue et al., 2007). Within an interdisciplinary model, school-based mental health professionals can provide additional training to healthcare providers (pediatricians and school nurses) on the impact of psychosocial concerns and management of symptoms across settings. Recent reviews of psychosocial intervention techniques (Bray et al., 2007; McQuaid & Abramson, 2009) noted benefits for asthma self-management training, family therapy, relaxation, problem solving, and biofeedback that can be implemented across settings. These techniques have demonstrated effectiveness for children and adolescents ranging from ages 6 to 15; however, the age of the child or adolescent impacts their ability to independently engage in the mentioned techniques, with younger children requiring more parental/teacher support.

The American Lung Association (2009) made a joint statement for improving asthma management in school settings, with school and health-based partners noting two primary focus areas for school-based asthma management: addressing the overall environment and comprehensive management of symptoms of children with asthma. It was recommended that all students with a diagnosis of asthma have an "Asthma Action Plan" to be used within the school setting. Teachers and staff interacting or having contact with the student should be notified of the plan, as appropriate, and receive adequate training of the plan's specifics to allow for high fidelity of implementation. Recommendations from the American Lung Association fit within the scope of selected prevention, with their overall school prevention and intervention program, the "Asthma-Friendly Schools Initiative Toolkit" (American Lung Association, 2007).

Diabetes Mellitus. Diabetes mellitus refers to overlapping conditions, including type 1 (T1), type 2 (T2), maturity-onset diabetes, and cystic fibrosis–related diabetes. Each of these involves metabolic glucose impairment due to insulin deficiency or resistance, but this review will focus on T1 diabetes (Wysocki, Buckloh, &

Greco, 2009). T1 diabetes is the result of insulin deficiency and is managed with daily insulin injections. Additionally, patients are expected to self-monitor blood glucose, maintain a recommended diet (including decreasing carbohydrate intake), and engage in daily physical exercise (Lasecki, Olympia, Clark, Jenson, & Heathfield, 2008). With proper management of symptoms, prognosis of T1 diabetes is quite positive. Improved adherence to treatment regimens have been shown with patient, family, and staff education; self-management training; coping skills; family therapy; and behavior modification (Wysocki, Buckloh, & Greco, 2009). The use of preventative educational and behavioral strategies to increase awareness, knowledge, and contingent reinforcement for adherence and use of self-management techniques has been shown to be highly effective. These strategies have demonstrated effectiveness across settings and may be more successful with collaboration across professionals and caregivers.

In a recent application of behavioral techniques to aid students with self-management of blood glucose levels, Lasecki and colleagues (2008) evaluated the use of behavioral consultation (BC) and conjoint behavioral consultation (CBC) paired with a mystery motivator. Students included in the study ranged from 8 to 12 years of age and had a diagnosis of T1 diabetes for approximately 4 to 6 years prior to the study. BC uses an indirect approach to provide assessment and consultation to parents or teachers of specific behavioral concerns of children and students (Bergan & Kratochwill, 1990), using a data-based problem-solving approach. CBC also uses an indirect approach, but, as previously mentioned, it expands the number of consultees and partners included in the process (Sheridan & Kratochwill, 1992). Thus, this model can include home, school, and medical professionals. A mystery motivator uses positive reinforcement and performance feedback for desired behaviors; mystery motivators have been widely used to increase appropriate behaviors (Robinson & Sheridan, 2000).

Lasecki and colleagues (2008) found that the use of behavioral interventions, specifically the mystery motivator, in addition to both CBC and BC, were successful in reducing blood glucose levels from baseline to treatment across all participants. Replication is needed, but given the individualized nature of the CBC and BC to specific target behaviors relevant for the identified student and the use of widely established evidence-based behavioral techniques within a problem-solving framework, results would likely generalize to adolescent populations. Within the present study, each participant was provided reinforcement for a specific behavior identified during either BC or CBC, such as percentage of insulin injections administered with supervision, incidents of snacking without permission, or percentage of compliance with checking blood glucose levels or taking insulin. Improvement was noted across each of the target behaviors. Identified behaviors are imperative to the management of T1 diabetes and the future independence of the child's own self-management of his or her healthcare. Results of the study demonstrated the need for and success of behavioral strategies within a school setting to improve management of T1 diabetes using both indicated prevention and evidence-based intervention within a multi-tiered service delivery model.

As previously mentioned, Sanders and colleagues (2012) have been extending the Triple P program to address behavioral pediatric and chronic health concerns across settings. In a recent evaluation, Doherty et al. (2013) conducted a randomized controlled trial of parents of 11- to 17-year-old adolescents with T1 diabetes and included them in an intervention or usual care group. The intervention consisted of a 10-week Teen Triple P self-directed behavioral intervention program, with an additional chronic illness tip sheet that addressed behaviors needed for the self-management of health concerns. The Teen Triple P behavioral intervention used a self-regulatory model that aims to increase positive interactions and appropriate behaviors, teach and acquire new desired behaviors, and remediate inappropriate or undesired behaviors. Results of the study indicated that the use of Triple P with the parents and adolescents with T1 diabetes reduced family conflict, whereas the usual care group saw no reduction in conflict; however, Triple P did not reduce parental stress. Future investigations of the use of multi-tiered interventions with this population are needed to support this preliminary evidence.

In addition to providing targeted intervention strategies to improve medical adherence, school personnel also need to consider accommodations for children and adolescents with T1 diabetes using a 504 plan. Examples suggested by Wodrich and Cunningham (2008) include addressing associated concerns of limited concentration, motor-skills, and excessive absences and missing work. Possible accommodations and modifications might include using a variety of teaching formats, assessing and matching student instructional level, preferential seating, alternative writing options, and schedule changes based on glucose levels. A comprehensive assessment of antecedent variables that may impact the student's behavior would be useful when considering relevant accommodations and/ or modifications. A preventative antecedent-based approach could identify particular times or settings where target behaviors of concern related to the student's T1 diabetes are more likely to occur. For example, problem behaviors may occur in the presence of certain setting events, and a link may be identified between the time of day (or the student's glucose level) and the student's off-task or disruptive behavior. The student's low glucose level may be decreasing the potency of available reinforcement, thus decreasing the likelihood he or she will engage in appropriate behavior.

As another example, sustaining attention during lecture-based courses covering advanced content in order to stay current with the class is less likely to occur when the student has low glucose, given the additional effort required to sustain attention; the reinforcement available is not as motivating as it could, given the student's current physical state (low glucose). Adjusting the student's schedule to provide less cognitively effortful material at certain times of the day, or classes that have more flexibility with the modality of the material, may allow a student to perform appropriately while decreasing the presentation of off-task and/or disruptive behavior. The previously mentioned accommodations and modifications are not an exhaustive list; however, it is necessary for school personnel to be aware of options and to consider using CBC to address the needs of the child. The use of CBC would allow teachers and parents to identify potential relationships between the behavior, the medical concern, and specific antecedents.

Pediatric Obesity. Pediatric obesity is a national epidemic with the National Health and Nutrition Examination Survey (NHANES) noting that the prevalence rates of obesity with adolescents has tripled within the past 30 years (Ogden, Carroll, & Flegal, 2008). Pediatric obesity has significant health complications, including, but not limited to, cardiovascular, pulmonary, and gastrointestinal concerns. Children and adolescents that present with pediatric obesity are at an increased risk for T2 diabetes (Daniels, 2006). An increase in school absentee-ism is noted as well. Pan and colleagues (2013) recently found an increase in annual sick days for obese adolescents compared to normal-weight adolescents. Additionally, obese children are at risk for impaired social, educational, and occu-pational functioning. Many of the associated risks for children and adolescents that are the result of obesity can be prevented or remediated with prevention and intervention efforts across medical, home, and school settings.

Many changes have been made in recent years to address school-based compo-nents targeting nutrition, health education, and activity requirements. Improving these components within the school system may improve healthy habits for ado-lescents later in life, which is particularly important, because obese children are likely to become obese adults. Prevention efforts and changing lifestyle choices may impact this trajectory. Many formal intervention programs exist, but not all have consistent findings. In a recent review, Brown and Summerbell (2009) evalu-ated school-based obesity intervention programs for children and adolescents 5 to 18 years of age that were implemented for a minimum of 12 weeks. Using body mass index (BMI) as the outcome measure, studies included dietary-only inter-ventions, activity-only interventions, and combined diet and physical activity interventions. Results indicated support for differences between control and inter-vention groups for some of the diet, physical activity, and combined interventions when evaluating changes in BMI, but there was limited evidence to determine differential effectiveness across intervention type. Importantly, insufficient data were available to determine how well these programs generalized to other settings or provided long-term effects. Clearly, there remains a need for tightly controlled evaluations of school-based efforts to manage obesity.

Although Brown and Summerbell (2009) noted limitations in the current litera-ture base for obesity prevention and intervention programs overall, one evaluation of a community-based intervention program looks promising. Rogers and col-leagues (2013) conducted a longitudinal (approximately four years) evaluation of Let's Go!, a mass media program and community-based intervention across mul-tiple settings. Let's Go! provides universal health education through mass media and targeted media messages. Specifically, Let's Go! encourages healthy eating choices, increased activity levels, modified use of appropriate rewards for desired behaviors, and increased parent education of nutrition and healthy lifestyles. Additionally, Let's Go! works with area partners, such as schools, day-care cen-ters and after-school programs, to follow-up on the strategies promoted through the media messages. Rogers and colleagues evaluated the effectiveness of the intervention across settings. Results indicated improvements in nutrition, includ-ing higher intake of appropriate foods/drinks and lower intake of inappropriate foods/drinks. Overall, community and parent awareness and implementation of the program increased. Thus, this is a promising intervention for treating obesity in children and adolescents, using a collaborative, cross-system service delivery model with an emphasis on education, prevention, and intervention.

Understanding Challenges and Advancing Current Practices

The need for schools to engage and accommodate students with chronic illness is increasing. This calls for innovative programs of service delivery and collaboration across systems that allow mental health professionals to tailor services to students with chronic illnesses and their families. However, several challenges exist as schools and their surrounding ecologies undertake such models. Some of these are discussed in the following section, such as the logistic and time challenges of creating collaborative teams across medical and school settings. As the benefits of integrated behavioral healthcare become more recognized, some medical training programs have increased opportunities for residents to acquire integrated behavioral health experiences. For example, Garfunkel, Pisani, leRoux, Phil, and Siegal (2011) surveyed medical school alumni who had previous experience with either a conventional or integrated behavioral health training models. Results indicated that trainees exposed to a clinic site that followed a collaborative, integrated behavioral health model reported higher levels of preparedness for collaborating with behavioral health professionals in practice. Thus, physician training will, in part, predict the likelihood of consultation and collaboration with other mental health professionals, including school personnel.

Limitations in knowledge, preparedness, confidence, and collaboration are apparent with both school and medical professionals, but differences in parenting behaviors are also noted for children with and without a chronic illness. Pinquart (2013) conducted a meta-analysis of parenting behavior for families of children and adolescents (mean age = 10.38) with and without chronic health concerns. These data suggested a less positive parent-child relationship when the child presented with a chronic illness. Overall effect sizes were small, but differences in parental responsiveness, overprotection, demandingness, and warmth were noted. Further research is needed in this area; however, the results suggest that parents of children with chronic health problems may need additional support and development of positive parenting behaviors. Such services could fit within the scope of a school-based model of service delivery. In addition, siblings may feel excluded or neglected when a brother or sister garners significant attention due to chronic illness. School mental health professionals should consider the needs of sibling social and emotional supports and advocate for their needs as well.

Another challenge involves privacy issues and family attitudes toward help-seeking. Collaboration across systems is the best way to support a student with chronic illness, but families must be willing to disclose health-related information, participate in problem solving, and give consent to allow the school system to share relevant educational information with medical or community care providers. Thus, issues of stigma surrounding some health conditions must be considered. Within the framework of prevention, schools should work to create a climate of tolerance and promote help-seeking behaviors for all students.

MODELS OF SERVICE DELIVERY

Children with chronic illnesses present with specific concerns that are difficult to manage within the framework of a traditional medical model, because this model carries specific theoretical assumptions that drive practice decisions. In brief, a medical model of illness or disability centers on the diagnosis of specific conditions from an in-depth clinical perspective, based upon the presence or absence of symptom clusters. This model tends to focus on deficits (as opposed to strengths), and on the adolescent as the source of the illness or disability, with less consideration of important contextual factors that influence one's functioning. Although diagnosing common health conditions (from diabetes to depression) is useful for understanding general intervention pathways and common outcomes, it is often too general and within-child focused to have utility in designing specific intervention strategies (Power, DuPaul, Shapiro, & Kazak, 2003).

In contrast, most school mental health professionals embrace a more behavioral and developmental-ecological framework to guide their service delivery (National Association of School Psychologists [NASP], 2009). Collaboration across systems via an interdisciplinary model allows providers to target concerns within the contexts that they occur (i.e., school and home). These models highlight contextual influences on behavior and an analysis of factors maintaining behaviors (both positive and negative), thus recognizing that a child's functioning can only accurately be understood by examining the dynamic interplay between school, home, and medical settings. This perspective is often more useful to interventionists because environmental events are more amenable to change than are fixed, within-child factors. Likewise, there is a greater focus on intersystem connections and systemic influences that impact child outcomes. Thus, schools are in a unique position to provide effective services for students with chronic health concerns if those involved can be proactive, build relationships across systems, and focus on strengthening existing supports.

The prevailing model of school psychological service delivery (monitoring response to intervention within multi-tiered systems of support) is one that mirrors a public health orientation that has long been used in community social service settings. Multi-tiered systems of support provide universal strategies for preventing problem behaviors for all students in a school by and systematic screening to identify students who fall behind expected benchmarks (academic or social-behavioral). For that group, more targeted interventions are then delivered, and the students' progress toward expected goals is carefully monitored so that intervention changes can be implemented. For that small percentage of students for whom these systematic efforts fail to yield progress, intensive interventions (perhaps through special education programming) are provided. At every stage of this multi-tiered system of support, rigorous problem-solving steps help to guide decision-making: What exactly is the nature of and function of the problem behavior? What interventions will be attempted? Do data suggest that the intervention worked? If not, what must we do differently to get at the problem? Thus, it is a recurring, data-based decision-making loop (NASP, 2009).

In recent years, a few specific models have been forwarded to link this prevailing "best practice" model of monitoring response to intervention within multi-tiered systems of support to students with chronic health issues (Grier & Bradley-Klug, 2011; Power & Bradley-Klug, 2013). One such collaborative and consultative model is the biopsychoeducational model proposed by Grier and Bradley-Klug (2011). This school-based model considers the school psychologist as liaison between family, school, and medical systems. Implementation of the model requires five steps; the first is to identify all key collaborators from the adolescent's total ecology (e.g., classroom teachers, parents, pediatrician, school nurse, school psychologist, etc.) and include them in collaborative problem-solving and open communication (Grier & Bradley-Klug, 2011). Once all players are invested, a traditional problem-solving model is followed: problem identification, problem analysis, intervention development and implementation, and treatment evaluation (e.g., Bergan & Kratochwill, 1990). Typical targets of concern that a team may address include excessive absences, academic performance, treatment adherence, anxiety and coping, pain management, social skills, and family conflict (Bradley-Klug et al., 2013). Within the context of the school environment, personnel can be involved in assessing and treating the impact of medical concerns on educational and social outcomes.

For the biopsychoeducational model, collaboration with system-level partners to support students with chronic health conditions is essential for providing quality and efficient care to adolescents. However, little is known about how school mental health professionals and pediatricians value communication across disciplines. In one survey, Bradley-Klug and colleagues (2010) examined pediatricians' perceptions of communication with school personnel. Pediatricians acknowledged the benefits of increased communication and collaboration, but mentioned several barriers that explain why such communications are relatively rare. These included inaccessibility of both parties, lack of time and reimbursement for consulting activities, and limited reception from schools.

Similarly, school psychologists were surveyed regarding their perception of pediatrician contacts (Bradley-Klug et al., 2013), and they also reported that communication with medical professionals was relatively uncommon. It was noted that when contact is made, the typical purpose is to obtain information and not to develop specific ongoing collaborations or interventions. School psychologists most often contacted the medical case manager or physician, whereas pediatricians most often communicated with teachers or principals. Both school psychologists and physicians saw collaboration for assessment and intervention as desirable, but time constraints were noted as the primary barrier (Bradley-Klug et al., 2013). Thus, although a more behavioral and developmental-ecological framework is best practice for working with chronically ill adolescents, it is more time-intensive and requires significant buy-in from collaborators across systems.

To address some of the communication barriers across settings, and to increase collaboration between schools and medical professionals, Sheridan and colleagues (2009) evaluated the use of conjoint behavioral consultation (CBC) with chronically ill students. CBC is a model of service delivery that links parents, teachers, and other providers (physicians) directly to the provision of services for children (Sheridan & Kratochwill, 1992). This model of consultation is a systematic process for addressing a variety of concerns (e.g., academic, social, emotional, and medical). Like Grier and Bradley-Klug's (2011) biopsychoeducational model, priorities are identified, defined, analyzed, and treated through a mutual and collaborative interaction, typically led by the school psychologist, with all necessary parties present. However, these models differ in that CBC emphasizes a true partnership model of service delivery, with greater time spent establishing joint responsibility for problem solutions, promoting capabilities, and exploiting existing strengths of each system player (Sheridan, Kratochwill, & Bergan, 1996). Thus, parents, educators, and medical service providers must collaboratively address concerns, actively provide treatments across settings, and identify and utilize their specific competencies to effectively solve problems with consistency across settings. This is typically achieved with the guidance and assistance of a consultant (e.g., school psychologist). Sheridan et al. (2009) used a sample of physician-referred children with medical concerns and ADHD to evaluate the effectiveness of the CBC model with a chronically ill population. Results of the study indicated encouraging effect sizes and goal attainment scores across both home and school environments. Home-based interventions had larger effect sizes than school-based interventions; however, parents, teachers, and medical professionals reported high acceptability (Sheridan et al., 2009).

Behavioral Health Screening (Prevention)

Implementation and use of behavioral health screening is recommended by the American Academy of Pediatrics (2009). Behavioral health screenings conducted within medical settings have increased mental health referrals from primary care practices. Unfortunately, patient compliance with physician referral recommendations is very low. Merikangas and colleagues (2011) found that only 36% of adolescents diagnosed with a mental illness receive ongoing mental health services. Rates are higher for those with a behavior disorder or ADHD, but with some cultural differences noted. Barriers to the receipt of mental health services include financial, cultural, transportation, and language barriers; stigma of mental health; and limited knowledge of mental health concerns and appropriate services.

In addition to developing universal screening protocols for emotional and behavioral issues, schools can provide indicated prevention for adolescents with health problems who are at risk for further complications. Often, this will involve establishing supports for the chronically ill student to deal with stress, develop coping skills, and create systematic opportunities for students to discuss their emotional state and fears surrounding a diagnosis (Kazak, 2006).

A Proposed Service Delivery Model for Secondary Schools

Medical treatments for students with chronic illness are more likely to involve more outpatient than inpatient care today as compared to earlier decades (Shaw & McCabe, 2008). This leaves families and schools to manage daily medical needs and health-related academic, social, and behavioral outcomes. Too often, adolescents who are chronically ill receive limited individualized support as they reintegrate into educational settings alongside their peers who are healthy (Clay, Corina, Harper, Cocco, & Drotar, 2004). Current pediatric models of treating illness already advocate for collaborations across the primary ecosystems of the child—medical, home, and school (e.g., Kazak, 2006)—as we are suggesting here. However, these models differ in their relative focus on the school setting, with many not recognizing it as a central context. In addition to cross-system collaboration, there needs to be significant communication and collaborative efforts by key members *within* the school system. Administrators, school psychologists, guidance counselors, school nurses, teachers, parents, and students must all work together to promote positive functioning and target specific concerns for an adolescent with chronic health concerns.

To this end, we recommend that schools utilize a cross-system collaborative model that uses a behavioral and developmental-ecological framework to guide integrated service delivery across home, school, and medical settings. Likewise, we recommend that these services be viewed through the lens of multiple tiers of support—from prevention to targeted intervention. We recognize the challenges of implementing such an integrated system of care, and thus recommend that schools use systematic consultation processes that have demonstrated success in building and maintaining cross-setting collaborations (e.g., CBC; Sheridan et al., 2009). Examples of a continuum of services (prevention to intervention) specific to adolescents with chronic health conditions were presented in the Evidence-Based Practice section of this chapter.

Although schools are an ideal setting to provide additional supports to adolescents and families experiencing chronic health concerns, classroom teachers often feel ill-prepared to meet the needs of these children (Clay et al., 2004; Nabors, Little, Akin-Little, & Iobst, 2008). School mental health professionals are in the best position to collaborate and consult across systems; to ensure comprehensive services to address behavioral, academic, social and medical concerns; and to help teachers who may not be confident in working with chronically ill students (Phelps, 2006).

Perhaps most challenging is the need to find creative ways to resource the cross-system collaborative programs recommended here. Initial efforts often arise via grant funding by local agencies (e.g., Children's Miracle Network) or university-led research projects to establish groundwork for systems-level implementation of models. But even if funding is acquired and groundwork is developed, issues of sustainability must be considered and proactively addressed (Hess, Short, & Hazel, 2012). Without proactive consideration of how service delivery models will be maintained over time, it is easy for systems to get side-tracked, bogged down on an issue, or simply run out of steam (Hess et al., 2012). To help maintain the viability of cross-system collaboration, some strategies can be employed. First, as with any systems change intervention, there will need to be buy-in from upper-level administrators if school-level personnel are to adjust their practices accordingly. Second, schools will need sufficient members to share the work and be invested in the collaborative problem-solving model. Third, maintenance will be more likely if the responsibilities for individual components are shared across the various system partners. If systems are managing their own components but still interacting with each other, there is greater likelihood that each will be invested in the overall goal (Hess et al., 2012). Fourth, Hess and colleagues also recommend that key stakeholders continually revisit and uphold the ideal of why these models are important. We must remind ourselves, school personnel, and community partners of the importance of utilizing a cross-system, collaborative model with a behavioral and developmental-ecological framework to guide integrated service delivery across home, school, and medical settings. Finally, Hess and colleagues recommend highlighting the efficiency of working together instead of having separate programs within schools, communities, hospitals, and outpatient centers. To support this claim, data can be collected by the team to determine if such integrated and collaborative models are, in fact, reducing medical treatments or doctor visits for chronically ill students, addressing their educational deficits, and/or precluding the need for more extensive mental health intervention due to neglected emotional or behavioral problems. That is, given the challenges of implementing such a model, teams are tasked with documenting the value added to the adolescent's education, care, and well-being.

A particular area of concern for adolescents and families who are managing a chronic illness is that of school re-entry following hospitalization and/or homebound care. Typical interventions include initiating community supports, educating peers, developing a support plan, and planning for follow-up communication. Although school re-entry is a known area of concern, limited empirical support is available for programs that are currently in use. Canter and Roberts (2012) conducted a review of the literature evaluating current re-entry programs' ability to increase teacher and peer knowledge of illness or injury-specific health conditions and attitudes toward the child presenting with the health condition. Researchers included rigorous inclusionary criterion for studies to be evaluated. Additionally, child-perceived self-worth was also assessed. Results indicated an increase in knowledge of the chronic health conditions upon re-entry with a larger effect size noted for teachers than for peers. A medium effect for an increase in self-worth was found for the child presenting with the medical concern. Results of the study emphasize the importance of re-entry programs for specific chronic conditions; however, results also suggest the need for further research in this area to provide a better system of collaborative care for children with chronic health conditions.

Shaw and McCabe (2008) explain how increased outpatient treatment for chronic illnesses has changed the way students experience healthcare. Instead of long hospital stays, students are more likely to have short inpatient stays followed by several outpatient visits over a month-long period, which brings new challenges to school transition planning (Shaw & McCabe, 2008). As such, they recommend that all transition programs for adolescents with chronic illness include four key components. First, homebound instruction (e.g., one hour of teacher contact per day) will often be needed to address frequent and lengthy absences while students receive outpatient treatment while based at home. Second, flexible school days can address limitations in vitality and pain-related crises. For both of these situations, technology can be used to allow students to have virtual visits with the classroom, to provide opportunities to send and receive schoolwork from the students, and to provide actual content/instruction when online lectures or computer-assisted instruction is available. Third, transition planning should allow for differentiated instruction to adjust the content, process, or required products based upon the specific sequelae of a chronic illness. For example, a student with Crohn's disease may require "stop the clock" testing or periodic rest periods. A student with an autoimmune disease may experience pain, difficulty reading or concentrating, and extreme exhaustion, requiring shortened assignments or longer timelines to complete projects. Finally, Shaw and McCabe (2008) recommend that transition plans address social support and affective issues. Social support from same-aged peers with chronic illnesses may be particularly valuable.

Although more research is needed to document effective hospital to school transition models, a few elements seem clear. Schools will need to be flexible and creative in addressing the unique needs of some chronically ill students. Additionally, parents and schools should proactively address transition needs by planning for peer education and supports, allowing outlets for the student to discuss affective issues, and creatively dealing with attendance issues. Likewise, warm, responsive teacher-student relationships will be important to promote academic and social functioning.

In conclusion, we recommend that schools be at the center of systematic, collaborative, and proactive efforts to work with adolescents with chronic health concerns. We believe that such cross-system, collaborative models are not only more efficient and effective ways to care for chronically ill students, but also more satisfying to students and their families than the disjointed interventions more commonly experienced. Increasing collaboration and integration of services should not only bring better outcomes, but also should reduce potential redundancies in care (Kazak, 2006). Schools are in a unique position to promote interdisciplinary collaboration for chronically ill students because they are central within the community and central to an adolescent's life. Likewise, schools have an existing multidisciplinary network of professional employees, including trained mental health professionals who can work to establish and maintain mutual partnerships for the benefit of chronically ill students.

REFERENCES

Agency for Healthcare Research & Quality. (2013). *2010 National Healthcare Quality Report*. Rockville, MD: Author. Retreived from http://www.ahrq.gov/research/findings/nhqrdr/nhqr10/index.html

American Academy of Pediatrics. (2009). Policy statement—The future of pediatrics: Mental health competencies for pediatric primary care. *Pediatrics, 124*, 410–421.

American Lung Association. (2007). *Asthma-Friendly Schools Initiative Toolkit*. Retrieved from http://www.lung.org/lung-disease/asthma/creating-asthma-friendly-environments/asthma-in-schools/asthma-friendly-schools-initiative/asthma-friendly-schools-initiative-toolkit.html

American Lung Association (2009). *Joint statement on improving asthma management in schools*. Retrieved from http://www.lung.org/lung-disease/asthma/becoming-an-advocate/national-asthma-public-policy-agenda/joint-statement-improve-asthma-mgmt-schools.pdf

American Psychological Association (APA) Presidential Task Force on Evidence-Based Practice. (2006). Evidence-based practice in psychology. *American Psychologist, 61*, 271–285.

Barkley, R. A. (2013). *Defiant Children: A clinician's manual for assessment and parent training* (3rd ed.). New York, NY: Guilford.

Bergan, J. R., & Kratochwill. T. R. (1990). *Behavioral consultation and therapy*. New York, NY: Plenum.

Berry, J. G., Bloom, S., Foley, S., & Palfrey, J. S. (2010). Health inequity in children and youth with chronic health conditions. *Pediatrics, 126*(Supplement 3), S111–S119.

Bloom, B. C., & Cohen, R. A. (2007). *Summary health statistics for U. S. children: National Health Interview Survey, 2006*. Hyattsville, MD: National Center for Health Statistics.

Boyle, C. A., Boulet, S., Schieve, L. A., Cohen, R. A., Blumberg, S. J., Yeargin-Allsopp, M., . . . Kogan, M. D. (2011). Trends in the prevalence of developmental disabilities in US children, 1997–2008. *Pediatrics, 127*, 1034–1042.

Bradley-Klug, K. L., Jeffries-DeLoatche, K. L., St. John Walsh, A., Bateman, L. P., Nadeau, J., Powers, T. J., & Cunningham, J. (2013). School psychologists' perceptions of primary care partnerships: Implications for building the collaborative bridge. *Advances in School Mental Health Promotion, 6*, 51–57.

Bradley-Klug, K. L., Sundman, A. N., Nadeau, J., Cunningham, J. & Ogg, J. (2010). Communication and collaboration with schools: Pediatricians' perspectives. *Journal of Applied School Psychology, 26*(4), 263–281.

Bray, M. A., Kehle, T. J., Grigerick, S. E., Loftus, S., & Nicholson, H. (2008). Children with asthma: Assessment and treatment in school settings. *Psychology in the Schools, 45*, 63–73.

Brown, T., & Summerbell, C. (2009). Systematic review of school-based interventions that focus on changing dietary intake and physical activity levels to prevent childhood obesity: An update to obesity guidance produced by the National Institute for Health and Clinical Excellence. *Obesity Reviews, 10*, 110–141.

Canter, K. S., & Roberts, M. C. (2012). A systematic and quantitative review of interventions to facilitate school reentry for children with chronic health conditions. *Journal of Pediatric Psychology, 37*(10), 1065–1075.

Clay, D. L., Corina, S., Harper, D. C., Cocco, K. M., & Drotar, D. (2004). Schoolteachers' experiences with childhood chronic illness. *Children's Health Care, 33,* 227–239.

Coyne, J. C., & Kwakkenbos, L. (2013). Triple P-Positive Parenting Programs: The folly of basing social policy on underpowered flawed studies. *BMC Medicine, 11,* 11.

Daniels, S. R. (2006). The consequences of childhood overweight and obesity. *The Future of Children, 16,* 47–67.

DePue, J. D., McQuaid, E. L., Koinis-Mitchell, D., Camillo, C, Alario, A, & Klein, R. B. (2007). Providence school asthma partnership: School-based asthma program for inner-city families. *Journal of Asthma, 44*(6), 449–453.

Doherty, F. M., Calam, R., & Sanders, M. R. (2013). Positive Parenting Program (Triple P) for families of adolescents with type 1 diabetes: A randomized controlled trial of self-directed teen Triple P. *Journal of Pediatric Psychology, 38*(8), 846–858.

Garfunkel, L. C., Pisani, A. R., leRoux, P., Phil, D., & Siegal, D. M. (2011). Educating residents in behavioral health care and collaboration: Comparison of conventional and integrated training models. *Academic Medicine, 86*(2), 174–179.

Grier, E. C., & Bradley-Klug, K. L. (2011). A biopsychoeducational model of consultation for students with pediatric health disorders. *Journal of Educational and Psychological Consultation, 21,* 88–105. doi:10.1080/10474412.2011.571522

Hembree-Kigin, T. L., & McNeil, C. B. (2011). *Parent-child interaction therapy* (2nd edition). New York, NY: Plenum Press.

Hess, R. S., Short, R., & Hazel, C. (2012). *Comprehensive children's mental health services in schools and communities: A public health problem-solving approach.* New York: Routledge.

Kazak, A. E. (2006). Pediatric Psychosocial Preventative Health Model (PPPHM): Research, practice, and collaboration in pediatric family systems medicine. *Families, Systems, & Health, 24*(4), 381–395. doi:10.1037/1091-7527.24.4.381

Lasecki, K., Olympia, D., Clark, E., Jenson, W., & Heathfield, L. T. (2008). Using behavioral interventions to assist children with type 1 diabetes manage blood glucose levels. *School Psychology Quarterly, 23*(3), 389–406.

Martinez, Y., & Erickan, K. (2009). Chronic illness in Canadian children: What is the effect of illness on academic achievement, and anxiety and emotional disorders? *Child Care, Health and Development, 35*(3), 391–401.

McMahon, R. J., & Forehand, R. L. (2003). *Helping the Noncompliant Child: Family based treatment for oppositional behavior* (2nd ed.). New York, NY: Guilford.

McQuaid, E. L., & Abramson, N. W. (2009). Pediatric asthma. In. M. C. Roberts & R. G. Steele (Eds.), *Handbook of pediatric psychology* (4th ed.). New York, NY: Guilford.

Meijer, S. A., Sinnema, G., Bijstra, J. O., Mellenbergh, G. J., & Wolters, W. H. G. (2002). Coping styles and locus of control as predictors for psychological adjustment of adolescents with a chronic illness. *Social Science & Medicine, 54*(9), 1453–1461.

Merikangas, K. R., He, J. P., Burstein, M., Swendsen, J., Avenevoli, S., Case B., . . . Olfson, M. (2011). Service utilization for lifetime mental disorders in U.S. adolescents: Results of the National Comorbidity Survey-Adolescent Supplement (NCS-A). *Journal of American Academy of Child and Adolescent Psychiatry, 50,* 32–45.

Nabors, L. A., Little, S. G., Akin-Little, A., & Iobst, E. A. (2008). Teacher knowledge of and confidence in meeting the needs of children with chronic medical conditions: Pediatric psychology's contribution to education. *Psychology in the Schools, 45*(3), 217–226.

National Alliance on Mental Illness. (2011). *A family guide: Integrating mental health and pediatric primary care.* Arlington, VA: Author. Retrieved from www.nami.org/primarycare

National Association of School Nurses. (2013). *Position statement: Individualized Healthcare Plans. The role of the school nurse.* Retrieved from: http://www.nasn.org/Portals/0/positions/2013psihp.pdf

National Association of School Psychologists. (2009). *Appropriate behavioral, social, and emotional supports to meet the needs of all students (position statement).* Bethesda, MD: Author.

National Survey of Children's Health. (2007). Data query from the Child and Adolescent Health Measurement Initiative, Data Resource Center for Child and Adolescent Health website. Retrieved from www.childhealthdata.org.

Nelson, T. D., & Steele, R. G. (2009). Evidence-based practice in pediatric psychology. In. M. C. Roberts & R. G. Steele (Eds.), *Handbook of pediatric psychology* (4th ed.). New York, NY: Guilford Press.

Ogden, C. L., Carroll, M. D., & Flegal, K. M. (2008). High body mass index for age among US children and adolescents, 2003–2006. *Journal of American Medical Association, 299,* 2401–2405.

Ogden, C. L., Carroll, M. D., Kit, B. K., & Flegal, K. M. (2014). Prevalence of childhood and adult obesity in the United States, 2011–2012. *Journal of American Medical Association, 311,* 806–814.

Pan, L., Sherry, B., Park, S., & Blanck, H. M. (2013). The association of obesity and school absenteeism attributed to illness or injury among adolescents in the United States, 2009. *Journal of Adolescent Health, 52,* 64–69.

Patterson, G. R., Chamberlain, P., & Reid, J. B. (1982). A comparative evaluation of a parent-training program. *Behavior Therapy, 13,* 638–650.

Perrin, E. C., Newacheck, P., Pless, I. B., Drotar, D., Gortmaker, S. L., Leventhal, J., . . . Weitzman, M. (1993). Issues involved in the definition and classification of chronic health conditions. *Pediatrics, 91,* 787–793.

Phelps, L. (Ed.). (2006). *Chronic health-related disorders in children: Collaborative medical and psychoeducational interventions.* Washington, DC: American Psychological Association.

Pinquart, M. (2013). Do the parent-child relationship and parenting behaviors differ between families with a child with and without chronic illness? A meta-analysis. *Journal of Pediatric Psychology, 38*(7), 708–721.

Pinquart, M., & Teubert, D. (2012). Academic, physical, and social functioning of children and adolescents with chronic physical illness: A meta-analysis. *Journal of Pediatric Psychology, 37*(4), 376–389.

Power, T. J., & Bradley-Klug, K. L. (2013). *Pediatric school psychology: Conceptualizations, applications, and strategies for leadership development.* New York, NY: Routledge.

Power, T. J., DuPaul, G. J., Shapiro, E. S., & Kazak, A. E. (2003). *Promoting children's health: Integrating school, family, and community.* New York, NY: Guilford.

Roberts, R. M., Robins, T., Gannoni, A. F., & Tapp, H. (2013). Survivors of childhood cancer in South Australia attending a late effects clinic: A descriptive report of psychological, cognitive, and academic late effects. *Journal of Psychosocial Oncology*, *32*(2), 152–166.

Robinson, K. E., & Sheridan, S. M. (2000). Using the mystery motivator to improve child bedtime compliance. *Child & Family Behavior Therapy*, *22*(1), 29–49.

Rogers, V. W., Hart, P. H., Motyka, E., Rines, E. N., Vine, J., & Deatrick, D. A. (2013). Impact of Let's Go! 5-2-1-0: A community-based multisetting childhood obesity prevention program. *Journal of Pediatric Psychology*, *38*(9), 1010–1020.

Sanders, M. R. (1999). Triple P-Positive Parenting Program: Towards an empirically validated multilevel parenting and family support strategy for the prevention of behavior and emotional problems in children. *Clinical Child and Family Psychology Review*, *2*(2), 71–90.

Sanders, M. R., Markie-Dadds, C., & Turner, K. M. T. (2012). *Practitioner manual for Standard Triple P* (2nd Ed.). Brisbane, Australia: Triple P International.

Shaw, S. R. (2003). Professional preparation of pediatric school psychologists for school-based health centers. *Psychology in the Schools*, *40*, 321–330.

Shaw, S. R., & McCabe, P. (2008). Hospital-to-school transition for children with chronic illness: Meeting the new challenges of an evolving health care system. *Psychology in the Schools*, *45*, 74–87.

Sheridan, S. M., & Kratochwill, T. R. (1992). Behavioral parent-teacher consultation: Conceptual and research considerations. *Journal of School Psychology*, *30*, 117–139.

Sheridan, S. M., Kratochwill, T. R., & Bergan, J. R. (1996). *Conjoint behavioral consultation: A procedural manual*. New York, NY: Plenum Press.

Sheridan, S. M., Warnes, E. D., Woods, K. E., Blevins, C. A., Magee, K. L., & Ellis, C. (2009). An exploratory evaluation of conjoint behavioral consultation to promote collaboration among family, school, and pediatric systems: A role for pediatric school psychologists. *Journal of Educational and Psychological Consultation*, *19*, 106–129.

Smith, K. E., Patterson, C. A., Szabo, M. M., Tarazi, R. A., & Barakat, L. P. (2013). Predictors of academic achievement for school age children with sickle cell disease. *Advances in School Mental Health Promotion*, *6*(1), 5–20.

Taras, H., & Potts-Datema, W. (2005). Obesity and student performance at school. *Journal of School Health*, *75*(8), 291–295. doi:10.1111/j.1746-1561.2005.00040.x

Thompson, R. J., & Gustafson, K. E. (1996). *Adaptation to chronic childhood illness*. Washington, D.C.: American Psychological Association.

U.S. Cancer Statistics Working Group. *United States Cancer Statistics: 1999–2010 Incidence and Mortality Web-based Report*. Atlanta, GA: Department of Health and Human Services, Centers for Disease Control and Prevention, and National Cancer Institute; 2013. Retrieved from http://www.cdc.gov/uscs

Walsh, A., & Chenneville, T. (2013). HIV in the school setting: Promoting mental health among youth through a school change model. *Advances in School Mental Health Promotion*, *6*(1), 21–34.

Webster-Stratton, C. (2011). *The Incredible Years parents, teachers, and children training series: Program content, methods, research and dissemination 1980–2011*. Seattle, WA: Incredible Years, Inc.

Wilson, P., Rush, R., Hussey, S., Puckering, C., Sim, F., Allely, C. S., . . . Gillberg, C. (2012). How evidence-based is an "evidence-based parenting program"? A PRISMA systematic review and meta-analysis of Triple P. *BMC Medicine, 10,* 130.

Wodrich, D. L., & Cunningham, J. M. (2008). School-based tertiary and targeted interventions for students with chronic medical conditions: Examples from type 1 diabetes mellitus and epilepsy. *Psychology in the Schools, 45,* 52–62.

Wysocki, T., Buckloh, L. M., & Greco, P. (2009). The psychological context of diabetes mellitus in youths. In. M. C. Roberts & R. G. Steele (Eds.), *Handbook of pediatric psychology* (4th ed.). New York, NY: Guilford.

PART III

Special Topics

12

Screening and Progress Monitoring in Secondary Schools

DENISE A. SOARES, CATHERINE C. GEORGE, AND KIMBERLY J. VANNEST ■

Mental health disorders in adolescence are known to be associated with poor school and life outcomes, including academic underachievement, school dropout, drug use, and physical aggression (Bradley, Doolittle, & Bartolotta, 2008; Brown & Grumet, 2009). A preventive approach to mitigating impairment and poor outcomes in school settings has been advised for at least four decades (Cowen et al., 1973). Despite a lack of widespread adoption and generally poor implementation, the field remains hopeful for a viable proliferation of preventive practices (Jamieson & Romer, 2005).

The first step in any systemic preventative approach includes universal screening for risk (Levitt, Saka, Romanelli, & Hoagwood, 2007). The current prevalence rates of universal screening for social, emotional, and behavioral problems is unknown, but in 2005 screening occurred in just 2% of schools (Romer & McIntosh, 2005). Some of the reported reasons for a lack of implementation of screening programs include limited staff training, competing foci and time commitments to educational reforms and priorities, and a lack of tools or methods (Fox, Halpern, & Forsyth, 2008; O'Connell, Boat, & Warner, 2009). These barriers indicate a need for greater awareness about adoption and implementation of universal screening (Glover & Albers, 2007; Harrison, Vannest, & Reynolds, 2013; Lane et al., 2013; Levitt et al., 2007).

Universal screening programs within multi-tier systems of support are most commonly implemented in elementary settings, where, unlike secondary schools, one teacher is responsible for a given student for the majority of the school day and provides a clear source of likely valid information. This may be happenstance or it may be due to differences (either real or perceived) in climate, personnel, and responsibilities. Elementary teachers are also responsible for fewer students in a day than secondary teachers, making them potentially more willing to complete screeners. Elementary school teachers also have nurturing and responsible dispositions (Wadlington & Wadlington, 2007) that may be more child-centered when compared to secondary teachers, whose disposition and training is typically more content-centered (Goe, 2007), theoretical, and investigative (Sears & Kennedy, 2001; Willing, Guest, & Morford, 2001). Additionally, the behavior and emotional regulation of elementary age students is viewed as more pliable and more available for prevention efforts, making the effort at screening seem more likely to produce effects. Rightly or wrongly, these issues contribute to barriers in attempting prevention and universal screening reforms in a high school setting. Logistics, exposure to students, teacher dispositions, and expectations about prevention efficacy related to the age of the student are not the only challenges for prevention programs in secondary settings.

CHALLENGES

Common High School Challenges

High schools face specific challenges in implementing screenings within multi-tier systems of support. The overall structure of high schools is quite different from that of elementary schools. High school students are expected to navigate a larger building with a larger number of people, they receive less personal attention from adults, and expectations can vary greatly from one setting to another (Lane et al., 2013). Historically, educators in secondary settings have posited a strong focus on academics with socio-emotional issues viewed as a secondary concern, or even as someone else's responsibility (Severson, Walker, Hope-Doolittle, Kratochwill, & Gresham, 2007). It can be difficult to convince teachers to invest their time and effort in implementing systems of support to address issues that are not perceived as their responsibility. Implementing mental health screenings may be seen as an imposition on the time of teachers who are already concerned with daily teaching and accountability demands (Glover & Albers, 2007; Lane et al., 2013; Levitt et al., 2007). Any added cost, which could include materials, training, additional personnel, and additional services for students, may be viewed as an extra burden on already limited resources (Glover & Albers, 2007; Levitt et al., 2007; Severson et al., 2007). Concerns regarding privacy and possible stigma associated with mental health screening and identification have also been noted in the literature (Levitt et al., 2007). The successful implementation screening as part of a multi-tier system for mental health will depend partly on how it is valued by stakeholders, including the adolescents themselves.

Adolescents are a vulnerable population and screening for social, emotional, and behavioral risk remains relevant for the 14–21-year-old age group. Mental health estimates on the incidence of emotional and behavior problems indicate the teen years are host to a large number of risk factors, and that prevention and early intervention programs are effective for this age group. Approximately 20% of adolescents have a diagnosable mental health disorder (Kessler et al., 2005), with up to 70% not receiving the care they need (Chandra & Minkovitz, 2006). Furthermore, it is estimated that fewer than 1% to 3% of students will ultimately be identified as eligible for special education support through the Individuals with Disabilities Education Improvement Act (IDEIA, 2004). However, there is evidence that the trajectory of a youth's social-emotional development can be changed, so early identification of youth with social-emotional needs is critical (Shonkoff & Phillips, 2000).

Mental Health Problems of Adolescents

Social, emotional, and behavioral issues among young people—including both diagnosable disorders and other problem behaviors, such as early drug or alcohol use, antisocial or aggressive behavior, and violence—have enormous personal, family, and societal costs. The annual quantifiable cost of such disorders among young people was estimated in 2007 to be $247 billion (O'Connell, Boat, & Warner, 2009). In addition, emotional and behavioral disorders among young people interfere with their ability to accomplish normal developmental tasks, such as establishing healthy interpersonal relationships, succeeding in school, and transitioning to the workforce. Mood or personality disorders, depression, anxiety, hyperactivity, and substance abuse are some primary areas of concern for the mental health of adolescents and reasons for universal screening in this age group.

Early identification of risk or problems is possible for each of these, and many other, areas. Screening programs are part prevention and part intervention, as the act of engaging in screening communicates indicators of risk to youth, parents, and teacher. This raises awareness and promotes dialogue and activities to prevent or intervene with risk and problems.

SCREENING AS A SOLUTION

Primary prevention systems of behavior support in schools require a systematic process for screening and identifying students who may be at risk for developing emotional and/or behavioral disorders. Social-emotional screeners are instruments that aid in the identification of students at risk for social-emotional problems. Early intervention based on this screening information allows for implementation of effective strategies to improve social-emotional skills that, in turn, are related to improved academic achievement (Barnett, 2011; Fleming et al., 2005; Gresham, Hunter, Corwin, & Fischer, 2013; Severson et al., 2007). Targeting students who are most in need of support, and delivering effective support to these students, significantly improves the overall effectiveness of prevention programs (Greenberg et al., 2003). Moreover, monitoring students' responses to social-emotional interventions provides formative assessment information that can guide effective practice. Thus, social-emotional screeners may be an important addition to a school's multilevel system of support as recommended by federal legislation.

Benefits of Universal Screening

The benefits of universal screening are threefold. First, screening allows schools and students to benefit by promoting an early intervention model as opposed to the "wait to fail" model (Glover & Albers, 2007). Second, screening may assist schools in a reduction of over-representation of children of color where African American students are twice as likely to be identified as having emotional behavior disorder (EBD) than white students (Alliance for Excellent Education, 2009). Lastly, screening addresses the issue of under-identifying girls and students with internalizing issues (Hosp & Reschly, 2004).

There is evidence that the trajectory of a child's social-emotional development can be changed, and that early identification of adolescents with social-emotional needs is critical (Shonkoff & Phillips, 2000). Primary prevention programs in school settings can enhance interpersonal competencies and prevent externalizing and internalizing problems (Durlak & Wells, 1997). Programs that developed students' problem solving skills and promoted positive school climates demonstrated improved interpersonal relationships, improved academic achievement, and reductions in problem behaviors (e.g., truancy, substance use, violence) among students (Catalano, Hawkins, Berglund, Pollard, & Arthur, 2002). Furthermore, there is a solid and growing empirical base indicating that well-designed, well-implemented, school-based prevention and youth development programming can positively influence a diverse array of social, health, and academic outcomes (Greenberg et al., 2003). Universal screening can be used to establish a school's risk level and allows for monitoring of responsiveness through shifts in the risk level (Lane, Kalberg, Bruhn, Mahoney, & Driscoll, 2008). Screening allows schools to appropriately target limited funds for interventions and provide preventative supports to reduce the need for more intensive supports later (Walker, Cheney, Stage, Blum, & Horner, 2005).

Available Screeners

Universal screeners are available across academic and behavioral domains, with evidence of providing robust and reliable data for identifying potential problems. By their very nature, most are calibrated to err on the side of false positives over false negatives, with the assumption that identification of elevated levels of risk has little to no stigma, and that providing additional instruction is not harmful, whereas a lack of preventative or remedial services could certainly be detrimental. This chapter focuses on emotional and behavioral screeners. Some are more mental health in nature; others are orientated to school or prosocial behavior. Some have a single target; others are broader and cover a range of potential problems.

Factor analysis and reliability and validity studies are available in the literature for these instruments, and although we reference some of these works, more are certainly available for those interested in a deep and broad analysis of any social, emotional, or behavioral screeners. This section is designed to present screeners available for adolescents (Grades 7–12) and provide sufficient descriptive and technical information for the reader to be able to identify which screener may be best for individual school needs.

Screeners Appropriate for Use With Adolescents

Eleven screeners for social, emotional, and/or behavioral challenges were initially identified through a review of commercial catalogues and published literature. What follows are the screeners identified as appropriate for use with adolescents (junior high and high school, or 7th–12th grade), based on manuals or published descriptions. We believe this to be an exhaustive and inclusive list at the time of publication. Where screeners have multiple editions, we have used the most recent version as a reference. The following screeners (listed in alpha order) are included in this chapter: the BASC-3 Behavioral and Emotional Screening System (BESS; Kamphaus & Reynolds, 2015); Behavior/Emotional Social Skills Tracking (BESST; Cicciarelli & Arity, 2008); Devereux Student Strengths Assessment—Mini Form (DESSA-Mini; Naglieri, LeBuffe, & Shapiro, 2008); Social Skills Improvement System (SSIS) Performance Screening Guide (Gresham & Elliott, 2008); Strengths and Difficulties Questionnaire (SDQ; Goodman, 1997); Student Risk Screening Scale (SRSS; Drummond, 1994); and Systematic Screening for Behavior Disorders, 2nd edition (SSBD-2; Walker & Severson, 2014). Additionally, the generic use of office discipline referrals (ODRs) is also included as a potential screening method.

The 25- to 30-item rating scales utilize a 4-point Likert-type scale (N = *never*, S = *sometimes*, O = *often*, A = *almost always*). A total score, percentile score, and corresponding risk classifications (normal, elevated, extremely elevated) provide for further planning steps. The Teacher form and Parent form have two levels: Preschool (ages 3–5) and Child/Adolescent (Grades K–12). The Student self-report form is one level: Child/Adolescent (Grades 3–12). Group and classroom administration can occur. Cut scores are customizable. T-scores are used to report results: T-score of 10–60 = normal, T-score of 61–70 is elevated, and T–score of 71 or above is extremely elevated. Test-retest reliability of scores from the BESS as reported in the technical manual were .80–.91, with internal consistency at .90 –.97 (Kamphaus & Reynolds, 2015). This screener is available from Pearson Education, Inc.

Behavior/Emotional Social Skills Tracking (BESST; Cicciarelli & Arity, 2008). The BESST is a universal screener (and progress monitoring tool) for behavior and social/emotional learning designed for use with kindergarten–8th grade students. Rating forms are available for completion by teachers. However, the developer reports they are in the process of developing a self-report for students in the 6th through 8th grades. All forms are available in English. The BESST has been normed on a large representative sample based on data submitted by registered districts.

The screening tool is the Universal Screener Benchmark Assessment Tool (BAT). Cut scores are customizable based on percentiles. Psychometric properties are unavailable. This screener is available from https://besstweb.com.

Devereux Student Strengths Assessment—Mini Form (DESSA-Mini; Naglieri, LeBuffe, & Shapiro, 2011). The DESSA-Mini is an initial summary of a student's social-emotional strengths and needs, designed for use with K–8th grade students. Rating forms are available for completion by teachers and after-school staff. This screener is available in English; however, the publisher indicates that a Spanish version is expected. The Dessa-Mini was normed against a nationally representative sample of 1,250 students in Grades K–8.

The DESSA-Mini can be used as a stand-alone tool or as part of the DESSA Comprehensive System. The 8-item rating scale utilizes a 4-point Likert-type scale (0 = *never*, 1 = *rarely*, 2 = *occasionally*, 3 = *frequently*, 4 = *very frequently*) and measures the following eight social-emotional areas: self- awareness, social awareness, self- management, relationship skills, goal-directed behavior, personal responsibility, decision–making, and optimistic thinking. The Social-Emotional Total (SET) scores are reported as T-scores, percentile ranks, and corresponding classifications. The classifications are strength (T-score of 60 or above), typical (T-score 41–59), and need for instruction (T-score 40 or below). Reliability coefficients of scores on the DESSA-mini range from .91–.92 with Test-Retest reliability correlations ranging from .88 to .94 (Naglieri, LeBuffe, & Shapiro, 2011). The DESSI-Mini is available from www.centerforresilientchildren.org/home/dcrc-resources/.

Office discipline referrals (ODR). Using discipline referrals as a means to record behavioral data is a general practice in many schools. Information recorded on discipline referrals can be used to track, examine, and monitor not only student behavior, but also the time and the place where the behavior occurred. Results can then be examined to determine if there is a need for school-wide intervention or staff development to address patterns in individual or group student behavior. In a study on the concurrent validity of discipline referrals, Nelson et al. (2002) found that the predictive validity was mixed and indicated concerns regarding the use of discipline referrals in making decisions regarding individual students. However, McIntosh, Campbell, Carter, and Zumbo (2009) examined the concurrent validity of discipline referrals and found a statistically significant correlation with broadband assessments for externalizing behaviors, but not internalizing behaviors.

This is likely due to the nature of internalizing behaviors, which are not as easily or as frequently recognized as externalizing behaviors. Irvin, Tobin, Sprague, Sugai, and Vincent (2004), examined the construct validity of discipline referrals and noted that, while the Nelson et al. (2002) findings are important, those findings do not preclude the use of discipline referrals for making school-wide behavioral intervention. ODRs are often considered the threshold for students who may be considered at risk (Horner et al., 2005). However, researchers found that for the 35% of students who qualified as at risk, the Systematic Screener for Behavior

Disorder (SSBD; Walker & Severson, 2007) did not have multiple ODRs (Walker, Cheney, Stage, Blum, & Horner, 2005).

Social Skills Improvement System Performance Screening Guide (SSIS-PSG; Gresham & Elliott, 2008). The SSIS-PSG is a class-wide universal screener used to evaluate four skill areas (prosocial behaviors, motivation to learn, reading skills, math skills), and is designed for use in children ages 3–18. Rating forms are offered in three versions available: preschool, elementary, and secondary. All forms are available in English. The SSiS is normed for students ages 3–18. This criterion referenced screener measures students' skills according to grade level expectations.

Teachers rate students' behavior on a Likert-type scale (*never, sometimes, often, always*) combined with a rating of significance of behavior. The rating is then compared to a cut score (1 = *high level of concern*, 2–3 [2 preschool] = *moderate level of concern*, 4–5 [3–4 preschool] = *at or above expected level*). Internal reliability is not provided; test-retest reliability of scores from the SSIS are adequate; and inter-rater reliability of scores from the SSIS are adequate, but decreases with increasing grade levels. Validity of scores range between limited and excellent (Gresham & Elliott, 2008). This screener is available from Pearson Education, Inc.

Strengths and Difficulties Questionnaire (SDQ; Goodman, 1997). The SDQ screener is used to evaluate internalizing and externalizing behaviors and is designed for use in students ages 3–16. Rating forms are available for completion by teachers, parents, and students (ages 13–16). All forms are available in English, and they are downloadable in over 80 languages. The statistical results are normed with both British and U.S. respondents and reports can be generated online or hand scored.

The rating scales utilize a 3-point Likert-type scale (*not true, somewhat true, certainly true*). All versions of the SDQ measure 25 attributes, some positive and others negative. These items are divided into five subscales. Score results yield a total difficulties score and five subscale scores: emotional symptoms, conduct problems, hyperactivity/inattention, peer relationship problems, and prosocial behavior. Subscale scores are totaled (range = 0–10), with cut scores used to determine normative behavioral level into three categories: 0–3 = *low*, 4–8 = *moderate*, 9 and above = *high*. Acceptable internal consistency has been identified (a = 0.73), as has test-retest reliability (0.62), and criterion validity has been judged adequate (Goodman, 2001). Internal reliability, as measured by Raykov's rho, is generally satisfactory (i.e., all > 0.70, except the Peer Problems subscale). The SDQ is available at www.sdq.com.

Student Risk Screening Scale (SRSS; Drummond, 1994). The SRSS is a brief universal screener designed to identify and rate patterns of externalizing antisocial behavior in Grades K–12. Rating forms are available for teachers and can be used three times a year for progress monitoring. All forms are in English. The SRSS has been validated and normed for use in kindergarten through 12th grade.

Teachers are instructed to rate only behaviors that they have observed directly. Teachers rate each student in their classroom on each item using a 4-point

Likert-type scale (0 = *never*, 1 = *occasionally*, 2 = *sometimes*, 3 = *frequently*). The seven items are steal, lie/cheat/sneak, behavior problems, peer rejection, low academic achievement, negative attitude, and aggressive behavior. Each student in the class will receive a risk rating based on the total screening score: *low risk* (0–3), *moderate risk* 4–8), or *high risk* (9–21) and then evaluated cut scores are applied. Test-retest reliability is .56–.80 with internal consistency at .78–.86. The SRSS is available from http://miblsi.cenmi.org/MiBLSiModel/Evaluation/Measures/StudentRiskScreeningScale.aspx

Systematic Screening for Behavior Disorders, 2nd edition (SSBD-2; Walker & Severson, 2014). The SSBD-2 is used to identify students who are at risk for externalizing and internalizing behavioral difficulties in PK–9th grade. Teachers identify students at risk through a three-stage, multi-gated system. There are two different screening packets available: one for Grades PK–K, and one for Grades 1–9. This screener is available in English and Spanish. It has been normed on a large representative sample of nearly 7,000 students, closely matching U.S. Census population characteristics.

This screener is designed to assist educators with early identification that will lead to implementation of interventions and supports for students before a critical event (e.g., steals, sets fires, exhibits cruelty to animals) occurs. Stage 1 teachers are asked to consider all students in their class, and to rank order the top 10 students with externalizing behaviors and the top 10 students with internalizing behaviors. Teachers will then choose the top three students from each of these lists to move on to stage 2. At stage 2, teachers will complete adaptive and maladaptive checklists for each of the six students nominated for stage 2 screening. Stage 2 results produce a critical event index (CDI) and a critical frequency index (CFI). Students who meet the criteria will then move to stage 3. Stage 3 screening includes student observations in both social and academic settings. Results at this stage produce cut scores and summary scores for academic engaged time (AET) and peer social behavior (PSB). Internal reliability, test-retest, and inter-rater reliability for scores on the SSBD-2 are all excellent, and validity ranges are from limited to excellent (Caldarella, Young, Richardson, Young, &Young, 2008). Stage 1 test-retest rank order correlations (one-month retest) averaged .76 for externalizers and .74 for internalizers (Caldarella et al., 2008). The SSBD is available from Cambium Learning Group.

MODELS OF IMPLEMENTATION

Models for implementing screening at the secondary level must take into account the unique features of the school and barriers to implementation. Secondary schools are characterized by segmented delivery of the academic curriculum and dictated by logistical considerations of scheduling. Course content is offered in isolation from other subject matter, including social, emotional, or behavioral skill programs. Secondary schools have more difficulty adopting and implementing programs targeting behavior and problem prevention than elementary schools, it seems. For example, while Positive Behavioral Interventions and Supports (PBIS), a multi-tier system of support, was reported to be present in 4,954 elementary schools, it was reported to be present in only 1,730 middle schools, and in just 828 high schools (Spaulding, Horner, May, & Vincent, 2008).

Screening can incorporate or rely on existing data in order to identify students who need additional support. Report card grades, universal formative assessments, benchmark assessments, state assessments, end-of-course exams, behavior and disciplinary referrals, retention rates, attendance (especially for ninth-grade students), and dropout or retention indicators (Muoneke & Shankland, 2009) are all sources of data for screening. Specific data are also available through commercially produced or university-published screeners; some are nationally normed, others use criterion references. These are discussed in greater detail later in this chapter.

There are several features of a universal screening program that require consideration, including student population, informants, permission or "consent" considerations, level of administration support, budget, time/resources, community support, and teacher support. Table 12.1 identifies these features based on our readings of the literature and experience implementing universal screening programs. Table 12.1 also provides considerations in the form of guiding questions so that school teams can organize and prepare their programs. In column three, we provide examples of how these questions might be addressed.

Implementing a universal screening program begins with a strong leadership team and administrator support. Students, parents, faculty, and staff should have consensus that screening is a worthwhile activity and a reasonable use of time in comparison to other priorities. Both short-term and long-term goal setting is appropriate to keep a new program on track and to recognize that systems change does not occur overnight, and certainly not in one year. Reasonable one-year goals may include education about the benefits of screening, review and selection of screeners, setting a calendar for implementation, forming a team, getting commitment from participants, assigning responsibilities, and planning review periods.

What follows is a four-month academic calendar for implementation (Table 12.2). This scenario assumes a beginning of the year start for purposes of implementing a program as quickly as possible, but some schools conduct screening in the spring to plan for subsequent-year programming or summer support. There is no definitive timeline; it depends on the goals of the screening program and the coordinated efforts and resources of the school.

One of the primary purposes of universal screening programs is not just to identify who is at risk, but also to initiate programs and monitor student progress. Intervention is beyond the scope of this chapter, but comprehensive programs are available from a variety of sources, and Table 12.3 presents some widely adopted programs with empirical support (Crone, Hawken, & Horner, 2010; Gresham & Elliott, 1993; Lane, Menzies, Barton-Arwood, Doukas, Munton, 2005; Storer, Evans, & Langberg, 2014; Vannest, Reynolds, & Kamphaus, 2015).

Table 12.1. SCREENER CONSIDERATIONS AND OPTIONS

Feature	Considerations	Options
Student population	Who will be screened?	One grade level, such as 9th grade; multiple grade levels, like Grades 8 and 9; or all grade levels (9–12). Existing students with plans for new student as they matriculate in.
Informants	Who will be reporting on the status of the secondary student? Who will score the completed screener?	Teachers, parents, students may all have rating forms available. Using multiple sources of information provides a more complete picture.
Permission/ Consent	At time of this printing, parental consent is not required by any state to engage in "universal" programs of screening. This means all students.	Consider if passive or active consent would be beneficial, in addition to notification for gathering support and educating family and community about efforts and priorities of the school.
Administrative support	What level of administrative support is present? Campus-based support? District-level support?	Individual administrators or leadership teams can model and provide direction regarding expectations of identifying and addressing problems and risk of problems in the student population. When possible, providing time, training, and resources are more effective leadership models than simple directives. Consensus building, education, and team building strengthen program foundation and influence longevity.
Budget	How much does our screener of choice cost? What are the pricing options? Does a publisher offer a scholarship for low-income schools or new projects? Where will the money come from?	Varies from no cost to about a dollar per student. Don't be hesitant to ask for assistance in initiating programs from commercial publishers, universities, or technical assistance centers.

Table 12.1. Continued

Feature	Considerations	Options
Time/Resources	How long will it take to screen a typical classroom? How long will it take to score the screener? Paper and pencil or computer-based?	When will teachers screen the class? During planning time, before/after school or on a staff development day? Will additional staff support be available?
Community Support	Consider partnerships or collaboration with outside agencies.	Mental health community agencies, local physicians, local mental health providers.
Teacher Support	Identify teacher leaders who can support others.	Teachers with experience or special interest in adolescent mental health.

PROGRESS MONITORING

In the context of a prevention model, after students are identified as at risk and interventions are implemented, educators are tasked with monitoring student progress. Traditional progress monitoring has been used to identify one's relative position within a group, rather than to evaluate individual progress across time (Deno, 1997). However, with the changes in accountability through No Child Left Behind (NCLB; 2001) progress monitoring is used to quantify a student's rate of improvement or responsiveness to intervention. Progress monitoring is a scientifically based practice that is used to assess students' academic and behavior performance (National Center on Student Progress Monitoring, n/d). Progress monitoring addresses the assumption that our decisions about students' behavior, learning, and performance need to be based on objective, reliable data.

Table 12.2. Fall Calendar for Implementation

Month	Tasks
Aug	Draft letters to students, parents, and teachers about program goals. Send permission or notification letters.
Sept	Host Q&A if desired, or back-to-school nights for permission signing. If students or parents are completing self-ratings, do this as early in the year as desired.
Oct	If teachers are completing self-ratings, do this around week 6. Too early in the early in the year is not enough time with a student, too late in the year delays program and service delivery. Collect and score the ratings.
Nov	Return results to teachers and discuss. Identify students to receive programming or additional services or identify school wide programs to teach new skills and support programs.

Table 12.3. PROGRAMS

Type of Program	Reference and Source
Social skills	Gresham, F. M., & Elliott, S. N. (1993). Social skills intervention guide: Systematic approaches to social skills training. *Special Services in the Schools, 8* (1), 137–158.
General externalizing behaviors	Crone, D. A., Hawken, L. S., & Horner, R. H. (2010). *Responding to problem behavior in schools: The behavior education program.* New York, NY: Guilford.
Developing schoolwide programs to prevent and manage problem behaviors	Lane, K. L., Kalberg, J. R., & Menzies, H. M. (2009). *Developing schoolwide programs to prevent and manage problem behaviors: A step-by-step approach.* New York, NY: Guilford.
Attention–deficit/ hyperactivity disorder and organizational problems	Storer, J., Evans, S.W., & Langberg, J. (2014). Organization interventions for children and adolescents with attention-deficit/hyperactivity disorder (ADHD). In M. Weist, N. Lever, C. Bradshaw, & J.S. Owens (Eds.), *Handbook of School Mental Health* (2nd ed). New York, NY: Springer.
Externalizing and Internalizing behavior problems	Vannest, K. J., Reynolds, C. R., & Kamphaus, R. W. (2015). *Intervention guide for behavioral and emotional issues.* Bloomington, MN: Pearson.

The increasing interest in fidelity of implementation related to interventions or instructional programs provides an opportunity to discuss not just progress monitoring for students, but monitoring of teacher behavior as well. The interaction between the two and the longstanding irrefutable data regarding the impact of teacher behavior on student outcomes necessitates this two-prong approach (Allen, Gregory, Mikami, Lun, Hamre, & Pianta, 2013; Allen, Pianta, Mikami, Gregory, & Lun, 2011; Brophy & Good, 1974).

Monitoring Tools

Existing data. Existing data includes grades, attendance/tardy records, office discipline referrals, and homework completion. Existing data is often insufficient alone to monitor student progress, but it can be a useful supplemental source of data on academic or behavioral performance (Wright, 2010). Existing data has the benefit of no additional resources expended, but it typically is taken infrequently (such as semester end) or on low-occurrence behaviors (like absences), so that the utility for quick decision-making is limited.

Checklists. Checklists contain a list of behaviors or specific steps that can be observed and recorded. Checklists come in more than one variety. A list can be of global skills or larger constructs, or it can be of specific skills and sub-elements of a construct. A checklist is typically a binary yes/no assessment of specific or global skills. In some cases, a teacher will use a checklist to observe the students. In other cases, students use checklists to ensure that they have completed all of the steps and considered all of the possibilities. The rater could be the student in a self-check, the parent, the teacher, or a relevant adult. Raters assess over a period of time, ranging from small instructional periods to a day or week, and record the appropriate evaluation. Although mostly dichotomous, some checklists may have a third category for "uncertain" or "unknown." Global skills checklists include both the larger skill and the sub-skill. Affirmation of majority or all sub-skills would indicate the presence of the global skill. Monitoring performance on a checklist would be as a percentage of possible skills. We suggest that educators avoid dichotomously monitoring each sub-skill, as there is a floor and ceiling problem and a lack of sensitivity. Instead, educators can monitor and graph the percentage of sub-skills for each global skill or the percentage of global skills. When more sensitivity is desired in measurement, a rating scale may be more desirable.

Rating scales. A rating scale (simply) is a checklist with greater degrees of measurement sensitivity, using three or more categories for decision-making about the demonstration of a skill. The greater the number of scores possible, the more sensitivity in the measurement. Scales with nine or more categories tend to have the most reliability when chance agreement is accounted for. Rating scales are commercially available and can also be locally created. Behaviors of interest are identified and a range of options for scoring is provided. Scales can be anchored at each point or only at the end. Scoring on a rating scale, like a checklist, is accomplished at the end of a specified interval, and this time period should remain consistent for graphing and monitoring (e.g., after each class period, at the end of the school day). One widely used example of a rating scale routinely used in classrooms is the daily behavior report card (DBRC). The teacher completes a rating scale each day, evaluating various target student behaviors.

Behavior frequency or rate. Direct observations, rather than retrospective ratings such as in a checklist or rating scale, often use basic behavioral measures such as frequency, rate, latency, or duration. These are each incident-based measures, sometimes with time related to the event. Operational definitions, sufficient to easily recognize the targeted behavior, are required for all direct observations of behavior frequency or rate. Behaviors best suited for frequency counting or rate are clearly observable, have discrete beginning and ending points, and are of limited and perhaps short duration. Frequency ratings are counts of the behavior occurring. Observation periods should be consistent in start and stop time, and consistent in the opportunities to engage in the behavior and the task demands that may precede the behaviors. When time periods are not consistent, frequency should be changed to rate for comparison across recording events. Hand-raising is a good behavior for counting, while off-task behavior is not. Frequency, duration, and latency are better suited to behaviors that have clearly observable start and end times, but may be longer in time of occurrence, or differ in their topography of occurrence.

Behavior log. Behavior logs are narrative "incident reports" that the teacher records when problem behaviors occur. The teacher makes a log entry each time that a behavior is observed. An advantage of behavior logs is that they can provide information about the context within which a behavior occurs. Behavior logs are most useful for tracking problem behaviors that are serious but do not occur frequently (Wright, 2010). There is no validity or reliability associated with a behavior log, as observations are typically from a single informant and reflect individual incidences. Behavior logs that include additional hypothesis about "why" behavior occurs can be problematic without functional analysis data.

Work products. Student work products can be collected and evaluated to judge whether the student is incorporating social, emotional, and behavioral skills to the school demands of in-classroom work tasks and homework. Skills like organization and attention, as well as characteristics such as motivation and effort, have clear social, emotional, and behavioral components or influences. These translate to academic performance, and work products can be a distal or proximal measure. Examples of work products are math computation worksheets, journal entries, and written responses to end-of-chapter questions from the course textbook. Whenever teachers collect academic performance data on a student, it is recommended that they also assess the performance of typical peers in the classroom. Performance information allows the teacher to directly estimate and track the skill gap that separates the target student from others in the class who are not having academic difficulties. Teachers should select students to serve as "comparison peers" whose skills represent the class average. Work products can be assessed in several ways, depending on the identified problem. The teacher can estimate the percentage of work completed on an assignment, for example, as well as the accuracy of the work actually completed. Additionally, the instructor may decide to rate the student's work for quality, using a rubric or other qualitative evaluation approach.

Self-Monitoring

Checklists, rating scales, and work products can be assessed by adults in the home or learning environment, but they can also be assessed and recorded by adolescent students. Graphing and monitoring progress is an intervention in and of itself, and students with behavioral disabilities or challenges respond well to the self-managed and self-control aspects of this type of progress monitoring. Self-monitoring has the added benefit of teaching the meta-cognitive skill of self-awareness (Hoff & DuPaul, 1998; Koegel, Koegel, Harrower, & Carter, 1999; Rhode, Morgan, & Young, 1983). Self-monitoring interventions are considered flexible, efficient, and effective strategies for students with a wide range of difficulties (Mitchum, Young, West, & Benyo, 2001; Pierce & Schreibman, 1994; Rock, 2005; Strain & Kohler, 1994; Todd, Horner, & Sugai, 1999).

Prior to initiating progress monitoring with adolescents in secondary settings, it is reasonable to expect that the students would be involved in selecting target behaviors and setting goals. The addition of self-identified rewards or self-selected reinforcers can increase the development of new skills or increase the demonstration of existing skills. Progress monitoring using any of the data described here is easily plotted on graph paper or Excel spreadsheets by adults or adolescents, and it provides an opportunity to learn a transferable skill set. If the adult is responsible for the progress monitoring, the adolescent can maintain involvement through a regular review of data. An in-depth discussion of the measurement considerations related to progress monitoring is beyond the scope of this chapter, and for most low- to medium-stakes decisions it is not crucial for engaging in the practice. However, if high-stakes decisions are involved (e.g., placement or changes in special education), then the data requires considerations of reliability and validity in the form of a second rater for 20% or more of all data collected, as well as an evaluation of the construct and social validity of the instrument used in addition to an awareness of the sensitivity of the measure for detecting growth and any potential effects from repeated measurement (Graham, Milanowski, & Miller, 2012; Gwet, 2001; Johnson & Svingby, 2007).

CONCLUSION

Universal screening programs and progress monitoring in secondary settings remain underutilized for any number of reasonable barriers. However, youth and adolescents are at risk for an equally impressive number of emotional and behavioral problems, most with disastrous consequences for individuals, their families, and our communities. Junior high schools and high schools have tremendous opportunities to identify risk before problems become intractable, implement programs, and progress monitor teacher and student behaviors and interactions. Doing so produces strong effects on problems and changes both trajectories and long-term outcomes. Universal screening and progress monitoring are cost-effective, proactive, positive methods for improving educational outcomes for youth. This chapter presented some data on types of common problems, justification for engaging in screening, and methods for screening and progress monitoring, including guiding principles and timelines. The authors fully hope that in a future revision of this book, screening programs will be present in more than half of schools, rather than below 15%, and that the focus of research efforts will be on the relative strengths and weaknesses of various methods and the efficiency of programing. Thomas Edison once said, "I have not failed, I have learned 10,000 ways not to succeed." Educators work and dedicate their time and energy because they want young people to be successful. Reactive punitive programs do not produce the changes and learning we desire to see in our students. Only the early identification of potential, emerging, and existing problems will create the opportunity to teach the social, emotional, and behavioral skills needed to be successful academically and socially.

REFERENCES

Allen, J. P., Gregory, A., Mikami, A. Y., Lun, J., Hamre, B. K., & Pianta, R. C. (2013). Observations of effective teaching in secondary school classrooms: Predicting student achievement with the CLASS-S. *School Psychology Review, 42*(1), 76–98.

Allen, J. P., Pianta, R. C., Gregory, A., Mikami, A. Y., & Lun, J. (2011). An interaction-based approach to enhancing secondary school instruction and student achievement. *Science*, *333*(6045), 1034–1037.

Alliance for Excellent Education. (2009). Teaching for a new world: Preparing high school educators to deliver college- and career-ready instruction. Washington D.C. Retrieved from http://all4ed.org/wp-content/uploads/TeachingForANewWorld.pdf

Barnett, W. S. (2011). Effectiveness of early educational intervention. *Science*, *333*(6045), 975–978.

Bradley, R., Doolittle, J., & Bartolotta, R. (2008). Building on the data and adding to the discussion: The experiences and outcomes of students with emotional disturbance. *Journal of Behavioral Education*, *17*(1), 4–23.

Brophy, J. E., & Good, T. L. (1974). *Teacher-student relationships: Causes and consequences.* New York, NY: Holt, Rinehart & Winston.

Brown, M. M. & Grumet, J. G. (2009). School-based suicide prevention with African American youth in an urban setting. *Professional Psychology: Research and Practice*, *40*(2), 111–117.

Caldarella, P., Young, E. L., Richardson, M. J., Young, B. J., & Young, K. R. (2008). Validation of the Systematic Screening for Behavior Disorders in middle and junior high school. *Journal of Emotional and Behavioral Disorders*, *16*(2), 105–117.

Catalano, R. F., Hawkins, J. D., Berglund, M. L., Pollard, J. A., & Arthur, M. W. (2002). Prevention science and positive youth development: Competitive or cooperative frameworks? *Journal of Adolescent Health*, 31(6 Suppl. S), 230–239.

Chandra, A., & Minkovitz, C. S. (2006). Stigma starts early: Gender differences in teen willingness to use mental health services. *Journal of Adolescent Health*, *38*(6), 754-e1.

Cicciarelli, P., & Arity, P. (2008). Behavior/ Emotional Social Skills Tracking (BESST) Web. Illinois. https://besstweb.com/?p=index

Cowen, E. L., Dorr, D. A., Clarfield, S. P., Kreling, B., McWilliams, S. A., Pokracki, P., . . . Wilson, A. (1973). The AML: A quick screening device for early identification of school maladaptation. *American Journal of Community Psychology*, *42*(1), 12–35.

Crone, D. A., Hawken, L. S., & Horner, R. H. (2010). Responding to problem behavior in schools: The behavior education program. New York, NY: Guilford.

Deno, S. L. (1997). "Whither thou goest: Perspectives on progress monitoring." In E. Kameenuii, J. Lloyd, & D. Chard (Eds.) *Issues in educating students with disabilities* (pp. 77–99). New York, NY: Lawrence Erlbaum Associates.

Drummond, T. (1994). *The Student Risk Screening Scale (SRSS).* Grants Pass, OR: Josephine County Mental Health Program.

Durlak, J. A., & Wells, A. M. (1997). Primary prevention mental health programs for children and adolescents: A meta-analytic review. *American Journal of Community Psychology*, *25*, 115–152.

Fleming, C. B., Haggerty, K. P., Catalano, R. F., Harachi, T. W., Mazza, J. J., & Gruman, D. H. (2005). Do social and behavioral characteristics targeted by preventative interventions predict standardized test scores and grades? *Journal of School Health*, *75*, 342–349.

Fox, J. K., Halpern, L. F., & Forsyth, J. P. (2008). Mental health checkups for children and adolescents: A means to identify, prevent, and minimize suffering associated with anxiety and mood disorders. *Clinical Psychology: Science and Practice*, *15*(3), 182–211.

Glover, T., & Albers, C. (2007). Considerations for evaluating universal screening assessments. *Journal of School Psychology*, *45*(2), 117–135.

Goe, L. (2007). The Link between Teacher Quality and Student Outcomes: A Research Synthesis. *National comprehensive center for teacher quality.*

Goodman, R. (1997). The Strengths and Difficulties Questionnaire: a research note. *Journal of child psychology and psychiatry, 38*(5), 581–586.

Goodman, R. (2001). Psychometric properties of the Strengths and Difficulties Questionnaire (SDQ). *Journal of the American Academy of Child & Adolescent Psychiatry, 40,* 1337–1345.

Graham, M., Milanowski, A., & Miller, J. (2012). *Measuring and promoting inter-rater agreement of teacher and principal performance ratings.* Washington, DC: U.S. Department of Education: Center for Educator Compensation Reform.

Greenberg, M. T., Weissberg, R. P., O'Brien, M. U., Zins, J. E., Fredericks, L., Resnik, H., & Elias, M. J. (2003). Enhancing school-based prevention and youth development through coordinated social, emotional, and academic learning. *American Psychologist, 58,* 466–474.

Gresham, F. M., & Elliott, S. N. (1993). Social skills intervention guide: Systematic approaches to social skills training. *Special Services in the Schools, 8*(1), 137–158.

Gresham, F. M., & Elliott, S. N. (2008). *Social Skills Improvement System (SSIS) rating scales.* Bloomington, MN: Pearson Assessments.

Gresham, F. M., Hunter, K. K., Corwin, E. P., & Fischer, A. J. (2013). Screening, assessment, treatment, and outcome evaluation of behavioral difficulties in an RTI Model. *Exceptionality, 21*(1), 19–33.

Gwet, K. (2001). *Handbook of inter-rater reliability.* Gaithersburg, MD: STATAXIS Publishing Company.

Harrison, J. R., Vannest, K. J., & Reynolds, C. R. (2013). Social acceptability of five screening instruments for social, emotional, and behavioral challenges. *Behavioral Disorders, 38*(3), 171–189.

Hoff, K. E., & DuPaul, G. J. (1998). Reducing disruptive behavior in general education classrooms: The use of self-management strategies. *School Psychology Review, 27,* 290–303.

Horner, R. H., Carr, E. G., Halle, J., McGee, G., Odom, S., Wolery, M. (2005). The use of single-subject research to identify evidence-based practice in special education. *Exceptional Children, 71,* 165–179.

Hosp, J. L., & Reschly, D. J. (2004). Disproportionate representation of minority students in special education: Academic, demographic, and economic predictors. *Exceptional Children, 70*(2), 185–199.

Irvin, L. K., Tobin, T. J., Sprague, J. R., Sugai, G., & Vincent, C. G. (2004). Validity of office discipline referral measures as indices of school-wide behavioral status and effects of school-wide behavioral interventions. *Journal of Positive Behavior Interventions, 6,* 131–147.

Jamieson, K. H., & Romer, D. (2005). A call to action on adolescent mental health. In D. L. Evans, E. B. Foa, E. Gur, H. Hendin, C. P. O'Brien, M. E. P. Seligman, & B. T. Walsh (Eds.), *Treating and preventing adolescent mental health disorders: What we know and what we don't know* (pp. 598–615). New York, NY: Oxford University Press.

Johnson, A., & Svingby, G. (2007). The use of scoring rubrics: Reliability, validity and educational consequences. *Educational Research Review, 2,* 130–144.

Kamphaus, R. W., & Reynolds, C. R. (2015). Behavior Assessment System for Children (3rd ed.) (BASC-3): Behavioral and Emotional Screening System (BESS). Bloomington, MN: Pearson.

Kessler, R. C., Berglund, P., Demler, O., Jin, R., Merikangas, K. R., & Walters, E. E. (2005). Life-time prevalence and age-of-onset distribution of *DSM-IV* disorders in the national comorbidity survey replication. *Archives of General Psychiatry, 62,* 593–602.

Koegel, L. K., Koegel, R. L., Harrower, J. K., & Carter, C.M. (1999). Pivotal response intervention 1: Overview of approach. *Journal of the Association for Persons with Severe Handicaps, 24,* 175–185.

Lane, K. L., Kalberg, J. R., Bruhn, A. L., Mahoney, M. E., & Driscoll, S. A. (2008). Primary prevention programs at the elementary level: Issues of treatment integrity, systematic screening, and reinforcement. *Education and Treatment of Children, 31,* 465–494.

Lane, K. L., Kalberg, J. R., & Menzies, H. M. (2009). Developing schoolwide programs to prevent and manage problem behaviors: A step-by-step approach. New York, NY: Guilford.

Lane, K. L., Menzies, H. M., Barton-Arwood, S. M., Doukas, G. L., & Munton, S. M. (2005). Designing, implementing, and evaluating social skills interventions for elementary students: Step-by-step procedures based on actual school-based investigations. *Preventing School Failure, 49,* 18–26.

Lane, K. L., Oakes, W. P., Ennis, R. P., Cox, M. L., Schatschneider, C., & Lambert, W. (2013). Additional evidence for the reliability and validity of the Student Risk Screening Scale at the high school level: A replication and extension. *Journal of Emotional and Behavioral Disorders, 21,* 97–115.

Levitt, J. M., Saka, N., Romanelli, L. H., & Hoagwood, K. (2007). Early identification of mental health problems in schools: The status of instrumentation. *Journal of School Psychology, 45,* 163–191.

McIntosh, K., Campbell, A. L., Carter, D. R., & Zumbo, B. D. (2009). Concurrent validity of office discipline referrals and cut points used in schoolwide positive behavior support. *Behavioral Disorders, 34*(2), 100–113.

Mitchum, K. J., Young, K. R., West, R. P., & Benyo, J. (2001). CSPASM: A classwide peer assisted self-management program for general education classrooms. *Education and Treatment of Children, 24,* 111–140.

Muoneke, A., & Shankland, L. (2009). Uncharted territory: Using tiered intervention to improve high school performance. *SEDL Letter, 21*(1). Retrieved from http://www.sedl.org/pubs/sedl-letter/v21n01/tiered.html

Naglieri, J. A., LeBuffe, P., & Shapiro, V. B. (2011). *DESSA-mini: Devereux student strengths assessment.* Lewisville, NC: Devereux Foundation.

Nelson, J. R., Benner, G. J., Reid, R. C., Epstein, M. H., & Currin, D. (2002). The convergent validity of office discipline referrals with the CBCL-TRF. *Journal of Emotional and Behavioral Disorders, 10,* 181–188.

No Child Left Behind Act of 2001 (2002). Public Law No. 107-110, § 115. Stat, 1425, 107–110.

O'Connell, M. E., Boat, T., & Warner, K. E. (2009). *Preventing mental, emotional, and behavioral disorders among young people: Progress and possibilities.* Washington, DC: National Academies Press.

Pierce, K. L., & Schreibman, L. (1994). Teaching daily living skills to children with autism in unsupervised settings through pictorial self-management. *Journal of Applied Behavior Analysis, 27,* 471–481.

Rhode, G., Morgan, D. P., & Young, K. R. (1983). Generalization and maintenance of treatment gains of behaviorally handicapped students from resource rooms to regular classrooms using self-evaluation procedures. *Journal of Applied Behavior Analysis, 16*, 171–188.

Rock, M. L. (2005). Use of strategic self-monitoring to enhance academic engagement, productivity, and accuracy of students with and without exceptionalities. *Journal of Positive Behavior Interventions, 7*, 3–17.

Romer, D., & McIntosh, M. (2005). The roles and perspectives of school mental health professionals in promoting adolescent mental health. In D. L. Evans, E. B. Foa, R. E. Gur, H. Hendin, C. P. O'Brien, M. E. P. Seligman, & B. T. Walsh (Eds.), *Treating and preventing adolescent mental health disorders: What we know and what we don't know, A research agenda for improving the mental health of our youth* (pp. 597–616). Oxford, England: Oxford University Press.

Sears, S., & Kennedy, J. (2001). Myers-Briggs personality profiles of prospective educators. *Journal of Educational Research, 90*(4), 195–202.

Severson, H. H., Walker, H. M., Hope-Doolittle, J., Kratochwill, T. R., & Gresham, F. M. (2007). Proactive, early screening to detect behaviorally at-risk students: Issues, approaches, emerging innovations, and professional practices. *Journal of School Psychology, 45*(2), 193–223.

Shonkoff, J. P., & Phillips, D. A. (2000). From neurons to neighborhoods: The science of early childhood development. Washington DC: National Academy Press.

Spaulding, S. A., Horner, R. H., May, S. L., & Vincent, C. G. (2008, November). Evaluation brief: Implementation of school-wide PBS across the United States. OSEP Technical Assistance Center on Positive Behavioral Interventions and Supports. Retrieved from http://pbis.org/evaluation/evaluation_briefs/default.aspx

Storer, J., Evans, S. W., & Langberg, J. (2014). Organization interventions for children and adolescents with attention-deficit/hyperactivity disorder (ADHD). In M. Weist, N. Lever, C. Bradshaw, & J.S. Owens (Eds.), *Handbook of school mental health* (2nd ed., pp. 385–398). New York, NY: Springer.

Strain, P. S., & Kohler, F. W. (1994). Teaching preschool students with autism to self monitor their social interactions: An analysis of results in home and school settings. *Journal of Emotional & Behavioral Disorders, 2*, 78–89.

Todd, A. W., Horner, R. H., & Sugai, G. (1999). Effects of self-monitoring and self-recruited praise on problem behavior, academic engagement, and work completion in a typical classroom. *Journal of Positive Behavior Interventions, 1*, 66–76.

U.S. Department of Health and Human Services, Substance Abuse and Mental Health Services Administration (2009). *Risk and protective factors for mental, emotional, and behavioral disorders across the life cycle*. Retrieved from http://dhss.alaska.gov/dbh/Documents/Prevention/programs/spfsig/pdfs/IOM_Matrix_8%205x11_FINAL.pdf

Vannest, K. J., Reynolds, C. R., & Kamphaus, R. W. (2015). *Intervention guide for behavioral and emotional issues*. Minneapolis, MN: NCS Pearson.

Wadlington, E., & Wadlington, P. (2011). Teacher dispositions: Implications for teacher education. *Childhood Education, 87*(5), 323–326.

Walker, B., Cheney, D., Stage, S., Blum, C., & Horner, R. H. (2005). Schoolwide screening and positive behavior supports identifying and supporting students at risk for school failure. *Journal of Positive Behavior Interventions, 7*(4), 194–204.

Walker, H. M., & Severson, H. H. (2007). *Systematic screening for behavior disorders.* Eugene, OR: Pacific Northwest.

Walker, H. M., & Severson, H. H. (2014). *Systematic screening for behavior disorders* (2nd ed.). Eugene, OR: Pacific Northwest.

Willing, D., Guest, K., & Morford, J. (2001). Who is entering the teaching profession? MBTI profiles of 525 master in teaching students. *Journal of Psychological Type,* 59, 36–44.

Weist, N. Lever, C. Bradshaw, & J. S. Owens (Eds.) (2014). *Handbook of school mental health* (2nd ed). New York, NY: Springer.

Wright, J. (2010). RTI: Teacher friendly methods for tracking student progress. New York, NY: Intervention Central Workshop.

13

Classroom-Based Services for Adolescents With Mental Health Needs

LEE KERN, BETH CUSTER, AND IMAD ZAHEER ■

INTRODUCTION

Providing classroom-based services to address the mental health needs of adolescents poses a number of challenges. First, although teachers at the secondary level are highly skilled in their respective content areas, few have parallel expertise in addressing their students' behavioral and mental health issues. Second, the structure of secondary settings, whereby teacher instruction is limited to a single content area, offers limited time with each student. This often provides insufficient time for teachers to become adequately acquainted with students and identify those who may be in need of additional supports. Unfortunately, universal screening remains extraordinarily unusual, particularly at the secondary level (Caldarella, Young, Richardson, Young, & Young, 2008). Third, we have found that teachers frequently view adolescence as a time when independence is expected, and they are reluctant to afford the supports that would greatly improve students' outcomes. Finally, the nature of many of the behavioral challenges common among adolescents, such as tardiness and truancy, can be frustrating and counterproductive, especially when teachers have made gallant efforts to assist those in need.

At the same time, the secondary school years are particularly important, representing the margins of adulthood, when success or failure paves the way for the future. For instance, high school completion is associated with a number of benefits, including higher employment rates and greater wages (U.S. Bureau of Labor Statistics, 2012). Conversely, high school dropout is associated with numerous detrimental outcomes, such as earning less yearly income, increased arrest rates, and chronic reliance on public assistance, compared to those who completed high school (Gasper, DeLuca, & Estacion, 2012).

There are many reasons why schools, and classrooms in particular, are ideally suited for the delivery of interventions that address mental health concerns. Because students spend a majority of their day in school, there are many opportunities to provide interventions. Further, among all of the staff in any given school, teachers have the most regular and consistent contact with students. This renders the potential for consistent intervention delivery both plausible and potentially consequential. In addition, student academic growth is intimately tied with domains of student mental health (e.g., social and emotional development), with positive growth in mental health impacting academic performance, and vice versa (Sameroff & Rosenblum, 2006).

Fortunately, there are a number of interventions teachers can readily implement in their classrooms that require limited expertise in the fields of behavioral and mental health, yet have a significant impact on student behavior. Importantly, research supports teacher effectiveness with respect to intervention delivery for students' emotional and behavior problems and also substantiates the manageability of such interventions in classrooms (Franklin, Kim, Ryan, Kelly, & Montgomery, 2012). In this chapter, we describe a tiered model of prevention and intervention in the classroom that is efficient and cost-effective. In addition, we detail specific interventions with solid or emerging evidence for effectiveness in secondary settings.

RATIONALE FOR A TIERED MODEL OF INTERVENTION

A tiered model of intervention, initially applied in the public health field, has now been widely used in schools in the form of school-wide positive behavioral support (SWPBS; Horner, Sugai, & Anderson, 2010). The model focuses on prevention and intervention through universal, secondary, and tertiary support, as dictated by student need. The strength of this system of service delivery is that it allows professionals to provide a full range of services, with the appropriate intensity matched to the level of need exhibited by each student. Furthermore, intervention at the universal tier is aimed at all students, thereby preventing the majority of behavior problems.

We recommend the same conceptual framework for individual classrooms as an efficient and effective way for teachers to both prevent emotional and behavioral problems from emerging and reduce the severity and impact of existing student problems. Tier I focuses on class-wide procedures that promote a safe and welcoming environment with clear expectations and structure. Tier II is aimed at preventing low-level problem behavior and can be used with specific individuals, groups, or, at times, an entire class of students. Finally, Tier III involves individualized and intensive interventions for students with the most serious needs. Beyond addressing the behavioral and mental health needs of secondary students, the interventions associated with this approach represent best practice in classroom instruction and foster a healthy and productive relationship between teacher and student.

We recommend that teachers introduce a tiered framework at the start of the school year or semester. This assures that students become familiar with classroom expectations and routines early on, and little time is wasted addressing problems that may have been prevented. Further, those students with greater intervention needs can be more readily identified. However, it is never too late to start. Introduction of a tiered model at any time in the school year, when implemented correctly, will improve the classroom atmosphere and can reduce emotional and behavioral problems. In the remainder of this chapter we describe specific classroom interventions organized within a three-tiered framework. We first provide a rationale for each intervention strategy, followed by specific implementation procedures. We then describe the existing research to support effectiveness of the intervention.

TIER I INTERVENTION: CLASS-WIDE PRACTICES

Tier I interventions are class-wide or universal practices that benefit all students. In addition, they represent best practice with respect to classroom organization and structure and maximize instructional time. The procedures can be easily integrated into the daily classroom routine. When class-wide procedures are solidly in place, fewer resources are needed for Tier II and III interventions and students with more intensive needs can be more easily and accurately identified. We describe four simple universal class-wide strategies below.

Class-Wide Expectations

Students spend the majority of their school day in the classroom setting. Unfortunately, most teachers receive limited, if any, formal preservice coursework in the area of behavior management (State, Kern, Starosta, & Mukherjee, 2011). Even in schools with school-wide positive behavior support in place, teachers may struggle adapting and applying universal expectations in their classrooms. Classroom expectations create a supportive environment where students feel comfortable and safe, which is essential for promoting academic growth and mental health. Expectations help students remember what they need to be doing in order to be successful. Furthermore, clear expectations can reduce stress and anxiety among students with internalizing problems by providing consistency and predictability.

Classroom expectations are unique to the teacher and subject matter, and they tell students what behaviors are desired in the classroom. Students will remember the expectations if there are no more than five (three to five is recommended). Effective classroom expectations should be positively stated, explaining to students what to do rather than what not to do. For example, "Students will arrive to class before the bell" is an instructive expectation, rather than "Students should not be late to class." Additionally, expectations should be observable and measureable. This means that expectations should leave little room for interpretation, even to new students with limited classroom exposure. For instance, asking students to "Be polite" could be interpreted in many ways, whereas the expectation to "Use materials as intended" is much more specific. Box 13.1 shows an example of expectations in a high school chemistry class.

For expectations to be effective, they need to be accompanied by consequences. It is most important that consequences follow appropriate behavior so that students are encouraged and reinforced for doing what is expected. When teachers let students know that they are meeting expectations, desired behavior is likely to increase. In addition, focusing on appropriate behavior and complementing students creates a positive classroom climate.

Praise is commonly used as a consequence for appropriate behavior in classroom settings. A useful way to quantify praise and balance it with the use of reprimands is the concept of "reinforcement ratio," which compares the number of positive teacher comments (praise) with the number of corrections or reprimands. The minimum ratio of positive to negative statements is 3:1 (Sprick, 1981, 1985); however some have recommended ratios as high as 10:1 (Nafpaktitis, Mayer, & Butterworth, 1985). Although there have been no published studies experimentally evaluating the specific ratio that is most effective for producing positive behavior, descriptive and correlational research indicates there are fewer behavior problems in classrooms with a high amount of positive statements and a low amount of negative feedback (e.g., Hall, Panyan, Rabon, & Broden,1968; Merrett, & Wheldall, 1992; Shores, Gunter, & Jack, 1993). Some adolescents prefer a discreet form of praise (Elwell & Tiberio, 1994), which can be delivered with a written note, gesture (smile, nod, high-five), or quiet compliment. Examples of other positive consequences include extra points for participation, free time at the end of the period, lunch with a teacher, reduced homework or free homework pass, listening to music while working, and computer time.

Box 13.1

EXAMPLE OF EXPECTATIONS IN A HIGH SCHOOL CHEMISTRY CLASS

Mrs. Smith's Classroom Expectations
1. Be in your assigned seat with only your book, pencil, and notebook on your desk when the bell rings.
2. All electronic devices not provided by the teacher stay inside zipped pockets between bells.
3. Raise your hand and wait for teacher permission to speak or to leave your assigned seat.
4. Keep your hands, feet, and objects to yourself.

Predetermined consequences also need to be in place for failing to adhere to the class-wide expectations. These must be clear and consistently delivered in order to discourage inappropriate classroom deportment. Examples include corrective feedback, loss of participation points, a phone call home, or an after-school conference.

It is important for students to fully understand the expectations and accompanying consequences, and teachers must provide such instruction. This can involve simply reviewing the specific behaviors associated with each expectation, along with the consequences. In classrooms with students who have difficulty following the expectations, this instruction may need to be repeated regularly (e.g., daily, weekly). The use of role-play with examples and non-examples is also an effective method of instruction.

There is a substantial amount of research indicating that providing clear expectations, instruction, and reinforcement for prosocial behavior has many benefits, including improvements in student behavior. For example, Klem and Connell (2004) found that student perception of these elements helps create a successful classroom environment. Students reported feeling engaged in school when they perceived that the learning environment was structured with high, clear, and fair expectations. Further, research on teacher aspirational expectations indicates that positive expectations lead to an increase in academic performance, whereas negative expectations have been associated with academic difficulties (Tyler & Boelter, 2008). Furthermore, Wentzel, Baker, and Russell (2012) found that adolescents' social and academic engagement was related to the extent that they believed their teachers and peers expected them to succeed.

In a study by Elwell and Tiberio (1994), 279 students between 7th and 12th grade reported feeling favorably toward teacher praise. Although all students generally liked receiving teacher praise, there were differences in how it was perceived among various grades, with 7th, 8th, 11th, and 12th graders reporting liking public praise whereas 9th and 10th graders reported preferring it more privately. Furthermore, Daniel, Duncan, and Harpole (2013) found that both public and private praise were effective in increasing on-task behaviors of high school students in the classroom, and in decreasing disruptive behaviors.

Improving Student-Teacher Interactions

A second class-wide strategy to prevent problem behavior is to engage in caring, positive, and supportive student-teacher interactions. Teachers can create a positive classroom community through their interactions with students. This occurs when teacher are accepting of individual differences, are friendly, and take the time to build a positive rapport with each student. There are simple strategies that are meaningful to students and set the classroom tone. These include addressing students by name, greeting them at the door when they enter the classroom, and smiling often. Moreover, talking with students about their interests or concerns demonstrates that teachers care about them beyond their performance in the classroom. This can be accomplished by asking a student what is troubling her or making it a point to acknowledge student success (e.g., grades, sports, other extracurricular activities).

Research shows that student-teacher interactions can help improve student outcomes, both academically and behaviorally, especially if they result in good student-teacher relationships. Improved teacher outcomes have been noted as well, such as reductions in work stress (Roorda, Koomen, Split, & Oort, 2011). Specific aspects of the interactions may be particularly important. For example, Anderman, Andrzejewski, and Allen (2011) surveyed 2,864 students in Grades 9–12 to determine how high school teachers can create motivating and engaging classroom environments. Three core themes emerged: (a) being supportive and understanding, (b) building and maintaining rapport, and (c) managing the classroom.

Embedding Choice

A central quality of self-determination is the perception of choice (Reeve, Nix, & Hamm, 2003). Choice is defined as the act of selecting or making a decision when faced with two or more possibilities. Offering choices can be used as a class-wide strategy to promote elevated levels of interest and attention and provide a sense of control, purpose, and competence. Furthermore, adulthood is a time when making choices is required, and providing adolescents with such opportunities prepares them to make effective choices as adults.

Teachers can embed choice in many ways without altering an assignment. For example, students may select the materials used to complete a task, their daily seating assignment, or their partner for a cooperative learning activity. Other choice options include allowing students to select the order of task completion or the medium for work completion (e.g., writing an essay by hand or on the computer). Broader types of choices include selecting the topic they would like to research or write about, or creating questions that the class will answer the following day.

Kern, Bambara, and Fogt (2002) illustrated the success of class-wide choice in a middle school classroom by allowing students to select the topical unit of study, how they would complete activities (e.g., on the computer, with a partner), and with whom they would work. The intervention resulted in higher levels of student engagement and a reduction in disruptive behavior. Research has also shown that choice can promote effort and persistence with tasks. For example, Carey, DeMartini, Prince, Luteran, and Carey (2013) demonstrated that when choice was provided to adolescents, their productivity and engagement increased.

Good Behavior Game

The Good Behavior Game is a class-wide intervention that promotes on-task behaviors and helps minimize undesired behaviors (Barrish, Saunders, & Wolf,

1969). This strategy reinforces students who demonstrate desired behaviors during instructional times. The Institute of Medicine report *Preventing Mental, Emotional, and Behavioral Disorders Among Young People* (National Research Council, 2009) stated that this strategy was one of the most influential prevention approaches that teachers can implement. We recommend this program, in conjunction with the approaches described above, for classrooms that are particularly challenging.

To implement the Good Behavior Game, the teacher typically divides the class into two groups that compete against each other for teacher recognition of target prosocial behaviors (Kellam et al., 2008). The original version used a response-cost paradigm in which students received "demerits" for breaking a publically posted classroom rule. We recommend a newer version in which the teams can earn bonus points to offset demerits (Rathvon, 2008).

Setting up this program involves four steps. The first step is to identify times or activities that are particularly problematic, and when the game would be beneficial (e.g., during teacher lecture when students tend to be inattentive). Next, the teacher or class operationally defines the behaviors that will result in a demerit (e.g., calling out or speaking without teacher permission) and behaviors that will earn a merit (e.g., encouraging a peer). Step three involves choosing how often students will be rewarded (e.g., daily, weekly) and the criteria for receiving the reward. If the team has earned fewer demerits than a preselected goal, students on the team will earn the reward; however, demerits can be eliminated by earning merits (e.g., every five merits erases one demerit). Merits and demerits can be monitored with tallies on the board or cards given to the students, which are collected and counted at the end of the period. Teachers should consider reinforcers that are a natural fit in the classroom context. The fourth step is to introduce the game by explaining the procedures and informing students of their teams (two or more).

Kellam and colleagues (2008) conducted a longitudinal study of first and second graders, who were randomly assigned to either the Good Behavior Game, an intervention aimed at academic achievement, or a control group. Positive outcomes among the group of students who engaged in the Good Behavior Game included lower rates of smoking, drinking and other substance use, antisocial behavior (violence and criminal behavior) and suicidal thoughts and increased service use for problems. These outcomes were maintained more than 12 years after intervention implementation. This research on the Good Behavior Game suggests it may have long-term benefits in multiple areas of the student lives.

Research on the Good Behavior Game has largely focused on positive effects for younger, elementary-age children. A study by Kleinman and Saigh (2011), however, was conducted in a multiethnic, New York City public high school in a ninth-grade classroom. The rate of all targeted disruptive behaviors decreased during intervention, and those reductions were maintained during follow-up. Further, social validity data indicated that (a) 100% of students felt they learned more when the GBG was implemented, b) 89% reported improvement in peer behavior, and (d) 66% reported improvement in their own personal conduct. This study provides evidence that the Good Behavior Game is a promising intervention for adolescents.

TIER II: PREVENTION WITH SELECTED STRATEGIES

Unlike Tier I interventions, which are delivered to all students in a classroom, Tier II strategies target just a few students in any given classroom. In other words, most of the students in a classroom should respond to Tier I strategies, when they are consistently delivered as designed. But those few who are not responsive will need additional support. Because Tier II interventions require individualization, they take more effort than Tier I interventions. At the same time, they can be implemented without gathering the assessment information required by Tier III. We describe three Tier II interventions that are age-appropriate for secondary students and benefit from research supporting their effectiveness.

Individual Goal Setting

Goal setting is a relatively simple intervention strategy that is particularly well suited to Tier II, because it can be easily individualized to address specific student needs. Goal setting is defined as student participation in planning a future goal, followed by self-evaluation of performance. Typically, goal setting involves evaluating what the student is presently able to achieve and determining what he or she would like to achieve in a preset length of time (e.g., a few days, weeks, a semester). The goal can involve increasing a behavior (homework completion, skill practice) or decreasing an undesired behavior (tardy to class, inappropriate social interactions). It is important to consider behavior changes that will be most meaningful and will positively impact the student's life. For instance, consider a high school senior who has difficulty completing class assignments, as well as social skills related to appropriate interactions with peers. Because gains in social skills could positively impact the student in all areas of his life (i.e., school, work, community), it may have a more meaningful effect for the student to establish a goal to increase positive interactions. Conversely, for a student experiencing difficulty getting along with just a few peers, but also with organization that results in a lack of turned-in classroom assignments and failing grades, organization might be a more meaningful goal, because failing grades would have a significant overall impact on the student's life.

Although teachers can establish goals for their students, we have seen that the outcomes appear more effective when goals are identified in collaboration with the student, particularly at the secondary level. The first step in goal setting is to determine a goal to be achieved (e.g. minutes on-task, assignments completed, kind acts), a time frame, and a reward if the goal is achieved within the designated time period. Sometimes rewards can be naturally occurring, as in the case of a student passing a test or class; however, students at Tier II often benefit from additional rewards, since they have a tendency not to be successful in school.

Goal Attainment Scaling (GAS; see Figure 13.1) is an effective and easy tool to monitor and record progress toward goal completion. Typically, GAS has five indicators of possible outcomes, ordered from least to most desirable. At regular

Goal Rating

At the end of the week, please use the following scale to rate how closely the above goal was met.

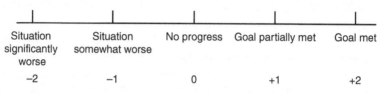

Situation significantly worse	Situation somewhat worse	No progress	Goal partially met	Goal met
−2	−1	0	+1	+2

Figure 13.1 Example of a goal attainment scale.

times, the teacher rates the student's progress in attaining his or her goal (Sheridan & Kratochwill, 2007). For example, to decrease Seth's interrupting, a goal may be that he will speak only with people who are not already engaged in conversation, or he will wait until his teacher or peers have completed a conversation. Because baseline data indicate he interrupts an average of five times during an academic period, a goal of no more than two interruptions might be initially established. Seth's teacher monitors progress toward his goal at the end of each class period, and he earns rewards if he receives a 1 or a 2. GAS provides a more detailed measure of goal progress than simply indicating whether or not a goal was attained.

Measuring goals can also be further enhanced by providing data-based feedback to students about their progress toward meeting their goals. Research indicates that when students receive positive feedback regarding their goals, they are more likely to set higher goals and to achieve their goals (provided the goals are perceived as attainable) (Krenn, Würth, & Hergovich, 2013). As such, teachers and students should make goals that are both challenging and attainable. Feedback should be specific, positive, and constructive to encourage student growth. Outcomes can also be embedded into ongoing procedures, such as grades. For example, points earned for assignment completion can be used to determine a student's participation grade. Finally, feedback can be provided through multiple formats, including written in a note, discussed in a brief conference, or tracked using other progress monitoring formats.

Research supports the effectiveness of goal setting for secondary students by making behavior change explicit and providing for continuous progress monitoring toward each goal (Codding & Smyth, 2008). Locke and Latham (2006) demonstrated that as goals become more specific, they are more likely to be accomplished. In addition, research suggests that goal setting may be most effective for tasks that are low in difficulty, with goals are specific, clear, and reachable (Krenn, Würth & Hergovich, 2013).

Self-Management

Self-management procedures are highly adaptable to address a wide range of behaviors, including decreasing problem behaviors and increasing appropriate behaviors.

Self-management procedures teach students to take responsibility for their actions, which places fewer intervention demands on teachers (Cole, 1992). The process involves observing and documenting occurrences of one's own behavior.

The first step in beginning a self-management program is to determine the targeted behavior and developing a measurable definition. The definition should clarify what the behavior looks like, making it distinguishable from other behaviors. Forms should then be created for the student to monitor his or her behavior (see Figure 13.2 for an example). Behavior can be monitored using yes-no responses or using rating scales (e.g., 1 = none of the period, 2 = some of the period, 3 = all of the period). Certain behaviors are better monitored with yes-no responses (e.g., "I completed my homework," "I was seated in my desk when the bell rang") while others may be more suited for scaling (e.g., "I worked well with my peers"). In addition, behavior can be monitored at different time intervals, depending on (a) the frequency of the behavior (i.e., higher frequency behaviors may require shorter monitoring intervals), (b) the time interval across which the student is able to accurately evaluate whether behavior occurred, and (c) the ability of the student to control his or her behavior (poor self-control requires shorter intervals). The student then needs to be taught to identify and monitor the target behavior by providing examples and non-examples of the behavior and practicing how occurrences will be coded. It may be necessary to allow time for practice with ongoing teacher support before the student begins to independently self-manage. This generally involves the teacher simultaneously monitoring occurrences of the student's behaviors, determining the extent to which those evaluations match with the student's evaluations, and providing feedback.

Daily Point Sheet

2 = Great

1 = Ok

0 = Goal Not Met

Points Possible   _____

Points Received   _____

% of Points   _____

Goal Met?   Y N

Name:

Date:

Behaviors	English	Chemistry	Algebra	Theater Arts	Economics
Work Completion	2 1 0	2 1 0	2 1 0	2 1 0	2 1 0
Appropriate Language	2 1 0	2 1 0	2 1 0	2 1 0	2 1 0
Active Listening	2 1 0	2 1 0	2 1 0	2 1 0	2 1 0

Figure 13.2 Example of behavior monitoring sheet.

When the student is reasonably accurate, he or she is ready to self-manage independently.

An abundance of research supports the effectiveness of self-management to improve the behavior of secondary students. For example, Snyder and Bambara (1997) assessed the effects of implementing a self-management with adolescent students with learning disabilities in both regular and special education classrooms. Following intervention, off-task behavior was reduced and students generalized targeted skills (working on the assigned task and following classroom rules) across settings. In a study by Dalton, Martella, and Marchand-Martella (1999), self-management was used with secondary students with poor academic performance who also displayed disruptive behaviors, were unprepared for class, and failed to turn in assignments. Behavior improvements were observed, including reductions in off-task behavior and increases in appropriate behaviors and the improvement generalized across subject areas.

Check In/Check Out

Check In/Check Out is an intervention strategy that provides students with daily monitoring and adult feedback beyond what the typical student would receive (Campbell & Anderson, 2011; Hawken & Horner, 2003). Teachers could consider using Check In/Check Out for a variety of student behavior problems, such as failing to complete work, poor organization skills, or difficulty focusing and paying attention.

Check In/Check Out is implemented in the following manner: First, target behaviors are identified and listed on a tracking form with accompanying behavior ratings (e.g., Campbell & Anderson, 2011; Hawken & Horner, 2003; see Figure 13.2). An adult "checks in" with the student upon arrival at school. This might be the student's homeroom teacher or another designated adult. During this morning check in, the adult checks the parent-signed tracking form from the previous day (see below). In addition, the student and adult make sure the student is prepared for the day (e.g., has needed materials) and the adult provides reminders or a review of behavioral expectations, along with encouragement and supportive comments (e.g., "It's nice to see you here today," "I'm so happy that you brought your tracker back with a signature"). At the end of each class period, the student brings his or her tracking form to the classroom teacher, who rates the student's behavior and provides brief feedback. At the end of the day, the designated adult reviews the points earned, sets goals with the student, and provides acknowledgement and encouragement (e.g., "You're really working hard," "I'm so proud of you for meeting your goal!). Each night the student takes the tracker home for his or her parent or guardian to review and sign.

Research on Check In/Check Out has found the intervention to be effective for reducing problematic behavior (e.g., disruptions, disrespect, disorganization, work completion, impulsive behaviors) and increasing prosocial behavior, including academic engagement. For example, Toms (2013) found that high school students who participated in Check In/Check Out showed improvements in their grades and decreases in school disciplinary problems. Additionally, Swoszowski, Jolivette, Fredrick, and Heflin (2012) found that Check In/Check Out helped to reduce escape-maintained behaviors (e.g. not completing work, head down) as well as other problems exhibited by adolescents in a residential treatment facility.

TIER 3: TARGETED INDIVIDUALIZED INTERVENTIONS

Students who fall in Tier III have not responded to interventions at Tiers I and II. These few students have intensive support needs and require much more complex interventions than those described above. To identify appropriate interventions and supports, an assessment-based approach is best practice, because of its long and successful track record in the school setting for guiding the selection of intervention and mental health services (e.g., Bambara & Kern, 2005). Because the needs of students at Tier III are usually complex, a support team with one or more individuals who have expertise in social, emotional, and behavioral problems usually develops intervention at this tier. For this reason, we will not detail Tier III intervention, but instead provide a brief overview of the process.

Assessment-Based Intervention Development

Because of the complex needs of adolescents with intensive behavior problems, we recommend assessment to evaluate both academic and classroom performance as well as mental health/social issues. Academic/classroom assessments should examine broad competencies, including organization and study skills. More specific skills that should be considered include attention and academic strengths and needs. In the area of mental health, assessments should determine whether a student is at-risk for major mental health disorders, including depression and anxiety. In addition, the assessment should identify any documented occurrences of behavioral outbursts. Finally, potential social skills deficits should be considered. Each of these areas of assessment should link directly to specific interventions. This multidimensional approach to assessment and intervention identification leads to a comprehensive multicomponent intervention plan. Kern and colleagues (2014) describe a comprehensive approach to assessment-based intervention for secondary students, developed by the Center for Adolescent Research in Schools (CARS). In addition, many of the chapters in this volume describe components of assessment-based intervention.

Accommodations

In the previous sections, we described a tiered system of intervention to match the level of support with student need. Accommodations offer another opportunity to facilitate learning. Accommodations, when implemented correctly, may potentially be the cornerstone of student success with the academic curriculum. That is, appropriate accommodations have the potential to make a difference in whether a student succeeds or fails.

The goal of accommodations is to remove barriers to learning and full participation, thereby offering students equal access to the curriculum, including course content and activities, similar to that afforded to their nondisabled peers. This is particularly important for students with emotional and behavioral disorders (EBDs) at the secondary level, because most spend at least some time in general education classrooms (Wagner et al., 2006). Furthermore, the majority of students with EBDs do not meet minimum standards on statewide assessments in core academic areas, suggesting the need to assure the validity of information derived from those assessment (e.g., Temple-Harvey & Vannest, 2012).

First and foremost, it is important to understand the exact meaning of accommodations, particularly since educators often confuse both the term and its practical applications. Accommodations are changes to some aspect of instructional delivery or student participation that does not substantially alter the curriculum or associated expectations (Thompson, Morse, Sharpe, & Hall, 2005). Importantly, accommodations are designed to maintain the academic standards required of students without disabilities while mediating the impact of the student's disability (Harrison, Bunford, Evans, & Owens, 2013). Stated in terms evoked by previous researchers, the goal is to "level the playing field."

Accommodations fall into four broad categories (Christensen, Braam, Scullin & Thurlow, 2011). These include presentation, response, timing/scheduling, and setting (Thompson et al., 2005). Presentation accommodations are those that modify the way in which material is presented. Some examples include reading directions, questions, or passages aloud; repeating or clarifying directions; providing visual cues; and providing prompts or encouragement. Response accommodations are those that change the manner in which students provide responses. Examples are using a scribe, responding via computer or other machine, writing in a test booklet, or using a tape recorder. Timing accommodations change some aspect of test timing or the way in which time is organized. Extended time and administration at a time most advantageous for a student are examples. Scheduling accommodations include breaks, assessments administered during multiple sessions or days, and flexible scheduling. Finally, setting accommodations change the location or environment where the assignment, test, or activity may be completed. Examples include reducing the number of students present in the environment (one, small group), providing a carrel or separate room (e.g., special education classroom), modifying seat location or teacher proximity, or minimizing environmental distractions.

The potential benefit of accommodations has not been realized for two primary reasons. First, there is inadequate research to support the effectiveness of accommodations, particularly for students with emotional and behavioral problems. In a recent, comprehensive review of accommodations, Harrison and colleagues (2013) concluded that research provides little evidence of the effectiveness of any approved accommodation for students with behavioral concerns.

The second is that accommodations are not often judiciously selected, nor do they necessarily align with student need. This concern is supported by research indicating that teachers report being unsure about how to provide accommodations and may be willing only to offer class-wide accommodations that do not risk disruption to their classroom routine (e.g., Polloway, Epstein, & Bursuck, 2003). In spite of these limitations, we believe that accommodations have the potential to make a significant difference in student outcomes. Therefore, we offer several recommendations for their selection and implementation.

First, it is critical that accommodations are individualized and linked to each student's specific deficits and skills. Accommodations should not be selected based on disability label, ease of implementation, or teacher preference. Teachers (in conjunction with the support team) should self-assess the manner in which they select accommodations to assure that they are not the result of the aforementioned processes. Unfortunately, there is an absence of models and procedures to guide teacher selection of accommodations. Until additional guidance is available, we recommend that teachers first determine the student's specific skill deficits and skill strengths. Second, they should identify an accommodation that addresses the deficit and capitalizes on the student's strengths. For example, if a student has difficulty reading instructions but has good oral comprehension, reading instructions orally would address her deficit and allow her to rely on a strength. Finally, teachers should closely evaluate whether the accommodation is actually providing a "differential boost" or compensating for the student's deficit such that his or her understanding, assignments, and test scores are improving.

Second, as noted above, the effect of accommodations should be evaluated on an ongoing basis. This means that teachers must periodically and regularly determine whether the accommodation is continuing to assist the student to demonstrate his or her skills. If the accommodation is not benefitting the student, the teacher must determine whether it needs to be changed or is no longer necessary and can be either faded or discontinued.

A third guideline is to assure that accommodations are applied to both daily academic classwork as well as testing. It is common for teachers to provide accommodations only for standardized tests and/or classroom tests. However, if a student needs testing accommodations, he or she almost always also needs the same accommodations to fully perform academically. An advantage of regularly providing academic accommodations is that it provides the teacher frequent opportunities to evaluate their effectiveness.

BARRIERS AND SOLUTIONS TO IMPLEMENTATION

In spite of extensive research and promise, classroom-based interventions for students with mental health needs are still not widely implemented in secondary settings Schaughency & Ervin (2006). There are several reasons for this, which can be broadly divided into the categories of teacher-specific barriers and external systemic barriers (Han & Weiss, 2005). Both categories of barriers need to be addressed to fully meet the promise of classroom-based mental health. In the remaining paragraphs, we outline specific barriers and offer suggestions for overcoming these barriers.

Teacher Barriers and Recommendations

Barriers specific to teachers fall in several distinct areas, including resistance to mental health programs, acceptability of interventions, knowledge and training, and teacher burnout and stress. Teacher resistance often stems from the belief that schools are not a place to address mental health concerns, or that it is the teacher's role to do so. As such, many teachers believe that their central role is academic education, and that mental health activities should be handled by mental health professionals in mental health facilities (Reinke, Stormont, Herman, Puri, & Goel, 2011). This is unfortunate for several reasons. First, teacher interactions have an impact on student mental health (Adelman & Taylor, 2000). Moreover, research has established a close relationship between academics and social, emotional, and physical health (Suldo & Shaffer, 2008). Therefore, addressing mental health concerns is likely to improve academic performance. Finally, among students who receive mental health services, the vast majority occur in school settings (Burns et al., 1997). Thus, schools are best positioned, and perhaps ethically obligated, to provide such services.

We believe that if teachers begin to implement interventions such as those described in this chapter, and in a tiered fashion, it will yield significant rewards, including improvements in class climate, student motivation, peer and adult interactions, and academic performance. A tiered approach to intervention is efficient in that it will eliminate low-level concerns, allowing teachers more time and energy on students with greater needs.

Another teacher-related barrier to classroom mental health is acceptability of interventions, which reflects a larger problem within the field of mental health. Even if teachers are motivated and willing to implement classroom mental health programs, many interventions are designed for clinical settings and do not offer a good fit in the classroom (Han & Weiss, 2005). Further compounding the acceptability problem is a lack of knowledge of interventions and insufficient training among teachers. Consequently, teachers do not have the skills to understand how interventions can be adapted or modified for their students and the classroom (Han & Weiss, 2005).

We recommend continuing to expand the emerging research, further demonstrating that simple and ecologically aligned classroom interventions can prevent and reduce mental health problems. In addition, we believe it is imperative that all teachers receive sufficient training, both pre- and in-service, to assure they can skillfully implement best practices in their classrooms to address the whole student. Such training is likely to interact with teacher acceptability of interventions, subdue anxiety, and raise teacher's self-efficacy (McCormick, Ayres, & Beechey 2006).

The final teacher-specific barrier is teacher burnout and stress, which can be attributed to many variables, including work overload and insufficient training to address students' social, emotional, and mental health concerns. An unfortunate cycle can result. Specifically, research has shown that high levels of teacher stress and burnout lead to reduced ability to implement interventions, lower morale, and high rates of staff turnover (Evers, Brouwers, & Tomic, 2002).

Fortunately, research has shown that teacher stress and burnout can be reduced through the use of directed stress management and supports (e.g., brief stress-management intervention), which also improves teacher self-efficacy (Van Dick & Wagner, 2001; Biglan, Layton, Jones, Hankins, & Rusby, 2013). Furthermore, teachers report feeling better, having higher levels of job satisfaction, and improved quality of life following stress-reduction programs (Leung, Chiang, Chui, Mak, & Wong, 2010).

We recommend teachers invest in a personal plan for stress management, including program participation. Again, we also recommend that teachers evaluate their skill at behavior and mental health management and obtain additional training, if needed. Further, we suggest that teacher preparation programs carefully evaluate their curriculum to ensure preservice teachers receive sufficient training to support students with social, emotional, and behavioral needs.

Systems Barriers and Potential Solutions

In addition to teacher-specific barriers, several institutional and systemic barriers can impede the adoption and successful implementation of classroom-based behavioral and mental health interventions. As previously mentioned, lack of teacher training can be caused by the system barrier of lack of opportunity. Other barriers include inadequate performance feedback, limited resources, and lack of flexibility and adaptability (Han & Weiss, 2005).

With respect to lack of training and supports, administrators play a key role in arranging for essential training as well as continued supervision with performance feedback (Han & Weiss, 2005). Moreover, administrators serve as gatekeepers for school-based interventions and programs and distribute funds toward practice (Hallinger & Heck, 1996). As such, it is critical that administrators are educated about the value and importance of classroom-based interventions and arrange for adequate training and resources.

Finally, lack of flexibility and adaptability can prove to be a significant systemic barrier. Flexibility within the school refers to the degree to which the system allows for modifications in plans and resources to provide needed supports, such as classroom-based and individual interventions to address emotional and behavioral needs. This may be partly attributed to the fact that schools have not traditionally focused on student mental health. We recommend capacity-building initiatives to allow for satisfactory levels of supports for mental health interventions, initiatives, and programs.

REFERENCES

Adelman, H. S., & Taylor, L. (2000). Moving prevention from the fringes into the fabric of school improvement. *Journal of Educational and Psychological Consultation*, *11*, 7–36

Anderman, L., Andrzejewski, C. E., & Allen, J. (2011). How do teachers support students' motivation and learning in their classrooms? *Teachers College Record, 113*(5), 963–1003.

Bambara, L. M., & Kern, L. (2005). *Individualized supports for students with problem behaviors: Designing positive behavior plans.* New York, NY: Guilford.

Barrish, H. H., Saunders, M., & Wolf, M. M. (1969). Good Behavior Game: Effects of individual contingencies for group consequences on disruptive behavior in a classroom. *Journal of Applied Behavior Analysis, 2*(2), 119–124.

Biglan, A., Layton, G. L., Jones, L. B., Hankins, M., & Rusby, J. C. (2013). The value of workshops on psychological flexibility for early childhood special education staff. *Topics in Early Child Special Education, 32*, 1–23.

Burns, B. J., Costello, E. J., Ekanli, A, Tweed, D. L., Farmer, E. M. Z., & Angold, A. (1997). Insurance coverage and mental health service use by adolescents with serious emotional disturbance. *Journal of Child and Family Studies, 6*, 89–111.

Caldarella, P., Young, E. L., Richardson, M. J., Young, B. J., & Young, K. R. (2008). Validation of the Systematic Screening for Behavior Disorders in middle and junior high school. *Journal of Emotional and Behavioral Disorders, 16*, 105–117.

Campbell, A., & Anderson, C. M. (2011). Check-In/Check-Out: A systematic evaluation and component analysis. *Journal of Applied Behavior Analysis, 44*(2), 315–326.

Carey, K. B., DeMartini, K. S., Prince, M. A., Luteran, C., & Carey, M. P. (2013). Effects of choice on intervention outcomes for college students sanctioned for campus alcohol policy violations. *Psychology of Addictive Behaviors, 27*(3), 596–603.

Christensen, L. L., Braam, M., Scullin, S., & Thurlow, M. L. (2011). *2009 state policies on assessment participation and accommodations for students with disabilities* (Synthesis Report 83). Minneapolis: University of Minnesota, National Center on Educational Outcomes.

Codding, R. S., & Smyth, C. A. (2008). Using performance feedback to decrease classroom transition time and examine collateral effects on academic engagement. *Journal of Educational and Psychological Consultation, 18*, 325–345.

Cole, C. (1992). Self-management interventions in the schools. *School Psychology Review, 21*(2), 188–192.

Dalton, T., Martella, R. C., and Marchand-Martella, N. E. (1999). The effects of a self-management program in reducing off-task behavior. *Journal of Behavioral Education, 9*(3/4), 157–176.

Daniel, B. J., Duncan, N., & Harpole, L. (2013). Effects of verbal and graphed feedback on treatment integrity. *Journal of Applied School Psychology, 29*(4), 328–349.

Elwell, W. C., &Tiberio, J. (1994). Teacher praise: What students want. *Journal of Instructional Psychology, 21*, 322–328.

Evers, W., Brouwers, A., & Tomic, W. (2002). Burnout and self-efficacy: A study on teachers' beliefs when implementing an innovative educational system in the Netherlands. *British Journal of Educational Psychology, 72*, 227–244.

Franklin, C., Kim, J. S., Ryan, T. N., Kelly, M. S., & Montgomery, K. (2012). Teacher involvement in school mental health interventions: A systematic review. *Children & Youth Services Review, 34*, 973–982.

Gasper, J., DeLuca, S., Estacion, A. (2012). Switching schools: Revisiting the relationship between school mobility and high school dropout. *American Educational Research Journal, 49*(3), 487–519.

Hall, R. V., Panyan, M., Rabon, D., & Broden, M. (1968). Instructing beginning teachers in reinforcement procedures which improve classroom control. *Journal of Applied Behavior Analysis, 1*, 315–322.

Hallinger, P., & Heck, R. H. (1996). Reassessing the principal's role in school effectiveness: A review of empirical research, 1980–1995. *Educational Administration Quarterly, 32*, 5–44.

Han, S. S., & Weiss, B. (2005). Sustainability of teacher implementation of school based mental health programs. *Journal of Abnormal Child Psychology, 33*, 665–679.

Harrison, J. R., Bunford, N., Evans, S. W., & Owens, J. S. (2013). Educational accommodations for students with behavioral challenges: A systematic review of the literature. *Review of Education Research, 83*, 551–597.

Hawken L. S., & Horner, R. H. (2003) Evaluation of a targeted intervention within a school-wide system of behavior support. *Journal of Behavioral Education, 12*(3), 225–240.

Horner, R. H., Sugai, G., & Anderson, C. M. (2010). Examining the evidence base for school-wide positive behavior support. *Focus on Exceptionality, 42*, 1–14.

Kellam, S. G., Brown, C. H., Poduska, J, Ialongo, N, Wang, W., Toyinbo, P., . . . Wilcox, H. C. (2008). Effects of a universal classroom behavior program in first and second grades on young adult behavioral, psychiatric, and social outcomes. *Drug and Alcohol Dependence, 95*(1), S5-S-28.

Kern, L., Bambara, L., & Fogt, J. (2002). Classwide curricular modification to improve the behavior of students with emotional and behavioral disorders. *Behavioral Disorders, 27*, 317–326.

Kern, L., Evans, S. W., & Lewis, T. J. (2014). Description of an iterative process for intervention development. *Education & Treatment of Children, 34*(4), 593–617.

Kleinman, K. E., & Saigh, P. A. (2011). The effects of the Good Behavior Game on the conduct of regular education New York City high school students. *Behavior Modification, 35*(1), 95–105.

Klem, A. M., & Connell, J. P. (2004). Relationships matter: Linking teacher support to student engagement and achievement. *Journal of School Health, 74*(4), 262–273.

Krenn, B., Würth, S., & Hergovich, A. (2013). The impact of feedback on goal setting and task performance: Testing the feedback intervention theory. *Swiss Journal of Psychology, 72*(2), 79.

Leung, S. S. K., Chiang, V. C. L., Chui, Y. Y., Mak, Y. W., & Wong, D. F. K. (2010). A brief cognitive behavioral stress management program for secondary teachers. *Journal of Occupational Health, 53*, 23–35.

Locke, E. A., & Latham, G. P. (2006). New directions in goal-setting theory. *Current Directions in Psychological Science, 15*(5), 265–268.

McCormick, J., Ayres, P. L., & Beechey, B. (2006), Teaching self-efficacy, stress and coping in a major curriculum reform. *Journal of Educational Administration, 44*, 53–70.

Merrett, F., & Wheldall, K. (1992). Teachers' use of praise and reprimands to boys and girls. *Educational Review, 44*, 73–79.

Nafpaktitis, M., Mayer, G. R., & Butterworth, T. (1985). Natural rates of teacher approval and disapproval and their relation to student behavior in intermediate school classrooms. *Journal of Educational Psychology, 77*, 362–367.

National Research Council. (2009). *Preventing mental, emotional, and behavioral disorders among young people: Progress and possibilities.* Washington, DC: The National Academies Press.

Polloway, E. A., Epstein, M. H., & Bursuck, W. D. (2003). Testing adaptations in the general education classroom: Challenges and directions. *Reading & Writing Quarterly, 19*, 189–192.

Rathvon, N. (2008). *Effective school interventions: Evidence-based strategies for improving student outcomes.* New York: Guilford Press.

Reeve, J., Nix, G., & Hamm, D. (2003). Testing models of the experience of self-determination in intrinsic motivation and the conundrum of choice. *Journal of Educational Psychology, 95*, 375–392.

Reinke, W. M., Stormont, M., Herman, K. C., Puri, R., & Goel, N. (2011). Supporting children's mental health in schools: Teacher perceptions of needs, roles, and barriers. *School Psychology Quarterly, 26*, 1–13.

Roorda, D. L., Koomen, H. M. Y., Split, J. L., & Oort, F. J. (2011). The influence of affective teacher-student relationships on students' school engagement and achievement: A meta-analytic approach. *Review of Educational Research, 81*, 493–529.

Sameroff, A. J., & Rosenblum, K. L. (2006). Psychosocial constraints on the development of resilience. In B. M. Lester, A. S. Masten, & B. McEwen (Eds.), *Resilience in children* (pp. 116–124). Boston, MA: Blackwell.

Schaughency, E., & Ervin, R. (2006). Building capacity to implement and sustain effective practices to better serve children. *School Psychology Review, 35*(2), 155–166.

Sheridan, S. M., & Kratochwill, T. R. (2007). *Conjoint behavioral consultation* (2nd ed.). New York: Springer.

Shores, R., Gunter, P., & Jack, S. (1993). Classroom management strategies: Are they setting events for coercion? *Behavioral Disorders, 18*, 92–102.

Snyder, M. C., & Bambara, L. M. (1997). Teaching secondary students with learning disabilities to self-manage classroom survival skills. *Journal of Learning Disabilities, 30*, 534–543.

Sprick, R. (1981). *The solution book: A guide to classroom discipline.* Chicago, IL: Science Research Associates.

Sprick, R.S. (1985). *Discipline in the secondary classroom: A problem-by-problem survival guide.* West Nyack, NY: Center for Applied Research in Education.

State, T. M., Kern, L., Starosta, K. M., & Divatia Mukherjee, A. (2011). Elementary preservice teacher preparation in the area of social, emotional, and behavioral problems. *School Mental Health, 3*, 13–23.

Suldo, S. M., & Shaffer, E. J. 2008. Looking beyond psychopathology: The dual-factor model of mental health in youth. *School Psychology Review, 37*, 52–68.

Swoszowski, N. C., Jolivette, K., Fredrick, L. D., & Heflin, L. J. (2012). Check in/Check out: Effects on students with emotional and behavioral disorders with attention- or escape-maintained behavior in a residential facility. *Exceptionality, 20*, 163–178.

Temple-Harvey, K. K., & Vannest, K. J. (2012). Participation and performance of students with emotional disturbance on a statewide accountability assessment in Math. *Remedial Special Education, 33*, 226–236.

Thompson, S. J., Morse, A. B., Sharpe, M., & Hall, S. (2005). *Accommodations manual: How to select, administer, and evaluate use of accommodations and assessment for students with disabilities.* Washington, DC: Council of Chief State School Officers.

Toms, O. M. (2012). The effects of Check-In Check Out on the social and academic planning and outcomes of African-American males in an urban secondary setting (Doctoral dissertation). Available from Proquest LLC. (UMI 3510233)

Tyler, K. M., & Boelter, C. M. (2008). Linking black middle school students' perceptions of teachers' expectations to academic engagement and efficacy. *Negro Educational Review, 59*(1/2), 27–44.

U.S. Bureau of Labor Statistics. (2012). Consumer Price Index: CPI Databases. Retrieved from http://www.bls.gov/cpi/data.htm

Van Dick, R., & Wagner, U. (2001). Stress and strain in teaching: A structural equation approach. *British Journal of Educational Psychology, 71*, 243–259.

Wagner, M., Newman, L., Cameto, R., and Levine, P. (2006). The academic achievement and functional performance of youth with disabilities: A report from the National Longitudinal Transition Study-2 (NLTS2). (NCSER 2006-3000). Menlo Park, CA: SRI International.

Wentzel, K. R., Baker, S. A., & Russell, S. L. (2012). Young adolescents' perceptions of teachers' and peers' goals as predictors of social and academic goal pursuit. *Applied Psychology, 61*(4), 605–633.

14

Consultation and Collaboration to Increase Integrity in School Mental Health

ERIKA COLES AND GRETA M. MASSETTI ■

Mental health services in school systems are delivered in a multitude of ways, most commonly in the form of consultation. Consultation has been conceived of as an indirect service delivery model in which school personnel (i.e., a consultee such as a teacher or school counselor) work with a consultant, and in turn provide direct service to the client. Most often, the consultation process is divided into a series of steps or stages to facilitate the identification of the main presenting concerns, development of an intervention plan, implementation and support of delivery in the naturalistic environment, development of a monitoring plan to determine changes in the child's functioning, and development of a plan for maintenance to ensure that the intervention is continuing to provide positive benefits to the child.

INTEGRITY

Treatment integrity, or the extent to which a treatment is delivered as planned, refers to the quality with which a particular intervention is implemented and delivered. In a school consultation model for school mental health, treatment integrity is an important construct to define and measure because of the complex dynamics involved in delivering an intervention. School mental health interventions using school consultation typically involve multiple individuals who are delivering treatment (e.g., consultants, teachers, other school staff) as well as multiple individuals who are receiving treatments or services (e.g., students, parents, teachers, school staff). The complex, multidimensional nature of school-based mental health through school consultation can create complications for delivering an intervention with high levels of treatment integrity.

Treatment integrity is typically conceptualized as a multidimensional construct for which several separate yet related constructs are subsumed. This includes adherence, competence, and differentiation (see Perepletchikova, 2009, for review). Adherence refers to the extent to which the consultant follows the intended procedures, while competence refers to the consultant's delivery of the treatment with flexibility and appropriate tailoring to the individual. Differentiation, on the other hand, is the extent to which a given treatment is different from other treatments. Initial empirical findings indicate that these separate constructs can be measured and may differentially predict student outcomes (Dusenbury, Brannigan, Hansen, Walsh, & Falco, 2005; Hirschstein, Edstrom, Frey, Snell, & MacKenzie, 2007; Manz, Bracaliello, Power, Mautone, & Kratochwill, 2010).

Numerous studies have demonstrated the link between treatment integrity and student outcomes (e.g., Biggs, Vernberg, Twemlow, Fonagy, & Dill, 2008), highlighting the importance of maximizing treatment integrity in school mental health. A key component of improving treatment integrity is its measurement, as accurate data is critical to providing accurate feedback and identifying opportunities to improve delivery of the intervention. To facilitate clarity in describing and measuring integrity, Noell (2008) suggests separating the concept of integrity into three distinct terms: treatment integrity (i.e., accuracy of implementation in the research context), intervention plan implementation (i.e., accuracy of implementation in a naturalistic setting), and consultation procedural integrity (i.e., the accuracy with which the consultation procedures are implemented).

Although integrity has been identified as an important predictor of student response to intervention, treatment integrity is not regularly assessed in schools (Cochrane & Laux, 2008; Sanetti & Kratochwill, 2009). There are several explanations for the lack of assessment of treatment integrity, including insufficient time, school personnel not understanding treatment integrity, lack of administrative support, and limited acceptability by school teachers to being monitored (Cochrane & Laux, 2008). Despite these barriers, research indicates that measurement of treatment integrity is an integral part of improving treatment integrity. Therefore, maximizing the quality of school-based mental health interventions depends heavily on a school's ability and commitment to measuring and tracking treatment integrity, and on using those data to inform and improve implementation.

Although the issue of treatment integrity, including ways in which treatment integrity can be measured and improved upon, has been widely studied in elementary school settings, to our knowledge there is no literature addressing this topic in middle or high school settings. This creates a particular challenge in making recommendations, as there may be unique aspects of either the settings themselves or the age of students that influence treatment integrity issues differently from elementary settings. Below we will highlight these issues as they are discussed in the existing literature and attempt to extrapolate recommendations, given the unique characteristics of secondary schools.

Measurement of Integrity in School

Although historically there has been a lack of agreement in the field about how to best assess treatment integrity (Schulte, Easton, & Parker, 2009), the most commonly used methods are observations, permanent products, and self-report. While multiple methods are considered effective, it is unknown what the relationship is among direct and indirect methods, and it has been suggested that this should be the focus of future research (Gresham, 2014).

Observations are direct measures of integrity (e.g., audiotaping, videotaping) in which observers code various aspects of treatment delivery. The function of observational measures is to accurately gauge the extent to which an intervention is implemented or to collect baseline data about the behavior of interest. Several studies have demonstrated the usefulness of using direct observations in assessing the integrity of an intervention (e.g., Jones, Wickstrom, & Friman, 1997; Mills & Ragan, 2000). While direct observations can help to provide an unbiased report of behavior, there are concerns about the representativeness of the data collected by direct observation (Gresham, 2014) and how much observational data is required to obtain a representative sample. Also, there may be reactivity in teachers, in that teachers increase integrity simply as a function of being observed (Codding, Livanis, Pace, & Vaca, 2008). In addition, there are questions as to whether that increase in integrity can be generalized to those times when the teacher is not being observed. One example of an observational coding scheme is the State-Event Classroom Observation System (SECOS), which is a systematic direct assessment procedure for observation of student and teacher behaviors in the classroom. SECOS has been shown to have adequate reliability and validity, and it has been used in several studies to illustrate treatment integrity (Saudargas, 1992; Saudargas & Creed, 1980). Also, McLeod and Weisz (2010) have developed the Therapy Process Observational Coding System for Child Psychotherapy Strategies Scale (TPOCS-S) to address limitations of self-reported uses of strategies during individual therapy sessions. It is important to note that, to our knowledge, there has been no systematic study of the use of observational measures in secondary school settings. There are several issues that may arise in the use of observations in these environments, including the limited time that any one individual teacher sees a child during the school day. On the other hand, this method may be more acceptable to teachers of these students, given the burden of completing rating scales or other measures.

Another common method of measuring treatment integrity is the use of permanent products, defined as concrete objects or outcomes. Permanent product review is a commonly used and accepted procedure for feasibly and efficiently assessing the daily treatment integrity of classroom-based interventions in applied research (Noell 2008). Typical permanent products include homework and classroom completion, attendance, and direct behavior reports (Chafouleas, McDougal, Riley-Tillman, Panahon, & Hilt, 2005; Gresham, 1989; Sheridan, Swanger-Gagne, Welch, Kwon, Garbacz, 2009). For example, Owens, Murphy, Richerson, Girio, and Himawan (2008) measured adherence to a classroom intervention by the collection of a daily report card (DRC), which showed that, on average, general and special education elementary teachers implemented (as evidenced by permanent products) the DRC on 77% of school days. While this average is respectable, the range of adherence across teachers varied widely (10% to 100%). In a similar study examining the DRC intervention with special education elementary-aged students, the average teacher adherence rate (as evidenced by permanent products) was 73%, with a range from 0% to 98% (Fabiano et al., 2010), suggesting that adherence to classrooms interventions is measurable. These methods may be particularly helpful in a secondary school setting, given the relatively shorter period of time that teachers are with the same students.

Although observations and direct monitoring have shown to increase treatment integrity, it is not without limitations, most notably the limited resources that may be available to provide ongoing observations. This can be particularly true in a secondary school setting, where students are frequently switching classes and may have multiple teachers and classes in which they are impaired or have interventions in place. One alternative is self-report measures of integrity, which involve teachers reporting, for example, what particular steps of an intervention were implemented. Adherence can be defined as the extent to which key intervention components are implemented as was originally designed (Dane & Schneider, 1998; O'Donnell, 2008). In most cases, adherence checklists have been used to simply demonstrate the percentage of treatment components that were completed, most often through self-report (Sheridan, Clarke, Knoche, & Edwards, 2006). Most research to date has relied on adherence only, without addressing issues of quality of implementation. Unfortunately, the extant literature suggests teachers are not accurate when self-reporting treatment integrity (Noell et al., 2005; Wickstrom, Jones, LaFleur, & Witt, 1998), although some studies have found more accurate self-reporting when asking teachers to report integrity on a daily rather than a weekly basis (Sanetti & Kratochwill, 2011), and that individuals are more accurate reporters as the time frame for self-reporting decreases and the specificity of the required responses increases (Burton & Blair, 1991; Riekert, 2006).

Although there are several challenges in assessing treatment integrity, one of the primary challenges is that interventions for students often occur at differing times of the day and, in many cases, include multiple steps (Noell, 2008). It is often necessary to develop integrity procedures unique to the intervention. Some work has been done to develop a protocol for treatment integrity planning (Sanetti & Kratochwill, 2009; Sanetti, Fallon, & Collier-Meek, 2011). This has involved a collaboration by a consultant and consultee(s) during the problem analysis stage of behavioral consultation (Bergan & Kratochwill, 1990; Sheridan & Kratochwill, 2010), where the consultant and consultee design an intervention, design treatment integrity assessment and evaluation strategies, and use treatment integrity and student outcome data to make implementation decisions (Sanetti & Kratochwill, 2009; Sanetti, Fallon, & Collier-Meek, 2011). Again, this work has not been done with middle or high school students.

Although the literature supports the idea that higher levels of treatment integrity are related to better student outcome, it remains unclear what the optimal level of treatment integrity is necessary in order to achieve success, and research is lacking in secondary schools. For example, in a review of 158 elementary school–based intervention studies, Gresham et al. (1993) found only a .58 correlation between treatment integrity and treatment outcomes. As noted by several authors (Sanetti & Kratochwill, 2009; Schulte et al., 2009; Gresham, 2014), 100% adherence to protocols may not be necessary (and in fact may be detrimental), and it remains unclear how much adherence is required, if not 100%.

Means of Increasing Integrity

Several means of increasing integrity have been identified, including performance feedback, negative reinforcement, and didactic training.

There are numerous studies that have highlighted the use of performance feedback as a mechanism to support the implementation of interventions to students (Casey & McWilliam, 2008; Codding, Feinberg, Dunn, & Pace, 2005; Rathel, Drasgow, & Christle, 2008). Performance feedback is generally thought of as a strategy to collect, summarize, and present data directly to teachers about the implementation of an intervention (e.g., Noell et al., 2005) with the goal of increasing the integrity with which interventions are implemented.

Performance feedback typically involves a four-step process, including (a) review of data, (b) praise for correct implementation, (c) discussion of corrective feedback, and (d) discussion of questions or concerns (Codding et al., 2005). Over the last 15 years, several studies have examined the impact of performance feedback on teacher adherence to a recommended procedure. Although some inconsistencies exist, in general these studies provide compelling data that performance feedback produces higher levels of teacher adherence relative to either baseline conditions or an alternative strategy (Codding et al., 2005; Jones et al., 1997; Martens, Hiralall, & Bradley, 1997; Mortenson & Witt, 1998; Noell et al., 1997, 2000; Witt, Noell, Lafleur, & Mortenson, 1997). One study found that, across teachers, the average adherence rates during baseline was less than 5%; average adherence rates during standard consultation were between 9% and 37%; and average adherence rates during consultation with performance feedback were between 60% and 83% (Jones et al., 1997). Four other studies, including one randomized group design, demonstrated that when teachers received performance feedback about integrity, integrity increased to above 80% and student performance increased (Noell et al., 1997, 2000, 2005; Witt et al., 1997). Some studies reported that integrity declined once performance feedback was removed (Noell et al., 1997), while others indicate that integrity is maintained longer following performance feedback conditions relative to training only conditions (Codding et al., 2005; Witt et al., 1997). However, given the brief time frame for the assessment of effects, there are insufficient data to draw conclusions about maintenance. Several other issues with regard to reasons that performance feedback works remain unclear and require additional research, including what variables may affect performance feedback (Noell & Gansle, 2014; Solomon, Klein, & Politylo, 2012).

In addition to performance feedback, negative reinforcement, defined as an attempt to increase a behavior (in this case, acceptable integrity) by removing an aversive stimuli (e.g., meeting being scheduled), is a strategy for maintaining therapeutic levels of treatment integrity has some empirical support (DiGennaro, Martens, & Kleinmann, 2007). Following treatment integrity assessment, if treatment integrity levels are below some predetermined criterion, a short meeting between the consultant and implementer is held, in which the consultant may review integrity data, including adherence checklists or observation data in order to identify areas of potential remediation and to practice intervention components with the consultee. If using the negative reinforcement strategy and treatment integrity levels are at or above the criterion, a meeting becomes unnecessary and the consultee continues to implement the intervention without the assistance of the consultant.

Finally, direct training, including strategies such as a didactic lesson, modeling, rehearsal, and feedback, has been found to facilitate high levels of treatment integrity (Sterling-Turner, Watson, & Moore, 2002), at least initially. While positive results have been shown in acceptable integrity during an initial training phase, studies also demonstrate that teacher intervention adherence decreases precipitously once consultation is removed. For example, despite demonstrating 100% adherence during the initial training phase, teachers in one study dropped below 80% adherence within three days (Witt et al., 1997) and below 60% adherence within one week following the training (Noell et al., 1997). Taken together, the literature seems to indicate that while initial inservice training is necessary for implementation of interventions, it is not sufficient.

Factors That Influence Treatment Integrity

There are several factors that have been identified as influencing treatment integrity in the context of the school setting and can potentially be targeted when trying to increase integrity. These includes contextual factors, materials that are used, and the relationship between the consultant and the consultee.

Contextual factors are factors of the learning environment that can manipulate the integrity of intervention. These are factors that are not directly related to the design of the intervention, but that may influence the implementation of the intervention (i.e., increase the likelihood of an intervention not being done consistently or with as much quality). Such contextual factors include teacher motivation for implementation, school climate and administrative support, and fit of the intervention in the classroom (Durlak & DuPre, 2008; Dusenbury, Brannigan, Falco, & Hansen, 2003; Fixsen, Naoom, Blasé, Friedman, & Wallace, 2005; Greenhalgh, Robert, MacFarlane, Bate, & Kyriakidou, 2004; Gresham, 1989; Perepletchikova & Kazdin, 2005; Stith et al., 2006). School consultation can identify contextual factors that are influencing implementation and address them directly through the consultation intervention process. For example, consultants can probe for teacher motivation and comprehension through the consultation process and address these issues directly. Consultants can also use observations and other data collection strategies to identify contextual factors that are barriers to high-quality implementation. We can think of contextual factors being particularly important in a discussion of treatment integrity in the secondary school setting. All of the methods for measuring and increasing treatment integrity described in this chapter were developed and evaluated in an elementary school setting, presenting us with the challenge of describing these processes and how the unique environment of the secondary school setting may affect them without a specific literature to refer to. For example, a secondary school teacher may only see a particular student for 40 minutes out of the school day, perhaps making her less aware of how impaired a student is or making her less motivated to implement an intervention, given the number of students she encounters during a typical school day. Ongoing assessment and considerations of these factors will be imperative when designing an intervention and monitoring plan.

Several factors with regard to materials have been identified that may affect increasing levels of treatment integrity in school-based mental health interventions using school consultation. These include providing teachers with all needed materials, "user-friendly" format of materials, and the thoroughness and clarity with which the materials are explained to the consultee (Bosworth, Gingiss, Potthoff, & Roberts-Gray, 1999; Durlack & DuPre, 2008;

Gresham, 1989; Perepletchikova & Kazdin, 2005). In the secondary school setting, consideration must be given to the balance of materials that are given to the teachers versus how much responsibility is given to the adolescent. For example, if a daily report card (DRC) is established for a student, it's imperative to consult with both the teacher and the student about whose responsibility it is to determine if goals were met, to bring the DRC to the teacher at the end of class, and to carry the DRC to the next class.

In addition to contextual factors and the use of appropriate and acceptable materials, a consultant's ability to develop a collaborative relationship with consultees has been hypothesized to influence treatment integrity (Durlack & DuPre, 2008; Fixsen et al., 2005; Stith et al., 2006). Collaboration in the context of a consultation relationship can be defined by the determination of joint goals, working together to problem solve, joint decision-making, and the assumption of an equal partnership between the consultant and consultee (Sheridan & Kratochwill, 2010) Without a sound foundation of this relationship, consultees may lack confidence in their ability to deliver an intervention, or they may lose motivation in the continued use of the intervention (Sheridan & Kratochwill, 2010).

Designing an Intervention

Several models for designing school-based mental health interventions through consultation have been recommended in the literature (e.g., Forman & Burke,

2008), although they contain common elements. An essential feature is the establishment of baseline data, which can be used to provide a justification for whether intervention is needed (e.g., functional behavior assessment, curriculum-based measurement; see Forman & Burke, 2008). Once the need for intervention is established, an intervention goal is developed (Forman & Burke, 2008) and an intervention related to the goal is determined, acknowledging that there may be several interventions that are appropriate. Determining whether a particular intervention is appropriate can be decided by considering how to best promote success, the empirical support for the intervention, and the feasibility of implementing the intervention in a particular setting (Kratochwill & Shernoff, 2004; Forman & Burke, 2008; Chafouleas, Riley-Tillman, & Sugai, 2007; Sanetti & Kratochwill, 2009).

BRIDGING RESEARCH AND PRACTICE: THE CONSULTATION AND COLLABORATION MODEL FOR IMPROVING INTEGRITY IN SCHOOL MENTAL HEALTH

As highlighted above, school consultation and collaboration can be effective strategies for assessing and improving the integrity of school-based mental health services. Schools can leverage collaborative relationships established in consultation to address the key elements in intervention planning, implementation, and evaluation. In this section we will provide a model or framework for using school consultation and collaboration to assess and improve intervention integrity in school mental health. The framework relies on the following key components:

1. Establishing collaborative and supportive teacher-consultant relationships.
2. Addressing intervention acceptability.
3. Developing an intervention implementation plan.
4. Establishing a system for implementation tracking metrics and providing feedback for continuous quality improvement.
5. Tracking outcome data to ensure that implementation is having the desired effects on intervention outcomes.

Establishing Collaborative and Supportive Teacher-Consultant Relationships

As previously noted, one of the key implementation challenges in school consultation involves the fact that different individuals are responsible for intervention delivery and implementation. In the case of secondary schools, teams of teachers or staff members are often responsible. This indirect service delivery model can sometimes result in challenges to ensuring that interventions are implemented as intended, and that they are implemented consistently across individuals and settings. Research indicates that teachers are likely to stop implementing interventions if attention and support from consultants is not maintained (Noell, Witt, Gilbertson, Ranier, & Freeland, 1997; Witt, Noell, Lafleur, & Mortenson, 1997). School consultation relies on changes in teacher behavior as a means of providing services, such as changes to instruction or classroom management. Interventions that are implemented through consultation often require teachers to learn new skills and make what are often significant changes in the way they interact with students. The establishment of a collaborative relationship is one way of facilitating, motivating, and supporting behavior change on the part of teachers and other school staff.

Collaborative relationships between consultants and teachers are an important foundation for implementation integrity through school consultation for school-based mental health services (Erchul & Martens, 1997). One of the key elements in establishing a collaborative relationship is to clarify the roles and responsibilities for each member of the team, including the consultant, teachers, and any other staff involved in delivering the intervention (Power et al., 2005). Additional strategies that consultants can use to promote a collaborative working relationship with teachers include using positive reinforcement for teachers' efforts, providing examples of successful use of similar interventions, and utilizing social-influence strategies, such as praising the teacher for successful implementation, to enhance teacher understanding of the intervention (Luiselli & Diament, 2002; Martens & Ardoin, 2002).

Addressing Intervention Acceptability

Another key component to promoting implementation integrity for school-based mental health interventions is the acceptability of the intervention for the individuals responsible for implementation and delivery. For teachers and school staff working with consultants, acceptability is often a prerequisite for buy-in. Lack of buy-in and poor acceptability can have a deleterious effect on the effectiveness of the intervention (Nastasi & Truscott, 2000). When teachers find an intervention acceptable, they believe it will be effective, practical, and feasible to implement (Truscott, Cosgrove, Meyers, & Eidle-Barkman, 2000). One strategy consultants can use to address intervention acceptability is to assess or measure teachers' perceptions of the intervention prior to implementation. This can serve as an indicator of how well an intervention will be implemented, along with the subsequent likelihood that the intervention will be successful. High levels of intervention acceptability reported by teachers pre-intervention can be a foundation for teachers to comply with intervention plans and have high implementation integrity (Truscott, Cosgrove, Meyers, & Eidle-Barkman, 2000). Assessments of intervention acceptability can be informal and brief, such as in the context of a conversation, and can measure how well the teachers understands the intervention, to what extent they feel the intervention will be effective, and their feelings of self-efficacy in implementing the intervention. If an assessment indicates any concerns in these areas, consultants can work through potential issues with the teachers and employ creative strategies to ensure proper buy-in. This dialogue and willingness to work collaboratively with teachers can be an effective strategy in further building a successful relationship. Implementer satisfaction with school-based interventions has been shown to be an important variable; interventions or practices that teachers perceive to be unacceptable will not be implemented with integrity, regardless of their effectiveness (Eckert & Hintze, 2000).

Developing an Intervention Implementation Plan

A well-constructed, explicit implementation plan can serve as a valuable blueprint for the intervention. From an implementation integrity point of view, the implementation plan plays a critical role in laying out the expectations regarding what is to be implemented, how, and by whom. The implementation plan thus provides a standard against which intervention integrity can be measured, so that implementation integrity data can be accurately assessed. Without a clearly defined implementation plan, it is difficult to determine whether implementation was consistent with what was intended. The implementation plan also defines the roles of the key individuals responsible for the intervention, including the consultant, teachers, other staff, and parents. It forms the groundwork for a common awareness and understanding for what the intervention will look like and how it will be pulled together.

One of the strategies used in the literature to establish an implementation plan involves the use of checklists or scripts to facilitate the implementation planning process. Studies have found that checklists and scripts can facilitate a structured intervention planning process (Ehrhardt, Barnett, Lentz, Stollar, & Reiffin, 1996; Hiralall & Martens, 1998). Implementation protocols appear to be effective at promoting intervention use by teachers, are easy to develop, and can be one tool for monitoring treatment integrity (e.g., Witt et al., 1997).

Tracking Implementation Metrics and Providing Feedback

The value of measuring intervention integrity is very often cited in the school psychology and school mental health literature (Power et al., 2005; Gresham et al., 1993; Dusenbury et al., 2003). However, studies show that intervention integrity is very rarely assessed in real-world settings. Cochrane and Laux (2008), for example, found that fewer than 15% of school psychology practitioners reported collecting integrity data for interventions. However, there is a strong and consistent relationship between integrity and treatment effect (Gresham et al., 1993), and measurement of treatment integrity provides valuable data regarding the intervention process (Gresham, MacMillan, Beebe-Frankenberger, & Bocian, 2000). These considerations highlight the critical need to ensure that intervention

integrity is monitored carefully, and that those data are used to inform intervention planning and improvement efforts. When measures of intervention integrity
provide data that are meaningful and useful for the intervention process, they
can be more easily collected (Hagermoser Sanetti & Fallon, 2011). For example,
research by Noell and colleagues (Noell & Gansle, 2014; Noell et al., 1997; Witt
et al., 1997) demonstrate that implementation measures provided to teachers that
have clear and easily interpretable information increase the consistency and quality of implementation for teachers.

One of the defining features of consultation as an intervention approach is the
fact that it consists of multiple levels of intervention. Essentially, a consultant
provides services to the teacher, and the teacher in turn provides services to the
student(s). There may be additional levels when parents or school administrators
are also involved. Given this multilevel structure, a well-designed integrity measurement system should take into account the various components of the intervention happening at different levels. For example, measures of the integrity of
the consultant's delivery of services to the teacher can be tracked in parallel with
the services the teacher delivers to the student. In establishing well-functioning
intervention delivery models for evidence-based interventions in schools, captur-
ing data on how interventions are being implemented at each level and by each
"node" in the intervention system can ensure that the different components are
working effectively across the intervention system.

Chafouleas, Christ, Riley-Tillman, Briesch, and Chanese (2007) provide a simple
framework for planning which data will be collected, and how. Their framework
is structured around four questions: (a) Why are data needed? (b) Which treatment integrity assessment methods are best matched to assess behaviors of interest? (c) What resources are available to collect the treatment integrity data? and
(d) What decisions will be made using the data? The answer to the first question,
regarding the purpose of data collection, can rely on tools in the school consultation literature for measuring integrity of consultant services (e.g., Kratochwill &
Bergan, 1990), as well as intervention materials. For the second question, the different methods for measuring integrity have been reviewed earlier in this chapter.
A well-designed intervention plan that is based on the best evidence can inform
decisions about the most crucial aspects of the intervention that need to be measured, but is also flexible so as to allow stakeholders to modify the intervention
and measure responses to help determine if those modifications are influencing
the outcomes and effectiveness of the intervention (Power et al., 2005).

Another key consideration here is the frequency of data collection. It may not
be feasible or necessary to collect daily data when a sampling of two or three
days per week provides sufficient information. The frequency of measurement
may also vary over the time course of an intervention, as implementation will
vary over time. A consideration of resources needed for measurement is important, as it provides information about what is feasible and doable. It is important
to consider the specific added value of different pieces of data, and whether the
resources needed to collect each are invested wisely. The needed resources must
also be balanced with a consideration of data quality. Some methods for data

collection are not resource-intensive, but they may not provide valid measures of integrity.

The final question in Chafouleas's model is critical from an implementation standpoint. Data collected must be useful, and it must be feasible to use it to inform implementation. Intervention integrity data at its best must drive decisions about implementation.

Tracking Outcome Data

Intervention integrity data provide important information about the implementation of an intervention, but ultimately the most important information is whether the intervention has been effective at addressing the mental health needs of students. Information about intervention integrity can capture information about adherence, exposure, dosage, and quality. However, well-implemented interventions may not be successful in achieving desired outcomes. Likewise, there may be some components of an intervention that are not well implemented, but students are responding well to other components. Data on how well students are responding to the intervention are needed to ensure that the intervention is having the desired effects (Brown & Rahn-Blakeslee, 2009). This information must in turn feed into a review of intervention plans to ensure that there is a consistent connection between the intervention plan, the integrity data, and the outcome data (Hagermoser Sanetti & Fallon, 2011).

CONCLUSION

In this chapter, we have described school consultation as a collaborative relationship in which treatment integrity can be measured and enhanced in several different ways. While the literature shows strong support for collaborative consultation and supports several techniques with which to improve treatment integrity, there is also a need for more research, in particular in the area of working with adolescents. For example, there is a strong emerging literature for the use of motivational interviewing strategies in the consultation process when working with teachers of elementary-age students interested in reducing disruptive behavior in the classroom (e.g., Frey et al., 2013). To our knowledge, these strategies have not been investigated at the middle or high school levels, which have different challenges than the elementary setting. Also, it is unclear how much integrity is sufficient to maximize treatment gains. Given limited resources in many school districts, it's important to be able to maximize the efficiency of consultation time. Of particular concern is how to maintain integrity in the absence of ongoing consultation.

AUTHOR NOTE

Dr. Massetti is currently at the Centers for Disease Control and Prevention.

REFERENCES

Bergan, J. R., & Kratochwill, T. R. (1990). *Behavioral consultation and therapy.* New York, NY: Plenum.

Biggs, B. K., Vernberg, E. M., Twemlow, S. W., Fonagy, P., & Dill, E. J. (2008). Teacher adherence and its relation to teacher attitudes and student outcomes in an elementary school-based violence prevention program. *School Psychology Review, 37,* 533–549.

Bosworth, K., Gingiss, P. M., Pottthoff, S., & Roberts-Gray, C. (1999). A Bayesian model to predict the success of the implementation of health and education innovations in school-centered programs. *Education and Program Planning, 22,* 1–11.

Brown, S., & Rahn-Blakeslee, A. (2009). Training school-based practitioners to collect intervention integrity data. *School Mental Health, 1*(3), 143–153.

Burton, S., & Blair, E. (1991). Task conditions, response formulation processes, and response accuracy for behavioral frequency questions in surveys. *Public Opinion Quarterly, 55,* 50–79.

Casey, A. M., & McWilliam, R. A. (2008). Graphical feedback to increase teachers' use of incidental teaching. *Journal of Early Intervention, 30,* 251–268.

Chafouleas, S. M., Christ, T. J., Riley-Tillman, T. C., Briesch, A. M., & Chanese, J. A. M. (2007). Generalizability and dependability of direct behavior ratings to assess social behavior of preschoolers. *School Psychology Review, 36*(1), 63–79.

Chafouleas, S. M., McDougal, J. L., Riley-Tillman, T. C., Panahon, C. J., & Hilt, A. M. (2005). What do daily behavior report cards (DBRCs) measure? An initial comparison of DBRCs with direct observation for off-task behavior. *Psychology in the Schools, 42,* 669–676. doi:10.1002/pits.20102

Chafouleas, S. M., Riley-Tillman, T. C., & Sugai, G. (2007). *School-based behavioral assessment: Informing instruction and intervention.* New York, NY: Guilford.

Cochrane, W. S., & Laux, J. M. (2008). A survey investigating school psychologists' measurement of treatment integrity in school-based interventions and their beliefs about its importance. *Psychology in the Schools, 45*(6), 499–507.

Codding, R. S., Feinburg, A. B., Dunn, E. K., & Pace, G. M. (2005). Effects of immediate performance feedback on implementation of behavior support plans. *Journal of Applied Behavior Analysis, 38,* 205–219.

Codding, R. S., Livanis A., Pace, G. M., Vaca, L. (2008). Using performance feedback to improve treatment integrity of classwide behavior plans: An investigation of observer reactivity. *Journal of Applied Behavior Analysis, 41*(3), 417–422.

Dane, A. V., & Schneider, B. H. (1998) Program integrity in primary and early secondary prevention: Are implementation effects out of control? *Clinical Psychology Review, 18,* 23–24.

DiGennaro, F. D., Martens, B. K., & Kleinmann, A. E. (2007). A comparison of performance feedback procedures on teachers' treatment implementation integrity and students' inappropriate behavior in special education classrooms. *Journal of Applied Behavior Analysis, 40,* 447–461.

Durlak, J. A., & DuPre, E. P. (2008). Implementation matters: A review of research on the influence of implementation on program outcomes and the factors affecting implementation. *American Journal of Community Psychology, 41,* 327–350.

Dusenbury L., Brannigan R., Hansen W. B., Walsh J., & Falco M. (2005). Quality of implementation: Developing measures crucial to understanding the diffusion of preventive interventions. *Health Education Research, 20*(3), 308–313.

Dusenbury, L., Brannigan, R., Falco, M., & Hansen, W. B. (2003). A review of research on fidelity of implementation: Implications for drug abuse prevention in school settings. *Health Education Research, 18*(2), 237–256.

Eckert, T. L., & Hintze, J. M. (2000). Behavioral conceptions and applications of acceptability: Issues related to service delivery and research methodology. *School Psychology Quarterly, 15*(2), 123–148.

Ehrhardt, K. E., Barnett, D. W., Lentz, F. E., Jr., Stollar, S. A., & Reifin, L. H. (1996). Innovative methodology in ecological consultation: Use of scripts to promote treatment acceptability and integrity. *School Psychology Quarterly, 11*(2), 149–168.

Erchul, W. P., & Martens, B. K. (1997). *School consultation: Conceptual and empirical bases of practice.* New York, NY: Plenum.

Fabiano, G. A., Vujnovic, R., Pelham, W. E., Waschbusch, D. A., Massetti, G. M., Pariseau, M. E., . . . Volker, M. (2010). Enhancing the effectiveness of special education programming for children with ADHD using a daily report card. *School Psychology Review, 39,* 219–239.

Fixsen, D. L., Naoom, S. F., Blase, K. A., Friedman, R. M., & Wallace, F. (2005). *Implementation research: A synthesis of the literature* (FMHI Publication No. 231). Tampa, FL: University of South Florida, Louis de la Parte Florida Mental Health Institute, National Implementation Research Network.

Forman, S. G., & Burke, C. (2008). Best practices in selecting and implementing evidence-based school interventions. In A. Thomas & J. Grimes (Eds.), *Best practices in school psychology* (pp. 799–812). Washington, DC: National Association of School Psychologists.

Frey, A. J., Lee, J., Small, J. W., Seeley, J. R., Walker, H. M., & Feil, E. G. (2013). The motivational interviewing navigation guide: A process for enhancing teachers' motivation to adopt and implement school-based interventions. *Advances in School Mental Health Promotion, 6*(3), 158–173. doi:10.1080/1754730X.2013.804334

Greenhalgh, T., Robert, G., MacFarlane, F., Bate, P., & Kyriakidou, O. (2004). Diffusion of innovations in service organizations: Systematic review and recommendations. *The Milbank Quarterly, 82*(4), 581–629.

Gresham F. M. (1989) Assessment of treatment integrity in school consultation and prereferral intervention. *School Psychology Review, 18,* 37–50.

Gresham, F. M. (2014). Measuring and analyzing treatment integrity data in research. In L. M. Hagermoser Sanetti & T. R. Kratochwill (Eds.), *Treatment integrity: A foundation for evidence-based practice in applied psychology* (pp. 109–130). Washington, DC: American Psychological Association.

Gresham, F. M., Gansle, K. A., & Noell, G. H. (1993). Treatment integrity in applied behavior analysis with children. *Journal of Applied Behavior Analysis, 26*(2), 257–263.

Gresham, F. M., Gansle, K. A., Noell, G. H., Cohen, S., & Rosenblum, S. (1993). Treatment integrity of school-based behavioral intervention studies: 1980–1990. *School Psychology Review, 22,* 254–272.

Gresham, F. M., MacMillan, D. L., Beebe-Frankenberger, M. E., & Bocian, K. M. (2000). Treatment integrity in learning disabilities intervention research: Do we really know how treatments are implemented? *Learning Disabilities Research & Practice, 15*(4), 198–205. doi:10.1207/SLDRP1504_4

Hagermoser Sanetti, L. M., & Fallon, L. M. (2011). Treatment integrity assessment: How Estimates of adherence, quality, and exposure influence interpretation of implementation. *Journal of Educational and Psychological Consultation, 21*(3), 209–232. doi:10.1080/10474412.2011.595163

Hiralall, A. S., & Martens, B. K. (1998). Teaching classroom management skills to preschool staff: The effects of scripted instructional sequences on teacher and student behavior. *School Psychology Quarterly, 13*(2), 94–115.

Hirschstein, M. K., Edstrom, L. V., Frey, K. S., Snell, J. L., & MacKenzie, E. P. (2007). Walking the talk in bully prevention: Teacher implementation variable related to initial impact of the Steps to Respect program. *School Psychology Review, 36*, 3–21.

Jones, K. M., Wickstrom K. F., Friman P. C. (1997). The effects of observational feedback on treatment integrity in school-based behavioral consultation. *School Psychology Quarterly, 12*, 316–326.

Kratochwill, T. R., & Bergan, J. R. (1990). *Behavioral consultation in applied settings: An individual guide.* New York, NY: Plenum.

Kratochwill, T. R., & Shernoff, E. S. (2004). Evidence-based practice: Promoting evidence-based interventions in school psychology. *School Psychology Review, 33*, 34–48.

Luiselli, J. K., & Diament, C. (2002). Behavior psychology in the schools: Innovations in evaluation, support, and consultation. New York: Haworth Press.

Manz, P. H., Bracaliello, C., Power, T., Mautone, J. A. and Kratochwill, T. R. (March, 2010). Monitoring multiple dimensions of intervention integrity in applied research. In *Monitoring Multiple Dimensions of Intervention Integrity in Applied Research*. Edited by: Manz, P. H. Chair. March, Chicago, IL: National Association of School Psychologists.

Martens, B. K., & Ardoin, S. P. (2002). Training school psychologists in behavior support consultation. *Child and Family Behavior Therapy, 24*(1/2), 147–164.

Martens, B. K., Hiralall, A. S., & Bradley, T. A. (1997). A note to teacher: Improving student behavior through goal setting and feedback. *School Psychology Quarterly, 12*, 33–41.

McLeod, B. D., & Weisz, J. R. (2010). The Therapy Process Observational Coding System for Child Psychotherapy Strategies Scale. *Journal of Clinical Child and Adolescent Psychology, 39*, 436–443.

Mills, S. C., & Ragan, T. J. (2000). A tool for analyzing implementation fidelity of an integrated learning system (ILS). *Educational Technology Research and Development, 48*, 21–41.

Mortenson, B. P., & Witt, J. C. (1998). The use of weekly performance feedback to increase teacher implementation of a prereferral academic intervention. *School Psychology Review, 27*, 613–627.

Nastasi, B. K., & Truscott, S. D. (2000). Acceptability research in school psychology: Current trends and future directions. *School Psychology Quarterly, 15*(2), 117–122. doi:10.1037/h0088781

Noell, G. H. (2008). Research examining the relationships among consultation process, treatment integrity, and outcomes. In W. P. Erchul & S. M. Sheridan (Eds.), *Handbook of research in school consultation: Empirical foundations for the field* (pp. 323–342). Mahwah, NJ: Erlbaum.

Noell, G. H., & Gansle, K. A. (2014). The use of performance feedback to improve intervention implementation in schools. In L. M. Hagermoser Sanetti & T. R. Kratochwill (Eds.), *Treatment integrity: A foundation for evidence-based practice in applied psychology* (pp. 109–130). Washington DC: American Psychological Association.

Noell, G. H., Witt, J. C., Gilbertson, D. N., Ranier, D. D., & Freeland, J. T. (1997). Increasing teacher intervention implementation in general education settings through consultation and performance feedback. *School Psychology Quarterly, 12*(1), 77–88. doi:10.1037/h0088949

Noell, G., Witt, J., LaFleur, L., Mortenson, B., Ranier, D., & LeVelle, J. (2000). Increasing intervention implementation in general education following consultation: A comparison of two follow-up strategies. *Journal of Applied Behavior Analysis, 33,* 271–284.

Noell, G. H., Witt, J. C., Slider, N. J., Connell, J. E., Gatti, S. L., Williams, K. L., . . . Duhon, G. J. (2005). Treatment implementation following behavioral consultation in schools: A comparison of three follow-up strategies. *School Psychology Review, 34,* 87–106.

O'Donnell, C. L. (2008). Defining, conceptualizing, and measuring fidelity of implementation and its relationship to outcomes in K–12 curriculum intervention research. *Review of Educational Research, 78*(1), 33–84.

Owens, J. S., Murphy, C. E., Richerson, L., Girio, E. L., & Himawan, L. K. (2008). Science to practice in underserved communities: The effectiveness of school mental health programming. *Journal of Clinical Child and Adolescent Psychology, 37,* 434–447.

Perepletchikova, F. (2009). Treatment Integrity and Differential Treatment Effects. *Clinical Psychology: Science and Practice, 16,* 379–382.

Perepletchikova, F., & Kazdin, A. E. (2005), Treatment integrity and therapeutic change: Issues and research recommendations. *Clinical Psychology: Science and Practice, 12,* 365–383. doi:10.1093/clipsy.bpi045

Power, T. J., Blom-Hoffman, J., Clarke, A. T., Riley-Tillman, T. C., Kelleher, C., & Manz, P. H. (2005). Reconceptualizing intervention integrity: A partnership-based framework for linking research with practice. *Psychology in the Schools, 42*(5), 495–507. doi: 10.1002/pits.20087

Rathel, J. M., Drasgow, E., & Christle, C. C. (2008). Effects of supervisor performance feedback on increasing preservice teachers' positive communication behaviors with students with emotional and behavioral disorders. *Journal of Emotional and Behavioral Disorders, 16,* 67–77.

Riekert, K. A. (2006). Integrating regimen adherence assessment into clinical practice. In W. T. O'Donohue & E. R. Levensky (Eds.), *Promoting treatment adherence: A practical handbook for health care providers* (pp. 17–34). Thousand Oaks, CA: SAGE.

Sanetti, L. M. H., & Fallon, L. M. (2011). Treatment integrity assessment: How estimates of adherence, quality, and exposure influence interpretation of implementation. *Journal of Educational and Psychological Consultation, 21,* 209–232.

Sanetti, L. M. H., Fallon, L. M., & Collier-Meek, M. (2011). Treatment integrity assessment and intervention by school-based personnel: Practical applications based on a preliminary study. *School Psychology Forum, 5*(3), 87–102.

Sanetti, L. M. H., & Kratochwill, T. R. (2009). Toward developing a science of treatment integrity: Introduction to the special series. *School Psychology Review, 38,* 445–459.

Sanetti, L. M. H., & Kratochwill, T. R. (2011). An evaluation of the treatment integrity planning protocol and two schedules of treatment integrity self-report: Impact on implementation and report accuracy. *Journal of Educational and Psychological Consultation, 21,* 284–308. doi:10.1080/10474412.2011.620927

Saudargas, R. A. (1992). *State-Event Classroom Observation System (SECOS).* Knoxville: University of Tennessee, Department of Psychology.

Saudargas, R. A., & Creed, V. (1980). *State-Event Classroom Observation System (SECOS).* Knoxville: University of Tennessee, Department of Psychology.

Schulte, A. C., Easton, J. E., & Parker, J. (2009). Advances in treatment integrity research: Multidisciplinary perspectives on the conceptualization, measurement, and enhancement of treatment integrity. *School Psychology Review, 38*(4), 460–475.

Sheridan, S. M., Clarke, B. L., Knoche, L. L., & Edwards, C. P. (2006). The effects of conjoint behavioral consultation in early childhood settings. *Early Education and Development, 17*, 593–618.

Sheridan, S. M., & Kratochwill, T. R. (2010). *Conjoint behavioral consultation.* New York, NY: Springer.

Sheridan, S. M., Swanger-Gagne, M., Welch, G. W., Kwon, K., & Garbacz, S. A. (2009). Fidelity measurement in consultation: Psychometric issues and preliminary examination. *School Psychology Review, 28*, 476–495.

Solomon, B. G., Klein, S. A., & Polityo, B. C. (2012). The effect of performance feedback on teachers' integrity: A meta-analysis of the single-case literature. *School Psychology Review, 41*, 160–175.

Sterling-Turner, H. E., Watson, S. T., & Moore, J. W. (2002). The effects of direct training and treatment integrity on treatment outcomes in school consultation. *School Psychology Quarterly, 17*(1), 44–47.

Stith, S., Pruitt, I., Dees, J., Fronce, M., Greeen, N., Som, A., & Linkh, D. (2006). Implementing community-based prevention programming: A review of the literature. *Journal of Primary Prevention, 27*, 599–617.

Truscott, S. D., Cosgrove, G., Meyers, J., & Eidle-Barkman, K. A. (2000). The acceptability of organizational consultation with prereferral intervention teams. *School Psychology Quarterly, 15*(2), 172–206. doi:10.1037/h0088784

Wickstrom, K. F., Jones, K. M., LaFleur, L. H., & Witt, J. C. (1998). An analysis of treatment integrity in school-based behavioral consultation. *School Psychology Quarterly, 13*, 141–154. doi:10.1037/h0088978

Witt, J. C., Noell, G. H., Lafleur, L. H., & Mortenson, B. P. (1997). Teacher use of interventions in general education settings: Measurement and analysis of the independent variable. *Journal of Applied Behavior Analysis, 30*(4), 693–696. doi:10.1901/jaba.1997.30-693

15

Mental Health Promotion
With Aboriginal Youth

Lessons Learned From the Uniting Our Nations Program

CLAIRE V. CROOKS AND CAELY DUNLOP ■

CHAPTER OVERVIEW

Aboriginal youth in Canada are at disproportionate risk for a range of mental health concerns compared to their non-Aboriginal counterparts. To address this disparity, communities, researchers, and policymakers have called for culturally relevant prevention and intervention programming to mitigate risk and promote well-being. A number of promising initiatives have been developed that are grounded in culture. The goal of these programs is to maximize the protective influence of multiple facets of culture in youth's lives, such as cultural identity, connectedness, and engagement in traditional practices. One such program is The Fourth R: Uniting Our Nations, a strengths-based, culturally relevant program delivered to Aboriginal youth in Canadian schools. This chapter outlines the rationale for promoting this type of programming with Aboriginal youth. We describe the development and evaluation of the Uniting Our Nations program. We also highlight the importance of authentic partnerships and committing to a timeframe that is sufficient for this work.

INTRODUCTION

The risks faced by Indigenous people have a deleterious effect on their health and wellness (Gracey & King, 2009a, 2009b). For example, Aboriginal[1] peoples in

1. The program described in this chapter was developed in Canada, and as such, references to Indigenous peoples are reflective of the Canadian context. We use the term Aboriginal to

Canada experience higher rates of poverty and substandard housing, lower educational attainment, higher unemployment rates and lower income, food insecurity and unreliable access to clean water, and higher rates of violent victimization (Adelson, 2005; Gracey & Kind, 2009b; First Nations Information Governance Centre [FNIGC], 2012; Health Canada, 2014;Perreault, 2011;Wilson & Cardwell, 2012). These and other risk factors are associated with disproportionately high rates of both physical and mental health concerns, such as shorter life expectancy, chronic health conditions such as obesity and diabetes, substance use and abuse disorders, psychological distress, major depression, and suicide (Adelson, 2005; FNIGC, 2012; Gracey & Kind, 2009a; Health Canada, 2014).

These same health disparities are evident among Aboriginal youth. Suicide rates among Aboriginal youth have reached crisis levels, with reported rates for First Nations youth in Canada[2] five to seven times higher than rates for non-Aboriginal youth (Health Canada, 2013). These rates are even higher for Inuit youth, where suicide rates are 11 times higher than national averages, and are among the highest in the world (Health Canada, 2013). Aboriginal youth also experience higher rates of substance use and abuse. Furthermore, they have higher rates of risky sexual behaviors, and higher levels of violence and victimization than their peers (FNIGC, 2012; Lemstra, Rogers, Redgate, Garner, & Moraros, 2011).

It is irrefutable that Aboriginal youth face profound health inequities and higher rates of mental health challenges than their non-Aboriginal peers. However, to understand the context for these numbers, it is critical to understand the historical, social, and political context that is inextricably linked to the structural inequalities Aboriginal peoples still face. In Canada, government-sanctioned systematic colonization and assimilation of Aboriginal peoples occurred for over a century (MacDonald & Steenbeek, 2015; Truth and Reconciliation Commission of Canada [TRC], 2015). These actions included the Indian Act of 1876 (which is an inherently racist piece of legislation), the "Sixties Scoop" of forced adoptions, and the residential school system, where Aboriginal children were forcibly removed from their homes and often subjected to physical, emotional, and sexual abuse.[3]

refer to peoples who identify as First Nations, Métis, and Inuit (FNMI). We use these terms (Aboriginal and FNMI) interchangeably. The term Aboriginal is defined in the Constitution as including Canada's three First Peoples. More recently, FNMI has been used in the educational policy context. We acknowledge that these are umbrella terms that denote overarching commonalities among Indigenous peoples, but that do not reflect the diversity of Indigenous individuals or their communities. Furthermore, significant research has been conducted in other countries, such as the United States and Australia, where different language may be utilized (e.g., Native American, American Indian, Alaska Native). When describing this research, we maintain the language used by the original authors. We use the term Indigenous to refer to First Peoples collectively on an international level.

2. These statistics for First Nations youth as a whole mask significant differences across First Nations communities (see Chandler & Lalonde, 1998).

3. The Gradual Civilization Act of 1857 created the official policy for removing children to residential schools. Schools were implemented across the country over a period of approximately

Collectively, these policies served to strip Aboriginal peoples of their land and their traditional languages, practices, and ways of knowing (MacDonald & Steenbeek, 2015). These attempts at extinguishing Aboriginal culture and identity have recently been deemed cultural genocide by the Truth and Reconciliation Commission of Canada (TRC, 2015).

This history (and similar colonial histories experienced by Indigenous peoples worldwide) has had lasting impacts on Aboriginal peoples. The enduring influence of colonial legacies affect determinants of Aboriginal health and well-being at multiple levels of society (Gracey & King, 2009b). These influences operate at different levels including distal factors (e.g., colonialism, racism, social exclusion), intermediate factors (e.g., community infrastructure, health and education systems), and proximal factors (e.g., food insecurity, education, employment) (Greenwood & de Leeuw, 2012; Reading & Wien, 2009).

The Case for Culturally Relevant Programming

Not only do Aboriginal youth face profound risks to well-being, there are also significant barriers preventing utilization of existing mental health services. These barriers include lack of, or restricted access to, services, and mismatch of Aboriginal and Western understandings of mental health (FNIGC, 2012; Vukic, Gregory, Martin-Misener, & Etowa, 2011; Wexler & Gone, 2012). Multiple authors have supported the notion of culture as intervention/treatment, suggesting that operationalizing culture for therapeutic use in Indigenous settings is a viable alternative or adjunct to Western approaches (Gone, 2013; Fiedeldey-Van Dijk et al., 2015; Wexler & Gone, 2012).

Moreover, culture has consistently been identified as a protective factor for Aboriginal youth. Culture has been explored through a number of mechanisms, including cultural continuity, which is a group-level process consistent with self-determination (Chandler & Lalonde 1998; Hallet, Chandler, & Lalonde, 2007). Cultural identity, engagement in traditional practices and language, enculturation, and bicultural competence have also been studied. These various facets of culture are associated with increases in positive functioning, mental health, and resilience, as well as reductions in psychological distress, substance use and abuse, and suicide (Kirmayer, Brass, & Tait, 2000; Kirmayer, Simpson, & Cargo, 2003; Lafromboise, Albright, & Harris, 2010; Lafromboise, Hoyt, Oliver, & Whitbeck, 2006; Smokowski, Evans, Cotter, & Webber, 2014; Whitbeck, McMorris, Hoyt, Stubben, & Lafromboise, 2002).

Researchers and community leaders have directed significant attention toward the development of culturally relevant prevention and intervention programming.

150 years. The last residential school closed in the mid-1990s. A condensed timeline of residential school events is available from the Aboriginal Healing Foundation at http://www.ahf.ca/downloads/condensed-timline.pdf.

A growing evidence base suggests that incorporating cultural content (including tribal-specific beliefs, traditions, and practices) is an essential component of effective prevention and intervention programming with Aboriginal youth (Brown, Baldwin, & Walsh, 2012; Hawkins, Cummins, & Marlatt, 2004; Kenyon & Hanson, 2012; Moran & Reaman, 2002; Okamoto, Kulis, Marsiglia, Steiker, & Dustman, 2014; Penn, Doll, & Grandgenett, 2008).

A multitude of culturally adapted or grounded initiatives for diverse groups of Aboriginal youth have been developed. Increasingly, we are seeing some of these evaluated in the research literature, with generally promising results. Programs that promote positive youth development and mental well-being have yielded positive initial results, including increases in self-esteem, positive coping strategies, and connection to culture and cultural identity (Goodkind, LaNoue, Lee, Freeland, & Freund, 2012; Gross et al., 2016; Langdon et al., 2016). Similarly promising effects have been found for culturally grounded, adapted, and informed alcohol and substance use prevention programs, including reductions in substance use and increased levels of hope, optimism and cultural identity (Donovan et al., 2015), and increases in drug-resistance knowledge and skills (Baydala et al., 2009; Kulis, Dustman, Brown, & Martinez, 2013). In addition, a review of interventions conducted by Rowan and colleagues (2014) found that culturally based interventions were effective at promoting well-being as part of addictions treatment for Indigenous peoples. Suicide prevention initiatives have also yielded encouraging primary findings, including reductions in suicidal ideation and hopelessness, as well as increases in problem-solving skills (Lafromboise & Lewis, 2008; Le & Gobert, 2015).

These initial evaluations are encouraging, but there are significant limitations to the existing research. For example, while individual program findings have often yielded positive results, reviews of the literature have failed to identify sufficient evidence to demonstrate program effectiveness (Clifford, Doran, & Tsey, 2013; Jackson & Hodge, 2010; Harlow & Clough, 2014; Walsh & Baldwin, 2015). These lackluster findings are due in part to challenges associated with meeting evidence-based evaluation design and methodological criteria while utilizing community-based participatory research approaches. Challenges include difficulty quantifying Aboriginal cultural practices and ways of knowing, a lack of culturally appropriate measures, tension between implementation fidelity and flexibility to integrate local knowledge, and difficulty obtaining large and diverse sample sizes (Crooks, Snowshoe, Chiodo, & Brunette-Debassige, 2013; Friesen et al., 2012; Gone, 2012). Nonetheless, these existing program evaluations highlight the feasibility of these interventions, the process of developing or adapting cultural content, key components of promising programs, and lessons learned from the implementation process, which are crucial to furthering our knowledge in this area. Moving past these feasibility and process questions takes considerable time and strong partnerships. We now turn to describing the Uniting Our Nations program, which have been developed, implemented, and evaluated with Aboriginal youth over a 12-year period.

DESCRIPTION AND DEVELOPMENT OF THE UNITING OUR NATIONS PROGRAM

Overview of the Fourth R Programs

The work with Aboriginal youth described in this chapter grew out of an evidence-based program called the Fourth R (Relationships). The Fourth R consists of a range of healthy relationships programs developed for school and community settings. These programs were designed to prevent violence and related risk behaviors among adolescents. In more recent years, a mental health promotion focus has been increasingly integrated into the programs. Fourth R programs differ with respect to age/grade level and format. All Fourth R programs are based on the contention that relationship skills can be taught the same way that many other academic or athletic skills are taught—through breaking down the steps and giving youth an abundance of guided practice (Wolfe, Jaffe, & Crooks, 2006). The Fourth R was developed by a consortium of researchers, educators, and psychologists. The original program was designed to align with the Ontario Ministry of Education curriculum expectations. Since 2001 the program has grown to be used from coast to coast in Canada. It has also been implemented in the United States and internationally. There is now Fourth R programming for students from Grades 7–12.

The Fourth R team (of which the first author of this chapter is a principal member) has published numerous studies evaluating the program. The initial cluster randomized controlled trial (RCT) with the Grade 9 program included 20 schools, with over 1,700 students aged 14–15 years. Students were surveyed before receiving programming, and 2.5 years after the program. Results indicated that physical dating violence was about 2.5 times greater among control (i.e., standard health education) versus intervention students at 2.5-year follow-up, and that the intervention impact was greater for boys than girls (Wolfe et al., 2009). The Fourth R intervention also improved condom use in sexually active boys compared to their counterparts in the control condition. In addition to reducing negative behaviors, observational data demonstrated an increase in effective peer resistance skills (such as delay, negotiation, and refusal) among Fourth R students compared to the control group (Wolfe, Crooks, Chiodo, Hughes, & Ellis, 2012). The Fourth R has consistently been identified as one of the few effective dating prevention programs for youth on the basis of these RCT findings (De Koker, Mathews, Zuch, Bastien & Mason-Jones, 2014; De La Rue, Polanin, Espelage, & Pigott, 2016; Ellsberg et al., 2015).

Beyond the universal impacts of the Fourth R, there is a protective impact for vulnerable youth. Analysis of the RCT data indicated that there was a protective effect for youth with a history of multiple forms of maltreatment with respect to lowering the likelihood of engaging in violent delinquency, even after 2.5 years (Crooks, Scott, Wolfe, Chiodo, & Killip, 2007; Crooks, Scott, Ellis, & Wolfe, 2011). Similarly, a quasi-experimental evaluation of the Fourth R in Alaska found a similar pattern of increased benefits for youth with significant histories of maltreatment and other adverse experiences (Siebold, Hegge, & Crooks, 2012). These findings provide a promising indication that Fourth R is not only beneficial for all youth, but that it may also be particularly beneficial for the youth who need it most.

The Fourth R was designed as a Tier I universal intervention. However, in light of the research findings, Fourth R programs may best be described as Tier I interventions that have significant impacts for Tier II youth (and possible some impacts on Tier III youth as well). Although the programs were designed for Tier I implementation, they have been adapted and implemented in many different ways. For example, we are currently working with the Manitoba youth justice system to pilot and evaluate our programming with incarcerated youth; these youth have significant trauma histories and mental health needs.

The Fourth R: Uniting Our Nations[4]

In 2004 the local school board approached the Fourth R team to discuss developing programming specifically for FNMI youth. The school board has a mixed rural/urban/First Nations catchment area. The Fourth R began working with the board and the three local First Nations communities[5] to develop and evaluate school-based, culturally relevant, relationship-focused programming for FNMI youth. An advisory committee identified the transition from elementary school to secondary school (which occurred between Grade 8 and 9) as a particularly difficult transition for many FNMI youth, and indicated a need for programming on either side of that transition. The team has since co-developed, implemented, and evaluated a range of program components for FNMI youth between Grades 7 and 12. These initiatives include the following: (1) Elementary Mentoring Program, (2) Peer Mentoring for Secondary Students, (3) Cultural Leadership Course, (4) Cultural Leadership Camp, (5) FNMI Student Leadership Committee, and (6) Aboriginal Perspectives Fourth R.

Elementary Mentoring Program. The Elementary Mentoring Program is an 18-week, school-based program for seventh- and eighth-grade students, facilitated by two First Nations young adults who mentor groups of students for one hour per week. The program is based on the Medicine Wheel[6] life cycles. The Medicine Wheel is a locally relevant teaching, but would not necessarily be applicable in other First Nations contexts. Beginning in the Fall (West/Spiritual

4. Although this full name distinguishes the culturally relevant programming from the more generic Fourth R, the short form (Fourth R) is often used by interviewees and stakeholders in quotes. All quotes used in this chapter refer to the culturally relevant Fourth R programming.

5. These include two First Nations reserves (analogous to Indian reservations in the United States) and one settlement.

6. Those unfamiliar with the Medicine Wheel teachings and who wish to understand the implications for education are referred to Bell, N. (2014, June). Teaching by the Medicine Wheel. *Education Canada* (available at http://www.cea-ace.ca/education-canada/article/teaching-medicine-wheel).

quadrant), sessions address student interests, the Creation Story (which is the locally relevant understanding of how a particular nation came to be), and creating positive attitudes and atmospheres. In the Winter (North/Physical quadrant), sessions address bullying, healthy eating, and First Nations' representations in media. In the Spring (East/Emotional quadrant), sessions address sharing and listening, goal setting, and positive decision-making skills. In the Summer (South/ Mental quadrant), sessions address communication skills, peer pressure, personal strengths, and handling peer conflicts.

Peer Mentoring Program for Secondary Students. The Peer Mentoring Program supports the development of healthy and positive relationships between junior (Grade 9) and senior (Grades 10–12) secondary students, who participate as mentees and mentors, respectively. This program facilitates student mentees and mentors meeting during lunchtime on a weekly basis over the course of the school year to engage in a range of activities together. Although it was designed for mentoring pairs, it is sometimes run in small groups to accommodate uneven numbers. There is also an option for an adult mentor from the First Nations community to facilitate a teaching circle with participants several times annually. This community mentor helps provide support to the school mentors, incorporates cultural teachings into the program, and serves as a role model.

Cultural Leadership Course. The First Nations Cultural Leadership Course incorporates the strengths of peer mentoring into the classroom setting, allowing youth to earn an academic credit for their participation. The course combines older and younger secondary students who are working on one of two credits (leadership or study skills) into the same classroom. Older students are explicitly taught how to provide mentorship and leadership to the younger students through joint activities. Furthermore, the course provides senior students with an opportunity to assume the roles of student leaders and volunteers for initiatives both inside and outside their schools.

Cultural Leadership Camp. The Cultural Leadership Camp was designed as a three-day, intensive, outdoor, experiential program designed to support FNMI secondary school students in developing leadership and healthy relationship skills through culturally significant, personally challenging, and fun activities. Elders, community leaders, and academics are invited to share traditional and contemporary teachings on hunting, land conservation, team building, creative arts, and healthy living strategies. The emphasis of the Cultural Leadership Camp is on experiential learning; youth have the opportunity to engage deeply in cultural activities rather than just learn about them. In 2015 the school board opted to change this component to a one-day event due to budget and other logistical considerations; however, the findings presented in this chapter pertain to the original three day version.

FNMI Student Advisory Committee. The FNMI Student Advisory Committee is composed of approximately 20 secondary students (Grades 10–12). Students apply for the positions and are selected on an annual basis. The group meets monthly to develop and implement a project at the school board level. They also undertake cultural and leadership development activities.

Aboriginal Perspectives Fourth R. One of our earliest efforts to create a culturally relevant Fourth R was an Aboriginal-informed version of the ninth-grade health curriculum. This program was developed in collaboration with a First Nations educator who has extensive experience in developing curriculum that is both informed by Aboriginal culture and meets Ontario Ministry of Education guidelines. The adapted curriculum addresses important issues with a resiliency lens, as students are encouraged to identify individual and community strengths within their cultural framework that will support them in making healthy choices. It includes historical context, such as the intergenerational impacts of residential school trauma, to help youth contextualize at-risk behaviors they may observe in their communities. Additional educational materials (such as the videos and role-plays) have been incorporated that reflect the realities of Aboriginal youth. Because there are many problems associated with attempting to develop a pan-Aboriginal version of anything (Proulx, 2006), we have worked with partners to develop an Anishinaabe-informed version, a Cree-informed version and a Dene-informed version of this program. Dene-informed versions of the Grades 7, 8, and 9 health programs are now being scaled up as a territory-wide initiative in the Northwest Territories, supported by the Department of Education. In addition, we developed a template and set of guidelines to assist other Nations in further adapting the materials for their own local contexts (Crooks, Hughes, & Sisco, 2015).

Comparing the Fourth R and Uniting Our Nations Program Components

Although the Aboriginal Perspectives Fourth R was adapted from the original Fourth R, all of the other programs were developed specifically for Aboriginal youth, with significant ongoing guidance from our advisory committee and community partners. All of the Uniting Our Nations programs share features with the original Fourth R programs in terms of the focus on healthy relationships and skill development. However, there are also important differences. The similarities to and differences from our original Fourth R program are depicted in Table 15.1. These differences are described in more detail below.

Cultural identity as an underlying framework. An emphasis on cultural identity is woven throughout all *Uniting Our Nations* programming. For example, in the mentoring program for secondary students, students approach mental health promotion from a Medicine Wheel context, looking at both stressors that arise in each of the four quadrants of being, but also supports and ways of coping that lie in each quadrant.

Culturally appropriate teaching methods. All of the programs utilize more culturally relevant teaching strategies than the original Fourth R. For example, students begin the Elementary Mentoring Program by learning the Creation Story, as shared by a local storyteller. Furthermore, the entire program is based on the cycles of the Medicine Wheel. Teaching methods have been adapted to include the use of sharing circles, which provide a culturally relevant means to facilitate discussion.

Table 15.1. COMPARISON OF ORIGINAL FOURTH R PROGRAM AND UNITING
OUR NATIONS PROGRAM COMPONENT

Similarities	Differences
Emphasis on healthy relationships	Cultural identity as an underlying framework
Focus on skills development (particularly SEL competencies)	Use of culturally appropriate teaching methods
Positive youth development framework	
School-based programs aligned with curricula expectations	Community inclusion
	Greater focus on mentorship
Commitment to documentation and development of manuals	Greater focus on youth voice

Community inclusion. Another key feature of Uniting Our Nations programs is the inclusion of community members who share their teachings and experience in culturally relevant ways. Community members are invited into the Aboriginal Perspectives (Grade 9) course, and Elders, community leaders, and academic experts are invited to share traditional and contemporary teachings at the Cultural Leadership Camp. Previous guests have spoken to students about traditional medicines, discussed personal cultural identity, shared traditional drum making, and led a drum waking ceremony. The unique benefits of including Elders in youth programming has been documented by other researchers, in terms of linking past to present and co-creating a shared vision for a healthy and positive future (Petrucka et al., 2016).

Mentoring. Another change from the original Fourth R program is the overarching emphasis on mentoring. Mentoring is a culturally appropriate and effective way to support healthy relationship development for First Nations youth, particularly when mentors share a cultural background with mentees (Klinck et al., 2005; Ware, 2013). Although peer and adult mentors may play different roles, both are recognized as protective influences in the lives of youth (Pridemore, 2004; LaFromboise et al., 2006). In addition to the two specific mentoring programs, mentoring is built into the Cultural Leadership Course. The Fourth R does not have mentoring programs for non-Aboriginal youth, so these programs are culturally grounded rather than culturally adapted.

Youth voice. Youth have historically been overlooked in the development, implementation, and evaluation of programs for them (Edwards, Jones, Mitchell, Hagler, & Roberts, 2016). Throughout the design of the Uniting Our Nations programs, we have actively looked for opportunities to honor youth voice. For example, we facilitated a number of video projects where students came together over several sessions to develop scenarios and solutions that are more relevant to their realities. These video resources are utilized in both the Uniting Our Nations and more general Fourth R programs. Ongoing youth leadership opportunities are available through the Student Leadership Committee.

UNITING OUR NATIONS RESEARCH EVIDENCE

Following the tradition of practice-based evidence, we employed a collaborative approach to identifying practices that work in real-life settings (Friesen et al., 2012), starting with a program based on the collective wisdom of group, yet also informed by the evidence-*based Fourth R. From* the outset, we wanted to build an evidence base through a progression of research questions and studies that increased in rigor over time. This approach is consistent with a comprehensive evaluation framework, which recognizes that there are several important evaluation steps to address prior to focusing on efficacy (Rossi, Freeman, & Lipsey, 2003). First and foremost, we wanted to know if the programs were feasible and engaging. Next, we conducted a cross-sectional study to look at whether youth and educators perceived the programs to be beneficial. Finally, we conducted a longitudinal study to evaluate impacts over time as youth transitioned into secondary school. Figure 15.1 depicts this line of questioning.

In this section we describe each phase of our evaluation work and the findings that emerged. We have included quotes from participants in our qualitative and mixed methods research to illustrate our main themes and maintain participants' and other stakeholders' voices.

Early Descriptive Work Assessing Feasibility and Fit

From the outset of the Uniting Our Nations initiative, we were committed to collecting data that could inform program improvement in an ongoing manner. Over the first five years of the programs, we invited youth to complete surveys and participate in focus groups to share their reactions to the programs. We worked closely with our advisory committee to fine tune the program. We prepared annual feedback reports for our partners outlining the results of these informal data collection procedures. Working with partners in this manner from the outset helped to build trust, which is critical in light of the history of exploitative research of Aboriginal peoples by non-Aboriginal researchers

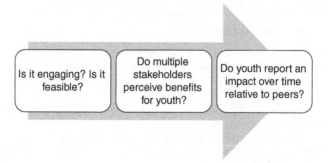

Figure 15.1 Developing an evidence base for Uniting Our Nations programs.

(Schnarch, 2004). We spent significant time documenting early program successes and challenges with input from all of our stakeholders (Crooks, Chiodo, Thomas, & Hughes, 2009; Crooks, Chiodo, Thomas, & Hughes, 2011). The time spent establishing feasibility and fit for the program during these early years provided an important foundation for further research, as successful research partnerships tend to evolve through various stages (Santiago-Rivera, Morse, Hunt, & Lickers, 1998).

Our first evaluation focused on the extent to which our programs for secondary students (namely mentoring and the Cultural Leadership Course) were shown to engage youth. Youth engagement is a framework that resonates universally with program developers and researchers, but it can be difficult to describe and quantify. The Centre of Excellence for Youth Engagement (CYE, 2008) defines youth engagement as the "meaningful participation and sustained involvement of a young person in an activity, with a focus outside of him or herself. For this study, we utilized our surveys and administrative data to look at behavioral, cognitive, and attitudinal indicators of engaged youth (adapted from CYE, 2007; see Figure 15.2).

Within this framework, we documented a number of indicators of high engagement (Crooks et al., 2009). There were several behavioral indicators of engagement: The mentoring program had a high retention rate, and students in the Cultural Leadership Course earned higher marks and accrued fewer absences in that course compared to the rest of their course load. Indeed, culturally relevant mentoring approaches have been promoted as a Tier 2 approach to promoting school attendance and decreasing absenteeism (Kearney & Graczyk, 2014). Cognitive engagement was demonstrated by mentors' comments about their role (Crooks et al., 2009). Mentors took pride in their role as leaders and role models to younger students, and saw the importance of their roles, as described by one of the student participants:

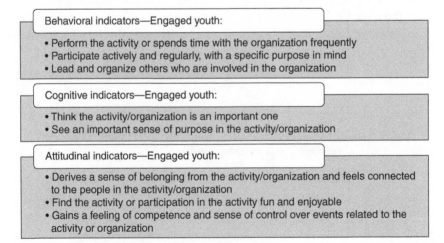

Behavioral indicators—Engaged youth:

• Perform the activity or spends time with the organization frequently
• Participate actively and regularly, with a specific purpose in mind
• Lead and organize others who are involved in the organization

Cognitive indicators—Engaged youth:

• Think the activity/organization is an important one
• See an important sense of purpose in the activity/organization

Attitudinal indicators—Engaged youth:

• Derives a sense of belonging from the activity/organization and feels connected to the people in the activity/organization
• Find the activity or participation in the activity fun and enjoyable
• Gains a feeling of competence and sense of control over events related to the activity or organization

Figure 15.2 Indicators of different types of engagement.

> *Treat this very seriously, even if the person you're mentoring is your friend,*
> *you must do everything you can and teach what you think would be helpful*
> *to them. It's their future that you're helping so don't think it's a joke because it*
> *won't have good results in the end.* (quoted in Crooks et al., 2009, p. 168)

Attitudinal engagement was apparent by the high levels of satisfaction and enjoyment endorsed by youth in their surveys. As a starting point for developing an evaluation base, this study documented a good fit between youth's needs for engagement and these programs.

Perceived Benefits for Youth

Once we were confident of the feasibility and fit of these programs, we turned toward identifying perceived benefits for youth. We employed a case study design to evaluate Fourth R programming in our local school board (Crooks, Burleigh, Snowshoe, et al., 2015). This study included surveys and individual interviews with youth participants of Fourth R programs, as well as educators and principals at schools involved in the programming. In total, 82 individuals participated in this study, including elementary and secondary students as well as educators and administrators from 15 schools. Students' involvement with programming ranged in terms of duration and intensity. In addition, the research team conducted interviews with two administrators and five Aboriginal educators.

Four organizing themes emerged from the qualitative data analysis and the related data from the quantitative surveys. These are presented in Table 15.2 with sample quotes from students and adult stakeholders. There was a high level of convergence between interview findings across stakeholders, and also between interviews and surveys.

Positive Impacts Over Time

In 2011 we began a longitudinal evaluation of programming in close partnership with our school board and community partners in order to evaluate the programs with more rigor. The purpose of this study was to undertake a mixed-methods evaluation of the impacts of two years of program participation on positive well-being and cultural identity, across the transition from elementary to secondary school (Crooks, Exner-Cortens, Burm, Lapointe, & Chiodo, 2016). We recruited an entire cohort of Aboriginal students from the local school board and surveyed them annually, starting in the 7th or 8th grade and ending in the 9th or 10th; 104 youth provided data at all three time points. In addition to the annual surveys, a subset of youth participated in annual interviews, and we obtained official school records.

At the end of the study, mentoring participants reported greater positive cultural identity and more positive mental health (Crooks et al., 2016). These results were maintained in multivariate models controlling for sex, school climate and

Table 15.2. Basic Themes Grouped Into the Four Organizing Themes, With Corresponding Qualitative Findings

Organizing Themes	Basic Themes	Qualitative Findings
Student Success	Feeling more supported Increased student self-advocacy Improved mood More student involvement Student behavior improved Reductions in suspensions and bullying Higher graduation rates	Participant: *"It [the program] really lifted my spirits. I was feeling kind of down but they always make me feel happy so that kinda ties into academics too. When you're happier your marks go up."* (Interview, female Grade 8 student, p. 7) Educator: *"Certainly many of the kids in the Fourth R program were in trouble quite a bit last year but not this year. One of those students went from being way below grade level in Grade 8 math and he is now right at grade level and he just maxed out the program he is on and he is an 85% math student now . . . and I know that was part of that intervention and prevention."* (Interview, female educator, p. 7)
Sense of Belonging	Positive health relationships established Meeting new friends Improved relationships Improved school activity involvement Increased comfort at school and with others Improved communication skills	Participant: *". . . it [the program] gives you that role model in your mentor, someone who can kind of guide you through your first year here at [school] so you can make a good transition with your mentor from Grade 8 to 9 because your mentor has a lot of knowledge about stuff like classes, and work load and you also have someone to talk to if they are feeling like they are behind in school, they can talk to their mentor. . . . The Fourth R helped me build relationships with my mentor and even the mentors even if they weren't mine. And I kind of knew a lot of people after that and kind of got to know their friends and make new friends myself."* (Interview, male Grade 12 student, p. 8) Educator: *"There are students that you saw in Grade 9 and its their first thing that they ever got involved in and then by the time they are in Grade 10 they are starting to go out to other clubs and then by Grade 11 and 12 they are leaders within the school and not just within the First Nations groups. For example, this year one of our former mentors is the co-president of the school."* (Interview, female educator, p. 8)

Table 15.2. Continued

Organizing Themes	Basic Themes	Qualitative Findings
Leadership Skills and Confidence	Speaking to groups Voicing opinions Opportunity to be a leader and mentor Pride Maturity Positive self-concept Increased involvement	Participant: *"It makes me feel good because I never really thought of myself as a mentor but I guess they must see something in me and it just feels good to be there and mentor the younger ones that are just starting and show them how to be a role model, something for them to look up to."* (Interview, male Grade 12 student, p. 9) Educator: *"There definitely has been a maturity in the way that they are approaching school and school life and their behavior here and their ownership here. I see them walking taller in the halls, I see a difference in them."* (Interview, male principal, p. 9)
Cultural Relevance	Positive FNMI role models Connecting to culture Sharing cultural knowledge with family/friends Experiential learning opportunities Gaining cultural knowledge	Participant: *"My most memorable experience was at the culture camp when we made the drums. Not only did I learn to make the drum, but I learned what all was involved during the process. I was also able to get the chance to awaken my drum and even learned to play a song. This is important to me because without that chance I would never have learned or even did it. It gave me a chance to learn about my culture which means a lot to me. I am able to teach my mom and grandparents who don't know very much about the culture either."* (Survey, male Grade 12 student, p. 10) Participant: *"Being open to challenging myself physically and being able to connect with my culture through smudging and the drum creation made me want to know more about our ancestry. I do not want to lose some valuable traditions for the future because I did not bother to learn them and the FNMI group that spiraled from this camp is proof that I'm not the only city Native who wants the same."* (Survey, female Grade 12 student, p. 10)

NOTE: All quotes retrieved from Crooks, Burleigh, Snowshoe, et al. (2015).

the baseline level of the dependent variable. Although we did not find a significant interaction between sex and mentoring in either model, post hoc analyses showed that the association between mentoring and positive mental health was only significant for females, and that for those not in mentoring, mental health by 9th or 10th grade was significantly worse for females than males. Similarly, in the identity model, the association between mentoring and greater positive identity was significant for females only, and for those not in mentoring, females had significantly lower identity scores at the end of the study compared to males. Collectively, these post hoc analyses suggested that female participants both needed the program more and benefited from it more. We also found that two years of mentoring participation was associated with significantly higher credit accumulation, although we consider those findings preliminary because of wide confidence intervals. The qualitative findings identified themes consistent with our cross-sectional analysis. In particular, mentoring participants identified both intrapersonal and interpersonal gains.

Research About Mechanisms of Change: Why Is Culturally Relevant Programming Effective?

Over the past decade, we have observed the success of strengths-based, culturally relevant programming in action. Youth, educators, and community partners have repeatedly conveyed the importance of the cultural aspects of the programs. Our research team wanted to better understand culturally relevant programming in terms of the *mechanisms* through which cultural activities promote well-being, and we undertook a qualitative study with adults who have deep knowledge of our programs and the youth involved (Crooks, Burleigh, & Sisco, 2015). We used purposeful sampling to identify and recruit stakeholders for this study who had close partnerships with the program, including Elders, teachers, First Nation counselors, school board staff members, and community members. Many participants held a combination of these roles and had been extensively involved with the local Aboriginal community and school board for numerous years. In total, in-depth interviews were conducted with 12 participants (3 male and 9 female). These interviews provided really rich data, in part because interviewers were able to reflect on their own experiences with schooling and the challenges they had faced as youth. Two interconnected themes about the importance of culture emerged from the interviews: (1) identity and belonging, and (2) cultural connectedness in promoting well-being among Aboriginal youth.

Cultural identity development. One important aspect of how participants viewed the role of culture in our programs was intrapersonal. Participants talked about this concept as student relational knowing of oneself, confidence, sense of belonging and engagement, and leadership. Several participants referred to the program's role in helping Aboriginal youth to "know themselves" and linked this with improved self-esteem and confidence. One male community partner explained that the program allowed students to embrace their cultural identities while learning:

I just think that they should be themselves when they are learning. The reason they remember the drum (a culture camp experience) so much is because it's who they are. You know when you're learning curriculum you are learning it as yourself, you are learning it as the person that you are and allowed to be. When you're struggling with your identity and trying to learn, you've got a problem. You're wondering who the heck you are, especially in high school (in Crooks, Burleigh, & Sisco, 2015, p. 108)

Cultural connectedness. The theme of cultural connectedness emerged through interviews and included stakeholders' perceptions of FNMI student identity, pride, and mentoring as well as culturally-specific program components. Cultural connectedness is linked with identity and sense of belonging. Specifically, participant data suggested that cultural connectedness enhances students' sense of identity, as one female educator stated:

I think . . . [cultural connectedness of the Fourth R] . . . gives them the identity that they are searching for. Who am I? Where do I come from? What am I about? I find that they don't feel so lost. They can ground themselves. It is hard to explain. They can ground their spirit. They know who they are. It is not like they are wandering around searching for an identity and then they can expand on that and find the sweat lodges and find the Elders and the teachings. (Quoted in Crooks, Burleigh, & Sisco, 2015, p. 111)

Participants framed FNMI pride as a counter-action to the shame so often expressed in relation to Canada's colonial history. For example, a female educator explained that the historical context provided allows students to overcome shame and embrace pride:

Residential schools are so important for students to know about. Not just the residential schools, but the aftermath and the before part too. It's the whole idea of colonization. When they have an understanding they can stop blaming, and they can say I deserve this pride and the shame changes because they can understand it in a context. (Quoted in Crooks, Burleigh, & Sisco, 2015, p.111)

Notably, the perspectives of these wise and highly involved Aboriginal adults converged well with the student interview responses in identifying both intrapersonal and interpersonal aspects of culture as protective factors.

LESSONS LEARNED

This chapter has described the development and evaluation of the Uniting Our Nations programs over the past decade. We have learned much over those years about how to best engage with community partners and schools to support the mental health and well-being of Aboriginal youth. Clearly, culturally relevant, strengths-based programming is feasible, engaging, and has the potential to promote well-being for these students. It is also important that this work occur in schools in particular, given the ugly role of education in Canada's colonial history (vis-à-vis residential schools). The opportunity to implement programming that celebrates Aboriginal cultures and recognizes the gifts of these cultures contributes to a new narrative about the relationship between Aboriginal and non-Aboriginal peoples in Canada (TRC, 2015).

Many lessons have emerged from this work with respect to programming and research. In addition to the lessons shared in this chapter, we have described lessons for program development, research, and policy in more detail elsewhere (Crooks, Chiodo, Thomas, Burns, & Camillo, 2010; Crooks et al., 2010; Crooks et al., 2013; Crooks, Burleigh, Snowshoe, et al., 2015). In both programming and research, the most important lessons have been those of patience and humility. There are no shortcuts to doing this work ethically and effectively. It has required our whole team to come with open hearts and minds, and be willing to question our own assumptions and biases. This openness is clearly important to our partners, as demonstrated in the following quote from a male community advisor:

What really won me over when I started working with the Fourth R is that they were open. They were open to learning and I think that they were probably typical Western researchers and not really knowing yet . . . I think the real strength from the Fourth R and the Fourth R team is that they recognize that there are greater compelling issues and they need to re-frame their thinking. (Quoted in Crooks, Hughes, & Sisco, 2015, p. 18)

Similarly, another male community advisor identified the importance of the duration of our team's commitment:

I have been happy to see that the Fourth R and their staff have engaged in the level of people and didn't see it as a short term thing, and that once their eyes were open they realized that there was a lot of work to do, and so that was nice to know and to encourage them to stay with that. (Quoted in Crooks, Hughes, & Sisco, 2015, p. 24)

This need to shift to a longer time frame for program development, implementation, and evaluation than we might be used to in other areas of work cannot be overstated (Fisher & Ball, 2005). Other successful community-research partnerships recognize the lengthy and critical process of building authentic partnerships (Santiago-Rivera et al., 1998).

In this chapter, we have highlighted the *Uniting Our Nations* programs for Aboriginal youth within a Canadian context. Although these programs were developed within a Canadian school context, the lessons contained herein could inform practice with Indigenous youth more broadly. Certainly in North America, the national border does not align with traditional territories for Indigenous peoples. For example, there are men and women's Haudenosaunee lacrosse teams that compete as a nation in the World Championships, with players drawn from both sides of the Canada/U.S border. Across the globe, the Indigenous population comprises a heterogeneous group of peoples with unique practices, beliefs, and experiences. However, Indigenous peoples also share certain common experiences as a result of similar colonial histories (Gone & Trimble, 2012), and challenges facing these youth are quite similar in different national contexts (Gracey & King, 2009a). Thus, while *Uniting Our Nations* was developed for a particular context (and then further adapted to other First Nations contexts), it is our hope that the strategies and lessons learned from this program will help those undertaking similar work in other Indigenous contexts.

REFERENCES

Adelson, N. (2005). The embodiment of inequity: Health disparities in Aboriginal Canada. *Canadian Journal of Public Health/Revue Canadienne de Santée Publique*, *96*(Suppl. 2), S45–S61. Retrieved from http://pubs.cpha.ca/pdf/p24/22247.pdf

Baydala, L. T., Sewlal, B., Rasmussen, C., Alexis, K., Fletcher, F., Letendre, L., . . . Kootenay, B. (2009). A culturally adapted drug and alcohol abuse prevention program for Aboriginal children and youth. *Progress in Community Health Partnerships: Research, Education, and Action*, *3*(1), 37–46.

Bell, N. (2014, June). Teaching by the Medicine Wheel. *Education Canada*. Retrieved from http://www.cea-ace.ca/education-canada/article/teaching-medicine-wheel

Brown, B. G., Baldwin, J. A., & Walsh, M. L. (2012). Putting tribal nations first: Historical trends, current needs, and future directions in substance use prevention for American Indian and Alaska Native youths.In S. R. Notaro (Ed.), *Health disparities among under-served populations: Implications for research, policy and praxis* (pp. 3–47). Bingley, England: Emerald.

Centre of Excellence for Youth Engagement (2008). *Youth engagement: A conceptual model* Retrieved from http://archives.studentscommission.ca/pdf/4pager_e2008FI-NAL_web.pdf

Chandler, M. J., & Lalonde, C. (1998). Cultural continuity as a hedge against suicide in Canada's First Nations. *Transcultural Psychiatry*, *35*(2), 191–219.

Clifford, A. C., Doran, C. M., & Tsey, K. (2013). A systematic review of suicide prevention interventions targeting Indigenous peoples in Australia, United States, Canada and New Zealand. *BMC Public Health*, *13*(1), 463–474.

Crooks, C. V., Burleigh, D., & Sisco, A. (2015). Promoting First Nations, Métis, and Inuit youth wellbeing through culturally-relevant programming: The role of cultural connectedness and identity. *International Journal of Child and Adolescent Resilience*, *3*(1), 101–116. Retrieved from http://in-car.ca/ijcar/issues/vol3/2015/Crooks_et_al_pp_101-116.pdf

Crooks, C. V., Burleigh, D., Snowshoe, A., Lapp, A., Hughes, R. & Sisco, A. (2015). A case study of culturally-relevant school-based programming for First Nations youth: Improved relationships, confidence and leadership, and school success. *Advances in School Mental Health Promotion*, *8*, 216–230. doi:10.1080/1754730X.2015.1064775

Crooks, C. V., Chiodo, D., Thomas, D., Burns, S., & Camillo, C. (2010). *Engaging and empowering Aboriginal youth: A toolkit for service providers* (2nd ed.). Bloomington, IN: Trafford Press.

Crooks, C. V., Chiodo, D. C., Thomas, D., & Hughes, R. (2009). Strengths-based pro-gramming for First Nations youth in schools: Building engagement through healthy relationships and leadership skills. *International Journal of Mental Health and Addiction, 8,* 160–173. doi:10.1007/s11469-009-9242-0

Crooks, C. V., Chiodo, D., Thomas, D., & Hughes, R. (2011). Strength-based violence prevention programming for First Nations youth within a mainstream school setting. In D. Pepler, J. Cummings, & W. Craig (Eds.), *Creating a world without bullying* (pp. 43–62). PREVNet Series, Vol. 3. Ottawa, ON: National Printers.

Crooks, C. V., Exner-Cortens, D., Burm, S., Lapointe, A., & Chiodo, D. (2017). Two years of relationship-focused mentoring for First Nations, Métis, and Inuit adoles-cents: Promoting positive mental health. *Journal of Primary Prevention, 1-2,* 87–104. Advance online publication. doi:10.1007/s10935-016-0457-0

Crooks, C. V., Hughes, R., & Sisco, A. (2015). *Fourth R: Uniting our Nations case study: Lessons learned from adaptation and implementation in Ontario and the Northwest Territories.* London, ON: Centre for School Mental Health.

Crooks, C.V., Scott, K., Ellis, W., & Wolfe, D. (2011). Impact of a universal school-based violence prevention program on violent delinquency: Distinctive benefits for youth with maltreatment histories. *Child Abuse and Neglect, 35,* 393–400.

Crooks, C. V., Scott, K. L., Wolfe, D. A., Chiodo, D., & Killip, S. (2007). Understanding the link between childhood maltreatment and violent delinquency: What do schools have to add? *Child Maltreatment, 12,* 269–280.

Crooks, C. V., Snowshoe, A., Chiodo, D., & Brunette-Debassige, C. (2013). Navigating between rigor and community-based research partnerships: Building the evaluation of the Uniting Our Nations health promotion program for FNMI youth. *Canadian Journal of Community Mental Health, 32,* 13–25.

De Koker, P., Mathews, C., Zuch, M., Bastien, S., & Mason-Jones, A. J. (2014). A sys-tematic review of interventions for preventing adolescent intimate partner violence. *Journal of Adolescent Health, 54*(1), 3–13.

De La Rue, L., Polanin, J. R., Espelage, D. L., & Pigott, T. D. (2016). A meta-analysis of school-based interventions aimed to prevent or reduce violence in teen dating rela-tionships. *Review of Educational Research, 20,* 1–28.

Donovan, D. M., Thomas, L. R., Sigo, R. L. W., Price, L., Lonczak, H., Lawrence, N., . . . Purser, A. (2015). Healing of the Canoe: Preliminary results of a culturally grounded intervention to prevent substance abuse and promote tribal identity for Native youth in two Pacific Northwest tribes. *American Indian and Alaska Native Mental Health Research (Online), 22*(1), 42.

Edwards, K. M., Jones, L. M., Mitchell, K. J., Hagler, M. A., & Roberts, L. T. (2016). Building on youth's strengths: A call to include adolescents in developing, imple-menting, and evaluating violence prevention programs. *Psychology of Violence, 6*(1), 15–21.

Ellsberg, M., Arango, D. J., Morton, M., Gennari, F., Kiplesund, S., Contreras, M., . . . Watts, C. (2015). Prevention of violence against women and girls: What does the evi-dence say? *The Lancet, 385*(9977), 1555–1566.

Fiedeldey-Van Dijk, C., Rowan, M., Dell, C., Mushquash, C., Hopkins, C., Fornssler, B., . . . Shea, B. (2015). Honoring Indigenous culture-as-intervention: Development and validity of the Native Wellness Assessment™. *Journal of Ethnicity in Substance Abuse.* Advance online publication.

First Nations Information Governance Centre (FNIGC). (2012*). First Nations Regional Health Survey (RHS) 2008/10: National report on adults, youth and children living in First Nations communities.* Ottawa: Author. Retrieved from http://fnigc.ca/sites/default/files/docs/first_nations_regional_health_survey_rhs_2008-10_-_national_report.pdf

Fisher, P. A., & Ball, T. J. (2005). Balancing empiricism and local cultural knowledge in the design of prevention research. *Journal of Urban Health, 82*(3), iii44–iii55.

Friesen, B. J., Cross, T. L., Jivanjee, P. R., Gowen, L. K., Bandurraga, A., Bastomski, S., . . . Maher, N. J. (2012). More than a nice thing to do: A practice-based evidence approach to outcome evaluation in Native youth and family programs. In *Handbook of race and development in mental health* (pp. 87–106). New York: Springer.

Gone, J. P. (2012). Indigenous traditional knowledge and substance abuse treatment outcomes: The problem of efficacy evaluation. *American Journal of Drug and Alcohol Abuse, 38*(5), 493–497.

Gone, J. P. (2013). Redressing First Nations historical trauma: Theorizing mechanisms for Indigenous culture as mental health treatment. *Transcultural Psychiatry, 50*(5), 683–706.

Gone, J. P., & Trimble, J. E. (2012). American Indian and Alaska Native mental health: Diverse perspectives on enduring disparities. *Annual Review of Clinical Psychology, 8*, 131–160.

Goodkind, J., LaNoue, M., Lee, C., Freeland, L., & Freund, R. (2012). Feasibility, acceptability, and initial findings from a community-based cultural mental health intervention for American Indian youth and their families. *Journal of Community Psychology, 40*(4), 381–405.

Gracey, M., & King, M. (2009a). Indigenous health part 1: Determinants and disease patterns. *The Lancet, 374*(9683), 65–75.

Gracey, M., & King, M. (2009b). Indigenous health part 2: the underlying causes of the health gap. *The Lancet, 374*(9683), 76–85.

Greenwood, M. L., & de Leeuw, S. N. (2012). Social determinants of health and the future well-being of Aboriginal children in Canada. *Paediatrics & Child Health, 17*(7), 381.

Gross, P. A., Efimoff, I., Patrick, L., Josewski, V., Hau, K., Lambert, S., & Smye, V. (2016). The DUDES Club: A brotherhood for men's health. *Canadian Family Physician, 62*(6), 311–318.

Hallett, D., Chandler, M. J., & Lalonde, C. E. (2007). Aboriginal language knowledge and youth suicide. *Cognitive Development, 22*(3), 392–399.

Harlow, A. F., & Clough, A. (2014). A systematic review of evaluated suicide prevention programs targeting Indigenous youth. *Crisis: The Journal of Crisis Intervention and Suicide Prevention, 35*(5), 310.

Hawkins, E. H., Cummins, L. H., & Marlatt, G. A. (2004). Preventing substance abuse in American Indian and Alaska Native youth: Promising strategies for healthier communities. *Psychological Bulletin, 130*(2), 304–323.

Health Canada. (2013). Acting on what we know: Preventing youth suicide in First Nations. Ottawa, ON: Health Canada. Retrieved from: http://www.hc-sc.gc.ca/fniah-spnia/pubs/promotion/_suicide/prev_youth-jeunes/index-eng.php

Health Canada. (2014). A statistical profile on the health of First Nations in Canada: Determinants of health 2006–2010. Ottawa, ON: Health Canada. Retrieved from: http://www.hc-sc.gc.ca/fniah-spnia/pubs/aborig-autoch/2010-stats-profil-determinants/index-eng.php

Jackson, K. F., & Hodge, D. R. (2010). Native American youth and culturally sensitive interventions: A systematic review. *Research on Social Work Practice, 20*(3), 260–270.

Kearney, C. A., & Graczyk, P. (2014). A response to intervention model to promote school attendance and decrease school absenteeism. *Child & Youth Care Forum, 43*(1), 1–25.

Kenyon, D. B., & Hanson, J. D. (2012). Incorporating traditional culture into positive youth development programs with American Indian/Alaska Native youth. *Child Development Perspectives, 6*(3), 272–279.

Kirmayer, L. J., Brass, G. M., & Tait, C. L. (2000). The mental health of Aboriginal peoples: Transformations of identity and community. *Canadian Journal of Psychiatry, 45*(7), 607–616.

Kirmayer, L., Simpson, C., & Cargo, M. (2003). Healing traditions: Culture, community and mental health promotion with Canadian Aboriginal peoples. *Australasian Psychiatry, 11*, S15–S23.

Klinck, J., Cardinal, C., Edwards, K., Gibson, N., Bisanz, J., & Da Costa, J. (2005). Mentoring programs for Aboriginal youth. *Pimatisiwin: A Journal of Aboriginal & Indigenous Community Health, 3*(2). Retrieved from http://www.pimatisiwin.com/online/?page_id=416

Kulis, S., Dustman, P. A., Brown, E. F., & Martinez, M. (2013). Expanding urban American Indian youth's repertoire of drug resistance skills: Pilot results from a culturally adapted prevention program. *American Indian and Alaska Native Mental Health Research (Online), 20*(1), 35.

LaFromboise, T. D., Albright, K., & Harris, A. (2010). Patterns of hopelessness among American Indian adolescents: Relationships by levels of acculturation and residence. *Cultural Diversity and Ethnic Minority Psychology, 16*(1), 68–76.

LaFromboise, T. D., Hoyt, D. R., Oliver, L., & Whitbeck, L. B. (2006). Family, community, and school influences on resilience among American Indian adolescents in the Upper Midwest. *Journal of Community Psychology, 34*(2), 193–209.

LaFromboise, T. D., & Lewis, H. A. (2008). The Zuni life skills development program: A school/community-based suicide prevention intervention. *Suicide and Life-Threatening Behavior, 38*(3), 343–353.

Langdon, S. E., Golden, S. L., Arnold, E. M., Maynor, R. F., Bryant, A., Freeman, V. K., & Bell, R. A. (2016). Lessons learned from a community-based participatory research mental health promotion program for American Indian youth. *Health Promotion Practice, 17*(3), 457–463.

Le, T. N., & Gobert, J. M. (2015). Translating and implementing a mindfulness-based youth suicide prevention intervention in a Native American community. *Journal of Child and Family Studies, 24*(1), 12–23.

Lemstra, M., Rogers, M., Redgate, L., Garner, M., & Moraros, J. (2011). Prevalence, risk indicators and outcomes of bullying among on-reserve First Nations youth. *Canadian Journal of Public Health/Revue Canadienne de Sante Publique, 102*(6), 462–466.

MacDonald, C., & Steenbeek, A. (2015). The impact of colonization and Western assimilation on health and wellbeing of Canadian Aboriginal people. *International Journal of Regional and Local History, 10*(1), 32–46.

Moran, J. R., & Reaman, J. A. (2002). Critical issues for substance abuse prevention targeting American Indian youth. *Journal of Primary Prevention, 22*(3), 201–233.

Okamoto, S. K., Kulis, S., Marsiglia, F. F., Steiker, L. K. H., & Dustman, P. (2014). A continuum of approaches toward developing culturally focused prevention interventions: From adaptation to grounding. *Journal of Primary Prevention*, *35*(2), 103–112.

Penn, J., Doll, J., & Grandgenett, N. (2008). Culture as prevention: Assisting high-risk youth in the Omaha Nation. *Wicazo Sa Review*, *23*(2), 43–61.

Perreault, S. (2011). *Violent victimization of Aboriginal People in the Canadian provinces, 2009* (Catalogue No. 85-002-X). Retrieved from Statistics Canada website: http://www.statcan.gc.ca/pub/85-002-x/2011001/article/11415-eng.pdf

Petrucka, P. M., Bickford, D., Bassendowski, S., Goodwill, W., Wajunta, C., Yuzicappi, B., ... Rauliuk, M. (2016). Positive leadership, legacy, lifestyles, attitudes, and activities for Aboriginal youth: A wise practices approach for positive Aboriginal youth futures. *International Journal of Indigenous Health*, *11*(1), 177–197.

Pridemore, W. A. (2004). Review of the literature on risk and protective factors of offending among Native Americans. *Journal of Ethnicity in Criminal Justice*, *2*(4), 45–63.

Proulx, C. (2006). Aboriginal identification in North American cities. *Canadian Journal of Native Studies*, *26*(2), 405.

Reading, C. L., & Wien, F. (2009). *Health inequalities and social determinants of Aboriginal peoples' health.* Prince George, BC: National Collaborating Centre for Aboriginal Health.

Rossi P. H., Freeman H. E., & Lipsey, M.W. (2003). *Evaluation: A systematic approach* (7th ed). London, England: SAGE.

Rowan, M., Poole, N., Shea, B., Gone, J. P., Mykota, D., Farag, M., ... Dell, C. (2014). Cultural interventions to treat addictions in Indigenous populations: findings from a scoping study. *Substance Abuse Treatment, Prevention, and Policy*, *9*(1), 1.

Santiago-Rivera, A. L., Morse, G. S., Hunt, A., & Lickers, H. (1998). Building a community-based research partnership: Lessons from the Mohawk nation of Akwesasne. *Journal of Community Psychology*, *26*, 164–174.

Schnarch, B. (2004). Ownership, control, access, and possession (OCAP) or self-determination applied to research: A critical analysis of contemporary First Nations research and some options for First Nations communities. *International Journal of Indigenous Health*, *1*(1), 80.

Siebold, W. L., Hegge, L. M., & Crooks, C. V. (2012). *Alaska Fourth R curriculum evaluation: Annual report 2011–2012*. Missoula, MT: Strategic Prevention Solutions.

Smokowski, P. R., Evans, C. B. R., Cotter, K. L., & Webber, K. C. (2014). Ethnic identity and mental health in American Indian youth: Examining mediation pathways through self-esteem, and future optimism. *Journal of Youth and Adolescence*, *43*(3), 343–355.

Truth and Reconciliation Commission of Canada (TRC). (2015). *Honoring the truth, reconciling for the future: Summary of the final report of the TRC of Canada*. Winnipeg, Manitoba: Truth and Reconciliation Commission of Canada. Retrieved from http://www.trc.ca/websites/trcinstitution/index.php?p=890

Vukic, A., Gregory, D., Martin-Misener, R., & Etowa, J. (2011). Aboriginal and Western conceptions of mental health and illness. *Pimatisiwin: A Journal of Aboriginal and Indigenous Community Health*, *9*(1), 65–86.

Walsh, M. L, & Baldwin, J. A. (2015). American Indian substance abuse prevention efforts: A review of programs, 2003–2013. *American Indian and Alaska Native Mental Health Research (Online)*, *22*(2), 41.

Ware, V. (2013). *Mentoring programs for Indigenous youth at-risk* (Vol. 22). Australian Institute of Health and Welfare. Retrieved from http://dro.deakin.edu.au/eserv/DU:30069871/ware-mentoringprograms-2013.pdf

Wexler, L. M., & Gone, J. P. (2012). Culturally responsive suicide prevention in indigenous communities: Unexamined assumptions and new possibilities. *American Journal of Public Health, 102*(5), 800–806.

Whitbeck, L. B., McMorris, B. J., Hoyt, D. R., Stubben, J. D., & LaFromboise, T. (2002). Perceived discrimination, traditional practices, and depressive symptoms among American Indians in the Upper Midwest. *Journal of Health and Social Behavior, 43*(4), 400–418.

Wilson, K., & Cardwell, N. (2012). Urban Aboriginal health: Examining inequalities between Aboriginal and non-Aboriginal populations in Canada. *The Canadian Geographer/Le Géographe Canadien, 56*(1), 98–116.

Wolfe, D. A., Crooks, C. V., Chiodo, D., Hughes, R., & Ellis, W. (2012). Observations of adolescent peer resistance skills following a classroom-based health relationship program: A post-intervention comparison. *Prevention Science, 13,* 196–205.

Wolfe, D. A., Crooks, C. V., Jaffe, P. G., Chiodo, D., Hughes, R., Ellis, W., . . . Donner, A. (2009). A universal school-based program to prevent adolescent dating violence: A cluster randomized trial. *Archives of Pediatric and Adolescent Medicine, 163,* 693–699.

Wolfe, D. A., Jaffe, P. G., & Crooks, C. V. (2006). *Adolescent risk behaviors: Why teens experiment and strategies to keep them safe.* New Haven, CT: Yale University Press.

Note: Page numbers followed by a *t* or *b* indicate material found in tables or boxes.